# Problems of Education in India

Ram Nath Sharma
Rajendra K. Sharma

PUBLISHERS & DISTRIBUTORS (P) LTD

Published by

**ATLANTIC**

**PUBLISHERS & DISTRIBUTORS (P) LTD**

7/22, Ansari Road, Darya Ganj, New Delhi-110002
Phones : +91-11-40775252, 40775214, 23273880, 23275880
Fax : +91-11-23285873
Web : www.atlanticbooks.com
E-mail : orders@atlanticbooks.com

**Branch Office: Chennai**
Phones : +91-44-48531784, 28291383
E-mail : chennai@atlanticbooks.com



Printed & bound in India by Atlantic Print Services

# PREFACE

This book deals with the problems of education in Indian society. Covering the courses prescribed by various Indian Universities and Institutes of Education in the following papers among others : (i) Problems of Indian Education and (ii) Education in Indian Society.

The book first of all deals with the problems of education : Pre-primary, Primary, Secondary, Higher Secondary, College and University level education. It discusses various the spheres of education like : Women Education, Adult Education, Education of the Scheduled Castes and Scheduled Tribes. The various Political, Technological and Social impacts on education are analysed. It examines various types of education : Population Education, Physical Education, Health Education, Religious and Moral Education, Technological Education, Teacher Education. Evaluating the different aims of education like — Education for Democracy, Education for National and Emotional Integration, Education for International and Inter-Cultural Understanding the book discusses problems peculiar to the entire structure of education: Administration and Supervision, Curriculum, Evaluation and Examination, Work Experience, Medium of Instruction. It deals with problems peculiar to expansion of education : Universalisation, Diversification, Text Book Nationalisation, Standardisation, Indianisation and Modernisation. And lastly presents, the latest position of education in India in its chapter 'Education in India Tody'.

Thus the authors have not left any stone unturned to make this book an ideal textbook on the subject. Suggestions from the readers are invited for improvement.

**RAM NATH SHARMA**
**RAJENDRA K. SHARMA**

# CONTENTS

# 1

# PROBLEMS OF EDUCATION

Problems of education are found in each and every country in the world. These problems vary in their kind and degree, but they are there throughout the world. However, some general questions pertaining to education arise in each country. Some examples of these questions are : Is the current system of education suitable to cope with the national needs and aspirations. Do the schools of today fulfil the expectations of the people? Have enough facilities and resources been organized for education? Thus people are everywhere aware of the basic problems of education. The teacher, taught, guardian and the governmental authorities feel that present educational efforts are not enough to cope with the needs of the people. In most of the countries of the world the following are the burning problems of education :

1. To correlate education with the problems of life.
2. To democratise education.
3. To cope with the problems arising out of the modern scientific and technical advancements.
4. To make education adequately efficient.

1. **To Correlate Education with Problems of Life** : Education should fulfil the needs of the society. When it does not produce self-dependent individuals, society begins to crack down under the load of its unemployed members. As the people in general suffer from various types of scarcities, education should not be only vocationalized, but also correlated with life. Only then can an educated youth understand his life-problems intelligently. Today, there is an explosion of knowledge. Now knowledge is increasing every day with an unprecedented speed. Informations have been revolutionized. In terms of the developing knowledge, various types of informations are now available for an individual. One has to acquire these informations in order to cope with the problems of life in general. The world is changing very fast. Within this changing world students are trapped with multifarious problems. An unrest is inevitably evinced in their behaviour. As the teachers also appear to be at cross-roads, the very foundation of education is shaken. The aims of education are being examined in every country of the world. The curriculum is being modified to suit the various demands. As Sweden and Spain believe the problem of change in education to be perennial, these countries have established centres of research in educational policies to give the necessary advice

after making the necessary investigations. The Arab States have introduced well-considered plans for reforms of education. Turkey, Thailand and Japan have established Central Committees for suggesting reforms in education. France and India have correlated their educational goals with social and economic plans. Brazil, Ghana, Spain and Yugoslavia have evaluated their educational systems and reorganized the same. Rumania has modernized education through an Act of Parliament. Albaina has introduced changes in its education in consultation with its public. Thus various countries of the world have consistently tried to modernize their educational systems for bringing it nearer to life.

2. **To Democratise Education** : Today every country professes to be a democracy. Everywhere the aim of education is to make it available to all. With the unprecedented growth of population in third world countries, education has to meet the needs of the teeming millions. In spite of the family planning programme in these countries, the population is ever on the increase. This has created the need of more teachers, more school buildings and more financial resources. Most of the developing countries are not having enough trained teachers. Many are not in a position to make education available to all. The socially, economically and culturally backward people are not being cared properly about their educational needs. Due to lack of the necessary resources the education of the handicapped and less privileged ones is being sidetracked.

3. **To Cope with the Problems Arising out of Modern Scientific and Technological Advancement** : The first half of the current century has seen two deadly world wars. Arms race in the developed countries is still at its peak. Battles have been fought in various countries, Indian sub-continent, South East Asia, Middle East countries, African countries and South America since the World War II. Regional pacts and associations have been formed for co-operating with each other in war time. Aligned and non-aligned groups have been formed for maintaining a balance of power that a country may protect itself during war. There has never been so much universal awareness and fear of war. The present industrial, scientific and technological advancements have led us to this juncture when the entire human civilization may be annihilated if a certain super power so intends. This has created a tension in each and every part of the world. The educationists and leaders all over the world are opining that the prevailing pattern of education has not helped man to find out his soul. It has rather led him into jealousies, rivalries, intricacies of diplomacy and Inter-State disputes on one point or another. Everywhere there is unhappiness, lack of accord and understanding, tension and miseries, disease and scarcities of various types. Leaders are everywhere sensing the necessity of redefining the fundamental aims and postulates of education, since education alone can put man on the right track. UNESCO has been very helpful in bringing together the educationists of the various countries for reformulating the basic objectives of education. The UNESCO and great educationists all over the world have rightly emphasized that education alone can save man from deterioration consequent of the modern technologically advanced civilization. This has led them to reformulate the following basic objectives of education :

(i) *To prepare man for readjustment* : Education has to prepare a man to adjust himself in the changing needs of the times. Thus education should meet the needs of the society. This is possible only when education prepares such individuals who can stand on their own legs. This will automatically put a check to the growing unemployment. Consequently, the economic balance of the society will also be maintained.

(ii) *To further economic development* : Education has now been accepted as an instrument for furthering economic development. This basic objective has been directly derived from the above first objective.

(iii) *To help human growth* : Education is now considered as a continual process from birth to death. Man has to grow every day. So Education has to help him in this growth all the time.

(iv) *To provide formal as well as informal education* : In order to fulfil the above three objectives, it has been further pointed out that education is not to be restricted to the four walls of a school. It has to be both formal and non-formal. Family, Community, Press, Cinema, Radio, Television and cultural and social organizations all play their constructive role in the education of an individual. If these fulfil their educational obligations, there will be no gulf between education and social needs.

(v) *To provide universal education* : Education is no longer a privilege of a few. It has to be made available to all, as each one must contribute to the growth and prosperity of the society. Due to the huge crowd of students desiring admission in schools, colleges and universities, it has been rightly pointed out that secondary education should be available to all.

(vi) *To vocationalize education* : For catering to the varying aptitudes and interests of the students and also to enable them to stand on their own legs after completing education, education should be vocationalised. This will also reduce the huge crowd of students trying for admission in colleges and universities. Today the importance of vocational and technical education has increased unprecedentedly.

(vii) *To provide liberal education* : Education has to prepare an individual who can adjust himself in the ever-changing civilization. This requires general intelligence much more than a skill in some practical or technical area. Hence, education is now supposed to emphasise the development of general intelligence and power of understanding alongwith specialization in some area. He should know something of everything and everything of something. Education has to be liberal as it has to educate the whole man.

4. **To Make Education Adequately Efficient** : Today it is generally felt that educational system is not so efficient as it should be. A number of individuals are deprived of opportunities of education in each country, though the expenditure on education per student has increased in each country. People have naturally begun to think about its efficiency. They have started thinking about introducing such innovations in education which may make it more effective and efficient.

## REMEDIES TO EDUCATIONAL PROBLEMS

For solving the problems of education discussed so far following efforts are being made:

1. New Structure of Education
2. Integrated Curriculum
3. Teachers Training
4. Better Teaching Methods.
5. Better School Buildings
6. Better Educational Administration
7. More Expenditure on Education
8. Functional Research
9. Functional Literacy of Adults.
10. Better Physical and Moral Health.

1. **New Structure of Education :**

(i) *Pre-primary* : Pre-primary education or nursery education is getting very popular these days. Numerous pre-primary or nursery schools are being run on commercial lines which is purely to earn profits. There is also a tendency to attach them with a primary schools as their interconnected units. In these nursery schools special emphasis is laid on developing vocabulary and power of expression.

(ii) *Primary* : Primary schools are growing in number. Their quantitative development has created the problem of qualitative development. New methods as group teaching through television and teaching the same class by a number of teachers are being adopted for qualitative development. In most of the countries class is accepted as a unit for teaching in a primary school. But in U.S.A. one finds many classless primary schools in which each child learns various subjects according to his own speed. Primary education has been made compulsory almost in all the countries of the world. In some countries like U.S.A. and U.S.S.R. secondary education has been also compulsory.

(iii) *Junior High Schools* : In junior high school classes all the subjects are compulsorily taught. Specialization starts from high school classes.

(iv) *High Schools* : Practical, vocational and technical and agricultural courses are being incorporated in the high school curriculum so that the student becomes self-dependent after receiving education. Secondary education is the terminus of education in many countries. In some countries a tendency is also perceived to open middle schools in between primary and secondary education and to run intermediate or junior college in between secondary and university education.

(v) *University Education* : Various types of courses are being taught at the university stage. The student unrest at the university level is attributed to unsuitability of the curriculum. An attempt is being made to pacify students by seeking their co-operation in the university administration. Students are opted to serve on some of the committees of the university. There is an increasing teacher-student co-operation at the university stage.

(vi) *New Experiments*: Evening schools, Correspondence Courses, Continuation classes are being run for extending facilities of secondary and university education. There is also a tendency to effect a smooth articulation between the various stages of education — primary, secondary and university — so that one stage may be lead to another and the whole system of education from primary to university may appear as one integrated whole. For this purpose the duration of primary education has been reduced in some countries and it has been connected with the pre-primary classes. At the same time some changes have also been introduced at the secondary stage.

(vii) *Utilisation of Equipment* : There is a tendency to utilise the school equipment to the maximum. This has lead to the opening of double shift classes. Hungary and Argentina are doing this for having the maximum advantage of the available school facilities. In some countries schools now remain open for six days a week instead of 5 days as before. There is a tendency to admit maximum number of students in a class. Small schools are being closed in Canada, U.S.S.R. and Spain. Bigger schools are being opened. In view of the huge number of students available for each class this has become necessary.

(viii) *Guidance and Counselling* : The necessity of guidance and counselling services is being relised to help students to solve their personal, educational and vocational problems. One find a good arrangement in this respect specially in U.S.A., Spain, Algeria, Rumania and Sweden.

2. **Integrated Curriculum** : If education has to meet the needs of modern conditions, necessary changes must be introduced in the curriculum. Curriculum must reflect the needs of the society and those of the individuals to be educated. The various courses of study should be integrated. Courses should not overload a student. The physical, emotional, mental and social development of the child should be taken into consideration in the curriculum organisation. Upto the primary stage the curriculum should be so liberal as to develop an awareness in the child about his immediate environment. The needs of the economic development of the society may be attended in the organization of the curriculum from the secondary stage. In U.S.S.R. the practicalness of the acquired knowledge is emphasised at the primary and secondary stage. In Mexico 'learning by doing' is emphasised at the primary level and 'learning by production' is the chief objective at the secondary level. In African countries education is being correlated with the needs of the rural environment. The students are taught how to keep the environment neat and clean and how to check the pollution of the atmosphere. Informations are also imparted regarding population control at educational institutions.

3. **Teachers's Training** : The central importance of the teacher is now recognized everywhere. In spite of the inventions of teaching machines, radio and television, the place of the teacher in education is as secure as ever. To meet the aspirations of the individual and society, special attention should be given to teacher education so that the newly prepared teachers may successfully meet the

new challenges facing education. Refresher and part-time courses are being organized all over the world for keeping the teacher-in-service adequately informed about the latest developments in educational theories and practices. There is a dearth of teachers of mathematics and science and also of the teachers for rural areas in many countries. An attempt is being made to prepare teachers for these purposes. For making their incomplete qualifications fuller diploma courses are provided in various allied areas of education. The teachers are now encouraged to participate in programmes of community development.

4. **Better Teaching Methods** : In view of integrated curriculum a change in the objectives of teaching methods has also been recognized. In the teaching of language the emphasis is placed on helping the child to pick up the language as a means of communication. Mother tongue has been everywhere accepted as the best medium of instruction. Besides, an international language and a classical language are also taught at the secondary stage in many countries. Language is being taught by the structural method. Audio-visual aids are being used as teaching devices in many subjects. New subjects are being devised for teaching of science and mathematics. It is hoped that these new methods will become more popular in due course. The developments in scientific and technological fields have had inevitable impacts on devising of new techniques of teaching. Programmed learning methods and laboratories have been organised for teaching languages as some of the latest innovations in the area of education technology. Universities on the Air or open universities have been organized in U.S.A. with the help of radio and television and correspondence courses. Those who have not obtained formal university education may obtain higher education through these 'open universities'. Such 'open universities' have been organised in some African countries and elsewhere. In course of time such universities will become more popular with further technological advancements.

5. **Better School Buildings** : The dearth of good school buildings is felt in most of the countries. In many countries the buildings of many schools and colleges are poorly built, and in a bad shape because of poor equipments. There are no good furniture and no good libraries and laboratories worth the name. These poor school and college buildings with inadequate equipments cannot adopt new techniques of educational science. While creating new school and college buildings special attention is being paid to their suitability for adopting latest developments in the educational technology.

6. **Better Educational Administration** : Expenditure on education is increasing because of quantitative development and the use of latest devices of teaching. Hence it insisted that the money spent on education is utilized effectively. There is an emphasis on decentralization of administration of education in such a way as to maintain a cordial relationship between various wings.

There is tendency to seek the co-operation of teachers, students and guardians in conducting some of the affairs of the school and college. In certain countries headmasters are authorized to take decision on many vital matters in consultation with students and teachers. By a Government order the school administration has been correlated with the life of students, teachers and the community surrounding it in Yugoslavia. In Arab countries the responsibility of effecting this correlation has been laid on the education authorities of the region concerned.

The inspectors are now considered as colleagues of their partner in achieving the objectives of education. They have to adopt a sympathetic attitude in giving suggestions to teachers for improvement of education. The inspectors are expected to study those factors which may help the students and teachers in their respective jobs. Efforts are now made to revolutionize the attitude of inspectors.

7. **More Expenditure on Education** : Expenditure on education is increasing every day. This has led to the development of 'economics of education' as a special branch of study which considers expenditure on education as investment. It makes an intensive study of educational planning and the internal wastage on education. Expenditure on education has become a State responsibility. However, it is felt that State has reached its limit of expenditure on education. So the government is encouraging private organisations for shouldering the responsibility of expenditure on education.

8. **Functional Research** : The trend of research in education is towards functional utility. The main objective of research should be to effect improvements in teaching. The intellectual type of research in education is being discouraged. Researches of problematic and reformative type are being encouraged.

9. **Functional Literacy of Adults** : In adult education programme the trend is to stress functional literacy and to increase the productive capacity of adults. Adults are being made aware of world affairs at the adults education centres through audio-visual method. This is done to effect their better adjustment in the immediate environment.

10. **Better Physical and Moral Health** : Special attention is being paid on the physical and moral health of children. Under the moral health programmes the children are taught principles of citizenship and the essential unity of all religions. Their attention is drawn on oneness of humanity so that this world may become a better place to live. In France five periods a week are allotted to games and physical education of children. In Hungary individual attention is paid to students for their mental and physical health. In Belgium sometimes classes are organized on sea-coasts or on ice to increase their physical endurance.

**Conclusions** : To conclude, one finds the emphasis on the following in order to solve the problems of education :

1. *Reforms* : There is a tendency towards reforms of education. The major emphasis is on redefining the objectives of education and reconstructing the curriculum in order that the same may meet the needs and aspirations of the individual and society.

2. *Equities* : There is an emphasis on equitable distribution of opportunities of education to all concerned according to their specific assets and limitations. It is insisted that all the regions of the land are adequately taken care of.

3. *Prosperity* : In the redefining of objectives of education and reconstructing of the curriculum, the demands of economic growth and the national prosperity are being specially considered. So all the types of technical, vocational, agricultural and scientific institutions are being reorganised according to the latest developments in the areas.

4. *National Integration* : Politically considered, education is now being considered as a means of national integration. For this, mother tongue is generally accepted as the medium of instruction. The student is required to learn at least three languages, *viz.* (i) his mother tongue, (ii) a regional language, and (iii) a foreign language.

5. *Morality* : Today moral values are more emphasised in education than ever. An attempt is being made to develop good moral attitudes in children. This will promote good character development.

6. *Regional Utility* : In the reorganisation of education the demands of the rural, coastal and hilly areas are carefully considered.

7. *Productivity* : Now in all educational efforts, the major objective is on productiveness, in order that the individual may feel self-dependent after completing his formal education.

8. *Harmony of individual and social demands* : It is felt that in view of the ever-developing scientific innovation and technological advancements, one cannot ascertain the shape of things to come. Hence there is a need of continual and consistence educational reforms in order that there may not be a gulf between education and individual and social demands.

9. *Decentralisation of control* : Since education has to be widely spread, a need is felt for decentralisation of education control and administration. It could meet the demands of all localities. Co-operation of all concerned is solicited in the educational administration. Each worker in the educational field, the inspector, director, the headmaster and others have to co-operate in the educational efforts of the teacher.

10. *Practical Bias* : In the educational efforts the student is given not only theoretical knowledge but practical experience as well. Now the practical aspects of education are also emphasised in order that the student may effect his better adjustment.

## PROGRESS OF EDUCATION IN INDIA

Education is integrally linked with the development process. There has been considerable progress in this sphere. The literacy rate increased from 18.3 per cent in 1951 to 52.2 per cent in 1991. The number of primary schools increased from 2.09 lakh in 1950-51 to 5.73 lakh in 1993-94. During the same period, the number of universities rose from 27 to 169.

A major concern is the gender-wise difference in literacy. The female literacy rate was 39.3 per cent as against 64.1 per cent for male in 1991 (Table 2). There are also wide variations among States, ranging from 86.2 per cent female literacy in Kerala to 20.4 per cent female literacy in Rajasthan in 1991. A similar situation prevails in the case of male literacy. The literacy rate for the Scheduled Castes increased to 37.4 per cent in 1991 from 21.4 per cent in 1981. Among the Scheduled Tribes, it increased from 16.4 per cent in 1981 to 29.6 per cent in 1991 (Table 1).

**Primary Education**

Substantial progress has been made in the area of primary education. The Gross Enrolment Ratio (GER) in the Primary Stage (classes I-V) increased from 42.6 per cent in 1950-51 to 104.5 per cent in 1992-93 and in the Upper Primary Stage (classes VI-VIII) from 12.7 per cent to 67.7 per cent. However, there are wide variations in the GER among major States. The GER in the Primary Stage is 76.1 per cent in Bihar, as against 145.0 per cent in Tamil Nadu (Table 2).

**Adult Education**

A Summit of Nine High Population Countries on 'Education For All' (EFA) held on December 16, 1993, adopted the Delhi Declaration and Framework of Action to make 'Education For All' a reality. Keeping in view demographic and other complex ground realities, the goals were framed in EFA in India are elucidated in Box 1.1

To attain the objectives laid down in the Delhi Declaration and also to follow up the NDC Committee Report on Literacy, a Special Conference of Chief Ministers of all States and Union Territories was held in February, 1994. The Conference emphasised the coordinated and concerted action on the part of the local community, State Governments and the Central Government for mobilisation of resources for education and high priority to primary and adult education.

**Universalisation of Education**

In order to achieve universalisation of elementary education, District Primary Education Programme (DPEP) has been initiated. The World Bank is providing IDA credit of US $260 million to support the Programme in 23 districts in six States of Assam, Haryana, Kerala, Tamil Nadu, Karnataka and West Bengal. The European Community is also providing credit of ECU 150 million (Rs. 585 crore) for supporting DPEP in Madhya Pradesh.

**Literacy Campaigns**

The Total Literacy Campaigns, constituting the principal strategy for eradication of illiteracy, have been extended to cover 282 districts and the Post-literacy Campaigns to 105 districts. The focus of the campaigns has now shifted to the Hindi-speaking States having bulk of the illiterate population. A total of 58.07 million people have been enrolled under various programmes of the National Literacy Mission (NLM) as of August, 1994.

**Women Education**

Women's education has always been a priority area. It has now been emphasised that gender concerns must be built into all educational programmes.

Emphasis has been laid on enrolement and retention of the girl child in formal and non-formal schooling, recruitment of female teachers and removal of gender bias from the curriculum. In the revamped Blackboard Scheme, provision has been made to recruit at least 50 per cent female teachers and 90 per cent assistance is given to centres reserved exclusively for girls.

TABLE 1

**Literacy Rate[1] among Scheduled Castes and Scheduled Tribes**

| Category | 1981[2] | | | 1991[2] | | |
|---|---|---|---|---|---|---|
| | Total | Male | Female | Total | Male | Female |
| 1 | 2 | 3 | 4 | 5 | 6 | 7 |
| (1) Scheduled Castes | 21.38 | 31.12 | 10.93 | 37.41 | 49.91 | 23.76 |
| (2) Scheduled Tribes | 16.35 | 21.52 | 8.04 | 29.60 | 40.65 | 18.19 |
| (3) All categories | 43.67 | 56.50 | 29.85 | 52.21 | 64.13 | 39.29 |

[1]Literacy rate relates to population aged 7 years and above.
[2]Excludes Assam in 1981 and Jammu and Kashmir in 1991.
*Source* : 'Education For All'. The Indian Scene 1993, Ministry of Human Resource Development.

**Plan Allocation**

Central Plan Allocation (BE) for education was raised from Rs. 952 crore in 1992-93 to Rs. 1310 crore in 1993-94 and further to Rs. 1541 crore in 1994-95. Total public expenditure, plan and non-plan, on education in 1992-93 by the Centre and States (including expenditure by Departments other than Education) was 4.2 per cent of GNP. Another significant development has been the recent shifts in intra-sectoral priorities, with substantial enhancement in the allocation for elementary and adult education, which are of direct relevance to the poor. The share of total plan expenditure (revenue) of the Centre and the States on elementary and adult education has increased from 48 per cent in 1990-91 to 51 per cent in 1993-94. This trend is a step in the right direction.

TABLE 2

**Gross Enrolment Ratio in Classes I-V and VI-VIII for Major States[1], 1992-93**

(Per cent)

| State | Primary (I-V) | | | Upper Primary (VI-VIII) | | |
|---|---|---|---|---|---|---|
| | Boys | Girls | Total | Boys | Girls | Total |
| 1 | 2 | 3 | 4 | 5 | 6 | 7 |
| Andhra Pradesh | 116.4 | 100.1 | 108.4 | 73.9 | 53.1 | 63.7 |
| Assam | 134.4 | 125.3 | 130.0 | 89.3 | 65.5 | 77.7 |
| Bihar | 95.9 | 54.4 | 76.1 | 47.4 | 21.0 | 34.7 |
| Gujarat | 131.4 | 106.0 | 119.1 | 82.8 | 55.5 | 69.6 |
| Haryana | 109.7 | 95.4 | 102.8 | 81.8 | 59.2 | 70.9 |
| Karnataka | 124.3 | 115.2 | 119.9 | 72.4 | 57.2 | 65.0 |
| Kerala | 103.8 | 100.8 | 102.3 | 108.3 | 105.7 | 107.0 |
| Madhya Pradesh | 116.7 | 91.3 | 104.5 | 82.5 | 50.0 | 66.9 |
| Maharashtra | 123.6 | 115.0 | 119.4 | 89.0 | 71.8 | 80.7 |
| Orissa | 116.8 | 77.6 | 96.8 | 67.5 | 46.9 | 57.0 |
| Punjab | 92.0 | 88.1 | 90.6 | 71.8 | 63.4 | 67.8 |
| Rajasthan | 119.5 | 60.9 | 91.0 | 76.8 | 28.9 | 53.9 |
| Tamil Nadu | 149.0 | 140.8 | 145.0 | 111.3 | 91.0 | 101.4 |
| Uttar Pradesh | 103.9 | 72.8 | 89.3 | 72.2 | 35.4 | 55.0 |
| West Bengal | 124.7 | 123.0 | 123.9 | 98.2 | 89.1 | 93.8 |
| **All India** | **115.3** | **92.9** | **104.5** | **79.3** | **55.2** | **67.7** |

[1]Major States include States with population of 10 million and above as per 1991 Census.

*Source* : Ministry of Human Resource Development.

Box 1.1

**The Goals of Education For All**

- Expansion of early childhood care and development activities especially for poor, disadvantaged and disabled children, through a multi-pronged effort involving families, communities and appropriate institutions.
- Universalization of Elementary Education (UEE), viewed as a composite programme of :
  - access to elementary education for all children up to 14 years of age;
  - universal participation till they complete the elementary stage through formal or non-formal education programmes; and
  - universal achievement at least of minimum levels of learning.
- Drastic reduction in illiteracy, particularly in the 15-35 age-group, bringing the literacy level in this age-group to at least 80 per cent in each gender and for every identified disadvantaged group, besides ensuring that the levels of the three R's (Reading, Writing and Arithmetic) are relevant to the living and working conditions of the people.
- Provision of opportunities to maintain, use and upgrade education, and provision of facilities for development of skills to all persons who are functionally literate and those who have received primary education through formal and non-formal channels.
- Creation of necessary structures and setting in motion of processes which would empower women and make education an instrument of women's equality.
- Improving the content and process of education to relate it better to the environment, people's culture and with their living and working conditions, thereby enhancing their ability to learn and cope with the problems of livelihood and environment.

The share of the Government in financing educational institutions has been very high. In 1985-86, it accounted for about 88 per cent of the total income of educational institutions, whereas the share from fees and endowments and other sources of educational institutions declined sharply (Table 3).

As bulk of the expenditure on education, including maintenance expenditure, is incurred by the State Governments, they must reprioritise expenditure and tighten fiscal discipline. Besides public spending, community financing of education needs to be encouraged. In view of the overall fiscal constraints, there is a need to mobile greater resources for the sector by revising fees and other user charges, especially for higher levels of education.

TABLE 3

**Source of Income of all Educational Institutions**

(Per cent)

| Year | Govt. Funds (Centre and States) | Local bodies[1] funds | University funds | Total Govt. (2+3+4) | Fees | Endowments and other Sources | Total |
|---|---|---|---|---|---|---|---|
| 1 | 2 | 3 | 4 | 5 | 6 | 7 | 8 |
| 1950-51 | 57.06 | 10.93 | - | 67.99 | 20.39 | 11.62 | 100.00 |
| 1960-61 | 67.97 | 6.53 | - | 74.50 | 17.14 | 8.35 | 100.00 |
| 1970-71 | 75.65 | 4.34 | 1.36 | 81.35 | 12.81 | 5.85 | 100.00 |
| 1980-81 | 81.70 | 4.71 | 1.37 | 87.78 | 8.20 | 4.03 | 100.00 |
| 1983-84 | 81.51 | 5.61 | 1.61 | 88.73 | 7.50 | 3.78 | 100.00 |
| 1984-85 | 79.98 | 5.40 | 2.08 | 87.46 | 6.47 | 6.07 | 100.00 |
| 1985-86 | 80.29 | 5.23 | 2.15 | 87.67 | 6.27 | 6.06 | 100.00 |

*Source* : Ministry of Human Resource Development.

## QUESTIONS FOR EXERCISE

1. Discuss any two major problems of education that have beset any country in the world.
2. How can education be correlated with life ? How can it be democratized? Give examples.
3. What are the major problems of education that arise because of the modern scientific technological advancements ? Suggest measures for their solution.
4. What are the principal tendencies perceptible in the current education of the world ? Explain any two of them in detail.

# 2

# ORGANISATIONS PROVIDING EDUCATION

India has been well-known in the field of education since ancient times. There were Ashrams during the Vedic, the Ramayan and Mahabharat periods. Institutions of higher education in the Buddhist period were centres of attraction for people all over the world. The famous universities of Nalanda and Takshila were autonomous though they received sufficient economic help from the States and the public. During the Muslim period, the Muslim rulers established Madarsas for the teaching of Arabic, Persian and Urdu languages in order to propagate their culture. These achieved success to some extent by adopting a hard and repressive policy towards the then prevailing educational systems. Those schools gradually became ineffective with the end of their rules. Till the advent of the British rule, the Indian educational institutions of all levels were run by voluntary organisations and providing free education. They received generous financial help from the various States, princes and public.

The advent of British Rule in India brought about several changes in Indian educational system. East India Company established Government Secondary Schools for teaching English to the Indians for administrative purposes. The Christian missionaries, established secondary schools and colleges alongwith Churches as a powerful means of propagation of Christianity. These educational institutions with Western influence spread throughout the country and indigenous educational institutions based on Indian traditions, were relegated to the background. Some Sanskrit Pathshalas can still be seen as their remnants at some places. The present Indian education is an outcome of Western efforts. During the British rule, several Indian educational enthusiasts established educational institutions which are active even today like other educational organisations. Some of them achieved high levels of efficiency. After Independence, the organisation of Government schools and colleges run by the British administration came under the State Governments. Educational organisations established by foreign missionaries, private and voluntary Indian organisations are even now functioning in the same manner.

**Kinds of Educational Organisations**

According to their organisations the present educational institutions can be classified as under :

1. Those established by the Central Government.
2. Those established by the State Governments.
3. Those run by private and social bodies.
4. Those run by the religious bodies.
5. Those run by the local bodies such as District and Municipal Boards etc.

**1. Educational Organisations Established by Central Government**

(i) *Schools and Colleges by Ministries* : According to the Indian Constitution, most of the responsibility of educational organization lies with the State Government. Some Central Ministries have established schools and colleges at some places under special circumstances. Railways, Defence and Education Ministries are main among them. As several big centres of Railway Service have been established in some towns and small cities where general education facilities are not easily available to the children of Railwaymen, so primary and secondary schools and colleges have been established by the Railway Ministry at such places according to the local needs. In these educational institutions the service conditions are like those for other Railwaymen. Regarding examinations and curriculum etc., these institutions are governed by the local government rules. Central Defence Ministry has established Military Schools (Academics) for preparing students for Military Services. Special attention is paid to the physical development of children in these schools. Alongwith it, the Defence Ministry has also established schools for the education of children of its servicemen. The Education Ministry has established secondary schools under the education development programmes and the entire burden of educational provisions in Centrally administered areas rests on the Centre. The condition of schools established by different ministries is much better than the average schools due to the attraction of better salaries, service conditions, better qualified and efficient teachers.

(ii) *Central Schools* : Kendriya Vidyalayas (Central Schools) were established in 1962 for education of children of parents engaged in various types of Central Services. These schools have been started to serve as model school in collaboration with the National Council of Educational Research and Training (N.C.E.R.T.) and Central Board of Secondary Education (C.B.S.E.). These schools admit children from any family if seats are not filled in by children of Central Government employees. However, preference is always given to the children of Central Government employees. Central Schools are running parallel to the secondary schools run under the jurisdiction of the Central Government. It is not easy to say that they are working as models to the schools established earlier for the wards of the employees of the Central Government.

**2. Educational Organisations Established by the State Governments**

The State Governments have received a long chain of Government Secondary Schools as legacy of the British rule. Since then, their number has also increased in various States. In some States their form has also changed. In States where there was sufficient number of educational institutions established by other organisations, fewer Government schools and colleges were opened as compared with the States which had less of these educational provisions. In some States, secondary schools for general education were converted into multipurpose and technical schools. Government Girls Schools were established for the development of girls' education in backward areas. After the establishment of new Government schools there were the two-fold aims of providing educational facilities to the people in all spheres and to inspire other organisations for establishing educational institutions. The new Government schools are established on the same basis even today. The greater the backwardness of a particular area, the greater is the number of government schools in that area.

### 3. Educational Organisation Run by Private and Social Bodies

In democracy, an individual is a part of the nation. The obligations of the nation are also the obligations of the individual. The number of persons co-operating in the national responsibilities denotes national progress. In India, the efforts of the different individuals and organisations in the field of education, reflect the developing feelings of nationalism in the country. Most of the Indian educational institutions fall in this category. Some schools of this category have been established and are being established even now by rich people. Some rich persons have appointed trusts by donating money for establishing schools. Other educational institutions have been established by persons and organisations interested in education. In the absence of personal property, some educational enthusiasts have established schools by collecting donations from the public. The same is true of other organisations. In the case of organisations most of the financial and other help has come from concerned organisations. The educational institutions of different levels, providing education to most of the children carry with them the stories of praise-worthy sacrifices of a number of people. Some institutions of this category have earned great reputation and some are centres of international attraction because of their special ideals and values in the field of education.

Barring a few institutions which are managed by the family members of the organiser, all other institutions are managed by various managing committees, the members on which are either elected or nominated. These institutions depend for their finances on Government grants, income from trust or endowment, attached personal property, or income from capital or subscriptions or donations etc. Before freedom, a sense of patriotism was attached with such institutions and inspired by it, the public, too, gave all possible help. After the attainment of freedom, the attitude of the public has changed and organisation of educational institutions is now considered as a state responsibility. So due to stringent financial conditions, private institutions are functioning with caution.

Some big industrialists have established some educational institutions for the education of the children of their workers in their respective factory areas and expenditure on this account is also borne by them.

### 4. Educational Organisations Run by Religious Bodies

(i) *Christian Mission Schools* : Educational institutions established by Christian missionaries for evangelisation are under the control of concerned missionaries even after the British Rule. The missions are financially sound. The educational institutions established by them also get Government grants. As such these institutions are well-off from every point of view. These institutions are managed by persons nominated by the missionaries. Most of such persons are connected with local Churches. These institutions have a better standard of teaching due to their better general conditions, facilities and attraction of better pay than that of other educational institutions.

(ii) *Schools by Hindu Organisations* : Beside Christian Missionaries some Hindu religious organisations such as Arya Samaj, Brahma Samaj, Sanatan Dharam, Ram Krishna Mission etc., have established educational institutions for the spread of both education and religion. With the passage of time, their programmes for the propagation of religion have slowed down but their efforts for the development of education are still useful. A long chain of educational institutions established by the Arya Samaj is running throughout the whole country. It is making significant contribution in the field of education. Before Independence, these institutions also received generous help from the public connected with the religion and inspired by the feeling of patriotism. After Independence, this tendency has slackened. Now, only those educational institutions connected with religious bodies are financially sound which are related to capitalist or businessmen and who get income tax rebate on donations. The sources of income of other organisations are reducing day by day. All educational institutions belonging to this category get government grants and except a few, the condition of all the institutions is average or below it.

**5. Educational Organisations Run by Local Bodies**

A large part of the educational responsibility of the State Governments is shared by local self-government bodies such as Zila Parishads and Municipal Boards. These receive financial help from the State Governments for a major portion of their expenditure. They have to supplement the rest from their own resources. In the rural areas of the district, the primary and junior high schools are established and provided for by Zila Parishads. In cities, the Municipal Boards organise primary schools and junior high schools according to local needs. In big cities Zila Parishads and Municipal Boards have organised secondary schools and colleges also. As the financial condition of most of the Zila Parishads and Municipal Boards are not good because of increasing needs of the time, limited sources of income and mismanagement, they find it difficult to meet their share of educational expenditure. So the schools run by them generally face the shortage of buildings, equipment and apparatus, teachers, etc.

## CRITICAL EVALUATION OF VARIOUS INSTITUTIONS

1. **Central Government Institutions** : The condition of institutions organised by the various ministries of the Central Government is good. They have good buildings, proper equipment and necessary apparatus and have suitable arrangement of games, sports, gymnasium, reading-rooms and hostels. But preference is given

to the admission of children of a particular class in these institutions. Such a provision is against the principle of 'equality of opportunity' of Indian Constitution and creates dissatisfaction in the society. The Central Government should provide educational facilities to the children of its employees through the State Governments. The amount thus spent will benefit a greater number of students.

2. **State Governments Institutions** : In the educational institution run by the State Governments, better salaries, service conditions and other facilities for the teachers and better buildings, equipment, apparatus, reading rooms, play grounds, gymnasium, hostels and such other facilities have created discontentment among the teachers and students of other educational institutions of the same place. The movement of teachers for same salary for same work is the outcome of such a system. The discontent among students is seen in the form of baseless movements and disruptive activities. As a government servant the teacher of government schools have to follow government orders which lead to disorder as follows : (i) They are transferred regularly from one school to the other and therefore, proper contact among teachers and students is not established. (ii) They have to obey the orders of their superior officers blindly whether the same are in the interest of school and students or not. They have no right to make amendments in the prescribed procedure. (iii) They have to show partiality sometimes in order to please local authorities besides their departmental authorities.

The State Governments should have uniform policy regarding educational institutions. Either all the educational institutions should be under the State Government or the local people should manage Government schools also and the State Governments should provide grants to all equally.

3. **Local-self Government Institutions** : The contribution of Zila Parishads and Municipal Boards in the field of education is particularly important.. Most of the defects in institutions run by them originate from financial shortage. This situation can be remedied by allowing them to levy education tax or by giving them sufficient financial help. There should be managing committees at different levels for the supervision of these institutions.

4. **Private Institutions** : One of the main drawbacks in the institutions run by private persons is that they themselves or their family members behave like autocrats while managing the schools. Hence, their management should be handed over to committee. Institutions run by various organisations have some other defects besides financial shortage. Influenced by the active cooperation of the institutions in the struggle for freedom, the members of different parties misuse them for their own vested interests by giving them the allurement of financial help. The groupism in the teachers of these institutions is an evil effect of the political influence. Sufficient financial help from the Government can remove many of these defects and the public should also cooperate in the fulfilment of other requirements.

5. **Religious Institutions** : In the educational institutions organised by the missionaries, the regular programmes for the propagation of religion and favouritism towards the students who follow that religion, are against Indian policy. According to the Constitution nobody can be forced to follow or study a particular religion. The

same favouritism is shown at the time of appointment and promotion of teachers. Such religious bias is the main drawback in the field of education. Educational institutions should be kept free from such influences of religion.

## QUESTIONS FOR EXERCISE

1. What are the different institutions run by Government and non-Government bodies? Describe them briefly.
2. What are the defects in educational institutions run by different bodies? What efforts should be made to improve them?
3. What problems of education do you generally face in view of various organisations for providing education? Explain briefly with suitable examples.

# 3

# PROBLEM OF EXPLOSION OF KNOWLEDGE

Now-a-days there is an explosion of knowledge due to unprecedented advancements in the fields of science and technology. These advancements have resulted into making a successful trip even to the moon. Old ideas are gradually changing giving place to new ones. Values and traditions are in the process of transformation. New knowledge has been discovered in each subject. Man's mind is disturbed with the question whether he should teach the new knowledge or the old. Should we teach the old for helping the student to learn the new ? How should we present the old and new knowledge in an inter-connected manner ? What type of knowledge should be imparted at a particular stage ? How should the knowledge given at the various stages of education be made as one connected whole? What methods should be adopted to facilitate the achievement of the objectives of teaching ? Under such a situation only that person can successfully give solutions to these issues who is thoroughly conversant with the knowledge we want to impart. This ever increasing store of knowledge has created following problems for education :

1. What should we teach ?
2. What is the purpose of teaching ?
3. When should we teach ?
4. How should we teach ?

## Principles of Knowing

1. *Structure of Knowledge* : In the methods of teaching today one finds emphasis on acquainting the student with the structure of knowledge and not to impart informations. This means that the student should be helped to grasp the structure of subject in such a way as to enable him to understand things related to it in a meaningful context. The student has to be taught how things are related. If he understands the inter-relationship between things, he will be able to grasp many other relevant things in a meaningful manner.

2. *Readiness for learning* : Today it is believed that any subject may be taught at any stage of education. The basic idea is that the fundamental principles of any subject may be taught in some form to a child of any age group. Many scientists,

technicians and machinists could be produced in U.S.S.R. through the theory of learning by conditioned response. This could be possible by creating a readiness in the individual for learning. Thus education in U.S.S.R. may be as an example of readiness for learning.

3. *Use of Intuitive Analytical Method* : Intuition is the method through which one reaches a relevant conclusion without analysing the situation. After reaching the conclusion one verifies it by analysis. Training should be given in hunches for developing intuition. Intuition is important in intellectual work, as well as in daily work. When a person tries to think intuitively and reach a possible conclusion, this habit refers to his intuitive ability. He at once grasps the intricacies of a situation and is able to go ahead in his chosen sphere of activity. Several great scientists and great persons base their thinking process on intuition in their respective fields. Intuition may be received in any mental activity higher or lower. The difference being only of the degree and not of the kind. Hence, training should be given in intuition in every school.

4. *Motivation* : In order to enable the student to learn, he must be motivated to learn. This motive may be a desire to learn or to win some reward or to get promotion to another higher class. The external incentives, like reward and promotion is not always helpful in stimulating the child to learn. One should depend upon the principles of child psychology, teaching methods and reorganizing the curriculum in an integrated manner for creating motivation in the child.

5. *Use of Teaching Aids* : A number of teaching aids have been developed these days. In order to be more effective, the teacher is now expected to select a proper teaching aid and use it relevantly. As there are so many aids to teach, the teacher naturally feels a problem of selecting the right one out of many before him.

## PROBLEMS OF EXPLOSION OF KNOWLEDGE

### 1. Structure of knowledge

A man studies not only for self-pleasure but also to benefit himself in such a way that he may use the earned knowledge in future for his betterment. In the process of learning he may acquire many such skills by virtue of which he may do many identical things later. In the same way through his studies he learnt many things and acquire many attitudes. These learnt things and attitudes are used later in various situations of life. The main purpose of various methods of education is to help the students to acquire certain useful principles of work, desirable attitudes and modes of good behaviour according to the accepted social norms. This will be achieved only when he acquires a grip over the structure of knowledge. Therefore, the major emphasis should be on helping the student to enter into the basic structural elements of the subject placed before him to learn. This creates the following two main problems before the teacher :

(i) How to reorganize the curriculum of the basic subjects in such a manner as to help the student to acquire the basic ideas effectively in order to develop the desired attitudes which may work as propellors of good behaviour.

(ii) The second problem is how to tailor the curriculum to suit each and every stage of education.

In order to solve in the above problems, the experts in the various subjects should sit together and reorganize the curriculum for the primary and secondary levels. These experts should be helped by experienced teachers of various primary and secondary classes. Experienced authors, film-producers and other experts may also be consulted in this work. Such a procedure has been followed in many advanced countries in the reorganising of the curriculum in mathematics, natural sciences, social sciences and literature.

When the general principles of a subject are learnt by a student he should be able to arrange the learnt things in a systematic and meaningful manner in his mind so that he may use the same when an occasion arises.

**2. Readiness to Learning**

It is assumed that any subject may be taught to any child at any stage of his development. There are three following bases of this assumption :

(i) *The process of intellectual development of the child* : In his process of development the child has his own characteristic way of viewing the world. He understands the world in his own way. Hence, a subject should be taught to the child according to his point of view. The teacher has not to teach a subject to the child according to the adult point of view. According to the demands of the development of the child, the subject matter may be made more inclusive and comprehensive gradually. At first the child is better able to understand concrete things through the help of concrete things or concrete examples. This is able to comprehend abstract ideas. At first the child absorbs only those ideas which are presented before him through some concrete instances.

(ii) *The psychology of learning* : There are three mental processes during the course of learning : (a) acquisition of knowledge or ideas, (b) transformation of the learnt knowledge of ideas in which the learner tries to arrange the learnt things in his mind in his own way. In this transformation he analyses the inherent points and introduces such changes in the same way which may be helpful to him later, (c) evaluation about whether the transformation made is such as to fulfil teaching purpose. All these three processes, acquisition, transformation and evaluation are involved in learning of any subject.

(iii) *The notion of spiral curriculum* : In the spiral curriculum the contents of a certain subject matter is arranged in such a logical and challenging manner that the learner is propelled to learn further about the subject once learnt. In this process even a small child is taught such things which will be suitable even for an adult to learn. Thus, through the spiral curriculum the child is helped to absorb many such basic and structural ideas which are challenging even to an adult. Therefore, those problems, principles, ideas and values should be incorporated in the spiral curriculum which the society consider suitable for adults to imbibe. As the problems, ideas and values prevailing in society are undergoing constant transformation the spiral curriculum should be continually changed and modified according to explicit or implicit demands of the society.

### 3. Intuitional Method

When one is working on a problem for a long time thinking about its solution, all of a sudden he gets the solution, though he has yet to provide a proof for it. This method of finding a sudden solution is a result of intuitional thinking. Hence, it is called intuitional method. In analytical thinking one proceeds step by step and he is conscious of this step all the time. The operations and informations involved in the analytical thinking are deliberately chosen and decided upon. It may also involve deductive reasoning. In contrast to this procedure of analytical thinking, the intuitive thinking is not well defined. It implies implicit perception of the total problem. The answer arrived at by intuitive thinking may be right or wrong, but the thinker cannot justify his conclusion immediately. Intuitive thinking is possible only if the thinker is familiar with the domain of knowledge and its structure. Due to this familiarity with the domain and structure of knowledge the thinker is able to leap about, skip steps and employ short cuts. Through intuitive thinking an individual may get a correct solution which he can never obtain by analytical method. But once the solution is obtained through intuition, the same must be checked and verified through analysis, induction and deduction. An intuitive thinker may discover or invent problems, but it is analysis that gives proper form to these problems. But unfortunately the formalism of the school atmosphere does not recognise the importance of intuition. As a result intuition appears to be devalued in the school. Hence, the teacher in the school must devise methods for developing intuitive thinking in his students. For this the curriculum has to be carefully reorganized.

*How to Develop intuitive Thinking* : After giving an answer through his intuition, the teacher should subject his answer to critical analysis to be made by his students. This procedure shall encourage the students to do their own intuitive thinking at times. It will energise the students and will bring life in the monotonous atmosphere of the class. The teacher must not analyse everything for his students rather the analysis should be made by the students themselves. One should remember that the emphasis in teaching or helping the students to grasp the structure or connectedness of knowledge will immensely facilitate intuitive thinking because the comprehension of structure will help the student to increase his effectiveness in grasping problems intuitively. Self-confidence and courage should be developed because effective intuitive thinking may be developed in the student on the basis of these traits. For the development of intuitive thinking the intuitive thinker must never feel shy if he makes mistakes in his intuitive answers. On the contrary, he should be willing to make honest mistakes in his endeavour to find out solutions to problems.

### 4. Motivation for Learning

Today every human society is exposed to continual changes. After the World War II, these changes have been revolutionary. The various countries are afraid of each other. There is an arms race. The world is divided in aligned and non-aligned groups, big and small powers, developed, developing and underdeveloped countries. The politicians categorise the human race into three major groups — first world, second world and third world. Each country of the world is facing political, cultural or social crises. There has been the impact of automatic machines, new sources of energy and space investigations. Never was the human society so much mrechanised. Never was it so near to annihilation which is dependent on the calculation of some super power. This state of affairs has revolutionized the very concept of the school offerings. People no more interested only in intellectual, cultural and physical activities in schools. They are now emphasising the teaching of science and technical subjects. Students offer these subjects, because these assure them positions in some technical establishments. More brilliant students are encouraged to offer science or technical subject whether or not he has an aptitude for the same. This trend has brought in many students who are not deserving on intrinsic merits study science and technical subjects. Many students are being neglected. The children whose growth is delayed or who are not able to complete their formal education because of adverse circumstances are totally neglected. One finds a new current of pursuit of excellence which has divided children into two classes — brilliant and dull. In every country there is a search of science talent and there is a test for it on in all country basis. National scholarships are being awarded to able students in science and technical subjects. This has led to the neglect of the studies of humanities and social sciences. It appears that a day will come, when there will be dearth of learned persons and really efficient teachers in these areas. Hence, the cultural traditions appear to be exposed to great harm. Thus, it is necessary to reorganise the curriculum of humanities, social sciences and literature in the same manner in which it is being done for science and technical subjects. Necessary reforms should be introduced in the examination system so that one may be able to classify students of various abilities on a scientific basis. If sciences and technical subjects are to be saved from unhealthy competitive spirit and over-importance, the Government must pay the same attention to the studies of humanities and social sciences. Incentive for learning should be made more comprehensive. Incentives should be energised by making the ability the basis of deservingness. Education should be saved from the ill effects of unhealthy competitions.

**5. Aids of Teaching**

Today one should find a number of aids to teaching and learning. Some of these enrich the students' experiences. Some help them to understand the basic structure of the curriculum. The various aids to teaching may be grouped into the following four categories :

(i) Devices of Vicarious Experiences;

(ii) Model Devices;

(iii) Dramatizing Devices; and

(iv) Automatizing Devices.

(i) *Devices of Vicarious Experiences* : These include films, television, microphotographic films, filmstrips, sound recording and the like which are ordinarily employed. Through these devices students are generally given such matters which are outside the prescribed courses. They are given experience pertaining to certain events directly. These devices enrich the experiences of the students and they also bring life in the educational procedure.

(ii) *Model Devices* : Through these the student grasps the fundamentals of an event or a certain context. These modes are generally shown as laboratory exercises. Certain wooden blocks have been devised for this purpose. Pictures and charts are also used for helping students to understand the basic structure.

(iii) *Dramatizing Devices* : These devices help the student in identifying a certain idea or phenomenon more closely. Some historical event or the life pattern of some great men may be dramatised. In the process of teaching the teacher himself may dramatise certain aspects of the subject matter or may read out certain portions of the text-book in a dramatic tone. This may bring life in the class-room. It may also help the student to grasp the essentials in a better way.

(iv) *Automatising Devices* : These include machines to aid in teaching. Through these machines certain problems are presented in a systematic manner. Alternative answers are also associated with the problems. The student is required to select the correct answer. With the selection the machine begins to respond. If the selected answer is correct, the machine moves on further and presents another problem or exercise. The exercises for the machines are so arranged that the student encounters both easy and difficult ones So if he fails in case of difficult exercises, in an easier exercise he succeeds immediately. Therefore he is not discouraged.

## QUESTIONS FOR EXERCISE

1. How has explosion of knowledge created certain problems for education? Explain.
2. What is structure of knowledge? What is its implication for modern education?
3. Distinguish between intuitive and analytical thinking. How can the teacher encourage intuitive thinking in students? Give examples.
4. Describe briefly the latest aids to teaching? Explain their uses and limitations.

4

# PROBLEMS OF EDUCATIONAL ADMINISTRATION AND SUPERVISION

Education is an important factor for the development of a nation. It is closely related with the public life of a nation. It enriches public life in a situation of development and expansion. In adverse circumstances the public life becomes unhappy and the national strength gradually becomes weak. Education should be an important part of national responsibility, for the smooth running of the programmes of national development.

**What is Educational Administration?**

Educational administration is that part of administrative set-up which is responsible for the development and expansion of different educational systems. Its function is to make the educational system useful and capable according to the needs of the people and to enable them to take maximum advantage from those systems. It is to regulate educational systems and to channelize them for public good and utility. Educational institutions prepare the ground for the future progress of nation. But educational administration has not been given any importance at the national or State administrative level in India. The Central Government has relieved itself of all responsibilities by delegating educational responsibilities to the States and by retaining only some special educational responsibilities. The Educational departments in the States are most neglected and inactive. Sanctioning grants and other economic help, budgeting and running of Government institutions is considered as their sole responsibility. Any civil servant is appointed on an important post of Education Department, irrespective of his qualifications, knowledge and suitability. Hence, while giving their approval for educational programmes and projects the authorities remain quite ignorant of the real situation. Instead of contributing to the development of education according to their rank, they remain an instrument of putting their signatures on departmental notes and often indulge in making unnecessary changes. Officers of the Educational Department should be different from other civil officers. Every education officer should have the ability of preparing budget, of planning and guidance, organisation, reporting, administration and coordination. He should be skilful, far-sighted and adept in observing men and situations. Certain moral virtues are necessary for education officers along with other qualifications. They should also have a knowledge of science of education. As educational administration is a complicated affair, the education officers should be equipped with above qualifications and qualities of distinct personality.

## ORGANISATION OF EDUCATIONAL ADMINISTRATION

The Indian Constitution has divided the responsibility of education between the Centre and States. The Central (Union) Government is responsible for certain specific provisions of education under special circumstances. The entire responsibility of education in the States rests with the State Governments. Following is the outline of educational organisation according to the Indian Constitution.

### Union Government

According to the Indian Constitution the responsibilities of the Union Government include educational organisation in Centrally administered areas or princely States, direction of Delhi, Aligrah, Varanasi and Vishva-Bharati Universities, direction of higher scientific and technical educational institutions and concerning research, specific educational programmes such as training for education of abnormal children, Criminology training and research, training of police personnel, educational projects, efforts for raising the standard of education, programmes concerning national language and culture, provision of international contact in educational sphere, education of labour and provision of scholarships etc. Besides these, financial help to the States for education is also the responsibility of the Centre.

*Central Agencies of Education* : These functions are performed by the Education Ministry and Ministry of Scientific Research and Cultural Affairs. The Railway Ministry makes separate arrangement for the education of the children of its employees at important railway centres. Under the Education Ministry fall Administrative Department, Secondary Education Department, Primary and Basic Education Department, Physical Education and Recreation Department, Social Education and Social Welfare Department, Research and Publication Department, Higher Education and International Relations Department. Scientific Research Department, Cultural Department, Technical Department, Foreign Relations and Administrative Department are under the Ministry of Scientific Research and Cultural Affairs. Central Hindi Directorate, Directorate of Extension Programme for Secondary Education, Directorate of Social Welfare and Rehabilitation are affiliated to the Ministry of Education. The Ministry of Scientific Research and Cultural Affairs has four main offices connected with technical education in Bombay, Madras, Calcutta and Kanpur. Apart from these, there are supervision committees attached to Education Ministry to look after the programmes of Union Government. The first Special Reorganisation Unit and the Second Plan Coordination Unit are connected with the organisation and implementation of educational projects of the Ministry of Education.

*Official Hierarchy* : The constitutional head of the Education Ministry is the Education Minister. For his assistance there are the Chief Administrative Officer, the Education Advisor and the Education Secretary. To look after the work of different constituents of Education Ministry, there are Joint Education Advisor and Joint Education Secretary. Under them are Deputy Education Advisor and Deputy Education Secretary, Associate Secretary, Assistant Secretary, Superintendent, Section Officer etc., and such other officers and employees. An Additional Deputy Secretary has been appointed to supervise the work connected with international relations and education abroad. An officer of the rank of Deputy Secretary or Associate Secretary shoulders the responsibility of all departments.

**State Government**

*State Ministry of Education* : According to the Indian Constitution, the entire responsibility of education in the States is that of the State Governments. All those subjects that have not been included in the Union list, come under the jurisdiction of State Governments. The structure of educational administration is almost similar in all the States. The Education Minister is responsible for giving necessary advice to the State Minister on matters pertaining to education and to implement the decisions of the Ministry. In the State Secretariat, there is a Department of Education for educational functions. Its highest authority is the Education Secretary. Besides, there are one or more Joint Secretaries, Deputy Secretary, Associate Secretary, Assistant Secretaries according to expediency. The main function of the Education Department is to formulate education policies. In University education matters, the University Grant Committee in the State advises the Education Minister on financial matters and if need be, on organisational matters, too. Otherwise, the Universities are autonomous bodies and make most of the provisions themselves. In State where text-books have been nationalized, the Education Minister holds the responsibility of composition, selection, permission, publication and fixing of price etc.

*The Directorate of Education* : The Directorate of Education holds a key position in State educational organization. Its highest officer is the Director of Education. For his help there are one Joint Director, Several Deputy Directors, Assistant Directors, Associate Deputy Directors and Special Officers with specific functions. The Director of Education advises the Education Minister or State Ministry on educational issues from time to time and makes necessary arrangements for education in the State. The Director of Education is the Chief of Educational administration and his representatives at the district level are District Inspector of Schools and at regional levels Regional Deputy Directors and Regional Inspectresses. At the district level, the post of Inspector of Schools is as important as that of the Director of Education. His duties include inspection and their general arrangement of schools in the district, sanction of grants and deficit grants, recognition of schools, organisation of examination upto senior basic stage, organisation of programmes for educational expansion etc. For his help, there are the Deputy Inspector, Sub-Deputy Inspectors and Inspectresses.

*Limitations of State Machinery* : The work-load of the Director of Education and District Inspector of Schools is so heavy that they cannot bear it well. In recent years, the number of their assistant officers has been increased but it is only an *ad-*

*hoc* arrangement. In Rajasthan, separate posts of Director of Primary Education and Director of Secondary Education have been created. But in most of the States, there is only one post. Different Education Commissions have given several suggestions to overcome organisational difficulties. The Secondary Education Commission 1953, had suggested to establish State Advisory Board of Education for co-operation and co-ordination between different educational bodies. The Kothari Commission has suggested to establish State Board of Education and State Institute of Education at the State level. But the State Governments have not taken any concrete steps in this direction.

## CONSTITUTIONAL PROVISIONS

According to Indian Constitution there are three units of educational administration in India. The first is the Union or Central Government, the second is State Government and third is local administrative units. The Constitution prescribes the jurisdiction of all the units. The Union Government has no direct concern with the administration of educational institutions. It is mainly concerned with financial help and specific education. The State Governments have the responsibility of education in the States, though educational administration is not centralised in the States. So the States Departments of Education and Director of Education have no direct control over the educational institutions. Local administration provides education only upto primary stage. The educational institutions managed by them are aggrieved by the double control of these and State Government both.

In education, the Western countries have a peculiar organisation. The individual freedom of educational institution is more emphasised while educational administration is nominal and decentralised. The constitutional provision in India favour decentralisation, yet the educational administration here is a mixture of centralisation and decentralisation. Hence, there is a complete lack of co-ordination in the different spheres of education. Therefore, educational administration is devoid of promptness. No unit of educational administration is fulfilling its obligations.

### Advantages of the constitutional division of responsibilities

1. Constitution has fixed the jurisdiction of all the administrative units and as such there is hardly any possibility of disputes of jurisdiction. No unit can monopolise in the field of arbitrary.

2. The idea of individual freedom may create democratic feeling in the people engaged in educational work. It is expected that the teachers and authorities of educational institutions may carry out their responsibility and working with free-will. Sincerity and co-operation will contribute more and more towards the public good. The same ideas and feelings should prevail amongst the officers and employees engaged in educational administration.

3. The constitutional division has provided opportunities to the people for contributing in the educational field. The people can show their educational awakening and liberal attitude towards education by giving all possible help to the

educational institutions of their region. The Union Government and State Governments, too, can lead them to progress by giving sufficient financial help and needed guidance to educational institutions and local self-government units without exercising special control.

4. As the constitution has tried to include the benefits of both centralisation and decentralisation systems, the educational organisations are saved from coming under some special monopoly or influence and it increases human relations between teachers and the students. It inculcates qualities of responsibility. It develops a sense of self-reliance.

**Disadvantages of the constitutional division**

1. The division is theoretical and ambiguous. Even after the division, the three units are interdependent. There is no clarity about their programmes.

2. There is indifference in the implementation of plans concerning educational development and expansion and regarding starting of various programmes. No unit tries to take initiative and come forward to work.

3. Lack of the feeling of co-operation amongst them has created several obstacles in the educational organisation. While some part of the union grants lapses due to non-utilisation, other educational institutions are in a very bad shape due to shortage of funds.

**Causes of constitutional difficulties**

The main cause of the difficulties arising out of the constitutional division is that at the time of framing the Constitution, no importance was attached to education. Whatever system of education existed before Independence was distributed to the three administrative units with some changes. Therefore, several difficulties have arisen in the execution of constitutional provisions. The entire system is based on the mutual co-operation of these units while practically this co-operation is totally absent.

**Tendencies of Educational Administration**

Generally, two types of tendencies are found in educational administration — centralisation and decentralisation.

1. *Centralisation* : Centralisation in educational administration amount to nationlisation. When the people are discontented with some individual or collective system, they demand nationalisation or centralisation. The ideology of centralisation is given by Communists or Socialist philosophy. According to it, centralisation of education is the most powerful means of providing equality of educational opportunities. It removes bad practices and mismanagement in the field of education. It helps equal educational development of the people in the country. Centralisation system is the most appropriate for the speedy development and expansion of education for nations backward in the educational sphere. It is found to be more convenient to make the educational system suitable to national needs. It is found in Russia and other socialist countries.

2. *Decentralisation* : Decentralisation in educational administration is opposite of the centralised system. In it, the main responsibility of educational organisation rests upon the regional people. The burden of its supervision and administration lies on the local administrative units. The responsibility of the State and Central Government is gradually reduced. Their relations with educational institutions are indirect. Their main functions are to formulate educational policies, to prepare plans for educational development and expansion, financial grants, recognition, equipment and permission for books. Educational institutions have comparatively more freedom.

## CENTRALISATION OF INDIAN EDUCATION

### Demand for Centralisation

When the people face scarcity of commodities of consumption and it is difficult to make both ends meet, they lean towards socialism. India is today suffering from scarcity of natural resources and artificial scarcity created by affluent and powerful persons to fulfil their vested interests. Due to the mismanagement in private organisations of production, industry and commerce, the incidents of strikes, movement etc. are increasing and the general opinion is in favour of nationalisation. In the educational field, the failure of people connected with the management of schools and their vested interests affecting the teachers as well as increasing educational expenditures affecting the students, have led them to demand centralisation of education. It is asked that Central Government should take the entire responsibility of education upon itself. Many educational institutions are slowly becoming commercial institutions. The tendency of exploitation is increasing. More and more money is being squeezed out from students in the name of fees though the teachers are paid inadequately. On the other hand, in the schools run by Central and State Governments, the teachers and students enjoy much more facilities. The difference of facilities and opportunities in similar Government and non-Government schools and colleges cannot be justified. According to some people, centralisation of education is necessary for removing such inequalities.

### Decentralisation during British Rule

During the British rule in India the Government was generally indifferent towards Indians. It did not like to earn the responsibility of education. It evaded this responsibility. It shifted the burden of educational organisation on religious bodies. While analysing the causes of disturbances in 1857, the British felt that education provisions made by Christian missionaries had been taken by the Indian people as a means of religious propaganda. The British administrators were against increasing the burden of Central Government. They handed over the educational responsibility to the State Governments. They did not take any concrete steps in this direction during the nineteenth century. Centralisation was attempted in the early years of the twentieth century. In the year 1910, a member for educational affairs was appointed in the Governor-General's Council. The Department of Education was opened in the Central Secretariate. After some years, it was amalgamated with the Health Ministry. It remained as such till the British regime lasted.

**Decentralisation after Independence**

After independence the Indian leaders felt the need of centralisation of education. A separate Ministry of Education was formed. Alongwith the development and expansion of educational organisations, it was necessary to have some control on them for national development. The easiest way for it was educational control through financial help. The Union Government gave financial help by providing money from several sources. It fixed programmes in the plans for educational development and expansion. It established several government and semi-government organisations and educational institutes for giving help and advise in the educational affairs. But it had always kept away from shouldering the burden of centralisation of education. At present the Central Government is taking special interest in education. Now, two Ministries, instead of one, are dealing in educational affairs. Several organisations and central institutions have been established for educational training and research. But the Central Government is still not prepared to take direct responsibility of centralisaton and educational administration. Constitutional provision is the main excuse for this. Some of the other attempts of the Central Government in the direction of centralisation are as follows :

1. *Centrally Administered Areas* : In Delhi and other centrally administered areas and princely states all educational provisions are made by the Union Government. In view of successes of education in these regions, it is desirable that education should be nationalised.

2. *Central Universities :* The Central Universities administered by the Centre are better than others in organisation and standard of education. These universities have made much progress after Independence. It indicates the fact that under Central administration the condition of the educational institutions will be leading towards development.

3. *Financial Aid to States* : The Central Government provides financial aid to the States for the development and expansion for educational projects. In return, the Centre does not try to exercise any direct control. As the State Governments honour the Central directives and suggestions and it is a kind of indirect control. Thus, the tendency of centralisation is increasing in the educational field. As a major part of the whole educational expenditure is met by the Central Assistance, the Centre can easily exercise educational control through financial help.

4. *All India Institutions* : The Central Government has established several all India Educational Institutions and institutes to fulfil its constitutional responsibility of establishing educational institutions. These institutions are making important contributions in the field of education. National institutions are helpful for research work in education. These provisions support centralisation of education.

5. *Central Educational Advisory Organisations* : The educational advisory organisations established at the Central level also exercise indirect control. It has led to the increase in Central administrative power. It is an initial step in the direction of centralisation. The State Governments and local administrative units depending more and more on Central assistance honour the suggestions and recommendations of the Central administration.

Thus, it is a right time for centralisation of education. Centralisation will become still convenient when the percentage of the Centre for educational expenditure will increase due to new educational projects. Even at present more than half of the whole educational expenditure is met by Central Grants while a major part of the remaining expenditure by fees from the students. Thus, the percentage of contribution by State Governments and local units is decreasing slowly. If expenditure and wastage on duplicate educational organisation is added, it will amount to the same. Thus, centralisation is necessary for better and satisfactory organisation, prompt administration and co-ordination in the educational sphere. Showing inclination towards centralisation the Kothari Commission has suggested to establish several type of advisory committees and boards at the Central level. The Union Government has decided to start an all Indian Educational Service which will be an important step in this direction.

## DECENTRALISATION IN INDIAN EDUCATION

### Historical Review

The British rulers did not like to take the burden of education upon themselves. They considered it a responsibility of religious organisations. They had no particular interest in the education of Indians as they were able to get educated persons for administrative needs from the then available educational institutions. After the disturbance in 1857, the British realized that the anger of the people against educational institutions established by Christian Missionaries was one of the causes of the revolt. As they did not like to increase the burden of the Central Government, so this subject was handed over to the State Governments. After Independence the interest of the National Government towards all the organs of administration increased. Necessary improvements, amendments and re-organisation were made in the available provisions. But educational administration remained more or less, the same because after independence, the leaders became more influenced by the attractive organs of administration and remained indifferent to educational administration. The Central Government shifted the burden to State Governments and the State Governments in their turn, placed the burden on the shoulders of local units and organisations. Present education suffers because of the duplicate arrangement and joint partnership. This is accepted as decentralised educational administration of Indian education according to the spirit of democracy.

The system of decentralization in educational administration has become popular as an ideal. In Indian life even poverty and scarcity is recognized as an ideal. Democracy means Government of the people. Therefore, people here have undertaken all those responsibilities in which administration has failed. Education is the responsibility of the State Governments but the State Governments have encouraged and given importance to non-government efforts.

### Requirements of Decentralization

In decentralization, the main responsibility of administration rests on local administrative units and lowest links of the chain of State educational administration, the officers and employees of the junior most cadres. Hence, the mutual relations between the officers and employees should be that of partnership or cooperation rather than subordination. The supervisory and controlling staff should be capable and well-versed with the situations of his sphere of work. They should have special qualities of establishing contacts with people, capable of understanding their viewpoint and make them understand their point of view effectively. In the formulation of administrative policies, they should give utmost importance to the advice of those who are in close touch with related matters and smaller units of local administration. Thus decentralized educational administration requires different arrangement from that of general administration. It requires confidence in big officers, honouring their views and transfer of own rights to these liberally. Though in the present situations it is really difficult to find such liberal officers but some such arrangements will have to be made for the success of decentralization.

**Advantages of decentralization**

1. It will create awakening and a feeling of self-dependence.

2. It will inculcate qualities of responsible behaviour and loyalty in the employees and authorities of administration.

3. It makes familiarity with the needs of the people easier and shape education accordingly.

4. It makes it possible regarding educational affairs and policies.

5. As the main responsibility of education lies with the people and local units, so the Government has to bear lesser burden of educational expenditure.

**Disadvantages of Decentralization**

1. As the educational system is generally influenced by local opinion, so often, the tendency of favouritism towards a particular class, caste, community, religion, race or political party is generated in and children of all the areas do not get equal educational opportunity.

2. Indian situation is not suitable for it. There is much difference in different regions. There are economic inequalities between different classes of society. All the local units are not equally rich in resources. While the rich local units can make better arrangements, poor units fail in their educational efforts. Decentralization at primary level is a glaring example of the fact that Indian conditions are not suitable for decentralisation in education.

## DIFFICULTIES OF EDUCATIONAL CONTROL AND SUPERVISION

In the decentralized Indian educational system educational supervision and control should be effective. However, the education Commissions appointed from time to time for studying the prevailing educational system and to advise improvement in it, have bitterly criticised the control and supervision system. Following is a critical estimate of the existing system.

1. *Too much work-load* : In every district, District Inspector of Schools is responsible for educational supervision and control. The list of his responsibility for educational organisation, administration and supervision at the district level is very wide. It includes supervision of the management and financial condition of the aided schools in the district, scrutiny of various educational fees and items of income and expenditure, provision and supervision of school building, hostels, libraries, educational instruments, laboratories, gymnasium and play-grounds and material, light and furnitures, appointment of principals and teachers, approval of promotions and prescribing of minimum qualification and training for them, inspection of their work, supervision of students, progress and discipline, recommendations regarding regular grants and other financial help, arrangement of examination at the senior basic level. Though the District Inspector of Schools has two or three Deputy Inspectors and some Sub-Deputy Inspectors for his help, there is so much work-load on a single unit that its practicability has become doubtful. Throughout the year the staff and officers of district remain busy in collecting different data, scrutinizing and sending it. Thus, no improvement will be effective without reducing the work-load of District Inspectors of Schools.

2. *Impractical Mode of Working* : The mode of working of the District Inspectors of Schools is far from the related needs. They consider the compliance of the departmental orders as the total fulfilment of their responsibility. Their main duty is to supervise and guide the different educational institutions but their method of supervision is unscientific and orthodox. In most of the educational institutions the inspection of the teaching work is done by inspection panels of teachers selected from different colleges. Often they do not perform their duty sincerely. The schedule of programme is sent in advance to the schools where the District Inspector of Schools pays his visit. So most of his time is spent in programmes organised by the schools for his welcome. He completes the inspection work simply by signing the registers and files of the school. The inspection is not real but only informal. The Inspector does not get time to see, hear or experience the problems of students and teachers. If he is anxious to know the real situation, then because of the advance information the persons connected with the schools manage things in such a way that the Inspector is unable to get a glimpse of real situation. Generally, he is shown only those places and arrangements which the managing staff wishes him to see.

3. *Lack of Qualifications and Experience* : The District Inspectors of Schools and their assistant Inspectors lack qualifications and experience which their posts demand. Generally, the District Inspectors are selected from the teaching or supervisory staff of the Department. Sometimes, their appointments are direct. As the promotions on the basis of departmental seniority or direct appointment system can never be suitable for this post, the District Inspector of Schools lack high professional ability training and experience. Promotion of direct appointees does not give them knowledge of various educational arrangements and problems. Therefore, they fail to see the organisational or academic shortcomings in schools. They are unable to solve organisational problems of schools due to lack of experience in the matter.

4. *Insufficient Sense of Responsibility* : District Inspector are more alive to their rights connected with their posts and their administrative powers than to their responsibility. Hence, they fail to behave properly with their subordinates and other capable and experienced persons. They do not get necessary co-operation and help from them. Their subordinate officers and employees also lack sincerity and proper behaviour. The attitude of the educational officers is authoritative and critical instead of co-operative and helpful in the matter of inspection of schools and its problems. So they do not help in solving the related problems.

## REMEDIES TO PROBLEMS OF ADMINISTRATION AND CONTROL

1. **Division of Work-load** : The work-load of the District Inspectors of Schools should be divided into several units. Different committees and councils should be formed for various types of control, inspection and guidance. The members of these committees and councils should be able and experienced persons connected with education. Their burden of collecting data and correspondence work should be reduced. Additional officers should be appointed for the same. The appointment of Extension Guides for the supervision of agriculture work in some States is useful step in this direction.

2. **Help by other Specialists** : The District Inspector of Schools cannot inspect all the schools and colleges of the district alone or with the help of his associates. The services of auditors should be available for auditing accounts, tuition fees and other registers. The system of panel inspection may be useful, if services of experienced teachers, professors and principals are utilised for the purpose. The work of panel inspectors may be more effective, if the services of retired persons are utilised by paying them some honorarium, in place of employed persons.

3. **Advance Information** : Real conditions of the schools is not known by giving prior information of inspection. All such inspections should be sudden. The moral character of Inspectors should be so high that they pay more attention to their responsibility than to their welcome programmes. The Inspectors should not stay in the concerning schools. They should contact local people for getting reactions to the existing educational provisions, before or after the inspection.

4. **Increase of professional ability and experience of the Inspectors** : The appointment of District Inspector of Schools should not be made on the basis of departmental seniority. The teachers having knowledge of science of education and possessing high professional ability and experience from amongst the teachers and Professors of Teachers Training College, should be appointed as District Inspector of Schools. At the time of appointment preference should be given to the constructive work of the candidate in the field of education. For acquainting the Inspectors and their Assistants with the periodical changes and improvements in education and educational planning, refresher courses, seminars etc. should be organised from time to time so that they may remain familiar with the national needs and social changes. They will be able to understand the shortcomings and problems of schools, to find solutions and give necessary guidance on the basis of their professional ability and experience.

5. **Necessary Traits of Inspectors** : The attitude of the District Inspector of School should be liberal towards his subordinate officers, staff and the teachers in educational institutions and other related persons. He should have such abilities as may command the respect of persons coming in his contact not because of his powers but his learning. His personality and behaviour should be so impressive that he is able to solve the educational problems effectively. Patience and tolerance should be his main tributes so that he may listen to and understand the difficulties of the people and take decisions accordingly. He should be sympathetic to all and his decisions should not create troubles for anyone.

## CO-ORDINATION IN EDUCATIONAL ADMINISTRATION

Centralisation of education increases the burden of educational expenditure on the Central Government. Hence, most of the educationists have the coordination as a valuable system.

### Meaning of Co-ordination

Co-ordination means a common system for all. Educational co-ordination means that there are equality of elements of national importance in the educational provisions of different levels and places. This equality may be of different kinds, such as equality of opportunity for students, equality in the classification of educational stages, equality of educational facilities, equality in industrial, technical and vocational education, equality in the qualifications of teachers, tuition fees and educational administration etc. Co-ordination in educational administration means that there should be a chain of contact throughout the country. At the centre of it information of educational activities in different parts of country is gathered and information of educational decisions at the national level may be diffused at the earliest to the different corners of the country. This co-ordination system may be compared to communication systems like telephone or telegraph. In the wider sense, it may be compared to the communication system of the human body.

### Importance of Co-ordination

Co-ordination is a national need in the educational sphere. It is a national responsibility that there should be equal facilities for students and teachers and equal opportunities of education for them in every part of the country in a democratic system. Uniformity or equality in all the system is very necessary for national integration. It is our constitutional aim and its fulfilment is our national responsibility. Hence, different national systems need co-ordination. Co-ordination in the educational sphere is more important because through education effective efforts are made for public awakening and progress of public life. The National Government of India is not taking entire burden of educational organization upon itself, because in the present economic crisis it is very difficult for the National Government to provide all kinds of facilities to the people of a vast land like India with a population nearing 900 million.

However, it is futile to hope for uniformity and equality in the context of the policy of decentralisation adopted in a helpless situation and efforts of non-government bodies and private efforts of various religious, social, political organisations for establishing educational institutions as well as schools and colleges established by foreign religious bodies. In all the institutions, the connected persons and organisations have made provisions according to their own beliefs and convictions. It is the responsibility of National Government to bring uniformity in such varied and complex situations. Through co-ordination, the National Government or the State Governments will be able to get information regarding educational activities in different regions. Programmes and projects for improvement in education can be successfully implemented through it.

**Efforts of Co-ordination**

Centralisation is the most effective method of co-ordination in educational administration. But the Indian Central Government is not prepared to bear the whole burden. It intends to shift the burden on State Governments on the pretext of constitutional provision. There is no agency of co-operation or contact among the State Governments through which uniformity may be maintained. Even if such an effort is made, it will not be practical and successful without centralised administration. So, the Central Government has following steps for co-ordination of existing educational administration in the country. The extension of Education Ministry, establishment of all Indian Education Boards and Committees and educational institutes are important steps in this direction. All these provisions indicate to the uniformity in the educational field and also to co-ordination in educational administration. The establishment of University Grants Commission is another important step through which efforts are made to bring co-ordination at the State level between the University Grants Committees and the Universities. UGC is not directly concerned with educational administration at the higher education level since universities are autonomous bodies.

**Recommendations by Kothari Commission**

1. *Boards of Education.* The Kothari Commission recommended for the establishing of National Board of Education at the Central level and State Board of Education and District Board of Education at State and district level respectively. These Education Boards will try to establish co-ordination between the educational administrators at their level along with other functions. At the State and district levels these bodies will try to bring uniformity in the educational institutions of their region. They will be co-ordinative links at the national level. They continue to apprise the Central administration with the educational activities of different regions. They will be able to diffuse programmes of educational improvement and development plans to the educational institutions in the different corners of the country. They will reduce the load of educational administration at different stages of education. They will do functions such as recognition of educational institution, distribution of grants, farming of curriculums for different stages, prescribing of teachers' qualifications, supervision of teaching methods and co-curricular activities, examination arrangements etc.

2. *All India Educational Service*. The Kothari Commission has recommended

for All India Educational Service for co-ordination in education so that there may be at least one representative of Central Educational Administration in every district who will be responsible for the implementation of Central Educational decisions and plans.

3. *Reorganisation of Education Ministry.* The Kothari Commission has also recommended for the reorganisation of Education Ministry. The suggestion for the establishment of Education Board is a part of that recommendation. These boards will function as a part of administrative units. Different advisory and research committees, boards and institutes and commissions will be joined with National Education Board.

4. *Government Central Schools.* Kothari Commission also recommended for the establishment of Government Common (Central) Schools. In the present system, there are several schools in the districts established by various persons and organisations. It is difficult to establish co-ordination among them. Their traditional ways are obstructions in the way of educational administration. Paucity of funds is their main helplessness. The establishing of Common (Central) Schools will create educational institutions which have no common teaching programme under the direct control of Central Government. The Central Government will bear the entire burden of their organisation. Non-government institutions will come to an end by themselves.

### Suggestion by Sapru Committee

Some time ago, some Members of the Parliament demanded that the Centre should take the responsibility of education by making necessary amendments in the Constitution. In this connection Sapru Committee suggested that at least higher education should be a Central subject. These proposals are very important and education can thus be made more useful.

## HUMANENESS IN EDUCATIONAL ADMINISTRATION

### Meaning of Humaneness

Learned persons, thinkers and educationists have always felt that the persons engaged in educational administration, generally lack human qualities. Humaneness means that compassionate dealing in which one person behaves liberally with the other. Humaneness in educational administration means that the administrators and other authorities should behave sympathetically with those engaged in education work. While considering their problems and difficulties they should have liberal attitude.

### Inhumaneness of Indian Authorities

In Indian administration after Independence change of regime has not changed the attitude of the authorities. The British administrators created a tendency of snobbishness in Indian authorities who are following the same traditions even to-day. The authorities appointed after Independence have fallen a prey to the same tendency. The method and rules of the administration remain the same. Though, educational administration envisages a different kind of method and rules from that of general administration but in India the same kind of rules are being used for all the systems without paying any attention to its practical aspect. Any officer of Indian Civil Service is sent to Education Ministry or Education Department. The tendency of authoritarianism and illiberality of rules create a sort of double inhumaneness.

**Defects of Present Set up**

Education is concerned with the development of the whole nation through the education and training of future citizens and development of their personality. Hence, educational administration should be more efficient and liberal than Civil Administration. Any slackness or carelessness in the programmes of development of the personality of children will affect the development programmes of the whole nation and cause a great loss to the nation. Hence, educational programmes should be changed quickly according to the need of the time. The changed programmes should be implemented even more rapidly. The prevailing administrative system suffers from red-tapism. Many useful projects and programmes, decided at the higher level could not be implemented because of this red-tapism. The money sanctioned in Five Year Plans for various ascertained projects was never utilised fully. Many important programmes remained tied in the departmental files at one stage or the other and finally that money was either spent on some work or returned as such.

## SUGGESTIONS FOR IMPROVEMENT

The following suggestions have been offered for improving school supervision and inspection :

1. More supervisory and clerical staff should be appointed.

2. More financial and administrative powers may be delegated to the inspecting officers.

3. Norms should be fixed, taking into account the size of the school, number of teachers, distance, etc. to make inspection more intensive, purposeful and systematic.

4. A panel of inspectors should visit schools instead of one inspector. Association of subject inspectors is likely to improve school standards.

5. In-service training programmes must be organised for supervisors to raise the efficiency of educational supervision.

6. The inspecting officer should adopt one good and one bad school and pay special attention to them for a year or so.

7. More inspection and surprise visits should be made to schools having low standards.

8. The inspector may organize demonstration classes and inter-school visits, strengthen reference libraries and arrange seminars, refresher courses, workshops, exhibitions, conferences, etc.

9. Due appreciation may be given to talented teachers. Demonstration lessons may be arranged by them.

## Kinds of Inspection

1. *Annual Inspection* : This is a comprehensive inspection of all aspects of the school such as staff, students, all subjects taught, equipment and organisation.

2. *The Follow-up Inspection* : This is conducted to ensure that the previous recommendations have been carried out.

3. *Partial Inspection* : This is concerned with the teaching of one subject only or some special aspect of the school life.

4. *Surprise or Unannounced Visits* : Supervisors visit schools without any prior notice to see that the working of the school under normal situations.

## Nomenclature

The Secondary Education Commission (1952-53) recommended that the nomenclature of the term 'Inspector' should be changed as 'Educational Adviser'. Thinking that the term 'Inspector' was unfortunate in the Indian context. Prof. S.N. Mukerji suggests that as the term 'Inspector' seems to have a bad connotation being associated with Police Inspectors, it should be changed into 'School Advisers' or 'School Visitors'. The Zakir Hussain Committee has substituted the word 'supervisors' for inspectors.

The present tendency among the educationists is to 'expel' the word 'Inspector' from the educational vocabulary in favour of 'Supervisor or Education Officer'.

However, what matters is not the designation but the functions they perform and more especially in what spirit they perform them.

## Types of Supervision

1. *The Corrective Supervision* : 'Fault-finding' is another name for this type. The supervisor looks at the activities of the school with an eye to pick holes. This does not serve any useful purpose. It makes teachers unhappy.

2. *Creative Supervision* : It encourages teachers to feel free to think for themselves in matters pertaining to objectives, curriculum, organisation and content, methods of teaching and methods of evaluation. It encourages the teachers to share voluntarily with the supervisor and co-workers. It gives scope to teachers to experiment with their own ideas. It inspires teachers to be themselves and to develop self-confidence in them.

3. *Autocratic Supervision* : Otherwise known as 'Authoritarian Supervision', makes the supervisor a 'supermaster'.

4. *Inspirational Supervision* : It inspires teachers and lifts them above themselves. 'Impression' rather than 'Oppression' is the essence of this supervision.

5. *Humanistic Supervision* : Its aim is to develop healthy human relationship among all the partners of the educational enterprise, namely, the pupils, the teachers, the parents, staff, personnel, etc.

6. *Democratic Supervision* : It emphasises the dignity and worth of the individual. Based on the democratic way of life, it gives importance to democratic values, and encourages freedom while providing direction, advice and suggestion.

**Suggestions for Creating Humaneness**

1. *Reorganisation of educational institutions.* The main objective of educational administration should be to organise the educational institutions to make people able to derive maximum advantage out of them. The educational administration should be made more efficient by making it free from red-tapism and delaying tactics. Special arrangement should be made for deciding educational matters speedily.

2. *Improvement of Behaviour.* The behavioural side of the authorities and employees of educational administration should be improved. Education department authorities should be sympathetic, liberal and tolerant. They should have no complexes so that they may meet all high and low equally. Ability of leadership, farsightedness and sense of responsibility should be their qualities. Educational officers should be appointed after special training.

3. *Winning Confidence.* The educational authorities should try to win confidence of their subordinate staff, teachers and students etc. They should behave in such a way that the people are able to consider them as their well-wishers. They should listen to the problems of the people patiently, consider them liberally and take quick decisions on them in order to win their confidence.

4. *Public Contact.* The work of the authorities should not be confined to office rooms. They should remain in contact with educational institutions and provide leadership and proper guidance to them.

## QUESTIONS FOR EXERCISE

1. Discuss the problems of educational administration in India.
2. Discuss the advantages and disadvantages of centralisation and decentralisation of education in India.

# 5

# PROBLEMS OF EDUCATIONAL METHOD

Educational efforts can yield the expected results only if they are based on appropriate methods. Evidently, the problem of educational methods cannot be overemphasised. It includes some basic problems which are naturally in the way of the teacher's job in the school, certain difficulties and wrong ways of doing things in the class by the teacher, and what the teacher should do to remove these difficulties and wrong ways. The following are the factors underlying the problem of educational method :

1. *Lack of Flexibility* : Some teachers appear to be very rigid in the use of educational methods. They are not prepared to make any change in the method according to the demands of the situation. They follow the methods that they have been taught in the training colleges days or that they have read in certain books. This helps them to finish the teaching of the subject-matter within the stipulated time limit, but it does not lead the student to acquire the fundamentals of the things taught. What is taught to them passes off their minds in due course.

It is difficult to recommend one single method of teaching that every teacher may follow. The teacher should be able to mould his methods according to the demands of the situation of the particular aspects of the subject-matter to be taught. The choice of a method depends upon the creative ability and progressive personality of the teacher. There should be a flexibility for introducing changes in methods if the situation so demands. The teacher should feel free to incorporate the desired aspect of the various methods of teaching and forge out his own particular method. For example, by accepting the planning procedure of the Project Method, the specific aspects as defined in the Dalton Plan and the discussion aspect of the unit method, the teacher may be able to formulate his own method of teaching in accordance with the situational demands. However, the training college methods should be accepted as the fundamental structure on which the teacher has to reconstruct his own educational methods and procedures.

2. *Multisided Process* : Generally, the teacher alone is active in the class and the students remain sitting as passive listeners. It should be remembered that it is the student who has to be benefited from any educational effort. If he is not a participant in the educational procedure the very purpose of education is likely to be defeated. The objective of any educational method is to establish an organic

relationship between the teacher and the taught and not only to impart informations. Hence, teaching is a two-way process involving the participation of both the teacher and the taught.

3. *Functional Teaching Method*: Thus in the teaching process the student has to remain all the time active. He has to learn by doing and not only through cramming. Through learning by doing he will understand the practical implications of what he learns. He will be able to apply the same in his life situations as and when necessary. Therefore, it is said that the student should learn by living.

4. *No Verbalism* : Teachers who use numerous words in making a point, mistake words for informations. In fact, there should be no verbalism in teaching method. The teacher should use minimum words in explaining a point. He has not to show that he can speak very fluently on any aspect. He should remember that he has not to establish his authority before the students, which is already recognised among the students. Therefore, the teacher has to see that acquisition of knowledge becomes functional in effect.

5. *Regards to Individual Differences* : There are individual differences in students. The students differ in their capacities, interests, aptitudes and abilities. Hence, the teacher has to adjust his teaching accordingly. If he does not do so, the brilliant and the dull both are likely to be ignored. There is no average student. The conception of average student is a myth. The teacher has to attend to individual differences found in students. He has to attend the more brilliant in some way. At other times he has to take care of the less privileged ones even in the group teaching procedure or afterwards. This will be possible through the active co-operation of the student. Each student should be given some special assignment according to his assets and limitations. Each student will acquire a functional attitude so that to adjust himself better in his environment. This will create in him a spirit of self-confidence, self-dependence and a sense of responsibility.

6. *Enlarging the Students' Scope of Interests*: There is a scope for the teacher to enlarge the interests of the students. Multi-sided interests enrich personality. The class-room, the play-ground, excursions and cultural programmes are some of the occasions which may be utilized for enlargements of interests of students while teaching any subject. A clever and successful teacher never misses a single opportunity of developing his students' interests.

7. *Developing Positive Attitudes and Good Character* : The teacher is responsible for developing positive attitudes and marks of good character in students. He must stimulate the student to examine fully a particular situation at hand and then proceed further for its solution. This will develop in the student an attitude to look at things with an open mind. It will help him to adopt a liberal attitude towards various things in life. Hence, the method of teaching by the teachers should be directed towards influencing the student's total personality by way of developing his emotional and intellectual capacities, giving him a criterion for making right judgements and developing in him desirable values of life.

8. *Practical Teaching*: In the teaching process the teacher generally concentrates his efforts in helping the student learn certain informations, facts and the subject-

matter of the course. This habit of teacher deprives the student from developing his faculties of discrimination, understanding of co-relationships between things learnt, classifying things and reaching relevant conclusions. The method of teaching should be such as to facilitate the development of all these faculties.

9. *The Burden of Home Work* : Assigning home work without due consideration of the burden that the student might be carrying in other subjects retards the balanced development of students. Generally at the end of the period a teacher gives some home work. Thus in various subjects the student is assigned some work. The total load becomes very heavy. Some students are able to do this home work somehow. Some other copy down the same from other student's note-book. As this home work is seldom examined by the teacher, the student is not adequately guided. He continues carrying wrong notions about many things. Hence, if any home work is given, that must be duly corrected, otherwise it will be better if the same is not given at all. The home work should be simple and small. It should be given according to a policy to be decided in consultation with other teachers. The major purpose of the home work should be to develop in the student a habit of self-study and to find out solutions of certain things which are within their reach. Therefore, the home work should be interesting, self-satisfying and stimulative.

10. *No Spoon-Feeding* : The teacher has to develop the qualities of self-reliance, critical observation and judgement and self-control through his method of teaching. At times the teacher has to leave the student to himself do things in the class, in experimental laboratories and in open fields and gardens. He must not fear that the student will make mistakes. He should leave him free to learn things through his own practical experience so long as he does not harm himself physically. There is no harm in the experimental process if he breaks some implements, tools or equipment. Through so doing he is likely to develop his creative imagination which should be regarded the sole purpose of any method of teaching.

## QUESTION FOR EXERCISE

1. Discuss the important factors remembered by the teacher while formulating an ideal method of teaching.

# 6

# PROBLEMS OF EDUCATION OF THE SCHEDULED CASTES AND SCHEDULED TRIBES

## CONSTITUTIONAL PROVISION

Indian Constitution has made the following provisions for education and improvement of scheduled caste and the tribal people :

1. *Clause 17* : Through the clause 17, untouchability has been declared as a social crime. The persons practising it may be prosecuted.

2. *Clause 15* : The clause 15 gives freedom to the scheduled caste people to use wells, ponds, hotels and river-ghats like people of other castes.

3. *Clause 25* : According to clause 25, all the worship places of Hindus have been opened for them as well.

4. *Clause 29* : The clause 29 gives equal right to admission in all schools and colleges maintained by public funds.

5. *Clause 16 and 335* : According to the clauses 16 and 335 reservations have been made in favour of scheduled castes and scheduled tribes in all public services.

## THE CONTRIBUTION OF SOCIAL ORGANISATIONS

Many social organisations are running educational institutions for education of scheduled caste and tribal people. These have instituted scholarships and freeships for encouraging children of scheduled caste and tribal people to receive education. Sometimes adequate financial assistance is also arranged for books, clothings, lodging and boarding. Fifteen crores of rupees in the First Five Year Plan, 41 crores in the Second Plan, 53 crores in the Third Plan, 70 crores in the Fourth Plan, over 100 crores in the Fifth and nearly 200 crores in the Sixth Five Year Plan were earmarked for education and improvement of scheduled caste and tribal people.

## THE DHEBAR COMMISSION OF 1960-61

The Government appointed a Commission under the Chairmanship of Dhebar in 1960-61 for finding out the condition and problems of the scheduled caste and tribal people. The Commission observed that adequate arrangements have not yet been made for the education of scheduled castes and scheduled tribes. It requested the Central Education Ministry to study this problem for doing the needful towards education of these people. It considered residential Ashram Schools useful for children of scheduled and tribal people, because they serve as centres of social and cultural education of these children. It recommended the expansion of such schools throughout the whole country.

**Recommendations**

The Commission made the following recommendations for the expansion of primary education :

1. The children of scheduled and tribal people should be trained in some handicraft or practical skills.
2. The teacher appointed to teach scheduled caste and tribal children should be given special allowances and residential facilities.
3. Children in schools for scheduled caste and tribal should be given food, clothing, books and stationaries free.
4. Teachers appointed for teaching scheduled caste and tribal children should be trained in training colleges established in their area in order that during the training period they may get acquainted with the life style of the scheduled and tribal people.
5. Teachers appointed to teach scheduled and tribal children should be fully conversant with their culture.
6. Primary education for scheduled and tribal children should be given through their mother-tongue. Suitable books should be published for this purpose in mother-tongue.

## THE KOTHARI COMMISSION, 1964-66

In addition to the recommendations of the Dhebar Commission the Kothari Commission has given welcoming suggestions for various levels of education of scheduled caste and tribal children.

1. *Primary Education* : Primary Education for scheduled caste and tribal children should be better organised. More schools should be opended in the densely populated areas of scheduled and tribal people.

2. *Secondary Education* : More secondary schools should be opened with facilities for hostels and stipends.

3. *Higher Education* : More scholarships should be instituted for higher education. Those engaged in the service for scheduled caste and tribal people should be assigned a separate cadre. In the beginning, non-scheduled and non-tribal people may be appointed in this cadre, but later on suitable persons from the scheduled and tribal groups alone should be appointed in this cadre.

The conditions of the scheduled caste and tribal people will be improved a great deal, if the recommendations of the Dhebar and Kothari Commissions are implemented.

## CRIMINAL TRIBES

*Meaning* : The criminal tribes include those who by way of habit are generally engaged in such crimes as committing theft at nights, looting passers-by and stealing away domestic animals. People of this tribe generally roam about from one place to another, as they have no permanent abode anywhere. They are landless and houseless.

### Efforts for Education

1. *Before Independence* : Prior to 1947 some Christian missionaries tried to educate and uplift the standard of living of criminal tribes. Through the Criminal Tribes Act passed by the Government, a right has been obtained to inhabitate these people at some particular places. Some of the people of these tribes have been encouraged to settle down at some places. Some boarding schools have been opened for education of their children. The Government has given financial assistance to missionaries and other organisations for looking after welfare of these people.

2. *After Independence* : After independence the Criminal Tribe Act was cancelled, as it was not considered proper to call any tribe criminal. Residential schools were opened for education of children of these tribes. An attempt was made to employ adults from this group at suitable places. The Government made some provisions for education of the tribes in the various Five Year Plans.

## THE NOMADS

### Meaning

The nomads do not have any specific place to stay at. In search of daily sustenance they remain wandering from one place to another throughout the whole country. They carry their children and the entire family with them. At times they may seek shelters beneath bridges, tunnels and footpaths of boards.

### Measures of Reform

Under the circumstances, it is extremely difficult to educate them and their children. However, following measures have been suggested for their reforms :

1. They should be encouraged to settle down at some specific place donated to them free of charge. In the State of Rajasthan some nomad people were given places to settle down at. But they could not stay there and moved out for other places.

2. Some provisions should be made for mobile schools for nomads' children. These schools should follow their movement from time to time. Thus their children will be getting education without any break. This experiment has succeeded in the State of Jammu and Kashmir. There the nomads people reside at hill-tops during summer and they descend down in valleys during winter. Mobile schools have been organised for education of their children. Upto 1961 there were 53 such schools in this State. Some persons of the same nomad group were appointed as teachers for their children. This arrangement could be accepted as a temporary measure only. The real solution requires getting them settled down at some specific places.

## PROGRAMMES FOR SCHEDULED CASTES AND TRIBAL PEOPLE

The following three types of programmes have been organised by the Government for the scheduled and tribal people :

1. The work directly done by the Central Government.

2. The work done under the supervision of the Government.

3. The work done by the various States in the country.

1. **The work directly done by the Central Government** : The Central Government grants reservations in government services in favour of scheduled and tribal people. But many reserved posts are not filled in by the scheduled and tribal people, because suitable hands from them are not available. For improving this situation, the Government has opened Coaching-*cum*-Guidance Centres at Madras, Jabalpur and Kanpur in order to transmit informations regarding employment opportunities and also to impart training to scheduled caste and tribal people for specific jobs. Since 1953 more than two dozen scholarships have been instituted for sending persons of scheduled and tribe groups to foreign countries for obtaining education. 17½ per cent of seats in educational institutions have been reserved for scheduled caste and tribal people. Some seats have been reserved for them in medical and engineering colleges also.

2. **The Work done under the Supervision of the Central Government** : (i) After passing high school examination the schedule caste and tribal students are granted scholarships for continuing the further education. These days about three lakh scholarships are awarded to students of scheduled castes and about a lakh scholarship to the students belonging to the tribal classes.

(ii) There are about 18 centres all over the country for coaching persons for scheduled and tribal classes for I. A. S. and I.P.S. services. About 2500 persons were prepared for these services and about 500 of them came out successful.

(iii) The Central Government gives grants to the various State Governments for instituting scholarships for scheduled caste and tribal students.

(iv) More than twenty centres have been established throughout the country for doing research on scheduled caste and tribal people.

(v) A Central Research Advisory Council has been established for correlating the activities of these research centres spread over the country.

(vi) The Central Government gives various kinds of financial assistance for rehabilitation and education of scheduled caste and tribal people. Through this assistance provisions have been made for meals, hostels, residential schools, examination fees, scholarships and tuition fees in favour of students from these groups.

3. **The Work Done by the Various States** : The financial assistance received from the Central Government by the various State Governments are treated as loans and block grants. Through this assistance the State Government run the following types of programmes for scheduled castes and tribal people :

1. To open Ashram Schools.
2. To organize teaching materials.
3. To establish schools and hostels.
4. To give stipends for primary and junior high education.
5. To arrange for mid-day meals.
6. To exempt from tuition and examination fees.

## SUGGESTIONS FOR IMPROVEMENT

The welfare of the scheduled caste and tribal people cannot be guaranteed through Government help alone. The co-operation of the society is very necessary for it, as their problem is a social problem which concerns the whole country. Their condition cannot be improved only through Government Laws and Regulations. In various States in our country, we find various types of scheduled caste and tribal people. A general consciousness has to be generated throughout the country for the reforms of people of this group. It has been suggested to introduce compulsory education for improving the condition of these people. But neither the Dhebar nor the Kothari Commission suggested the introduction of compulsory education. The following programmes may be suggested for education of scheduled caste and tribal people :

1. To make survey of places for opening schools for children.
2. To open residential schools for children of these people.
3. To organise suitable teaching materials in all the schools meant for scheduled caste and tribal children.
4. To provide free meals, books, stationaries and other facilities to the children of these people.
5. To prepare favourable atmosphere for compulsory education of their children.

## QUESTION FOR EXERCISE

1. What recommendations have been made by Dhebar Commission and Kothari Commission for the education of scheduled castes and scheduled tribes.

# 7

# THE PROBLEMS OF WOMEN EDUCATION

### Historical Review

In India woman education was encouraged in ancient days. One finds mention of numerous learned women in the Vedic and Upanishadic periods who were well versed in various disciplines of study. But situation changed during the Muslim period in India. The women were sent behind Purdah under the Muslim influence and the unsafe conditions prevailing in their society. But by the middle of the nineteenth century some progressive Indians and Englishmen started working for their reawakening. This encouraged the development of their education. According to the recommendations of the Education Commission of 1882 some schools for women were opened with government grants. Certain private organisastions also came forward and opened many schools and colleges for girls. By the beginning of the twentieth century there were about 6107 schools for girls and there were 4,47,470 girls studying in them. Out of these 6107 schools, twelve were colleges, 467 secondary schools and the rest were primary schools. In 1904 Mrs. Annie Besent took a historical step for women education by starting the Central Hindu Girls School in Varanasi. In 1916 Lady Hardinge Medical College was established in Delhi. Henceforward many new schools and colleges for girls were opened and a number of stipends for girls were instituted as encouragement to poorer ones. Arrangements for transport for girls were also made. The government opened many schools for girls. Inspectress of schools were also appointed by the government for looking after the newly opened schools for girls. By 1917, there were about 12,30,419 girl students in 18,827 schools. The number of high schools for girls was 689. Few vocational schools were also opened for girls. The number of colleges for girls remained 12. The rest were primary schools for girls.

After the First World War was over in 1918, great efforts were made for expansion of women education. Mahatma Gandhi was the leader of this expansion. With him there were many top leaders and ladies of the country. Their efforts bore fruits and by 1947 there were 31,14,860 girls studying in schools. Out of this number 40,843 were in vocational and industrial schools and 16,284 were in general schools. Thus by 1947 the progress in women education was three times.

After Independence the government considered its sacred duty to expand women education and many voluntary organisations also came forward to work for expansion of the same. In various Five Year Plans separate funds have been allocated for women education. An attempt has also been made to introduce changes in the curriculum at all the levels of education corresponding the special interests and life-duties of girls.

### Aims of Women Education

While good progress has been made in the sphere of women education but this progress is not very heartening keeping in view the high number of women in the country. However, during the last fifty years India has produced great women in different walks of life, science, literatures, various disciplines of studies in the universities and in political life of the country. These great women are comparable to any woman in any part of the world in their specific spheres concerned. Various Committees and Commissions on education appointed by the government have emphasized the unique need and nature of women education. Evidently, the curriculum for girls should not be the same as that for boys. Happily, the educationists in our country are conscious of this due necessity. So suitable recommendations have been made by the various commissions on education for reforms of women education.

## THE GOVERNMENT EFFORTS FOR WOMEN EDUCATION

### General Structure

In India the Central Government has been constitutionally made responsible for women education. But since women education is considered as a part of general education, it is regarded as the responsibility of the State. It is the State government that does everything for expansion of women education. The administration of women education is just like that of education for boys. There are regional inspectresses of schools and other government officers for the inspection and supervision of girls' schools. The Director of Education is the chief of women education as he is for boys' education. In 1959 a National Council for Women Education was established for looking after the education of girls. It recommended that the women education should be treated as a separate unit of education and the State Governments should establish Advisory Council for Women Education and there should be a Joint Director for women education. It is hoped that the situation will go on improving as time passes.

### Higher Education for Women

In view of the great zeal shown by girls for higher education it is hoped that their number in universities and degree colleges will ever be on increase. Some necessary changes are also being introduced in the curriculum in order to suit their special interests and aptitudes. The girls are also attracted towards various professional courses, such as medical, engineering, teaching and nursing, etc.

### Secondary Education for Girls

At the secondary stage the growth of women education has been more satisfactory. As the time passed the old conservative traditions were relaxed and the girls were encouraged to get education which they desire. The curriculum has also been suitably modified at the secondary stage in order to suit their special requirements and tastes.

### Primary Education for Girls

Primary education is the base for the development of secondary and higher education. Its development ultimately affects the development of onward stages of education. However, it has been estimated that only 30 per cent of the girls of primary school reach the fifth class, *i.e.*, they drop out earlier for one reason or the other. The government has a special responsibility for enforcing compulsory education for girls up to the secondary stage.

## VOCATIONAL, SPECIAL AND ADULT EDUCATION

Today, women are showing an interest for professional education. Hence, it is a sacred duty of leaders and rulers to provide adequate opportunities for professional education of women in order that they may also contribute to the national prosperity. Girls show special inclination towards teaching profession, after this their choice falls on nursing and medical profession than on some others. So special provisions have to be made for attracting them to the professions of their choice. For this suitable stipends and other necessary facilities must be provided so that the desirous ones are not deprived of the education they want. Of course, there must be some norms which they must meet. But after they meet these norms, they must be given all the facilities for education of their choice. For this some institutions must be opened offering courses of their choice. Recently, it has also been observed that the women are showing inclination for social services. Hence, their interests in this area, too, should be developed by giving them the necessary training. Specially trained women may also be encouraged to take up assignments in rural areas for some time. This will also promote the development of our villages.

## PROBLEMS OF WOMEN EDUCATION

Indian women are as capable as any women in any part of the world. But unlike women in many Western countries, Indian women are denied equal opportunities for working with men in many spheres of life. Constitutionally, Indian women have been granted equal rights with men, but practically speaking they are kept much behind men in various life activities. Hence, the women should be given equal rights with men everywhere according to their special interests and legitimate demands. While framing the courses of study for girls special care should be taken of their unique life responsibilities and domestic demands. Accordingly, the curriculum should be modified. Co-education should be permitted. But for secondary education separate schools should be opened in various parts of the country as many parents do not like co-education at the secondary stage. So women should be specially trained in various professional courses. India requires a large number of women teachers for primary and secondary schools. Hence, more training colleges should be opened for training of women teachers and more seats for women should be reserved in training colleges. Similarly, more seats should be reserved for women candidates in medical, engineering and other professional colleges. This will facilitate the growth of women education in various areas. If trained women workers or lady doctors and teachers are sent to work in rural areas, they should be given higher salaries and immediate facilities of residence and other minimum amenities for obvious reasons.

## COMMITTEE ON WOMEN'S EDUCATION (1957-59)

### Introduction

At its meeting held in July, 1957, Education panel of the Planning Commission recommended that, "A suitable Committee should be appointed to go into the various aspects of the question relating to the nature of education for girls at the elementary, secondary and adult stages and to examine whether the present system was helping them to lead a happier and more useful life." This was placed before the Conference of the State Education Ministers (held in September, 1957). They agreed that a special committee should be appointed to examine the whole question of women's education. Accordingly the National Committee on Women's Education was set up by the Government of India in the Ministry of Education, with Smt. Durgabai Deshmukh, Chairman, Central Social Welfare Board as chair person.

### Terms of Reference

(a) To suggest special measures to make up the leeway in women's education at the primary and secondary levels;

(b) To examine the problem of wastage in girls' education at these levels;

(c) To examine the problem of adult women who have relapsed into illiteracy or have received inadequate education and who need continuation of education so as to enable them to earn a living and participate in projects of national reconstruction;

(d) To survey the nature and extent of material and other facilities offered by voluntary welfare organisaitons for education of such women and to recommend steps necessary to enable them to offer larger educational facilities to them.

## MAJOR RECOMMENDATIONS

### A. Special recommendations needing top priority

1. *Determined Efforts* : The education of women should be regarded as a major and a special problem in education for a good many years to come and a bold and determined efforts should be made to face its difficulties and magnitude and to close the existing gap between the education of men and women in as short a time as possible. The funds required for the purpose should be considered to be the first charge on the sums set aside for the development of education.

2. *National Council* : Steps should be taken to constitute as early as possible a National Council for the education of girls and women.

3. *Rapid Development* : The problem of the education of women is so vital and of such great national significance that it is absolutely necessary for the Centre to assume more responsibility for its rapid development.

4. *State Council* : The State Governments should establish State Councils for the education of girls and women.

5. *Comprehensive Plans* : Every State should be required to prepare comprehensive development plans for the education of girls and women in its area.

6. *Cooperation* : It is also necessary to enlist the cooperation of all semi-official organisations, local bodies, voluntary organisations, teachers' organisations and members of the public to assist in the promotion of the education of girls and women.

7. *Permanent Machinery* : The Planning Commission should set up a permanent machinery to estimate, as accurately as possible, the woman-power requirements of the Plans from time to time and make the results of its studies available to Government and the public.

**B. Other Special Recommendations**

1. *Primary Education* (*age group* 6-11) : (i) Concessions in kind (not in cash) should be given to all girls, whether from rural or urban areas, of parents below a certain income level.

(ii) The Government should formulate a scheme for awarding prizes to the village which shows the large proportional enrolment and average attendance of girls.

2. *Middle and Secondary Education* (*age group* 11-17) : (i) At the middle school stage, more and more co-educational institutions should be started.

(ii) Separate schools for girls should be established specially in rural areas, for the secondary stage, at the same time giving parents full freedom to admit their girls to boys' schools if they so desire.

(iii) All girls (and all boys also) of parents below a prescribed income level should be given free education upto the middle stage.

(iv) Free or subsidized transport should be made available to girls in order to bring middle and secondary schools, within easy reach.

3. *Curriculum and syllabi* : (i) There should be identical curriculum for boys and girls at the primary stage with the proviso that, even at this stage, subjects like music, painting, sewing, needle work, simple hand-work, and cooking should be introduced to make the courses more suitable for girls.

(ii) At the middle school stage, and more especially the secondary stage, there is a need for differentiation of curricula for boys and girls.

4. *Training and employment* : (i) Immediate steps should be taken to set up additional training institutions for women teachers in all such areas of the country where a shortage exists at present.

(ii) With a view to inducing women from urban areas to accept posts of teachers in rural schools, women teachers serving in rural areas may be provided with quarters and a village allowance may be given to such teachers.

(iii) The maximum age limit for entry into service may be relaxed, and the age of retirement may be extended to 60 provided the teacher is physically and otherwise fit.

5. *Professional and vocational education* : (i) The employment of women on part-time basis, wherever feasible, should be accepted as a policy.

(ii) Girls should be encouraged to take up courses in commerce, engineering, agriculture, medicine, etc., at the university stage by offering them scholarships and other concessions.

(iii) It is important to organise campaigns to mobilise public opinion for creating proper conditions in offices and establishments in which women can work freely.

6. *Facilities of adult women* : (i) Education facilities in the form of condensed courses (a) that prepare women for the middle school examination, and (b) those that prepare them for the high school or higher secondary examination, should be provided more extensively in all stages.

(ii) Provision should also be made of condensed courses, which train women for suitable vocation after completion of necessary education.

7. *Voluntary organisation* : The services of the voluntary organisations should be extensively used in the field of middle, secondary, higher, social and vocational education of women. The existing grant-in-aid codes of the States need a thorough revision. There should be a substantial and significant difference in the rates of grants-in-aid as between girls' institutions and boys' institutions at all levels. The conditions of aid for girls' institutions should be made easier.

**C. General Recommendations**

1. *Free* : Whenever primary education is not free, immediate steps should be taken to make it free.

2. *Wastage and Stagnation* : (1) The Ministry of Education should carry out special studies of this problem in all parts of the country.

(2) The following steps should be taken to reduce the extent of stagnation in class I : (i) all fresh admissions to class I should be made in the beginning of the year and not later than sixty days after the beginning of the first session; (ii) it should be a specific responsibility of teachers to see that proper attendance is maintained in the school; (iii) the age of admission should be raised to six plus, (iv) standards of teaching should be improved.

(3) The stagnation in classes II to V can be reduced if (i) attendance of children is increased; (ii) standards of teaching are improved; (iii) internal examinations are introduced; (iv) books and educational equipment needed by poor children are supplied in good time.

(4) About 65 per cent of the case of wastage at the primary level are due to economic causes. It can be illuminated only if provision for part-time instruction is made for those children who cannot attend on a whole-time basis.

(5) About 25 to 30 per cent of the cases of wastage at the primary level are due to the indifference of parents. This can be eliminated partly by educative propaganda and partly by a rigorous enforcement of the compulsory education law.

3. *Employment of teachers* : (1) The present scales of pay of teachers should be suitably revised.

(2) There should be no distinction between the scales of pay and allowances paid to teachers in Government and local board or municipal institutions and those that are paid to teachers working under private managements.

(3) The triple-benefit scheme called the Pension-*cum*-Provident Fund-*cum*-Insurance Scheme should be made applicable to every teacher who is employed permanently in an institution.

## COMMITTEE FOR GIRLS' EDUCATION AND PUBLIC CO-OPERATION (1963-65)

At its meeting held in April, 1963 the National Council for Women's Education endorsed the suggestion made by the Union Education Minister that a small committee be appointed to look into the causes for lack of public support, particularly in rural areas, for girls' education and to enlist public cooperation. The Chairman of the National Council for Women's Education accordingly appointed in May, 1963, a Committee with Shri M. Bhaskavatsalam, Chief Minister, Madras as Chairman the Committee to suggest ways and means of achieving substantial progress in this field. The Committee submitted its report in 1964 and the report was published in 1965.

### Recommendations

It is only through a willing, educated and informed public that any progress can be made at all. Not only is the need urgent, but the ground is also ready for a comprehensive programme for mobilizing public cooperation to promote girls' education and giving it constructive channels for expression. It is essential that official action and the programme based on public initiative must move forward in close harmony. There has to be a sense of partnership and shared responsibility between official and voluntary agencies. There is also the need for a systematic and sustained programme with an adequate organisation for mobilizing community effort.

1. *Public Co-operation* : Direct cooperation of the public should be encouraged in the following fields :

(i) Establishing private schools;

(ii) Putting up of schools buildings;

(iii) Contributing voluntary labour for construction of school buildings;

(iv) Helping in the maintenance of school buildings;

(v) Helping in providing suitable accommodation for teachers and students, particularly in the rural areas;

(vi) Popularising co-education at the primary stage;

(vii) Creating public opinion in favour of the teaching profession and to give greater respect to the teacher in the community;

(viii) Undertaking necessary propaganda to make the profession of teaching for women popular;

(ix) Encouraging married women to take up at least part-time teaching in village schools and to work as school mothers;

(x) Initiating action and participating in educative propaganda to break down traditional prejudices against girls' education;

(xi) Setting up and organizing school betterment committees, improvement conferences;

(xii) Supplying mid-day meals;

(xiii) Supplying uniforms to poor and needy children; and

(xiv) Supplying free text-books and writing materials to needy children.

2. *The State Council for Women's Education* : These are the most suitable agencies for providing the organisation and leadership for mobilising community effort. They should function as a part of the network of which the District Councils at the district level, and the Mahila Mandals and similar voluntary bodies at the town and village levels would be strong and active links. These agencies should look upon mobilising of community effort and educating public opinion to promote girls' education as their main and primary responsibility. They should aim at building up in villages and towns' teams of voluntary workers, men and women, who are willing to devote themselves to this cause and work actively for its promotion.

3. *State's Responsibility* : The State should educate public opinion in favour of girls' education through —

(i) School improvement conferences;

(ii) Seminars;

(iii) Radio talks, audio-visual aids and distribution of informative pamphlets;

(iv) Enrolment drives, generally in June and special additional drives for girls' education during Dussehra; and

(v) Assisting voluntary, welfare and other organisations, private individuals and associations engaged in the field of education of girls and women.

4. *School Improvement Conferences* : These should be arranged widely throughout the States and particularly in the less advanced States in order to encourage people to contribute to educational awakening and advancement.

5. *State Help* : The State should continue to help in an abundant measure in providing necessary schooling facilities in all the areas and in the habitations, however small, so that the local population can make use of them.

6. *Pre-Primary Schools* : It is necessary that in rural areas particularly, pre-primary schools should be attached to primary schools so that children get accustomed to schooling even at the tender age.

7. *Reform and Inspection* : The existing functional deficiencies of schools should be remedied by replacing buildings which are totally inadequate to modern educational needs. There should be periodical inspection of school buildings and hostels so as to ensure their structural soundness and suitable sanitary facilities.

8. *More Attractive* : School work should be made more attractive and should present education in terms more acceptable to pupils.

9. *Recruitment of Women teachers* : Concerted efforts have to be made to recruit as many women teachers as possible. Women are by general consent the best teachers for the primary classes in all schools. It should be the aim of all states to appoint women teachers in primary schools and a greater number of women teachers in mixed schools. A school staffed by women will inspire greater confidence in the parents and make them willing to send their children to mixed institutions.

(i) *Conditions of Recruitment* : The basis of recruitment of women teachers should be widened and their conditions of work should be made more attractive. Financial incentives like special allowances for hilly, isolated or any other specific backward rural areas should be given to teachers. Each State may specify areas where such allowances would be available.

(ii) *Married Women Teachers* : Attempt should be made to bring back to the teaching profession married women who have left it in recent years and to bring women from other occupations to supplement the teaching staff.

(iii) *Condensed Courses* : Condensed courses should be organised on a large scale for adult, women particularly from rural areas so that they could take up teaching jobs in the villages.

(iv) *Recruitment age limit* : In order to attract more women teachers the age-limit for the unmarried and married women teachers should be relaxed in the case of those working in village schools. The service conditions of such married women who do part-time teaching work should be made more attractive.

(v) *Posting* : As far as possible women teachers should be posted in or near their own villages.

(vi) *Pay Scale* : The pay scales of all teachers should be improved and the teachers should be paid an economic wage, so that they may be retained in the profession.

(vii) *Special Attention* : Special drives should be organised to attract people in rural areas to the teaching profession as the best form of social service needed for the upliftment of the villages.

(viii) *Training Schools* : Training Schools with hostels need to be located in the rural centres and near 'different' areas where girls from the villages are trained and sent back to work in their own or neighbouring villages.

(ix) *Training* : During selection of trainees for training schools and colleges, special preference should be given to women from rural areas seeking admission.

(x) *Sufficient Facilities* : The training facilities available in each State should be of such a magnitude that the annual output of trained teachers would be equal to the demand for additional teachers.

(xi) *Inspection* : The inspecting staff should be adequate and strong if improvement is to be secured and waste reduced. A separate woman inspectorate will help to bring in more girls to school.

(xii) *Lodging* : It is only by providing women teachers with quarters near the schools that we can attract many educated women to the teaching profession.

(xiii) *Hostels* : The absence of hostel facilities as also the slow progress in the construction of those that have been undertaken, have affected the hostel. The construction of hostels should be included as one of the priority objectives in the Plans of the States and necessary financial assistance for the construction of hostels and maintenance stipends be made available more liberally to local authorities and voluntary organisations working in the field of education of girls and women.

10. *Building and Equipment* : Local bodies should be made responsible for the provision of school buildings, equipment, playing fields and the like and observance of the educational code in the State.

11. *Social Education* : In the field of social education, a determined effort should be made to increase the number of literacy classes for women in rural areas and to carry out intensive campaigns for the spread of literacy amongst women. Activities in this field should be administered by the education departments of the State Governments.

12. *Central Assistance* : Such Central assistance should be —

(a) At the elementary stage for : (i) preparation and employment of women teachers; (ii) grant of free books, writing material and clothing to girls; and (iii) twin quarters for women teachers.

(b) At the secondary stage for : (i) provision of separate schools for girls; (ii) hostels; (iii) Grant of free books, writing materials and clothing to girls; and (iv) preparation and appointment of women teachers in increasing numbers.

13. *Compulsory Education* : Compulsory Education Act should be introduced in States where it does not exist. In addition, State Governments should provide sufficient incentives and carry on propaganda to attract all children to school.

14. *Curriculum* : While the curriculum can be the same for both boys and girls at the primary and middle stages, provision should be made for offering of electives comprising subjects which would be of special interest to girls and which would help them later in their fields of activity.

15. *Shift System* : In schools that lack accommodation but have a rush of admission, the double shift system may be tried as a temporary measure.

16. *Seasonal Adjustment*: Changing of school hours and school holidays to seasonal requirements has been found in some places to be a helpful concession to parents who would otherwise not be in a position to spare the children for attending classes.

## COMMITTEE ON THE STATUS OF WOMEN (1971-74)

Various new problems relating to the advancement of women which had not been visualized by the constitution makers and the Government in earlier days have emerged. Therefore, with the changing social and economic conditions in the country, the Government of India felt that a comprehensive examination of all questions relating to the rights and status of women in this country would provide useful guidelines for the formulation of social policies including education. For this purpose the Government of India, Ministry of Education and Social Welfare constituted this Committee on September 22, 1971. The Committee submitted its report entitled 'Towards Equality' in December, 1974 with Dr. (Smt.) Phulrenu Guha as chair-person.

### Terms of Reference

1. To examine the constitutional, legal and administrative provision that have a bearing on the social status of women, their education and employment.

2. To assess the impact of these provisions during the last two decades on the status of women in the country, particularly in the rural sector, and to suggest more effective programme.

3. To consider the development of education among women and determine the factors responsible for the slow progress in some areas and suggest remedial measures.

4. To survey the problems of the working women including discrimination in employment and remuneration.

5. To examine the status of women as house-wives and mothers in the changing social status and their problems in the sphere of further education and employment.

6. To undertake surveys of case studies on the implications of the population policies and family planning programmes on the status of women.

7. To suggest any other measures which would enable women to play their full and proper role in building up the nation.

## RECOMMENDATIONS

### 1. Co-education

(i) Co-education whould be adopted as the general policy at the primary level.

(ii) At the middle and secondary stages separate schools may be provided in areas where there is a great demand for them.

(iii) At the university level co-education should be the general policy and opening of new colleges exclusively for girls should be discouraged.

(iv) There should be no ban on admission of girls to boys' institutions.

(v) Wherever separate schools/colleges for girls are provided, it has to be ensured that they maintain required standards in regard to the quality of staff, provision of facilities, relevant courses and co-curricular activities.

(vi) Acceptance of the principle of mixed staff should be made a condition of recognition for mixed schools. This measure may be reviewed a few years after it is implemented.

(vii) Wherever there are mixed schools, separate toilet facilities and retiring rooms for girls should be provided.

**2. Curricula**

(i) There should be a common course of general education for both sexes till the end of Class X.

(ii) At The primary stage, simple needle craft, music and dancing should be taught to both sexes.

(iii) From the middle stage, differences may be permitted under work experience.

(iv) In Classes XI-XII girls should have full opportunity to choose vocational and technical courses according to local conditions, needs and aptitudes.

(v) At the university stage there is a need to introduce more relevant and useful courses for all students.

**3. Pre-school education**

(i) The provision of three-year pre-school education for all children by making a special effort to increase the number of 'balwadis' in the rural areas and in urban slums.

(ii) In order to enable them to fulfil the social functions discussed above, an effort should be made to locate them as near as possible to the primary and middle schools of the locality.

**4. Universalisation of education for the age-group 6-14**

(i) Provision of primary schools within walking distance from the home of every child within the next five years.

(ii) Establishment of ashram or residential schools to serve clusters of villages scattered in difficult terrains. Where this is not immediately possible, preparatory schools may be provided for the time being.

(iii) Provision of mobile schools for children of nomadic tribes, migrant labour and counteraction workers.

(iv) Sustained propaganda by all types of persons, preferably women officials, and non-officials, social and political workers, to bring every girl into school in Class I preferably at the age of 6.

(v) Provision of incentives to prevent drop-outs. The most effective incentive is the provision of mid-day meals. The other important incentives are free school uniforms, scholarships or stipends and free supply of books and other study material. For schools which do not prescribe any uniform, some provison of clothing is necessary.

(vi) Special incentives for areas where enrolment of girls is low.

(vii) At least 50 per cent of teachers at this stage should be women.

(viii) Provision of at least two teachers in all schools, and conversion of the existing single teacher ones as early as possible.

(ix) Developing a system of part-time education for girls who cannot attend school on a full time basis.

(x) Adoption of the multiple entry system for girls who could not attend school earlier or had to leave before becoming functionally literate.

(xi) Provision of additional space in schools so that girls can bring their younger brothers and sisters to be looked after, either by the girls themselves in turn, or by some local women.

(xii) Opening of schools and greater flexibility in admission procedure in middle schools (multiple only) to help girls to complete their schooling.

**5. Sex education**

(i) Introduction of sex education from middle school.

(ii) Appointment of an expert group by the Ministry of Education to prepare graded teaching material on the subject.

(iii) This material may be used for both formal and non-formal education.

**6. Secondary education**

(i) Free education for all girls up to the end of the secondary stage.

(ii) Improving the quality of teaching and provision of facilities for important subjects like science, mathematics and commerce.

(iii) Introduction of job-oriented work-experience, keeping in view the needs, the resources and the employment potential of the region *e.g.* courses leading to training as ANM, typing and commercial practice, programmes oriented to industry and simple technology, agriculture and animal husbandry.

**7. General recommendations**

(i) Provision of mixed staff in all mixed schools.

(ii) Adequate provision of common-rooms and separate toilet facilities for girls in all schools.

(iii) Adequate arrangements for co-curricular activities for girls in all schools.

(iv) Provision of more need-*cum*-merit scholarships and hostel facilities for girls.

**8. Higher education**

(i) Development of more employment opportunities, particularly of a part-time nature, to enable women to participate more in productive activities.

(ii) Development of employment information and guidance service for women entering higher education.

## RECOMMENDATIONS ON NON-FORMAL EDUCATION

The greatest problem in women's education today is to provide some basic education to the overwhelming majority who have remained outside the reach of the formal system because of their age and social responsibilities as well as the literacy gap. For the sake of national plans for development, it is imperative to increase the social effectiveness of women in the 15-25 age-group. *Ad hoc* approaches through the adult literacy, functional literacy and other programmes of the Government have proved inadequate. As for vocational and occupational skills, the needs of women are greater than those of men. The skills differ according to the industrial and market potential of regions and it is imperative to relate the training to local needs, resources and employment possibilities instead of adopting an artificial sex-selective approach.

## QUESTIONS FOR EXERCISE

1. Discuss the recommendations of the Committee on Women's Education (1957-59).
2. Discuss the recommendations of the Committee for Girls Education and Public Cooperation (1963-65).
3. What were the recommendations of the Committee on the Status of Women (1971-74).

# 8

# POPULATION EDUCATION

The nett addition to Indian population between 1921-1981 was around 13 millions equal to the population of the continent of Australia. Following are the main causes which contribute to this rapid growth of numbers :

1. As India has a large population, even a small and nominal rate of increase adds quite a few millions to the total population.
2. Indian population is young. Forty per cent of Indians below 14 are likely to get married with a decade or two.
3. As marriage in Inda is not optional but a duty, so also is parenthood.
4. Early marriage is widely prevalent. In rural areas girls married when they are hardly 14 or 15. As fertility rate is high in that age group, the size of their family is also large.
5. Social reforms like widow remarriage have also contributed to population growth.
6. In the absence of social security measures, the poorer sections believe that having many children particularly sons, is an insurance against old age.
7. Science has helped man to conquer diseases. Thanks to improve sanitation, health and medical facilities death rate has come down from 42.6 per thousand in 1901, to 13.9 per thousand in 1979.
8. Infant mortality (*i.e.* death before the first year of birth) has come down from 215 per thousand in 1901-05 to 74 in 1964.
9. Longevity has increased. Now the average expectation of life at the birth is 52.

**Social and Economic Implications**

Unless the Governments take timely action, the situation may well be out of control. Let us consider the consquences of unchecked population growth.

1. India has only 2.4 per cent of the world's land but 14 per cent of the world's population. One in seven is an Indian.

2. A new baby arrives every 1½ seconds. In 1979 birth rate was 33 per thousand. Indian population has grown around 2.5 per cent per annum.

3. Dependency ratio is very high. Roughly half the number of the people (the very young and the very old) depend heavily upon the other half. This will be clear from the following population profile of India.

**Population Profile**

| Age Group | Males | Females | Combined (%) | Male | Females (%) | Combined |
|---|---|---|---|---|---|---|
| 1 | 2 | 3 | 4 | 5 | 6 | 7 |
| 0.14 | 41.86 | 42.19 | 42.02 | 48.84 | 38.54 | 38.69 |
| 15.59 | 42.20 | 51.82 | 52.01 | 55.79 | 55.63 | 55.71 |
| 60.0 | 5.95 | 5.99 | 5.87 | 5.83 | 5.83 | 5.60 |

4. India has a very low per capita income (Rs. 712 only). 48 per cent people live below poverty line.

5. The problem of unemployment is a serious challenge to social and political stability.

6. Food production has doubled since independence, but the population has also increased by 75 per cent in 35 years.

**Population Dynamics and Pressing Needs**

To cope with the rapid strides in population, India needs additional resources for each and every year as noted below:

1,26,500 Schools
3,72,500 Teachers
25,06,000 Houses
187,44,000 Metres of cloth
125,45,300 Quintals of food
40,00,000 Jobs.

Five year plans could succeed, only if the growth of population is held under check. Poverty could be eradicated only when economic growth is much ahead of population growth. The famous demographer Dr. S. Chandrasekhar had said :

"History bears witness to the fact that man, when threatened, is capable of extraordinary endeavour. Now, that man's very survival is at stake, let us hope he will control his numbers, stop polluting his environment, and finally learn to live at peace with his fellow beings. Let us hope man will endure."

*State and Population Control* : Mysore was the first Government in the world to open a family planning clinic as early as 1930. India and China have launched nation-wide programme to arrest population explosion. United Nations Funds for Population Activities (UNFPA) is giving aid to all developing countries.

More information on population trends may be secured from the following agencies :

1. Family Planning Association of India, New Delhi.
2. Demographic Research Centre, Baroda.
3. Demographic Training and Research Centre, Bombay.
4. Population Education Cell, NCERT, New Delhi.
5. Population Education Cell in SCERT of Your State.

## National Population Policy (1976)

1. Increase in the age of marriage from 15 to 18 years for girls and from 18 to 21 for boys.
2. Freezing of the population figures at the 1971 level until the year 2001 for purposes of representation in the National Parliament as well as for allocation of Central assistance, devolution of taxes etc. to the States;
3. Linking of a part of Central assistance to the States for their development with their performance in family planning;
4. Greater attention to girl's education;
5. Proper place for Population Education in the total system of education;
6. Involvement of all Ministries/Departments of the Government in the family planning programme;
7. Increase in monetary compensation for sterilisation;
8. Institution of group awards as incentives for various organisations and bodies representing women, with the implementation of the programme;
9. Greater attention to research; and
10. Greater use of motivational media, particularly in rural areas, for increasing acceptance of family planning.

## Education and Population Growth

Education is an input fundamental to the success of economic development. In the last thirty years, primary education has increased three times, secondary education by six times and higher education by seven times. The number of universities has increased from 19 in 1950 to 118 by 1981. Despite the increase in number of educational institutions and their intake capacity, the number of illiterates has also increased from 38 millions in 1971 to 446 millions in 1981.

'Eternal vigilance is the price of democracy'. Illiteracy and ignorance hamper the successful functioning of democracy. Education enriches the human potential. According to Prof. Kenneth Bounding, "From the social and cultural points of view, the development of human resources helps people lead fuller and richer lives, less bound to superstition and unscientific beliefs. In short, the process of human resources development unlocks the door to modernisation."

Education has a bearing on population growth. This is clear from the following table.

**Literacy and Population Trends**

| | Rural Kerala | Rural U.P. |
|---|---|---|
| 1. Female literacy | 63% | 10% |
| 2. Birth rate | 27 per thousand | 40 per thousand |
| 3. Death rate | 7 | 18 |
| 4. Mean average age at marriage | 21.7 | 15.5 |

## Population Education

India seeks to establish an egalitarian society through constitutional means. Education has a dynamic role to play by including right values, beliefs and attitudes in children, who are the future citizens. They should be made aware of the trends in population growth, the gap between the available resources and increasing numbers, the negative effects of population growth on social and natural environment and the blessings of a small family.

Population Education is not a sophisticated name for family planning. It is not sex education, either. It expects the students to be sensitive to the problem of population explosion and how it affects the happiness and well being of their future.

## Definition of Population Education

1. *UNESCO (Bangkok Conference, 1970)* : "Population Education is an educational programme which provides for a study of the population situation of the family, community, nation and world with the purposes of developing it the students' rational and responsible attitudes and behaviour towards that situation."

2. *Population Reference Bureau, Washington, 1971*: "Population Education is an attempt to create a deep, universal action guiding perception of the consequences of demographic change. It seeks to bring about a realization of the individual, family, social and environmental effects of the explosive increase in human population, the rapid shift in the construction and distribution of people, the implications of changing age and other demographic patterns and the conceivable options that may be open to mankind to cope with the consequent problems. While it is confined exclusively to a particular group, it is focused primarily on students, who will become the principal, child bearers within one or two decades."

## Goals of Population Education

*Dr. Simmons Observes* : "Population education holds promise not only as means of diffusing information about population problems more pervasively in a given country than can be done by the channels ordinarily available to family planning programmes, but as a means for bringing about the desired changes in attitudes,behaviours and values in the next generation (which is almost here)." Dr. Sloan R. Wayland has given the following list of possible goals of Population

Education "For the individual's own personal behaviour-pattern and attitudes :

(a) Acceptance of the small family norm.

(b) Understanding that the size of the family can be controlled

(c) Acceptance of marriage at a mature age as a desirable pattern.

(d) Appreciation of the advantages of planning, including health and economic gains from spacing and limitation in total number of children, and of the health, education and other opportunities for children that may be more adequately provided for in the small family."

## NATIONAL SEMINAR ON POPULATION EDUCATION (1969)

The National Seminar on Population Education was organized by the Ministry of Education and Youth Services in collaboration with the Ministry of Health and Family Planning, on 2nd and 3rd of August, 1969 at Bombay, with Smt. Dhanwanthy Rama Rao, President, International Planned Parenthood Federation, Bombay as the chairperson. The Department of Social Sciences and Humanities of the NCERT provided the academic services to this Seminar. It was attended by the representatives of Ministry of Education and Youth Services, Ministry of Health and Family Planning, State Representatives, USAID, Ford Foundation, Pathfinder Fund and NCERT and twenty-two other specialists in allied fields.

### Aims and Objectives

1. To review the work already done so far in population education by the different agencies, official and non-official, in the country;

2. To clarify the concept and objectives of population education; and

3. To develop a practical and realistic plan of action for the introduction of population education in the curricula at different stages of education.

### Recommendations

1. *Challenge* : The country is faced with a new challenge which arises out of the enormous increase in population, the needs of which are not being met adequately by the economic development.

2. *Education* : Steps should be taken to educate the students at various levels to meet these challenges. Population education should be an integral part of education at all levels.

3. *Objectives of Education* : The objectives of population education should be (i) to enable the students to understand that family size is controllable, (ii) that population limitation can facilitate the development of a higher quality of life in the nation, and (iii) that a small family size can contribute materially to the quality of living for the individual family.

4. *Information* : Students at all levels have a right to accurate information about the effect of changes in family size and in national population on the individual, the family, and the nation so that this body of knowledge is utilized to control family

size and national population with beneficial impact on the economic development of the nation and the welfare of the individual families.

5. *Curriculum* : Population education should be introduced unto the curriculum of schools and colleges by including it in so far as it may be possible, in the areas of study now common in the educational curriculum such as social studies, sciences, health education, mathematics, languages, etc. It may be possible to achieve all the objectives in view by including population education suitably in the curicula of appropriate subjects already comprised in the curriculum.

6. *Correlation* : Careful attention must be given to offering ideas and information which are appropriate to the age levels and the cultural orientation of children, adolescents and adults in schools and colleges and outside the educational system.

7. *Gradual development* : Population education is a new area of curriculum to most schools and colleges. Steps will therefore, have to be taken to introduce it gradually so that the curriculum is developed, teachers trained and pilot projects conducted and evaluated.

8. *Population Education Cell* : A separate "Population Education Cell" should be established in the NCERT in order to develop suitable curicula on population education at the school stage. This cell should work in close collabration with the Central Health Education Bureau, Central Family Planning Institute and other agencies interested in the programme, both official and voluntary.

9. *Implementation.* Immediate steps must be taken:

(a) To clearly define the content of population education at different stages and evolve suitable methods for teaching and examination; and

(b) To prepare books, supplementary reading materials, audiovisual aids, teacher's guides, etc. needed for the successful implementation of the programme.

10. *Education out of schools* : Special steps may be taken to draw a suitable programme in population education for the youth who are not enrolled in the schools and use the facilities as well as the personnel available in all education institutions for this purpose.

11. *Training* : (a) Immediate steps should be taken to organize courses on population education in teachers' colleges at the primary as well as the secondary levels.

(b) Suitable steps should be taken to organize in-service training for the teachers who are already working.

(c) There should be specialists on population education among the teacher educators at the post-graduate level.

12. *Research* : Efforts should be made to promote research on population education in the teachers' colleges as well as in the liberal arts colleges and other institutions of higher education. In the universities efforts have to be made to develop inter-disciplinary research on population problems.

13. *Courses, Guidance and Extension* : (a) At the college level, steps should be taken by the universities to design a course in demography at the undergraduate stage so that those who are interested in population problems could specialize at the post-graduate level in demography.

(b) College level guidance bureau should be strengthened by qualified staff who would help the students to solve personal problems in connection with family relations, marriage counselling, etc.

(c) Extension lectures should be organized on population problems in each college and university every year in order to ensure a widespread awareness of the problems among the youths and the teachers.

14. *Steps by U.G.C.* To achieve the purpose in the two resolutions stated above, *viz.* Resolution Nos. 12 and 13, University Grants Commission may be requested to take the necessary steps to enable the affiliated colleges and the universities to take up these tasks-courses of study, research and extension lectures.

15. *Parent-Teacher Co-operation.* Teachers' organizations and parent-teacher associations should discuss the problem and help in the implementation of population education proprammes.

16. *Step for Govt. Experiments.* The seminar welcomes the willingness of the States to try this programme on an experimental basis provided the details of the curricula, materials and necessary guidance were made available. The Seminar, therfore, recommends that the following steps may be taken:

(i) *Statement.* The Government of India, Ministries of Education and Health in consultation with the State Governments should draw up a statement showing the broad objectives of the programme, its broad content as it would be introduced at different stages, and the manner in which the pilot projects for the programme would be developed, administered and financially supported.

(ii) *Programme.* On the basis of this statement, the NCERT and the Central Health Education Bureau, Central Family Planning Institute collaborating with the State Education Departments and other organizations interested in the programme — official and voluntary — should go into the details of the programme and produce (a) detailed curricula,(b) hand-books for teachers dealing with among other things, methods of teaching and examination, and (c) other materials which should be available in English, Hindi and other Indian languages, in good time.

(iii) *Introduction on a pilot bases.* The programme should then be introduced on a pilot basis in different categories of institutions of the various categories and levels.

17. *Support to Projects.* The Seminar notes with satisfaction that some unversities and other organizations have already started pilot projects and recommends that they should be supported.

18. *Evaluation and Improvement.* Adequate arrangements should also be

made to watch the progress of these pilot projects to evaluate them and improve the materials and techinques in the light of the experience gained.

19. *Standing Committee*. The Government of India should take immediate steps to set up a standing committee which could watch the progress in the implementation of these recommendations by various organizations at different levels.

## POPULATION EDUCATION IN INDIA

Experts are of the view that population studies should not be made a separate school subject, but should be judiciously interwoven with all subjects. It should not smack of propaganda. No separate period need be allotted. There is no need for appointing special teachers. Necessary information should be given in a natural way. An intelligent resourceful teacher can integrate relevant population problems while teaching his own subject. Following are a few topics which automatically crop up whenever one discusses problems of national welfare in the classroom :

1. Population growth-census figures.
2. Economic development and population.
3. Social development and population.
4. Impact of population growth on environment.
5. Nutritional standards and population.
6. Education, social justice and population growth.

### Instructional Objectives of Population Education

1. To develop an understanding of some demographic concepts and processes.
2. To develop among younger generation an understanding of the most important phenomenon of the modern world *viz*. rapid growth of population and its causes.
3. To develop an understanding of the influence of population trends on the various aspects of human life, political, social cultural and economic.
4. To develop an understanding of the close interaction of population growth and development process with particular reference to developmental programmes for raising the standard of living of the people.
5. To develop an understanding of the evil effects of overpopulation on the environment and the concomitant dangers from population.
6. To develop an understanding of scientific and medical advancement enabling man to get an increasing control over famines, diseases and untimely death and the imbalance thus created between death-rate and birth-rate.
7. To develop an understanding of biological factors and phenomenon of reproduction which are responsible for the continuation of the specie.
8. To develop an appreciation of —
   (i) the small family norm as proper and desirable;

(ii) the relation between population size and the quality of life;

(iii) the fact that family size is a matter of deliberate choice and human regulation rather than of accident or forces beyond human control.

9. To develop as appreciation of the relationship between the preservation of the health of the children and the small size of the family.

10. To develop appreciation of the fact that the actions of each individual member of the society affects others as well and personal and national decisions concerning family size and population have a long range of consequences for the whole world.

**Teaching Points at Secondary Level**

**A. Lower Secondary Level**

| | *Understanding* | *Content* |
|---|---|---|
| 1. | Food, shelter and clothing are basic necessities of life. | Per capita requirements of basic necessities — malnutrition and chronic illness. |
| 2. | Availability of the basic necessities varies from place to place. | Rapid population — lack of availability of basic necessities — high prices. |
| 3. | Standard of living differs from country to country depending upon the stage of economic development. | Nutritional requirements of serveral groups — per capita availability of essential commodities in a few select countries. |
| 4. | Relation between production and population. | (i) Both are subject to human control.<br>(ii) Depletion of natural resources. |

**B. Higher Secondary Level**

| | | |
|---|---|---|
| 1. | Increase in production is nullified by rapid increase in population. | Rate of growth of population and production — Gross National Product Contribution of Agriculture and Industry to national income. |
| 2. | Rapid growth of population adversely affect the ecomomic life of country. | Natural resources allocation exploitation of nature by man. Unemployment. |
| 3. | Standard of living — relationship between production and population. | Standard of living is relative — minimum need programme. |
| 4. | Low standard of living results in lower production. | Vicious circle — low production, low standard of living, decrease in production. |
| 5. | Effective ways to check population explosion. | Agencies involved in arresting population. |

**Enrichment Activities in Population Education**

Following activities may be emphasisd in the subjects taught to bring home the messages of Population Education after modifying them to suit the school needs:

1. Language :
   - (i) *Precis-writing* — condensing a passage which describes the population situation in India.
   - (ii) *Comprehension* — Let the students silently read an article or an instructional material prepared by you and answer a few questions to test their understanding.
   - (iii) *Essay-writing* — An essay on a relevant social or economic problem and its links with the country's population growth.
2. Mathematics :
   - (i) *Growth of population in the school, town or village* — comparison of census figures.
   - (ii) Family budgets in relation to size and income of the family.
   - (iii) Comparing national income with those of other countries.
3. General Science :
   Man and his physical environment — sanitation and health-conservation of natural resources — pollution — protecting the environment. These topics may be explained through suitable illustrations. Discussions may be held on the above themes to develop the skill in scientific analysis.
4. History :
   - (i) Citizenship training.
   - (ii) Overpopulation-migration wars. This relationship may be illustrated from history.
   - (iii) Preparing a chart to show the growth of population of the world from the dawn of history.
5. Geography :
   - (i) Studying the density of population in different countries.
   - (ii) Using suitable shades to make the population density in all the States of India.

(iii) Comparison of natural and human resources in select countries.

(iv) Scarcity and famine conditions Where they exist? Why?

6. Arts :

(i) Songs and dances to depict the effects of unchecked population growth.

(ii) Simple diagrams to illustrate population growth, availability of accept-commodities and the need to accept the small family norm voluntarily.

## Instructional Material for Population Education

1. *Printed Text and Reference Materials* — Illustrated work-books supplementary books, comics etc.
2. *Inexpensive Supplementary Materials.*
3. *Projected Material*—Films, film strips, transparencies, T.V. Presentations etc.
4. *3-D Materials* — Dolls, models etc.
5. *Displays*—Flannel boards, display boards, cutouts etc. Some of the above mentioned aids are available with the Health and Family Welfare Department. Press clipings and pictures can be effectively used in all schools.

## Role of the Teacher in Population Education

Teachers not only serve the cause of education, but also lend a helping hand to all nation-building activities. Many teachers are real 'opinion-leaders' in their villages and command much respect. In their informal chat with the people in the community, they can stress the concept of the 'small family norm'.

In the words of Dr. Chandrasekhar, "The teachers are the backbone of this educational movement and the success of this innovation will depend largely on the ability of these pioneers to put across the concept of small family norm to the young intelligently and effectively. This means that the teachers themselves must learn a great deal about the dynamics of population problem and what is equally important, must master techniques of imparting such information in an attractive and compelling manner."

## QUESTION FOR EXERCISE

1. Discuss the recommendations of the seminar on Population Education, 1969.

# 9

# SOCIAL EDUCATION OR ADULT EDUCATION

**Definition of Adult Education**

1. *S.N. Mukherjee.* "Adult education may be defined very broadly so as to include all instruction, formal or informal, to adults."

2. *K.G. Saiyeden.* "Adult education includes political and civil as well as moral education." What was called adult education before winning Independence is today called social education. But the aims of social education are more comprehensive than those of adult education. Its main aim is to bring a socialistic pattern of society through education.

3. *Abul Kalam Azad.* The erstwhile Education Minister Maulana Abul Kalam Azad explained the meaning of adult education while inaugurating the UNESCO seminar on village adult education in 1949. He said that social education implied education for making a man complete. It will make him literate so that he has acess to the knowledge of the world. It will tell him how he should adapt to his environment and how he should take maximum advantage of his physical circumstances. It will teach him handicrafts and more efficient method of production so that he may achieve economic prosperity. It will teach him the fundamentals of personal and social hygiene so that his domestic life may be happy and prosperous. And finally, this education will train him in citizenship so that he may be able to cooperate with his government in making the country strong and in establishing peace in the world, for which some knowledge is essential. In the beginning, social education or adult education was interpreted only in the sense of granting literacy to the unread adult, but now it has come to comprehend every kind of education for the adult.

4. *Biharee.* "Social education is the stimulation in each citizen of a greater awareness of the advantages of the pattern of society as conceived in the constitution and a persistent desire for progress towards a pattern socially, economicaly and culturally."

## PURPOSE OF SOCIAL EDUCATION

In the past, adult education limited itself of creating some limited literacy in the adult so that he could read and write letters, read religious texts and comprehend accounts. But social education today is far more comprehensive. In this connection, the following aims of social education have been stated in a booklet *Social Education in India* published by the Government of India. The following are the aims set down there :

(a) *Individual Objectives* : Social education, from the individual standpoint, aims at the achievement of the following objectives:

1. Mental development of adults.
2. Development of their professional ability.
3. Their physical development.
4. Development of their social skills.
5. Their cultural development.
6. Their self-development.

(b) *Social objectives.* Social education has the following social objectives:

1. Development of social unity.
2. Protection and development of national resources.
3. Organization of co-operative communities and institutions.
4. Inclusion of the social ideal.

## AIMS OF SOCIAL EDUCATION

It is evident from the foregoing list of the purpose of social education that its aim is very comprehensive. In India after independence, a committee was appointed under the chairmanship of Mr. Mohan Lal Saxena to advise the Government on the expansion of adult education in the country. This Committee re-christened adult education and called it social education, and determined the following aims for it :

1. To awaken the citizens towards their rights and duties, and to encourage the sense of social service among them.
2. Creating love for democracy among the citizens and training them in democratic Government.
3. Acquainting the citizens with the problems confronting the country and the world.
4. Creating a sense of respect and admiration for Indian culture through the teaching of history, geography and culture.
5. Providing the citizens with an opportunity for cultural mixing and getting pleasure through organization of songs and dramatic activities.
6. Acquainting the citizens with specific moral values through community discussions and teaching.
7. Providing necessary knowledge of language and arithmetic and encouraging the spread of knowledge.

8. Educating the citizens to use their leisure for economic production and prosperity through teaching handicraft and other skills.
9. Continuing the educational programme among the citizens through the use of libraries, discussions, educational committees and public universities.
10. Creating a sense of co-operation among the citizens.

## FOUR POINT PROGRAMME

The Government evolved a four point programme to achieve these targets of social education:

1. Spread of literacy.
2. Education in health and hygiene rules.
3. Training in industry and professions for economic progress.
4. Awareness of rights and duties along with sense of citizenship.

According to Humayun Kabir, "Social education may be defined as a course of study directed towards the promotion of consciousness of citizenship among the people and the promotion of social solidarity among them. It is not content with the introduction of literacy among the grown-up illiterates but aims at production of educated mind among the masses. As a natural corollary, it seeks to inculcate in them a lively sense of right and duties of citizenship both as individuals and members of the community."

## NEED OF SOCIAL EDUCATION

Social education fulfils the need of the following:

1. **Illiterate Adults** : Though Indian Constitution has granted the right of equality and equal rights of freedom to all the citizens many of them are not able to exercise their rights on account of their illiteracy. Social education tries to make the illiterate adults literate.

2. **Complete Education** : Present education does not develop the necessary abilities in the persons to lead their lives successfully in different fields. It does not give any type of training in respect of health, family and proper utilisation of leisure. Social education fulfils this need of complete education.

3. **Recreation** : In the cities lack of means of entertainment is not a problem. But there is a great lack of means of entertainment in the villages. Social education has taken upon itself a task of providing different types of entertainment to the rural people.

4. **Political Need** : The present time is the period of reorganisation, rehabilitation, development and progress for our country. To achieve this aim, it is necessary that the common people should be given proper education and proper literature should be made available to them for study. Hence there should be proper provision of education of adults of India. Unless we are able to bring about the consciousness among the adults, we will not be successful to achieve our cherished goal. Social education has taken upon itself the task of educating the adult Indians.

5. **Social Need** : The structure of the society rests on the foundation of co-operation. It protects the society and also builds and develops it. The existence of all the institutions, committees and organisations of the society depend upon co-operation. This need is fulfilled in adult education.

6. **Economic Need** : The majority of Indian people is poor. The condition of the rural people is more miserable than that of the urban people. Hence, the Government of India have devoted their attention to the financial uplift of crores of poor Indians. It has been decided to raise their economical status by giving them different types of training through the programme of social education.

7. **National Need** : If the people are not educated, then it is not possible to make a full use of constructive power of the country. Social education fulfils this national need.

## PROBLEMS OF SOCIAL EDUCATION AND THEIR REMEDIES

1. **Illiteracy** : India is the second most populated country of the world, next only to China. Nearly 48% of Indian people are groping in the dark because of their illiteracy. In view of the existence of so widespread illiteracy, it is futile to hope any type of social, economic and political development.

**Remedy : Liquidation of Illiteracy**. Although, the liquidation of illiteracy of 48% of the illiterate adults is not a simple task yet success can be achieved by adopting social education.

Obviously, the liquidation of illiteracy is the responsibility of our Government. It is, therefore, necessary that either through the successful method experimented By Dr. Laubach or any other method which seems to be proper should be adopted to completely liquidate illiteracy from our sub-continent.

2. **Unsuitable Curriculum** : The work of social education is not making much progress due to the unproper and unsuitable curriculum. The curriculum which is used for the education of the children cannot be used for the adults because their interests, needs and viewpoints towards life are completely different. Again, same curriculum cannot be adopted for all the adults. Some are illiterates and some are half illiterates and for them teaching of some special subject is necessary. Lastly there are some neo-literates who know some reading and writing and require the curriculum including subjects such as civilization, culture, history, geography, civics, etc.

**Remedy : Construction of proper Curriculum.** Proper and suitable curriculum can be prepared only after carefully and minutely studying and considering the needs of complete illiterate, and neo-literates. The curriculum should include all those subjects which may ensure their political, economic, social and cultural development. Several curricula will have to be prepared keeping in view the needs, interests, mental tendencies and standards of the adults of different ages. Although the curricula will be different yet their subjects will ordinarily be the same, subject to their short or detailed studies according to the needs of adults of different age group. The first importance should be given to the teaching of writing and reading. Then provision should be made for imparting education of mother tongue, mathematics, history, civics, economics, geography, culture, animal husbandry general science, hygiene, literature, physical education, etc. According to local needs, each adult should be trained in some or the other crafts, so that he may be able to make it a means of his income.

3. **Lack of Suitable Method** : If the teaching method is uninteresting or against their feeling of 'self', freedoms, principles or habits then it will certainly unsuccessful. That is why, it is not possible to determine a single method of teaching for the adults.

**Remedy : Suitable method of teaching**. The teaching should be interesting and may attract adults. Following are some of good teaching methods:

(i) *Letter acquaintance method.* In this method the adults are first made acquainted with the knowledge of the letter. This system is prevalent in our primary schools.

(ii) *Sentence method.* In this method the adults are first made acquainted with the knowledge of two words and thereafter given in the form of different sentences by joining them or the letters.

(iii) *Lauback method.* A missionary named Dr. Lauback has evolved a new method which is known as sentence method. This method has been experimented in different parts of the world. In this method education of the whole sentence is given with the help of the chart.

(iv) *Story method.* Sri Sangam Lal Agarwal has the credit of evolving this method. In this method the education of the letters is given through certain stories based on the construction of letters.

(v) *Simple word method.* This method has been evolved by Sri Pathak. In this method prominence has been given to the songs. The songs are first sung and then the letters and the words are recognised by seeing them in the charts.

It is necessary that the letters of Indian language should be made easy so that the adults may have convenience to write, understand and recognise them. Roman letters should be used for all the Indian languages. This will give the adults the knowledge of European languages along with their own languages and the obstacles which are there in the unity of the country on account of diversity of the languages will also come to an end. Kamal Ataturk solved the problem of illiteracy of the people of Turkey by making use of the Roman letters and thereby developed the feeling of unity in them.

4. **Dearth of Teachers**. The teachers who are appointed in the adult schools are generally the teachers of primary schools. They do not possess necessary ability to teach the adults. They are ignorant of the psychology of adults. They are not trained in the suitable teaching method of the adults.

**Remedy : Supply of good Teachers**. Teachers should be appointed for imparting method of adult education and the psychology of the adults. They should have sufficient knowledge of agriculture, animal husbandry, cottage industry, hygiene, spinning and weaving, etc., so that the rural adults may be benefited by their teaching.

Under the guidance of Mahatma Gandhi, the volunteers successfully and properly performed the work of imparting education to children of the village in the District Champaran. If the students and teachers, educational institutions, employees of the office, members of the N.C.C. and A.C.C. and other selfless social workers take inspiration from the example of Mahatma Gandhi and adopt the principle of 'each one teach one', then there will be sufficient number of teachers for the adult schools.

5. **Lack of Suitable Literature** : The responsibility of social education cannot end with only making the adults literate. It is not sufficient only to teach reading and writing and simple mathematics to the adults. It is necessary that after giving them preliminary education some literature should be made available to these neo-literates as may develop their capacity to examine things, power of criticism and the social feelings. Such type of literature of the neo-literates as may develop their capacity to examine things, power of criticism and the social feelings. Such type of literature of the neo-literates is not very much available. According to K.G. Saiyeden, "The work of social education is greatly handicapped both at its literary stage and in this wider sense by the paucity of suitable reading materials, graded to apply to the adults. There is urgent need for producing large number of booklets, folders, charts, journals, newspapers, wall papers and other illustrated material which will capture adult's interests.

**Remedy : Production of suitable literature**. This work can be performed and completed with the help of learned writers who should be encouraged with every possible way to prepare suitable books and booklets for the adults. Illustrated newspapers and magazines should be published. Monthly magazines should be published containing news relating to games, health, culture and news of the world because there is utmost need of such a magazine for the neo-literates, The report of the Literary work in the production of Literature for Neo-literates 1958 of U.P. has made the suggestion that while preparing literature for the Neo-literates following 5 things must be kept in mind: (a) aims of social education, (b) distinction of age, (c) distinction of sex (d) distinction of religion, and (e) demand and need.

6. **Insufficient Agencies of Education** : According to 'Teacher's Hand Book of Social Education', "By agencies of social education is meant the bodies or institutions which deliver the goods, which contract the 'consumer' of social education and satisfy their needs." A special caution is required for selecting these means of social education. Persons specialised in knowledge of adult psychology should be engaged to solve this problem.

**Remedy : Proper agencies of education**. In this connection Report of the Literary workshop in the Production of Literature for Neo-literates, 1958 of U.P. has suggested the following: (a) descriptive prose, (b) poetry, folk-song and riddles, (c) drama, dialogues, etc. (d) stories, (e) newspapers, (f) interesting discourses, and (g) reading.

Other means will also have to be used for giving education to the adults. The following means can prove sufficiently effective :

(a) Audio-visual aids, radio, cinema, gramophone, dramas, etc.

(b) Collective songs and dances.

(c) Literary and debating conference and seminars.

(d) Historical and cultural programmes, etc.

7. **Lack of Funds** : Availability of funds is a stupendous problem for making adult literate. Generally the argument is put forward that sufficient money cannot be made available for making literate nearly, crores of adults in our poor country. Shri K.G. Saiyeden has rejected this argument. According to him, there is only one type of poverty which cannot be removed and that is the poverty of enthusiasm. If we make sincere efforts, other types of poverty can be removed. It is the responsibility of the Finance Department of the Government and the framers of the National Economic Schemes to make provision of the necessary money required for the purpose of adult education.

8. **Irresponsibility** : Who should be responsible for social education : Central Government, State Government, Education Departments, District Boards or Public Educational Institutions? The Central Government have shifted this responsibility on the State Government and thus they have tried to free themselves from the responsibility of 'social education'. This has created problem.

**Remedy : Joint responsibility**. Social education should be the joint responsibility of the Central Government, State Government and the different institutions of the people of this country. According to K.G. Saiyeden,'' It is, obviously a responsibility which neither the Education Department nor the Government Machinery as a whole can take on by itself, it needs the closer and most cordial co-operation of all agencies, official and non-official and of all individuals of good will and social sense who are interested in the welfare of India. There is so much work to be done and it is of such varied kind that there is scope for every one who cares to join the cavalcade of service students, teachers, men of leisure, political leaders, writers, labourers, craftsmen, professional men, everybody.''

## ADULT EDUCATION — A POLICY STATEMENT (1977)

The policy statement was made on the floor of Parliament on April 5, 1977. It declared that highest priority in educational planning would be accorded to adult education. As a result of the policy statement a national Adult Education Programme was launched in the country on October 3, 1978. It was envisaged to cover the entire population in 15-35 age group by the end of 1983-84.

### Policy Statement

1. *Universalization* : Educational facilities must be extended to adult population to remedy their educational deprivation and to enable them to develop their potentiality. Indeed, universalization of elementary education and of adult literacy are mutually inter-dependent.

2. *Assumptions* : Literacy ought to be recognized as an integral part of an individual's personality. The present thinking on adult education is based on the assumption (a) that illiteracy is a serious impediment to an individual's growth and to country's socio-economic progress; (b) that education is not coterminous with schooling but takes place in most work and life situations; (c) that learning, working and living are inseparable and each acquires a meaning only when correlated with the others; (d) that the means by which people are involved in the process of development are at least as important as the ends; and (e) that the illiterate and the poor can rise to their own liberation through literacy, dialogue and action.

3. *Relevant to Environment* : Adult education should emphasize imparting of literacy skills to persons belonging to the economically and socially deprived sections of society. Stress should be laid on learning rather than teaching, on use of the spoken language in literacy programmes and on harnessing of the mass media. Adult education should also be relevant to the environment and learners' needs; flexible regarding duration, time, location, instruction, arrangements, etc; diversified in regard to curriculum, teaching and learning materials and methods; and systematic in all aspects of organization.

4. *Priority to Illiterates* : Highest priority in adult education needs to be given to the illiterate persons. A massive programme should be launched to cover the vast segment of population in 15-35 age-group as far as possible within five years of its launching. This implies organization of special programmes of women and for persons belonging to scheduled castes and scheduled tribes. The regions which have a concentration of illiteracy will also require special attention.

5. *Mass Movement* : The need to view the programme as a mass movement must also be underlined. From the organizational point of view it is of utmost importance that elaborate preparations are made before launching a massive programme. Identification and motivation of the instructors, preparation of curriculum and teaching/learning materials and training have been the main areas of deficiency in adult education programmes in the past. Besides, adult education must cease to be a concern only of the educational authority. It should be an indispensable input in all sectors of development, particularly where participation of the beneficiaries is crucial to the fulfilment of development objectives. A pre-requisite of an adult education movement is that all agencies, Governmental, voluntary, private and public sector industry, institutions of formal education , etc., should lend strength to it. Voluntary agencies have a special role to play and necessary steps shall have to be taken to secure their full involvement. To ensure effectiveness and systematic analysis of the problems, the programmes should have built-up mechanisms for monitoring and evaluation as well as for applied research. Finally, importance must be laid on follow-up measures such as production and distribution of reading materials, organized learning and group action.

6. *Provision of Resources* : Provision shall have to be made for a programme comprising literacy as well as environmental and social education, extending to approximately 300=350 hours or about 9 months, and also taking to be provided by the Government, local bodies, voluntary agencies, trade and industry, etc.

7. *Programmes for Special Groups* : In addition to organizing a massive programme for adult illiterates, it is necessary to provide programmes for special groups based on their special needs. For example, programmes are needed for :

(i) Urban workers to improve their skills, to prepare them for securing their rightful claims and for participation in management;

(ii) Government functionaries such as office clerks, field extension workers and police and armed forces personnel to upgrade their competence;

(iii) Employees of commercial establishments such as banks and insurance companies to improve their performance;

(iv) Housewives to inculcate a better understanding of family life problems and women's status in society.

Programmes for these and several other categories of persons could be organized through classroom participation, correspondence courses or mass media, or by a combination of all these.

8. *Decentralisation* : It is of the greatest importance that implementation of adult education programmes is decentralized. A National Board of Adult Education has been established for this purpose by the Central Government. Similar Boards should be established at the State levels. Suitable agencies should be created at the field level for coordination and for involvement of the various agencies in the programme.

## PHILOSOPHY OF ADULT EDUCATION

Adult education does not imply only to make adults literate. It means to educate to total personality of the adult. As a first step towards the achievement of this objective adults should be made literate. In other words they should acquire command over the tools of knowledge or reading, writing and arithmetic. When they succeed in acquiring this command, they may be educated into economic, social and political problems of the day so that they may become intelligent citizens for taking right decisions when they are faced with a number of alternatives. If they fail to acquire this skill, the mean and self-seeking people will exploit them for their own interests. Consequently, democracy will fail and will yield place to dictatorship.

Thus the purpose of adult education is not merely to impart bookish knowledge. Philosophy of adult education aims at the education of the total personality of the adult. This will be possible only when they develop various types of skills to make them successful and socially useful members of the society. There is no limit to adult education. The adults should be helped to acquire useful knowledge in professional, political, economic and social spheres. This is what philosophy of adult education stands for.

So far in India in the field of adult education our main emphasis has been to make the adult literate. But adult education is worth the name only if it helps the adult to understand all the social, economic, cultural and political problems and their solutions. For this a well-planned programme has to be thought of and executed.

## SOCIAL EDUCATION IN INDIA

Adult education began in India with the beginning of the current century. But nothing remarkable could be done for the first 20 years. In fact, the people did not exactly understand the correct meaning and purpose of adult education. In the provinces of Madras, Bombay and Bengal some night-schools were started for those boys who were not able to get education due to working in the day in offices and factories. In 1909, there were 775 such night schools in Madras, 1028 in Bengal and 167 in Bombay. During the coming years the number of these schools came down. This situation continued till 1920. In 1921, some representatives of the people went to legislative councils. They raised their voice against the prevailing illiteracy and tried to do something for adult education. They established some libraries and reading rooms for adults.

### Progress under British Rule

Upto 1927, adult education work was especially done in Madras, Bombay, Punjab and Bengal. In 1927 there were 5604 adult schools in Madras, 193 in Bombay, 3784 in Punjab and 1519 in Bengal. U.P. also did something in this field.

Due to financial stringency many adult schools were closed in 1927, but certain missionaries continued their efforts in this direction and did commendable work.

Bombay alone continued its efforts for adult education and its progress was maintained till 1937. Many social organizations of Bombay promoted the expansion of adult education. In these organizations, Adult Education League of Poona, Social League and Bombay City Literacy Committee of Bombay are worthy of mention. In 1932-33 there were 143 adult schools in Bombay. The number became 180 in 1937. The number of students in these schools were 5660 in 1932-33 and in 1937 the number rose to 6299. In Baroda and Travancore adult education was encouraged and many libraries were opened for adults.

### Progress under Congress Rule

In 1937 Congress Ministries were sworn in 8 of the provinces of the country according to the Government of India Act of 1935. The Congress Ministries in all the provinces showed immense interest in adult education and it was promoted unprecedentally. The popular ministries widened the scope of adult education and it was not limited to literacy alone. Now adult education was understood as social education and accordingly the programmes were planned. Such audio-visual materials as Magic shows and cinemas were also used along with suitable books especially prepared for the purpose.

Under the adult education programme 'Let an educated one make another literate' scheme was started in 1937. Due to this adult education progressed in various provinces. By 1939-40 following progress was made in various provinces under this new scheme:

1. *U.P.*: Education Department was first established in this State in 1930. The popular Congress ministry in 1937 gave a special impetus to the adult education

programme. For this purpose several night schools, libraries, reading rooms and training centres were opened under the supervision of the government. In order to generate interest in the public for adult education every year "literacy day" and "literacy week" used to be organized. On the first literacy day in U.P. 768 libraries and 2600 reading rooms were opened. Forty libraries were started for only women in 1940. About 272 additional libraries were opened in 1941-42. Many books in Hindi, Urdu, Geography, History, Mathematics and Handicrafts for adults were published by the government. In the district of Faizabad 500 rupees per centre were distributed to fifty Women Welfare Centres. Thus commendable work was done by the U.P. Government for adult education during a short period.

2. *Punjab* : In Punjab 'Learn and Educate' movement was started and Rs. 28,800 were given as a grant for adult education in the First Five Year Plan. This money was utilized in opening some new adult schools and helping some old ones.

3. *Orissa :* 425 centres of adult education were opened in Orissa in 1940-41. 8147 adults were educated by these centres.

4. *Bihar* : In Bihar 'Make Your Home Literate Movement' was started with great enthusiasm. Dr. Saiyed Mahmud led this movement. 24289 adults were made literate during 1941-42. This work was continued even during the Second World War period and a Provincial Public Education Committee was established for looking after this work. During the period every year at least two lakh adults were educated in Bihar. In 1942-43 in the Adult Post Literacy Examination 1,11,000 adults passed this examination. When the Congress Ministry was again sworn in 1946, the adult education programme was again started with great zeal.

5. *Bengal* : Adult education programme was quite popular in Bengal amongst farmers, because this was entrusted to the Adult Education Rural Reconstruction Department. Under the adult education curriculum were included agriculture, animal husbandry, co-operative work, health and other useful subjects for the villagers.

6. *Assam* : In Assam a separate department was started for adult education under a mass literacy officer. About 1,200 centres were opened for adult education. In 1941 libraries were opened for further education of those adults who had received some education.

7. *Bombay*: In 1927 adult education programme was started in Bombay along with the establishment of provincial education board. In 1937 the Congress ministry took active interest in the adult education programme. During 1942-43 the Bombay Government granted Rs. 50,000 for adult education in villages. In 1945 a number of centres were opened for adult education and each centre was to educate 1,000 adults. On this programme Rs. 9,400 were allocated for each year.

8. *Princely States* : Baroda, Travancore and Mysore did commendable work in the field of adult education. In Baroda and Travancore the progress was better than in the British India. The Mysore University and the Mysore State Literacy Board did commendable work. In 1942-43, 4050 centres were opened in Jammu and Kashmir for adult education. In the hilly areas and in Sind as well some work

was done for education of adults. An attempt was made to educate Harijans and tribal people.

## ADULT EDUCATION IN INDEPENDENT INDIA

The scope of adult education was widened after independence. It was decided that adult education should be termed social education, because adult literacy should aim at educating the total personality of the adults. Accordingly, some literature was prepared for education of adults and new methods of teaching were also adopted.

### Objectives of Social Education

After independence social education was divided into the following three parts:

1. To make the illiterate literate.
2. To encourage writers for writing books for social education.
3. To acquaint the adults with their social rights and duties.

Accordingly the following points were specially emphasized in social education:

1. To impart the knowledge of civic rights and duties in order that the necessary ability may be developed for running a democracy.
2. To give a knowledge of historical and geographical background of the country.
3. To acquaint with the current social traditions and circumstances.
4. To impart knowledge of the things that promote good health.
5. To develop ability for helping in the economic growth of the country.
6. To foster the feeling of co-operativeness and internationalism.
7. To develop aesthetic sense.

### Twelve Points Programme

The following twelve points programme was chalked out for fulfilling the above objectives :

1. To make the village school a centre of education, recreation, sports and social service.
2. To fix up different time for education of different age groups.
3. To fix certain days in the week for ladies and girls.
4. To utilize audio-visual aids at least once a week.
5. To provide Radio sets to schools and to organize special programme for school children.
6. To stage dramas of educational value in schools and to award prizes to participants.

7. To organise national and folk-song programmes.
8. To give training in handicrafts according to local needs.
9. To impart knowledge about agriculture and health through departmental government officers.
10. To organize lectures for leaders on national problems to stage cinema shows by the Information Department.
11. To organize group sports and games.
12. To organize exhibitions and fairs.

**Progress in States**

To implement the above twelve points programme a conference of education ministers of various States was organized in 1949. This conference decided that within three years 50 per cent of the persons within the age group of 12 and 50 years of age would be educated. Due to financial difficulty this objective could not be achieved, although the Central Government gave a grant of one lakh rupees for this purposes. The Central Government established the Mohan Lal Sexena Committee for educating persons within the age groups of 12 and 40 years. This Committee recommended that both the Central and State governments should equally share the financial burden involved in adult education. Under this plan some work was done in adult education in some States.

1. *Delhi* : Around 1950 a number of adult education centres were opened. Sixty centres were opened in the adjoining rural areas for which 62 teachers were trained in the methods of adult education.

2. *Madras* : In 1949-50 six rural colleges and 100 schools were opened for adult education. Some centres were also opened for training teachers for teaching Tamil, Telgu, Kanar and Malayalam languages.

3. *Bombay* : In this province there were many labourers in various cities. In Ahmedadabad, Sholapur, Khandesh and Hubli good work was done in adult education. For experimental work in social education 80 centres of rural areas were chosen. Adult Education officers were appointed. Each officer was entrusted with the responsibility of educating at least 1000 adults. In Bombay city also good work in adult education was done. Labour Welfare Centres were opened in labour colonies.

4. *Madhya Pradesh* : Adult Education Camps were organized at various places in this State. In 1948-49, 451 such camps were opened and 41274 men and 20924 women were educated in these centres during the year. To encourage the expansion of adult education every adult was given an allowance of Rs. 2.00, women Rs. 5.00 and teacher Rs. 20. 1,000 Radio sets were given to village centres of adult education.

5. *Uttar Pradesh* : A separate department was established for adult education in U.P. This department opened 62 schools for women and a number of schools for men for imparting adult education. In 1948-49, 49382 adults were educated. In 1951-52 there were 2200 adult schools and 3600 reading rooms for men and 935

for women were established. Besides, there were 1518 libraries. Within 1948 and 1952, 13,50,000 adults were educated and 1,75,000 books were distributed to adults.

6. *Others* : Some work in adult education was also done in Rajasthan, Hyderabad, Jammu-Kashmir and West Bengal after independence. Some work for educating the handicapped and blind was also done and for training the blind a school was opened in Dehra Dun.

## UNESCO Plan

Our Indian Government accepted the UNESCO Plan for adult education with a little necessary modification. Accordingly, a number of camps were organized in villages for adult education. An attempt was also made to educate lakhs of refugees who fled from Pakistan.

Under the camp programme three objectives had to be achieved :

1. To spread literacy.
2. To generate the sense of civic rights and duties.
3. To develop thinking power through recreational programmes.

1. *Literacy* : The adult was enabled to write his name and names of his relatives, mohalla, village, tahsil, block, district, State, and country, etc. to write simple letters.

2. *Civic Rights and Duties* : It enabled the adult to read and understand the related books, newspapers.

3. *Developing Thinking Power* : It sought to teach to count up to 100 and do simple additions, subtractions, multiplications and divisions and to measure weight, length and to understand values of coins.

Cultural functions, sports, games and exhibitions were to be organized to attain the above objectives.

It was decided that the Adult Education camps will be established throughout the whole country. A scheme was made in Madhya Pradesh to train volunteers who should be at least 16 years of age and at least seventh class passed. A director was also to be appointed to supervise the work of these volunteers. A camp was to be run for five weeks. This scheme of running camps went on very well in Madhya Pradesh.

The above scheme was started in other States also. In some of them the duration of a camp was made of eight weeks. The college and school teachers were encouraged to work in these camps during their leave or leisure period.

Under the social education scheme it was aimed to educate the villagers in civic duties and responsibilities and to educate their total personality. Some arrangements were also made for their recreation and to impart them general knowledge. Some pilot projects were opened in some states for giving social education. In various Five Year Plans much work was done towards the achievement of the objectives of social education.

**Institutions for Social Education**

For social education Janata colleges, libraries and social centres were opened. A programme was drawn for producing social education literature and its distribution amongst adults.

1. *Social Centres* : The purpose of a social centre was to impart social and cultural education to adults. In it there was an arrangement for healthy recreation. It was generally opened in the Panchayat centre, school and other places of social gatherings.

2. *Libraries* : For libraries such places were selected where there could be good gathering. Books relating to agriculture, industries, civic principles, literature, business and trade, health and domestic science were kept in these libraries in order that the adults could benefit themselves by these.

3. *Janata Colleges* : The purpose of Janata colleges was to train workers for working at the social centres in villages. These workers were to function as leaders in social and public work. Simplicity and utility was emphasized in these colleges with a view to give cultural and social education to trainees who will guide the adults for achieving the purpose of social education.

A conference was arranged in Mysore for seven days in 1956 for framing the curriculum for Janata Colleges. This conference made the following recommendations :

1. The Janata colleges should be run in such a away that the teacher and taught may live together. Sufficient land should be given to each Janata College for agricultural work.
2. The Government should take its entire responsibility or it should be entrusted to good voluntary organizations.
3. The Government should give adequate financial aid and other facilities to Janata colleges.
4. Persons within the age group of 15 and 40 years alone should be admitted in them. There should be separate colleges for men and women.

The Government of Indian has produced more than 300 books for social education in different Indian languages. Literature for children has also been published under the supervision of the government. The Central Government has introduced a scheme of giving 15 prizes of Rs. 500 each to writers of literature for adults. The Government also gives awards to writers producing books for mass education.

## QUESTIONS FOR EXERCISE

1. Define adult or social education. Discuss its purpose, aims and programme.
2. What is the need of social education? Discuss its problems and suggest remedies.
3. Discuss the Policy Statement of the Government of India on Adult Education in 1977.

4. Write a short essay on social education in India.
5. What is the importance of social education for democracy?
6. Write short notes on Janata Colleges, Social Centres and UNESCO Education Plan for adults.

# 10

# PROBLEM OF PRE-PRIMARY EDUCATION

Froebel founded a Kindergarten school at Blackenberg in 1837 which was the beginning of pre-primary education. Besides Froebel's Kindergarten system, Nursery system and Montessory system also give the pre-primary education.

In ancient India, the system of pre-primary education was not so organized as it is to-day though in the Mahabaharata there is the example of Abhimanyu who was taught the art of demolishing the circular fort (Chakravyuha) while he was still in his mother's womb. But with the advent of modern period the formal pre-primary education began in India.

## KINDS OF PRE-PRIMARY SCHOOLS

1. *Kindergarten Schools* : Froebel's system pre-primary adopted play-way method in education. In this system the children of four years of age are admitted. They are taught many things pertaining to good behaviour through various plays. Children are taught 3 R's through a psychological method. During the first six years of life the child is able to develop many such sentiments which become almost permanent with him. Froeble studied child psychology and made it the basis of education for young children.

2. *Nursery Schools* : Mrs. Margret Macmillan founded a Nursery School for physical and mental development of young children. Qualified lady teachers were appointed in these schools for giving the necessary protection and guidance to young children. Ordinarily chidden of two to four years of age are admitted in Nursery Schools. They are provided healthy environment for their development.

3. *Montessori Schools* : Maria Montessori started these schools. Children from two to six years of age are educated here. They get eduction on their own through didactic materials and toys.

### Merits of Pre-primary Schools

The above types of pre-primary schools provide good opportunities to young children for their sensory training and education in good conduct and behaviour. Their physical and mental development is ensured through psychological methods. The impression and habits acquired during this period of nursery schools last lifelong. These schools provide medical care, healthy food and healthy environment for good character development. The children acquire many good social traits through plays. Language, art, music, dance and rudimentary mathematics are taught to children in these schools on psychological lines.

## PRE-PRIMARY EDUCATION IN INDIA

In India pre-primary education was started in the third decade of the current century. By 1952 there were about 330 nursery schools in the country. This number rose to about 800 by 1957. Since then their number has been increasing approximately 150 every year. Nursery schools are getting popular in the public. Its expansion is ever on increase. These schools are run on Nursery, Montessori and Kindergarten lines. All these schools are individual and voluntary. As the government does not give any financial aid to them. These schools suffer from want of necessary material equipments, good buildings and other facilities. Trained teachers for infant education are also very few in number.

Today people have begun to realise the importance and utility of pre-primary schools. Sargent Report of 1944 recognised the merits of nursery schools in India. It encouraged the people to adopt this for young children. Therefore, the Government has also become interested in its development.

### State of Pre-primary Education

On the basis of some experiments and investigations pre-primary education has been classified into the following four stages:

1. From conception to birth.
2. From birth to 2½ years of age.
3. From 2½ to 4 years of age.
4. From 4 to 6 years of age.

1. *From conception to birth* : In this stage the baby is influenced by mental and physical dispositions of the expectant mother. Mother-welfare centres have been established in order to educate the mother in the right direction affecting the would-be baby in the desired manner. In these centres the expectant mothers are given good environment inducive to healthy impact on the would-be baby.

2. *From birth to 2½ years of age* : During this age the child learns something under the guidance of the mother. If the mother is of good nature and culture, the child will also be influenced by the same.

3. *From 2½ to 4 years of age* : Now the child may receive education in some pre-primary school. This type of school provides the necessary environment for healthy development of children in psychological lines.

4. *From 4 to 6 years* : During this stage the children are taught through plays, language, music, dance, art, arithmetic and general science along with manners of good behaviour.

**Problems of Pre-primary Education**

In India the pre-primary education is run on western lines. Hence, new techniques should be devised suited to Indian conditions. In the Kindergarten, Montessori and Nursery systems in pre-primary schools, the children should be taught manners and social etiquettes according to Indian traditions. New stories should be written with Indian themes for young children since at present young children are told stories with themes imbued with European cultures.

So far Indians have started some pre-basic schools on the Montessori lines. The Child Education Society of Bhavanagar has done Commendable work in this direction. It has adopted a new system of nursery education by drawing the best from the Basic and Montessori Systems. Some educationists of Sarvodaya Society have expressed many good ideas about nursery education. These may be thoughtfully considered and incorporated as far as practical and desirable.

## QUESTION FOR EXERCISE

1. What is pre-primary education? What are various types of schools imparting this education?
2. Discuss the status of pre-primary education in India. How should it be Indianized?

# 11

# PROBLEMS OF PRIMARY EDUCATION

Apart from being a constitutional obligation in India the provision of universal primary education is crucial for spreading mass literacy, and an indispensable first step towards the provision of equality of opportunities to all the citizens.

**Objectives of Primary Education**

The following are the major objectives of Primary Education :

1. To give an adequate mastery over the tools of learning.
2. To bring about a harmonious development of the child's personality by providing for his physical, intellectual, social, emotional, aesthetic, moral and spiritual needs.
3. To prepare the children for good citizenship, to develop in them a love for their country, its tradition and its culture and to inspire in them a sense of service and loyalty.
4. To develop in the children the spirit of international understanding and universal brotherhood.
5. To inculcate scientific attitude.
6. To inculcate a sense of dignity of labour.
7. To prepare children for life through the provision of worthwhile practical activities and experiences, including work-experience.

## PROBLEMS OF PRIMARY EDUCATION

1. **Natural Problems** : The geographical enrolment has a great impact on man life. His ways of living, food habits, profession and means of transport and communication are very much influenced by geographical environment. As the facilities enjoyed by the people in the plains are not available for those in hilly areas and deserts, the geographical conditions of hilly areas and deserts demand new steps in life. Hills, plateaus, deserts, rivers, lakes, forests isolate people of one area with those of another. Means of transport are scattered in deserts and hills. In these areas there is no dense population. Hence, it is not economically feasible to open a primary school for a few people. Primary schools with very few children will be

impracticable due to the meagre funds at the disposal of the authority responsible for providing education. Children from one area cannot go to school founded in another area because of difficult and inadequate means for transport. Hence, children in unfavourable geographical environment do not get sufficient primary education. India is a land of villages. More than 70 per cent of the population reside in villages. People in villages have not yet been provided with educational facilities. Teachers do not like to work in schools of difficult geographical surroundings. Hence, natural obstruction has come in the way of expansion of primary education.

2. **Political Problems** : The British Government was indifferent to primary education in India. It did not try to remove illiteracy prevailing in the land. After independence the Indian Government became keen to spread primary education throughout the whole country. It was provided in the Constitution to make primary education free and compulsory. Hence, primary education was encouraged throughout the whole country. But due to political difficulties the efforts in this direction have been faulty. The policy followed by the government for the expansion of primary education had been impractical. The concerned authorities do not take much interest in its expansion. There is no co-ordination in the various Government departments. The work of primary education has been entusted to local bodies such as municipal boards, district boards and town areas. These local bodies do not cooperate with the government officers appointed for looking after primary education. Many of the schemes pertaining to primary education remain incomplete due to want of money. It has not yet been surveyed as to how many primary schools are necessary. The literacy expansion schemes are closely related to free and compulsory education. If the two are linked together primary education will expand. Indian public opposes any move for taxation for education. Hence, the village Panchayats are not fulfilling their objectives. All the local bodies are suffering from paucity of funds. They are not free from local and regional politics. The public and government should co-operate with the local bodies and education should be freed from all sorts of politics.

3. **Social Problems** : One finds many social evils in India such as untouchability, caste differences, narrow religious beliefs, conservatism, illiteracy, communalism, neopotism and jealousy. People of different castes, religions and communities seek to open schools only to educate their own children. At some places children of Harijans and the down-trodden are not admitted to schools as children of higher caste do not like to mix up with the children of Harijans studying in the same schools. Language problem also obstructs some children from going to schools. Separate schools are demanded for girls due to Purdah system. Conservative parents do not send their girls to boys school. Social workers and efficient government officers should establish personal contacts with parents for removing their wrong notions which hamper the growth of primary education.

4. **Economic Problems**. The national income is the index of the income of the common man. Indian national income is not satisfactory. The common man is spending difficult days. The distribution of wealth is very uneven. While some people have so much wealth that they do not know how to spend it, many others

do not know how to manage the two square meals a day. Such poor people do not send their children to school, because they cannot meet the involved expenses. They persuade their grown-up children for earning to supplement the family income. The Government, also has not been able to spend as much money on primary education as needful. Thus, economic problems have come in the way of expansion of primary education in India.

5. **Problems of Teaching System**. The atmosphere of an ideal school should be so attractive and natural that the children may themselves like to spend much of their time there. Such an atmosphere can be available only when the teaching methods, devices and materials are organized on psychological lines. Indian Primary schools do not have suitable teachers and appropriate teaching materials. Hence, they have failed to provide a suitable atmosphere for attracting young children. The cruel and unpsychological behaviour of teachers and harsh corporal punishment force many children to leave the school in the middle of the session. Suitable teaching materials are not organized due to paucity of funds and ignorance. Most teaching methods emphasise craming. The students are seldom encouraged to participate in educative activities. The basic education scheme has not been implemented in any real sense. The children do not get any vocational orientation. Many guardians regard primary education as useless and unprofitable and they employ their young children in their own professions.

6. **Problem of Wastage and Stagnation**. In India there is too much of wastage and stagnation at the primary stage of education. Many children leave school or fail due to the above difficulties. Money, labour and time are wasted. Stagnation is there when children repeat classes due to failure.

7. **Problem of Dearth of Teachers**. In India suitable teachers for primary schools are not available in adequate number. Most of the teachers are intolerant. They behave very harshly with children. Children are very much afraid of them and do not like to go to school. Even after obtaining training, there is no change in the behaviour of some teachers. It appears that training has not produced any impact on them. Their ability to teach young children is doubtful. Many primary schools are single-teacher schools. A single teacher cannot teach five classes of the primary school. Thus, lack of teachers vitiates the atmosphere of the school.

## REFORM OF PRIMARY EDUCATION

Indian Constitution provides for free and compulsory education for all children between 6 and 11 years of age. This may be extended up to 14 years of age. Some States have implemented it for the children up to 14 years of age. It was planned that this scheme of free and compulsory education should be implemented up to the junior high school stage by 1960-61. Later on it was decided that free and compulsory education should be made available for children between 6 and 11 years of age. But when even this objective could not be achieved by the end of the Second Five Year Plan, its programme was extended in the Third Five Year Plan. For the Fourth Five Year Plan the scheme was revised for children between 6 to 14 years of age. But even by the end of the Seventh Five Year Plan this could not be achieved due to following difficulties :

1. **Shortage of New Schools** : For expansion of primary education new schools should be opened within the easy approach of children so that they may not have to face the problem of transport. India have more than seven lakh villages. In order to cater to the educational needs of children of these villages lakhs of schools will have to be opened within the easy reach of most of the children. Each of these schools will have a number of teachers, one teacher for each class. Thus there should be five teachers for five classes of each primary school. These teachers should be well qualified and willing to serve in the area concerned. The school building should also be suitable. A new school may be established in the locality inhabited by at least 500 people. As in India 65% of the villages have less than 500 inhabitants a school may be established at a central place which may serve a number of villages.

2. **Lack of Interest**. There is not much interest for education in Indian villages. Illiterates do not understand the importance of education. Others do not send their girls to school because of the Purdah system. Some keep their children at home so that they may help them in earning their bread. Others are not able to educate their children because of paucity of funds. Some wants to train their children in their hereditary trade and do not send them to school. Hence, the schools for villages should be so organized as to help the villagers to get solution of their educational problems. The curriculum of the school should be vocationally-oriented according to the needs of the locality which it is supposed to serve. This will help the people to realise the utility of the school and they will start taking interest in the education of their children. The school should function as a community development centre. It should try to develop all skills in children which the villagers want them to pick up in view of their agriculture and allied professional occupations.

3. **Catering to Local Needs** : Keeping in view its religious, cultural and social traditions, the schools should be organized for a particular area. Then alone the public will feel a belongingness to the schools. If the public so desires, separate schools should be run for girls. But it will be better if co-education is encouraged up to the primary stage. The primary school should be established for educating the children of scheduled castes, tribes and backward classes according to their particular social and cultural traditions. Private enterprises forthcoming in this direction, should be fully encouraged.

4. **Insufficient School Buildings** : Suitable buildings are very necessary for primary schools. In India very few primary schools have buildings worth the name. The buildings should be in open, healthy and clean places. There should be big playground adjoining it to facilitate adequate physical activities of the school children. There should be separate space for agricultural workshops and practices in cottage industries. Till suitable school buildings are provided, free and compulsory primary education may be imparted at such public places which may accommodate the teachers and students for the purpose such as Village Panchayat building, Dharmshalas and Parks etc.

5. **Lakh of Sufficient and Suitable Teachers**. For free and compulsory education, it is necessary that suitable teachers from the adjoining areas or local persons are appointed who are willing to work in rural areas. They should be

conversant with the local cultural, religious and social traditions. They should be fully familiar with language of the area. They should have the capacity to make the school environment healthy, attractive and useful. They should be master of subjects so that the teaching of various subjects may be done satisfactorily.

It is estimated that there are only 8 lakhs of teachers for primary schools today, while India actually needs more than 35 lakhs of them. This need cannot be met by local teachers. Hence teachers have to be recruited from distant places. If teachers for primary schools in the rural area are appointed from distant places, they should be provided residence near the schools. For the time being the Higher Secondary Examination passed persons may be given preliminary training to work as teachers in rural primary schools. In the absence of training facilities, even untrained hands may be appointed as teachers and they may be given in-service training later.

If the students cannot be managed in one shift, the school may be run in two shifts. This will not require appointment of additional teachers. The one teacher-school may be permitted at only those places where the students are very few and number of teachers is inadequate.

6. **Inappropriate Curriculum**. The purpose of primary education is to equip children in fundamental processes so that they may be able to receive further education. The social needs have changed with changes in society. Hence, the curriculum of the primary education should also be modified accordingly. The Basic education curriculum should be implemented at the primary stage. Local needs should be the basis of organizing the curriculum on the Basic pattern so that students acquire some vocational bent of mind while receiving training in the principles of citizenship and healthy living along with the acquisition of command over the 3 R's. *i.e.*, reading, writing and arithmetic. The primary schools of the rural area should have a curriculum different from that in the urban, because the needs of the two differ.

7. **Lack of National and Local Co-Operation** : The co-operation of the government and of the public is very necessary for the development of primary education. In India both the Central and State Governments are trying for the expansion of primary education, but success has not yet been achieved due to the defective policy and the lack of necessary co-operation from the government officials responsible for running the primary education scheme. The public also does not extend sufficient co-operation. Even some voluntary organizations extend helping hands, the government is not able to utilize it. Now the government departments should stop such policies which obstruct the growth of primary education. The co-operation of the public should be enlisted and the government officials should invite it. The inspectors of schools should contact the primary school teachers and the public. They should guide the teachers and create an awakening in the public for primary education. They should study the local needs and arrange for primary education accordingly.

The co-operation of the public is very necessary in the expansion of primary education. Only the public understands its needs. It should co-operate with the government by giving financial aids, land and building for expansion of primary education. In the context of the needs of the locality concerned the school should also be made a centre of community work.

8. **Inadequate Research in Primary Education** : The expansion and development of primary education depends upon the satisfactory solution of the above problems which should be based on research in primary education organized in Universities, teachers training colleges and in government research institutes. The State governments should encourage research in primary education. The research scholars in this area should be given handsome stipends for successfully carrying out their research projects.

## QUESTIONS FOR EXERCISE

1. What are the problems of primary education which obstruct the expansion of free and compulsory primary education in India? Suggest remedies.
2. Suggest measures for the reform of primary education in India. How can the same be implemented?

# 12

# PROBLEMS OF WASTAGE AND STAGNATION IN PRIMARY EDUCATION

Since the attainment of freedom Indian Governments both at the Centre and in the States have tried to improve and expand primary education. However, the desired success has not yet been achieved. Many children leave the schools even before completing the primary education which means a waste of money and energy spent over their primary education. Hartog Committee has called it a waste in its report. In 1955-56 the percentage of children having left primary education in the middle was 57. This wastage in primary education has been due to following causes.

## CAUSES OF WASTAGE IN PRIMARY EDUCATION

1. **Absence of Methodical Approach**. Primary education in India lacks a methodical approach. There is a dearth of suitable school buildings, trained teachers, essential equipments, libraries and necessary amenities. Lack of bare necessities at the primary stage lead the students to lose interest in their education. They, therefore, leave primary education unfinished. It is also difficult for the teachers to step-up efforts aimed at the mental, physical and moral development of the personality of their students in the absence of basic thing necessary for primary education.

2. **Indifference of Guardians**: Nearly 70 per cent of the population in India is still illiterate. These illiterate people do not understand the worth of education. When the parents are illiterate and the primary education is not capable of enabling the children to earn money, the guardians soon make their children leave the schools and join some work or trade to earn wages.

3. **Faulty Administration** : Lack of good administration has adversely affected the development and quality of primary education. There has been an emphasis on the expansion of primary education without equal emphasis on the number of teachers and supervisory administrative personnel, equipment and buildings. Hence, whereas the number of students has increased manifold, the strength of teachers has not increased proportionately. The strength of inspecting staff and administrative officers has also not proportionately increased. The teachers-students ratio has gone up so that the teachers find themselves unable to pay

personal attention to each student. Lack of efficient transport system also tells heavily on primary education. It helps to increase waste of funds and deepen stagnation in the sphere of primary education.

4. **Absence of Proper Planning** : Another major cause of waste and stagnation is that there are no rules regarding age of admission and conditions for staying in classes for a certain period. Students with different age join primary education and leave it when they desire. There are boys of different age group in the same class which creates difficulty in teaching. It also acts as a handicap for the psychological development of the children who cease taking interest in their education and finally give up studies. In rural areas the children absent themselves too often due to the poverty of their guardians. They particularly absent themselves during sowing and harvesting seasons. The remedy lies in preparing a proper holiday list keeping the needs of rural people in mind as also the problems of guardians.

5. **Poverty**: Poverty of the Indian people is the most important factor responsible for wastage in the sphere of primary education. Most of the guardians are so poor that they cannot manage even two square meals a day for their families. It is too much to expect from them to arrange books, note books etc. for their children. On the contrary they find it easy to stop their children's education and put them into some trade to earn money. Thus a large percentage of promising children become the victims of poverty and deprived of primary education.

6. **Lack of Suitable Curriculum** : Many of the Indian primary schools have yet not been converted into newly patterned basic schools. They still teach the old curriculum which is not interesting but monotonous to children. The boredom creates in them a desire to leave the school.

7. **Old Traditions** : Indians have yet not been able to give up conservative practices and adopt a more liberal and progressive attitude. Old traditions still governing the Indian social life, include child-marriage, untouchability, secondary position of women-folk, purdah etc. The majority of people do not favour co-education even at the primary stage. This results in wastage. People consider girl's education a waste as they feel that girls should not take up jobs and earn livelihood. Marriages of boys and girls give a severe jolt to education because most of the students give up studies as soon as they are married.

## REMEDIES TO WASTAGE AND STAGNATION

1. **Reorganization of the Curriculum** : Primary Curriculum should be so prepared as to be appealing to the children and generating in them an interest for education. It should be reorganised according to local conditions, problems and traditions. Its number of subjects should not be too many. It should be practical and useful for the life. Its subjects for girls and boys should not be the same. It should be liberal and flexible so that proper changes and adjustments may be easily made. For providing impetus to the creative attitude of the student it must include a craft. It should help the children to understand the dignity of manual labour.

2. **Reconstruction of the Educational System** : The present educational system involves wastage in education due to the following shortcomings :

(i) Shortage of good books.

(ii) Unhealthy atmosphere in school.

(iii) Lack of suitable play-grounds.

(iv) Lack of trained teachers.

It is impossible to achieve alround development of a child's personality in the presence of these drawbacks. The child cannot complete his primary education in such an environment. In single-teacher schools, where the teacher is expected to teach a number of subjects, the condition is more pathetic. If he is absent on some day, the students, too, go on a holiday.

3. **Education of Guardians**. An uneducated guardian does not realise the worth of education. He cannot make sacrifice for the education of his children. Therefore, the guardian should be made aware of the importance of education so that he develops a desire to educate his children. For this purpose part-time and night schools should be opened to educate guardians.

4. **Administrative Reforms**. The present educational administration system needs a thorough overhaul to stop waste and stagnation. The inspection method should be improved. The number of inspectors should be increased. Rules should be framed for admitting children at uniform age as far as possible. Due attention should be paid towards the age, ability and intelligence of the children while admitting them. The standard of education should be improved. Attendance should be regularly checked. The local bodies should be asked to take more interest in expansion of primary education.

5. **Ban of Child Marriage and Child Labour**. People should be encouraged to adopt a more liberal and progressive outlook. Laws should be enacted to enforce to eradicate the evils of child marriage and child labour. People should be encouraged to patronise girls' education and co-education in the interest of the society.

6. **Elimination of Poverty**. Foreign rule made the evil of poverty penetrate the entire country in India. The economic condition of people is pathetic though the national government is doing its best to remove poverty through five year plans, but no success has been attained so far. The galloping inflation is neutralising the economic progress. India is essentially an agricultural country. The pressure on land is too much. To eradicate poverty emphasis should be laid on village and cottage industries and industrialisation, besides agriculture.

## STAGNATION IN PRIMARY EDUCATION

### Meaning of Stagnation

Stagnation means failure to complete the prescribed course within the prescribed time. It also means failure of students in the class once or for a number of times. It also means wastage of time. It is waste in primary education both directly and indirectly. For example, if a student completes five years course in eight years, it means that he has wasted three years money, labour and time. Repeated failures in a class produces frustration in the student who then gives up studies and tries to find employment. If he fails to earn money through honest efforts, he indulges in anti-social activities and becomes a burden on the society. In India stagnation has considerably harmed primary education. It is 60 per cent in the five classes of primary education while only 40% students could avoid it.

**Causes of Stagnation**

1. *Many Unattractive Courses* : For the primary classes there are as many as five subjects including arithmetic and science which are dry for children belonging to tender age group of six to eleven years. This leads to failure of many students in a class and increases stagnation.

2. *Dissimilar Age for Admission in the Same Class.* Lack of any definite rule relating to admission in primary classes is also a factor responsible for stagnation. Absence of any age restriction allows any child of any age to get admission to any class he desires for. Hence, children of different age groups and mental calibre are found in a class. Their physical and mental development does not take place in a balanced manner. Many students fail in their classes, thus causing stagnation.

3. *Uninteresting Atmosphere.* A child joining a school finds an atmosphere quite different from the atmosphere prevailing in his home. He faces a difficult adjustment problem. Those children who fail to adjust themselves in the new environment develop an anti-social outlook and turn into juvenile delinquents and truants. It spoils other children as well and leads to stagnation. Sometimes the home and school environment is so disturbing that the child is left with no interest to pursue his studies. He fails to complete his home work and falls prey to stagnation.

4. *Physical Weakness.* Physical weakness caused by unhealthy environment, malnutrition or diseases is also a cause of stagnation. Physically underdeveloped children cannot study hard to cover their courses. Their memory gets weak and they fail in their examinations.

5. *Evil Social Practices.* Evil social customs like early marriages also prove a cause for stagnation. Married boys and girls stop or neglect their studies.

6. *Inadequate Provisions in the School.* In Indian primary schools the number of teachers is too small. In many schools there is only one teacher who cannot do justice to various subjects. Hence, it is very difficult for the children to complete their courses. The shortage of teaching and reading material, insanitary conditions of school building and unhealthy environment play havoc with children's studies causing stagnation.

7. *Defective Examination System.* The present system of examination is defective as it does not take into account the work done and labour put in by the student throughout the year. It evaluates the child's worth within a few hours. If for any reason the child is unable to answer questions within examination hours satisfactorily his whole year's labour is lost. This out-dated and defective examination system causes stagnation.

**Remedies to Combat Stagnation**

1. *Reconstruction of Curriculum* : Primary school curriculum should be reconstructed. Arithmetic and Science, dry and unattractive to majority of students should be made simple and interesting to prevent stagnation.

2. *Proper Admission Policy* : Educational administrators should lay down a rational policy for admission age to primary classes. The age, mental development and the speed of child's development in relation to other faculties should be taken into consideration while determining the admission age. Application of rational rules will prevent stagnation in primary education.

3. *Revolutionised Atmosphere* : The atmosphere of home, society and schools should be totally revolutionised so that co-ordination may exist between them. This can be achieved only when there exists a co-ordination between the people, the teacher and the administrators. Social evils and unhealthy traditions may be removed through intensive publicity. Healthy entertainment should be provided to students under the supervision of teachers. Adult education should be provided to guardians.

4. *Improved Health of Children* : Mental health is related to the physical health. Good health is a must for possessing a healthy mind. As Indian people are extremely poor parents find it difficult to provide nutritious food to their children. Hence, it is the duty of the State to arrange the needful food for the future citizens of India. The State should take the responsibility of providing nutritious food to children to prevent stagnation.

5. *Psychological Teaching Methods* : The current teaching system is unscientific and unpsychological. It, therefore, causes stagnation. Its replacement with a psychological teaching system will involve money. The affluent section of the society should be approached to help for the change.

6. *Ban on Child Marriage and Child Labour* : Law alone cannot succeed in stopping this bad practice. Society should boycott such marriages and people responsible for these marriages. Although the Act of 1930 bans child marriage, yet in the absence of social help it has not achieved the desired goal. The people and leaders must join hands with the government to put a stop to this evil practice.

7. *Reform in Examination Pattern*. The present system of examination is defective in as much as it tries to find out within a few hour the progress of the child. Promotion should be given after taking into consideration the entire sessions work and achievements.

## QUESTIONS FOR EXERCISE

1. What do you understand by 'waste' in primary education? Enumerate its causes and suggest remedies.
2. Differentiate between waste and stagnation.
3. Explain 'stagnation' in primary education. What are its causes? Give suggestions to prevent it.

# 13

# UNIVERSALISATION OF PRIMARY EDUCATION

In 1950 the Indian Constitution provided that all States should provide free and compulsory education to the children of every section of the society up to the age of 14 years in ten years time. As the literacy then was only 16 per cent in India the decision was timely, important and according to the need of the land. The success and prosperity of a democratic system of government depends on enlightened and educated people. Equal opportunity to all is the salient feature of a democratic set up. Hence, it is necessary that all people should get education. There should be no discrimination between rich and poor, touchables and non-touchables, low caste or high caste, Hindus and Muslims, Sikhs or Christians etc. People become aware of their duties and responsibilities, rights and obligations only through education. Knowledge generates in them the feelings of nationalism, patriotism and sacrifice. Education changes people's behaviour for better. They become civilized, and learn and practise noble behaviour towards others.

**Historical Review**

1. *Pre-British Primary Education* : The old system of primary education was prevailing throughout the country under the British rule. However, by the eighteenth century, it had lost much of its glory and utility. When the Britishers gained a solid victory at Plassy in 1757 A.D. one lakh Indian educational institutions were engaged in the expansion of education in Bengal alone.

2. *Aim of British Schools* : Because of the British policies this state of affairs of education, did not last long. The Britishers aimed at tightening the shackles of slavery by destroying the social, cultural and literary base of India and replacing it by their own culture, social traditions and literature. They started new schools in order to consolidate their political and commercial gains and put the same on a permanent footing. These schools spread Western culture, civilization and literature. The Britishers achieved success to a large extent in destroying the old system. In this destructive work they were helped by Christian missionaries who opened public schools to popularise Western culture, civilization, literature and Christianity in a very subtle manner. They tried to impose their culture and religion through the medium of primary, secondary and higher educational institutions.

3. *Primary Education Under East India Company* : Under the Charter of 1813

issued by the Government in England the East India Company was authorised to spend a paltry sum of rupees one lakh annually over scientific education and Indian Literature. The East India Company's sole interest was in developing its trade and earn more and more money. In the field of education it remained content with the efforts being made by the missionaries and completely neglected the Indian education. Its indifference was also due to the fact that in proportion to the huge population the sum sanctioned for education was too small. The company was unable to make up its mind as to which part of the country or in which direction this amount should be utilised. These problems were reconsidered in 1824. It was accepted in Woods despatch in 1854 that all Charters relating to education issued from time to time till 1857 under the company's rule were inadequate. According to Woods despatch, the company was responsible for the education of Indians. It was asked to encourage Indian schools and give financial help for the expansion of primary education. It was further charged with the responsibility of providing useful and practical education for Indian people. During the short period before the revolt of 1857, some financial help was given for the expansion of secondary and higher education. But no monetary help worth the name was extended for the expansion of primary education.

4. *Primary Education Under British Govt.* After the revolt of 1857, the administration passed into the hands of the British Parliament which was more liberal than the East India Company. It paid due attention to education and the next three decades proved very important for primary education. Under the Stanley Charter of 1859 the Indian administration was saddled with the responsibility of primary education. It was authorised to levy tax in order to collect money for the purpose. By the year 1882 nearly 29,000 primary schools were opened for educating 21 lakhs of children. This provision could give education to only 1.2 per cent of children.

One of the oldest Viceroys of India Lord Curzon, agreed that despite the administration having passed into the hands of British Government not much work could be done in the sphere of primary education during the nineteenth century. According to him the aim of primary education was to provide education to every one through the medium of mother tongue or local dialect and the facility of receiving primary education was to be available to anyone desiring to receive it. The primary education needed government patronage, but completely disregarding the recommendations of the Indian Education Commission, the government entrusted the local bodies with the responsibility of primary education in 1882. This step created financial difficulties for the local bodies. The desired success did not take place despite the efforts of the local bodies. In the 20 years from 1882 to 1902 only an increase of 6.6 lakh children could be achieved at the primary education level.

Lord Curzon truly gave a boost to efforts for the expansion of primary education. He made sincere efforts in this direction. His term can be called the first phase in the expansion of primary education. His bold confession in respect of meagre efforts made by the government in the sphere of primary education gave courage to the people to demand expansion of primary education. But the unfortunate division of Bengal set at naught the efforts of Curzon. In the Calcutta session of the Congress held in 1905 the policies of the government were bitterly criticised. No plans whether good or bad could be implemented successfully. However, a start was made in the right direction so for as primary education was concerned.

5. *Efforts to Make Primary Education Compulsory* : (i) *British Viewpoint* : Believing that the government's responsibility in the sphere of education was only to give direction and guidance, the British Government became indifferent towards primary education after handing over its charge to the local bodies. However, three educationists, William Adams, Capt. Wingate and T.C. Hope, urged the government to declare primary education as compulsory. It gave further encouragement to Indians to press their demand for making primary education compulsory. The expansion of education programme became a part of national movement. Sir Ibrahim Rahimtoola and Sir Chiman Lal Setalwad gave birth to this movement. As a result of this movement the government of Bombay constituted a committee in 1906 in order to examine the progress and condition of education. The Committee found that the people in general were not prepared for compulsory education. Hence, the old policy remained unchanged.

(ii) *Baroda Ruler's Initiative* : In 1893 the ruling prince of Baroda State, Maharaja Sir Sayaji Rao Gaikwad, took initiative and introduced compulsory education in 52 villages of his State. In 1906 a rule was framed to introduce this scheme. It covered all the boys within the age group of 7 to 12 years and all girls in the age-group of 7 to 10 years.

(iii) *Efforts of Gopal Krishna Gokhale*: Inspired by the noble example of the Maharaja of Baroda, Gopal Krishna Gokhale proposed in the Central Assembly the introduction of free and compulsory primary education throughout the country. For a year this proposal remain tagged with red-tapism. On March 16, 1911 Gokhale brought a Bill in the Central Assembly to this effect. The main feature of this Bill was that the local bodies, with the sanction of the governments should introduce free and compulsory education for boys in the 6 to 10 years age group in those areas where a certain number of such children might be available. Unfortunately this Bill could not be passed due to lack of adequate support.

(iv) *Efforts By Vithal Bhai Patel* : Vithal Bhai Patel presented a Bill in the Bombay Legislative Assembly to introduce free and compulsory education in the area falling under the jurisdiction of Bombay Municipal Board. In 1918 the Bill became an Act with a far reaching effect. By 1930 primary education became compulsory in the whole country for boys within the 6 to 10 years age group. Primary education was entrusted to the local bodies who were empowered to levy taxes for meeting the expenditure over primary education.

## PROBLEMS OF UNIVERSALISATION

J.C. Aggarwal in his book *Development and Planning of Modern Education with reference to India* has listed the following major problems of universalisation of education :

1. Uneven spread of education.
2. Low enrolment of the backward section of the society.
3. Stagnation
4. Wastage.
5. Low enrolment of girls.
6. Apathy and poverty of parents.
7. Defective curriculum.
8. Uninspiring methods of teaching.
9. Lack of reading and writing material for children.
10. Lack of qualified teachers.
11. Frequent transfer of teachers.
12. Lack of effective inspection and academic guidance by the inspecting staff.
13. Failure to enforce compulsory attendance.
14. Lack of suitable admission policy.
15. Conservative attitude towards co-education.
16. Inadequate and unattractive school building.
17. Poor nutrition.
18. Existence of large number of incomplete primary schools.
19. Lack of part-time facilities.
20. Group involving local bodies.
21. Meagre financial outlay.
22. Overpopulation.

**Pattern of Inequality**

The total number of non-enrolled children at the elementary stage (Classes I to VIII) is of the order of 470 lakhs. Most of them belong to the weaker sections of the country like Scheduled Caste, Scheduled Tribe, Agricultural landless labourers and urban slum-dwellers. Even in states where overall enrolment has been satisfactory, low enrolment was observed in respect of girls, Scheduled Caste, Scheduled Tribe and in backward areas. In certain States, the very low enrolment of girls had become a problem. In all States some districts were advanced, whereas others were lagging behind. Similarly in the same district, there were differences in the provision of educational opportunities in different Community Development Blocks. The pattern of inequality of educational opportunity may be considered at several levels and with reference to different sections of society as follows :

(i) Inequality between one State and another.

(ii) In a State the prevailing inequality between one district and another.

(iii) In a district, inequal educational opportunity in different areas.

(iv) Inequality of educational opportunity between boys and girls.

**Causes of Inequality**

Inequality of educational opportunity in India prevails between the different sections of society, advanced castes *Vs.* Scheduled Castes and Scheduled Tribes, upper and middle classes *Vs.* lower classes, economically better off classes *Vs.* poorer sections, etc. On the basis of the experience reported in the different states, the following causes of inequality may be listed :

1. Some States are economically advanced while others are lagging behind. Consequently, the income per head of population in different States varies considerably. The same is true of district, block and local level.
2. Social and psychological reasons, *e.g.*, apathy towards girls' education, particularly in socially backward groups of people.
3. Varying literacy levels in States, districts and localities.
4. Existence of inaccessible and isolated small habitations particularly in hilly and forest areas.
5. Varying occupational opportunities prevailing in different areas.
6. Lack of suitable and adequate accomodation for running schools.
7. Dearth of suitably qualified teachers, particularly women teachers and teachers for tribal areas.

**Suggestions for Equality in Educational Opportunity**

The financing of Elementary Education should be separated from financing of other sectors of education and treated on a special footing. Special financial assistance should be given to all States on the Principle of Equalization in order to enable them to fulfil the directive of Article 45 of the Constitution. While adopting this principle, the Equalization Authority should consider both developmental and committed expenditure on elementary education. The extent of State effort and the quantum of assistance from the Centre should both be decided by the Equalization Authority *i.e.*, the Central Government while equalising at the State level. Similar principles should be adopted by the State when equalising at the District level and by the District, when equalising at the local level.

**Aims of Universalization**

1. Free distribution of mid-day meals to the poor and needy children.

2. Supply of free text-books and clothing to the poor children.

3. Directives may be issued by the centre to backward States to concentrate on the clearance of the backlog of non-attending boys and girls.

4. Setting up of School Improvement Committee for undertaking intensive drive for bringing not-attending children to schools and also to see to it the enrolled

children are retained in schools. Where School Management Committees already exist, they may be entrusted with this task.

5. Steps may be taken to enforce attendance, at least to the extent of issuing warning notices and attendance orders to the parents of defaulting children.

6. Whenever necessary, the prescribed teacher-pupil ratio may be relaxed while sanctioning new schools and additional teacher units in backward areas.

7. Provision of part-time schooling may be arranged for those children who are unable to attend regular schools.

8. Intensifying social education programmes in backward areas and among socially backward groups of people for educating the parents.

9. Special targets may be fixed for enrolment by the State Government from year to year for each district; greater attention being paid to backward districts and areas.

10. Separate targets for the enrolment of children of groups of backward classes may also be fixed at State and District levels.

11. It may be made obligatory for teachers to stay in the vicinity of the school as far as possible. As an incentive, payment of rural accommodation allowance to teachers of rural areas who live within the vicinity of the school may be considered.

12. Suitable facilities may be given to the children of rural elementary school teachers studying in high schools.

13. Residential type of schools (Ashram Schools) may be established for children of teachers working in very backward areas and the full cost of their education may be borne by the Government.

**Measures for Improving Enrolment**

Concerted efforts should be made for improving enrolment at the elementary stage. The following measures can help :

1. *A system of multiple entry* : It should be introduced so that children could be admitted at different points. This flexible arrangement will keep their interest alive as they can be admitted to the class for which they are fit.

2. *Part-time classes* : There are more drop-outs at the age of nine, and this is due to economic reasons. If part-time classes are organized, many children may get education at the time most convenient for them. The duration and timings of these classes should be determined in the light of local conditions.

3. *Own-time education* : This means self-instruction through special work-books prepared for the purposes. This method can work well if some teachers are put in charge of some areas to help students in needs.

4. *Provision of incentives* : A variety of incentives should be provided, like free distribution of text-books and stationery, mid-day meals, uniforms and attendance scholarship. For promoting education in the tribal areas, an increasing number of Ashram schools should be established. Special training should be given to teachers

in the tribal life and culture, provision of audio-visual aids, suitable curriculum, economic incentives to parents etc., should be made.

**Steps to Improve Quality of Primary Education**

1. *Broad-based education* : The objective of teaching in the primary schools should be the 3 R's, good manners, healthy habits, some skill with hands, general knowledge and develop qualities like sense of responsibility, co-operativeness, discipline and patriotism.

2. *Reformed curriculum* : Through the adoption of suitable curricula and appropriate teaching methodologies, the schools should inculcate in the students, such qualities as are relevant to the entire spectrum of occupations and would ultimately improve their adjustability and employability and make them more capable of setting down in self-employment, work-experience should form an integral part of the curriculum.

3. *Improvement in buildings and equipment* : School building should be constructed with the help of the local community. School should be provided with science-kits, radio sets, T.V. etc.

4. *Experimental schools* : Experimental schools should be set up to improve the content and methology of teaching. NCERT, SCERT, Colleges of Education can take up these projects.

5. *Better status of the teacher* : Only trained teachers should be appointed and in-service training must be systematically provided. Social and economic status of teachers should be improved. There must be scope for further promotion.

6. *Reform in educational administration* : The administration should be decentralized as far as possible. The inspecting authorities should provide leadership to the schools.

7. *Adequate financial provision* : The Central and State Governments should ensure that primary education is given adequate share out of the total outlay on education.

8. *Local resources to help primary teachers* : For example, if there is a good local singer available, his services may be utilized for teaching music to children.

9. *Research* : Research programmes on various aspects of primary education should be taken up for the improvement of primary education, *e.g.*, wastage and stagnation, curriculum, methods of teaching, action, research, etc.

**Causes of Shortfalls in Education of Girls**

The causes for shortfalls in the enrolment of girls at the primary and middle stages of education are manifold.

1. *Economic Reasons* : Mothers are reluctant to send their daughters to schools as they are very useful at home for carrying out domestic duties. Under-nourishment and inadequate clothing and books in rural area is yet another reason. Hence, free uniforms and free books to the needy and deserving children should be given.

Attendance scholarships should also be given as a compensation to parents. Mid-day meals should be provided.

2. *Social Customs* : Certain harmful social customs such as purdah system, caste barriers, etc., stand in the way of girls' education. Many parents who like to educate their girls are unable to do so because of co-education. To remedy these problems, research in women's education should be taken up, separate schools for girls should be established at Middle and High school stages, creating public opinion in favour of girls' education. Mass media, PTA may also be of help.

3. *Lack of Girls Schools.* One of the factors responsible for lower enrolment of girls is non-availability of a school in rural localities and lack of separate sanitary facilities for girls in mixed schools, lack of suitable school buildings and equipment. The following measures would overcome these difficulties :

(i) one primary school within a radius of one mile from every home;

(ii) hostel for girls;

(iii) stipends to girls who are residing in hostels;

(iv) transport facilities;

(v) free education for girls up to SSLC Examination.

4. *Lack of Qualified Women Teachers* : At present the proportion of women teachers to men teachers is very low. In Kerala it is 45%, Tamil Nadu 33%, Karnataka 25%, and West Bengal 14%. In the backward States the position is much worse. It is 5% in Orissa and 10% in Rajasthan. The following steps may be taken to increase the number of women teachers : (i) Special training institutions for women must be started and they must be located in rural areas. (ii) Condensed courses should be started to enable unqualified women for employment as teachers. (iii) In rural areas, quarters for women teachers should be provided. (iv) Rural allowance should be given to women teachers who are employed in rural areas. (v) In-service training must be given systematically.

5. *Lack of Lady Teachers.* The number of lady officers is far too small, to shoulder the responsibility of speeding up the progress of girls' education as envisaged in our plans. The offices are poorly staffed and ill-equipped. They lack conveyance facilities. To overcome these problems : (a) Women inspecting officers should be increased. (b) Adequate transport facilities should be provided. (c) Adequate office staff and equipment must be available. (d) Residential facilities provided to all woman officers.

## DEVELOPMENT OF COMPULSORY EDUCATION

(i) **Rapid Expansion** : After the passing of the 1918 Acts primary education made rapid strides. The then prevailing sense of nationalism along with the political and social condition further accelerated the expansion programme. This rapid expansion of primary education was due to following reasons :

(a) Greater co-operation by the government after the formation of popular ministries;

(b) The efforts of All India Women's Education Conference which in its session of 1927 demanded equal rights with men.

(c) Awakening in Harijans due to the efforts of Mahatma Gandhi and Dr. Ambedkar. The Harijans became conscious of the importance of education and their rights.

(d) Acts passed by many governments declaring primary education compulsory during this period.

(ii) **Slowing down of Expansion Tempo** : The expansion of primary education proceeded at a fast pace and uninterruptedly till 1930. Unfortunately Hartog Committee in its recommendations pleaded for quality and not quantity. It recommended that primary schools should be well equipped. The government accepted its recommendations. This slowed down the tempo of primary education expansion.

Another factor responsible for slowing down the tempo was the economic depression because the government was not in a position to spend adequate money.

(iii) **Resurgence of Primary Education** : In 1937 the speed of development of primary education gathered momentum with the formation of Congress ministries in six provinces. The Congress ministries laid emphasis on the expansion of primary education in rural areas so that it may come within the health of common man. By 1947 primary education became compulsory in 10,017 villages and 229 towns. Besides, it was made compulsory for girls in 1405 villages and 10 towns.

(iv) **After Independence** : After the country achieved independence the responsibility of administering the country devolved upon the popular ministries. The leaders realised that unless and until the people knew the aims and objects of the popular government democracy would not succeed. The people could know the objectives before the national government only through education. The importance of literacy and education was realised. In article 45 of the Indian Constitution the principle of compulsory education was defined. The Union Government started giving 30 per cent expenditure involved in the compulsory education to State Governments as grant. Primary education was made compulsory and free for children in the 6 to 14 years age group. A target of 60 per cent for children in the 6 to 11 years age group and 19 per cent for children in the 11 to 14 years age group was fixed for compulsory education under the Second Five Year Plan. Despite financial hardships the achievement in respect of this target was satisfactory.

## PROBLEMS IN COMPULSORY EDUCATION

1. **Indifference of British Administration** : The Britishers did not want to educate the general public in India for fear of awakening in them the feelings of nationalism and patriotism, besides the knowledge of their rights. They did not want that the Indian masses receive education and raise the voice of protest against injustice and exploitation. They wanted Indian clerks to help in their administration. So they made arrangements for education to produce clerks. They ensured that their trade and commerce continue to flourish. Hence, they completely neglected compulsory education.

2. **Political Problems :** In the wake of independence the Indian leaders had to face a number of major problems. The British left the country in chaotic political, communal and economic conditions. They had ruled India by adopting the policy of 'divide and rule' so when they left the sub-continent they partitioned it on communal basis. With the formation of Pakistan, the change of population created a refugee problem of unparallel magnitude and communal passions reached the highest pitch. The price paid was too heavy although the national government rose equal to the occasion and got the situation under control. Other major problems related to princely States, Zamindars and linguistic agitations. These problems taxed the country's resources to such an extent that due attention could not be paid to compulsory education.

3. **Defective Administrative Policy :** The government faced two major problems in the sphere of education, while the first one was to provide compulsory education to children within the 6 to 14 years age group, the second one related to change of the present primary schools into basic schools. Since the very beginning, attention was paid to the first problem. It was also mentioned in the Indian Constitution. But due to lack of adequate funds the scheme for compulsory education could not make much headway. The policy of changing the primary schools into basic schools was responsible for unsatisfactory progress of compulsory education. Due to lack of resources both the problems remained tagged with red-tapism and the needed progress was not made.

4. **Dearth of Teachers** : The pay scale and service conditions of teachers were so poor that educated persons were not attracted towards teachers' job. This shortage was more glaring in rural areas where avenues of part-time employment were practically nil. In urban areas the shortage of teachers was not so much because of opportunities to earn from other sources as well. This problem was more acute so for as lady teachers were concerned. The shortage of teachers training schools was also a cause of dearth of teachers.

5. **Non-availability of Necessary Funds** : The British rulers handed over the responsibility of primary education to local bodies. Unfortunately the only change in this policy that has come after freedom is that the grant to local bodies in this matter has been increased by 4 or 5 per cent. On the basis of this paltry increase in grant it is difficult to expect good results because the financial condition of the majority of the local bodies in the country is extremely poor.

6. **Unsuitable Educational System** : The responsibility of primary education in States lies with the local bodies which are semi-autonomous bodies. Their financial condition is far from satisfactory. The elected members and chairmen do not show courage to levy taxes to implement the policy of compulsory education lest the people will not vote for them again in elections. Therefore, they avoid increase in taxation and hence compulsory education remains neglected. Although the number of institutions has increased, but these schools lack adequate equipment and, good administrators. The compulsory education has not made the desired progress under such a defective system.

7. **Low Teaching Standard** : Because the pay scales are low and training

facilities inadequate, there is a dearth of good and trained teachers in primary schools. Most of the teachers in the primary schools are educated only up to the Junior High School standard and therefore their teaching efficiency is almost nil. The shortage of funds results in lack of reading materials and other equipments in the schools. Hence, the teaching standard in these schools is low. It does not attract the guardians to send their children to such primary schools.

8. **Unsuitable Curriculum** : The curriculum of primary education is unsuitable in as much as it neither develops the creative and constructive faculty of the child nor provides him opportunity for practical education. Some improvement has been effected in schools curriculum which have been changed into basic schools. However, due to shortage of funds the programme of basic schools has not made much progress.

9. **Impediments in Building New Schools** : The opening of new schools, needed most in rural areas where the majority of the population resides, is a complicated problem. First of all, the building material is costly and scarce. Secondly, it is difficult to decide about the site of the school, as villages are small in size and the population of children in each village is not enough to run a school in every village. So the choice of a site where enough children may be able to come for a school is obviously a difficult matter.

10. **Waste and Stagnation :** Statistics reveal that only 43 per cent students completed the primary education within the prescribed time due to lack of attractive equipment and reading materials, unsanitary school buildings, heavy curriculum etc. The poverty of parents often compels them to make their children share their work or to earn money. This hampers their study. Many leave the school before completing the studies. This is a serious impediment to the expansion of primary education.

11. **Shortage of School Buildings** : Due to lack of financial resources there is a great shortage of school buildings. Those which exist are insanitary, old and dilapidated. Many schools are run in temples or charitable buildings which have no play grounds. This is detrimental to the health of the children. Such buildings and disturbed environment are an impediment in expansion of primary education.

12. **Problem of Medium of Instruction** : Although only 14 languages have been mentioned in the related article in the Indian Constitution, yet as many as 845 languages or dialects are in vogue in the country. Many of the languages are such as have no literature or even alphabets although these are spoken by quite a large number of people. Under such conditions, it is difficult to determine the medium of instruction for compulsory primary education.

13. **Varying Social Values** : In India due to people's ignorance their daily routine is influenced to an undesirable extent by some social customs and values such as child-marriage, religious fanaticism, untouchability etc. The national leaders have tried much to eradicate these evils by making laws, but the laws remain ineffective as long as society does not act. Even to-day the entry of Harijans in the schools is prevented on one reason or the other in many schools. Early marriage

does not spare enough time to the couple to receive education. Such couples also lack interest in education. A large number of people in India do not like co-education even in primary classes. Hence, there is no wonder if compulsory education has not achieved the desired progress.

14. **Geographical Difficulties** : In India one finds a number of rivers, nullahs and rivulets, mountains, forests and other physical barriers. In mountaineous terrain the villages are far flung and snowy. It is difficult for children to cross rivers and rivulets or walk on snow bound ground for miles to attend the schools. In these regions the dream of compulsory education is difficult to materialise.

15. **Poor Condition and Ignorance of the Masses** : Even after so many years of independence the Indian masses are poverty-striken. They do not have enough to eat or to clad themselves. In many cases the head of the family carries over his shoulders the burden of as many as ten persons. Despite this gruelling condition wage-earning by women particularly in higher castes is looked down with contempt in the society. Ignorance of the masses do not allow them to realise the real worth of education. The guardians prefer to employ their children in some job than to send them to schools. This attitude is a big impediment in the development of compulsory education.

## REMEDIES TO PROBLEMS

1. **Provision of Adequate Funds** : The main factor responsible for the unsatisfactory progress of compulsory education in India is the poverty of the masses. Lack of funds is the reason for the absence of good buildings in healthy surroundings, shortage of trained and well qualified teachers and inadequacy of equipment and reading material in schools. Keeping in mind the poor financial condition of the country Shri Gopal Krishna Gokhale did not press the qualitative aspect of teaching, but advocated for increasing the number of schools. His contention was that primary education should be made easily available to larger number of people in order that illiteracy could be wiped off. This object may also be partially achieved by saving the money spent over changing the primary schools into basic ones. To solve the economic problem it has also been suggested by educationists to reduce the five years' course into four years. In the circumstances the programme of conversion of primary schools into basic schools should be postponed for some years and illiteracy and ignorance should be first removed from masses through plain primary education. The government should also give serious consideration to the suggestion mooted out by educationists.

2. **Reorganization of the Administrative Set-up** : In order to ensure progress of compulsory primary education some administrative changes in the policy and set-up are necessary. The State government should themselves take the responsibility of meeting the entire expenditure incurred over the compulsory primary education, because it is not possible to achieve the desired success by simply giving grants to the local bodies only when a central committee has been set up at the State level to compel them to implement the policy enunciated sincerely. The local bodies will not object to the directives of the central committee if the entire expenditure

incurred over the primary education is met by the State government. These steps, it is hoped, will ensure rapid progress of compulsory primary education.

3. **Consistent Education Policy** : The Government policy for compulsory primary education has not been consistent. The reason is that compulsory primary education policy is more idealistic and less practical. The implementation of this policy with prior assessment of financial resources and then conversion of primary education into basic education has adversely affected the entire programme. It will be more rational to first ensure complete success of compulsory education and then its conversion into basic education, should be thought of.

4. **Appointment of Trained Teachers in Large Number** : It is not possible to train a huge number of teachers required for implementing the compulsory education programme within a short period and with limited number of training schools. Hence, it is not advisable to withhold the compulsory education programme for want of trained and qualified teachers. The programme should be carried out with the available teachers who should be trained turn by turn. The pay scales of primary teachers should be made attractive to attract better persons for serving as teachers.

5. **Temporary Shift System Allowed** : In view of shortage of buildings the shift system should be introduced in schools. This practice is in vogue in even advanced European countries, like U.S.A., Germany, Japan, Denmark etc. The timing may be from 7.30 A.M. to 11.30 A.M. for the first shift and 1 P.M. to 5 P.M. for the second. This will also help children from farmers, and labourers families who can come in the second shift and also help their parents. The teachers may be paid additional emolument for extra hours. The shift system should be organised keeping the weather in the mind. It should be flexible also so that necessary changes may be made according to climatic changes.

6. **Special Schools for the Backward :** A good percentage of India's population belongs to the backward group. These people have remained illiterate since centuries. After independence the national Government made special efforts for the uplift of scheduled castes and tribes. The children of these families were granted money for the purchase of books besides receiving scholarships. Special schools were opened in areas predominantly inhabited by these families. However, the masses in general will have to co-operate to remove the ignorance and illiteracy from amongst them.

7. **Reorganization of the Curriculum :** As the present curriculum is not suitable for introducing compulsory primary education, it needs reform and improvement. It is lop-sided. A local craft should be included as a subject in the curriculum in order to make it attractive. In the curriculum of basic schools crafts have been given a place of honour. Till all the schools are converted into basic schools, at least one local craft should be included in the curriculum of primary education.

8. **More Schools** : In proportion to country's huge population the number of primary schools in India is insufficient. Efforts will have to be made to utilise spare

space in temples, mosques, panchayatghars, chaupals and other public places to open new schools. People will not object to these schools, as in ancient India schools were run in Ashrams and cottages of saints.

9. **Planning** : In India Five Year Plans have helped the development of education both directly and indirectly. Indirectly, they have helped the expansion of education by improving means of communication and by increasing the per capita income of the people. The Plans have executed many programmes which have helped education. Funds have been made available for the construction of school buildings, purchase of essential equipments and for setting up libraries and laboratories. Assistance has been given to start a large number of different subjects. Efforts have been made under the Five Year Plans for the rapid expansion of education for giving strength to the roots of democracy.

10. **Teacher's Realisation of Increased Responsibility** : The country's financial position is not such as to give good salaries and emoluments to the teachers. However, in the national interest it may be assumed that the teachers' community will ungrudgingly bear the additional burden as it was in countries like Italy, China, England etc. The number of children may be raised from 33 to 60 in the class. Care should be taken to see that teacher is not asked to teach many classes time as this will affect his efficiency.

## WASTAGE AND STAGNATION IN PRIMARY EDUCATION

Wastage means a pre-mature withdrawal of children from school at any stage before the completion of primary course. Stagnation means detention of a child in the class for period of more than one year.

Stagnation discourages the child as well as his parents who think it better to withdraw the child from the school.

At the primary stage, there is a huge wastage and stagnation. A poor country like India cannot afford such a great wastage and stagnation. This is an acute problem of Indian primary education.

### Causes of Wastage and Stagnation

1. *Economic Causes* : The parents are unable to afford the expenses of education of their children. Children at the age of 9 or 10 are a source of income to parents. Thus poverty of the parent is the main cause of wastage and stagnation.

2. *Social Causes* :

(i) Because of the social set up and inadequate social facilities, scheduled caste and scheduled tribe people are reluctant in sending their children to schools.

(ii) Illiterate parents do not understand the importance of education.

(iii) Some orthodox people do not like girls' education. They withdraw their daughters from the schools at an early age.

(iv) Early marriage system is another hurdle.

(v) Orthodox people are against co-education.

3. *Educational Causes.* The present primary education is not worthwhile both for the children and the parents :

(i) The curriculum is not suited to the real life of children.

(ii) Due to heterogenous group of students in a class, the higher age-group students cannot adjust properly and they leave the school.

(iii) Admission in Class I continues throughout the year. The children who join late cannot pass the examination.

(iv) The psychological needs of children are not properly satisfied. Many children play truant.

(v) Teaching methods are dull and boring

(vi) Teachers do not take interest in their jobs.

(vii) The fear of the examination remains always in the minds of children.

(viii) Individual attention is not paid to children.

(ix) Punishment inflicted upon children is very severe.

(x) Some of the existing schools are incomplete.

(xi) Lack of provision for instructional material.

(xii) Lack of healthy contact between parents and teachers.

(xiii) Most of the parents feel that education imparted to their children is useless. It does not train them for better work. On the contrary it isolates the children from habit of work.

**View of Indian Education Commission**

The Indian Education Commission has mentioned the following causes of wastage and stagnation:

(i) The heterogeneity of the age composition among the students in the first class.

(ii) The practice of making fresh admission throughout the year.

(iii) Irregularity of attendance.

(iv) Lack of educational equipment in the school as well as with the children.

(v) Overcrowded classes.

(vi) Unsuitable curricula.

(vii) Inability of the teacher to use play-way techniques which can assist in initiating the children pleasantly to school life.

(viii) Poor teaching.

(ix) Inadequately prepared teachers.

(x) A wrong system of examination.

**Recommendations By the Education Commission**

Kothari Commission has made the following recommendations :

(i) Examination at the end of Class I should be abolished and first two classes (and where possible, even class I to IV) should be regarded as one unit.

(ii) Introducing a year of pre-school education.

(iii) Providing part-time education for poor children so that they can work as well as learn.

(iv) Adoption of Play-way techniques in Class I.

(v) Providing 'Literacy classes' for a period of one year at least to all children in the age-group 11-14 who are not attending schools.

(vi) Providing similar facilities of part-time education for children who have completed the lower primary stage and desire to study further.

**Measures Taken by the Ministry of Education for Universalization of Primary Education**

1. Special Central assistance to backward States for their progress of non-formal education for primary school children. The total central sector outlay for this scheme was Rs. 25 crores for 1980-85. Under this scheme financial assistance was extended to voluntary agencies in the nine educationally backward States for running non-formal educational centres.

2. A modest programme for early childhood education was envisaged in the Sixth Plan by way of broad-basing universalization of elementary education, including training of teachers needed for the programme.

3. A 20-year programme (1980-2000) has been initiated under IYDP for disabled children. The main plan of the educational programmes for the disabled is to integrate education in schools along with normal children.

4. Under Central initiative, a few innovative projects have been in operation to improve the school curriculum. These programmes are being assisted by UNICEF. For the period of 1981-83, a Master Plan of Operations (MPO) was drawn up as follows :

(i) *Nutrition, Health, Education and Environmental Sanitation* : Launched as a pilot project in 1976, this project has been implemented till 1980 through 5 regional centres at Coimbatore, Jabalpur, Baroda, Calcutta and Ludhiana. The curricular materials developed were tried in 2308 primary schools involving training of 7091 primary teacher educators and supervisors. There is a proposal to extend this scheme to 14 States and Union Territories.

(ii) *Primary Education Curriculum Renewal* : Implemented since 1975 in 15 states in 30 primary schools in each State, this project aims at a qualitative improvement of the curriculum. During the MPO period, this project is being extended to another 100 schools in the existing 15 States/Union Territories. There is a proposal to take up this in an experimental phase in remaining States/Union Territories with three schools in each of the selected districts.

(iii) *Development Activities in Community Education* : The project was initiated in 1976. Till 1980, the experimental phase was in operation in 30 centres, at 2 per State. The project aims at developing non-formal educational programmes for various target groups, particularly for out-of-school children and adults. It proposed to increase the number of community centres to 102.

(iv) *Comprehensive Access of Primary Education (CAPE)* : This was taken up for implementation in 29 out of 31 States/Union Territories with a view to decentralising the curriculum according to the needs and life situations of out-of-school children. The learning materials developed will be utilised in the network of one-formal learning centres, 3500 teacher educators and 550 education officers in the participating States have been trained by NCERT, SCERT, etc.

(v) *Children's Media Laboratory — Early Childhood Project* : This project aims at developing new capacity for the training of pre-school educators, extension of research and developing activities, and development of model, pre-school centres, play materials and Audio-Visual materials for pre-school children have been devised.

(vi) *Non-Formal Education Programme for Women* : This project aims at introducing a substantial component of maternity and child care training in the programme of Adult Education. An important feature will be to link child care centres with adult education centres so that women can attend adult education classes simultaneously leaving their children to the child care centres.

## QUESTIONS FOR EXERCISE

1. Trace the development of primary education during the British rule till the formation of popular ministries in 1937.
2. What do you understand by compulsory primary education? What are the impediments in its path? Suggest remedies.
3. Write short notes on the part played by the following persons in the development of primary education in India :

   Sri Gopal Krishna Gokhale, Lord Curzon, Sri Vitthal Bhai Patel, Maharaja Sir Sayaji Rao Gaikwad.

# 14

# PROBLEMS OF SECONDARY EDUCATION

## Meaning of Secondary Education

Secondary education is the kind of education which is given after primary education and before university education. It includes all the classes after the primary school and before the university. Education has been grouped into primary, secondary and university stages in different countries, though the duration of secondary education may differ in one country from that in other. At some places secondary classes begin from the sixth class and go up to twelfth. Elsewhere upper primary classes go up to the eighth class and secondary classes start from the ninth and go up to eleventh or twelfth. Before Independence secondary education was classified in different manners, such as vernacular middle school, matriculation, entrance, high school and intermediate, etc.

## Form of Secondary Education

Before independence the form of secondary education in India was prescribed by foreign educationists. Primary classes were designed up to fifth class though they generally stopped at the fourth class. Middle classes were run from fifth to seventh. High school and intermediate classes were run from eighth to twelfth. The form of secondary education changed after independence. Now the seven year secondary education is generally current. With some modification secondary education has been divided into three groups — from sixth to eighth, Junior high school, from ninth to tenth, high school and eleventh and twelfth have been regarded as higher secondary or intermediate classes. The Mudaliar Commission (1952-53) termed secondary education as higher secondary education while ninth to eleventh classes were included in it the twelfth class was pre-university class.

## Structural Reform

1. *Calcutta University Commission (1917-19)* : Popularly known as the Sadler Commission it recommended replacement of the then prevailing 10+2+2 pattern by a 10+2+3 one. It had come to the conclusion that the two year intermediate course really belonged to schools. It also desired the increase in the duration of the undergraduate course to make it comparable to that in the advanced countries. It did not suggest vocationalisation of education.

2. *The University Education Commission (1948-49)* : It took up the discussion of the problem once again. The Commission accepted the 10+2+3 pattern, but added the vocational spectrum. Unfortunately, no steps were taken to implement the recommendations of the Commission.

3. *Secondary Education Commission (1952-53)* : The Commission recommended a school duration of 11 years followed by three years of the first degree course. Perhaps the decision was dictated by the compulsion of economy.

4. *The Central Advisory Board of Education (1955).* It expressed the desirability of establishing parity of standard of schools in different states and advised on the lines already recommended by the Secondary Education Commission.

5. *The Planning Commission (1960)* : It felt that "the duration of the school-course should be 12 years and not 11 years so that the total span of education from Primary to Higher Educational level should be 15 years (12+3) and it was very desirable that mature students of the age of 18 should go to the University."

6. *The Committee on Emotional Integration (1960)* : It gave considerable thought to the problem and suggested that in the higher secondary stage there should be provision for specialisation. The higher secondary stage should include vocational and semi-vocational courses.

7. *The All India Council for Secondary Education* : It recommended 12 years for total schooling, with the last four years consisting the secondary stage of education. Two examinations, Higher Secondary I and Higher Secondary II, should be conducted at the end of the first year and second year of Secondary stage respectively.

8. *Education Ministers Conference (1964)* : It was decided that the entire education at the Secondary stage should be done in the schools. Pre-University classes started in Universities as a temporary measure should be transferred to the schools as soon as possible.

9. *The Education Commission (1964-66)* : It came to the conclusion, and saw academic considerations for the adoption of the uniform pattern of 10+2+3 for schools and colleges in all parts of the country. It recommended a higher secondary stage of two years of general education or one to three years of vocational education. The idea was also supported by the Sampurnanand Committee of National Integration (1966).

10. *A Committee of the Members of the Parliament (1968)*: Formed to spell out a National Policy on Education in India it endorsed this national pattern.

11. *The Central Boards of Secondary Education* : At its meeting (1972) passed a resolution in favour of 10+2+3 pattern.

12. *Shukla National Committee* : The Government of India appointed the National Committee on 10+2+3 educational structure under the Chairmanship of Dr. P.D. Shukla. The report was submitted in 1973. The following are the salient features of the new pattern of education, as enunciated by the Shukla Committee :

1. Uniform national pattern of education will strengthen National Integration.
2. This new pattern will rationalise and strengthen school education.
3. The students entering Universities will be more knowledgeable and mature.
4. Pressure for admission in Universities and other centres of higher education will be reduced.
5. Provision for introducing appropriate vocationalisation at the higher secondary stage will be made.
6. It will modernize and strengthen school curricula, secure the social and economic needs of the adolescents and youth in a better manner.
7. A broadly uniform pattern will facilitate implementation of educational programmes.
8. It will help to solve educational problems of the minorities.
9. Students take decisions regarding the particular stream to be studied by them at a suitable age.
10. It will contribute to raise the general standard and quality of education at all stages.

**Features of Secondary Education**

The following important features of education at the secondary stage have been pointed out in the booklet entitled "10+2+3 — A major change in School education", published by the Ministry of Education, Government of India (1975).

1. The goals of national, integration training for democratic living, co-operativeness, cultural and religious tolerance have been duly emphasised in the courses of Languages and Social Sciences and find ample scope in community service.

2. For intellectual development of students, provision has been made by way of teaching subjects like Languages, Mathematics, Sciences and Social Sciences. For fuller development of the physical, emotional and other aspects of the students' personality, provision has been made for work-experience, community service, health and physical education and other activities.

3. The contents which have been given in the syllabi of these subjects are forward looking. Important developments in the respective areas have been incorporated. Stress has been laid on recent scientific, technological, social and economic developments in sciences and social sciences. To broaden the outlook, developments in other parts of the world, too have been put in proper limelight, while changes of the national scene receive importance.

4. A significant feature of the plus-two education is the provision of opportunities to students to be productive and self-reliant. With the introduction of work-experience a step in the direction of inculcating right attitude towards work has been taken. The important areas to which work experiences relate are : Engineering,

Agriculture, Domestic Science, Commerce, Fine Arts and other trades which have great utility in domestic and other areas of work.

5. The schools may undertake suitable activities of community service in addition to work-experience. Such activities may include projects of village uplift, slum clearance, adoption of a locality for its improvement, work in hospitals to help and nurse the sick and poor, attending to the families of a group of workers of a factory, removal of illiteracy, etc.

## ORGANIZATION OF SECONDARY EDUCATION

On the Basic education pattern secondary education has been divided into basic and non-basic groups. Basic education, too, was divided into pre-basic and post-basic. Within the basic scheme it was planned to teach the curriculum of the seven or eight years secondary school in six years. In this system the three year Higher Basic course was considered equivalent to the three year higher secondary school course. To implement this scheme it was planned to establish Model Higher Secondary schools in rural and urban areas. The introduction of the three year degree course was also planned in this educational organization.

### Recommendation of Mudaliar Commission

Emphasising the need of reorganization of secondary education, Mudaliar Commission had recommended the introduction of three year degree course by changing the prevailing intermediate system into Higher Secondary. The Central Government accepted the recommendation of the Mudaliar Commission. It advised the various States to introduce the three year degree course. The Commission also emphasised the need of establishing multi-purpose schools for introducing an occupational approach. For this purpose, the Government of India gave financial help to the States. In partial acceptance of recommendations of the Mudaliar Commission classes 6, 7 and 8 were grouped under junior high school and 9, 10 and 11 were placed under the Higher Secondary.

*Types of Secondary Schools* : The following types of secondary schools are generally found in India :

1. Intermediate Colleges,
2. High School and Junior High School,
3. Higher Secondary Schools,
4. Multi-purpose Schools, and
5. Special Schools.

1. *Intermediate Colleges* : In U.P. intermediate education system has been accepted. Under it classes 6, 7 and 8 are grouped under lower secondary, class 9 and 10 are termed as High School and class 11 and 12 are known as Higher Secondary. The college itself conducts the examination at the end of the Junior High School stage, *i.e.* at class VIII. In intermediate colleges, there are two public examinations — one at the end of class X and the other at the end of class XII. Both the public examinations are conducted by the U.P. Board.

2. *Junior High School and High School* : The Junior High School examination is conducted by the institution itself. In these schools classes 6, 7 and 8 are grouped under junior high school. High Schools are those secondary schools where the final examination of class X is conducted by the U.P. Board of High School and Intermediate Education. Classes IX and X are known as high school.

3. *Higher Secondary Schools* : According to the recommendations of the Mudaliar Commission the Government of India advised the States to run three-year Higher Secondary Schools and three-year degree courses. On financial grounds many State governments expressed their inability to introduce this scheme. In the States where this new scheme has been accepted in principle the progress of changing of high schools into higher secondary schools is very slow. Although the Central Government has agreed to shoulder the 60 per cent expenditure of this change-over, but some State governments have not been able to manage for the remaining 40 per cent.

The State governments are not taking interests in opening higher secondary schools, as they are unable to appoint the necessary number of teachers. Another difficulty is that they will have to make corresponding changes in the university system as well by way of running three-year degree courses. The three-year degree courses have been organized at places where three-year secondary courses are in operation. The secondary education board conducts the public examination at the end of class XI. After passing this examination the candidates are admitted to the three-year degree course.

4. *Multipurpose Schools* : Mudaliar Commission recommended the opening of multi-purpose schools for giving a more meaningful and pragmatic bias to education at the secondary stage. It was very expensive, because a multipurpose school requires a special school building, various types of tools and implements, laboratories, spacious land for farming, workshops, reading rooms and other reasonable facilities. These things involve heavy expenditure. Arranging for at least two or more types of vocations in the school becomes all the more expensive.

Many subject-groups will have to be organized because of the various types of curriculum in these schools. Such teachers will have to be appointed who can forge a co-operation between the teaching of various subjects. They should be trained in vocationally-oriented courses. So far no arrangement has been made by university or any other State organization to produce such trained teachers.

Multipurpose schools may be opened as model government institutions only. The private institutions cannot run such schools. Some courses of the multipurpose schools may be taught in some vocational and industrial institutions. A synthesis may be created between the general and vocational courses and the two are taught together in some industrial institutions.

There have been numerous difficulties in opening multipurpose schools, though there is no denying of the fact that they are very useful and important. They create self-dependence and vocational skill and develop both general intelligence and vocational aptitude. A student is more likely to get subjects of his special bent of mind. When students of various subjects and trade study together, they acquire better social sense. They may easily develop the spirit of mutual co-operation and brotherhood.

5. *Special Schools* : According to the recommendations of the Secondary Education Commission (1952-53) the Government of India planned to change the prevailing secondary schools into single-purpose schools and new higher secondary schools. It was also planned to open the high schools in the rural area.

In U.K. the single-purpose schools are very important, so the policy of establishing single-purpose schools was also accepted in India. In the single-purpose school the inadequacies of the multipurpose schools may be avoided. It was considered more practicable to establish single purpose schools of literature, commerce, engineering, fine arts and agriculture etc.

Since more than 70% of the population of India lives in villages, opening of agricultural higher secondary schools in rural areas should be emphasised. By the end of the Fifth Five Year Plan only about 500 secondary schools of agriculture, cottage industries, gardening and animal husbandary could be organized in the country.

## PROBLEMS OF SECONDARY EDUCATION

The problems of secondary education may be enumerated as below :

1. Organization and form of secondary schools.
2. Determination of aims of secondary education.
3. Construction of the curriculum.
4. Examination and evaluation
5. Management and administration.
6. Finance.
7. Number of teachers.
8. Inadequate supervision.

1. **Organization and Form of Secondary Schools** : There is no similarity in the forms of various secondary schools in India. If the forms of secondary schools in the various States of the country were the same, the students will not feel much difficulty in going for education from one State to another.

2. **Determination of Aims of Secondary Education** : The Indian Constitution provided for free and compulsory primary education. This feature has an impact on secondary education. Hence, the number of students at the secondary stage has increased. The government has tried to make provision for secondary education for students coming after passing primary schools. Many new secondary schools have been opened during the various Five Year Plans. The number of students at the secondary stage has increased. But education imparted to them has been merely theoretical. To-day, after having received secondary education the student has only following two options :

1. To enter some university for further education.

2. To roam about here and there in search of job.

In many Western countries secondary education has been so organized that after obtaining it the student is able to stand on his own legs in some vocational area. But in India the current secondary education is aggravating the unemployment problem. Therefore we have to make our secondary education so useful that the students having passed this stage do not run only for admission to universities or remain unemployed and they become economically independent by having acquired some vocational skill of productive nature. India needs able citizens for making democracy a success. Hence, the ultimate aim of secondary education should be to prepare self-dependent and dutiful citizens imbued with the spirit of intelligent patriotism contributing to the prosperity of the country.

In secondary education special attention should be paid to the programmes contributing to the formation of character. The purpose is not only to offer opportunities for acquiring certificate but to produce youths of character. Education has not only to impart bookish knowledge but to give a knowledge which may contribute to personal, social and national prosperity. There should be an all-round development of children. They should be made physically, mentally, economically, morally and spiritually strong. They should be made citizens who may think for themselves and who may acquire such experiences which they may fruitfully utilize.

3. **Construction of Curriculum** : (i) *Aim and Objectives* : In order to achieve the above objectives of secondary education, its curriculum should be more practical and useful. Though due to geographical variations, the needs of one State differ from those of another, however, we may prepare a curriculum for the whole country which is helpful in meeting the national goals. The Government of India is conscious of this objective. The All India Board of Secondary Education has suggested that some subject should be compulsorily taught in all the secondary schools in the country. It is trying to forge out such a curriculum which may achieve the national goals and also meet the regional needs of all classes and groups.

(ii) *Language Teaching*. The problem of language-teaching is a difficult issue in the curriculum construction. In India Hindi has been accepted as the national language of the country. But some non-Hindi speaking States are opposing Hindi on the plea that it is being imposed on minorities. Many groups in South India favour English in place of Hindi. India is a religious country. Its basic scriptures are in Sanskrit. Hence, there are many who still love Sanskrit. Hence, it has been proposed that at least three languages should be taught at the secondary level. This is known as the Three Language Formula which is given below :

1. National language or regional language for non-Hindi speaking people.
2. If Hindi has not been taken as a national language, then Hindi or any other Indian language or Sanskrit.
3. Sanskrit or any Indian language, if not taken a Western language (English, French, or German).

In three language formula the student will study the national language along with a regional language and as a third language Sanskrit or any foreign language.

(iii) *Integrated Curriculum.* It has been considered necessary to understand the problem relating to the aptitude and interests of students, regional needs, mother tongue as the medium of instruction, arrangement for counselling and guidance and the appropriate method for implementing the curriculum so that some uniformity may be forged in the curriculum at the secondary stage. General science and social studies were included as the compulsory subjects keeping in view the understanding capacity of the students at the secondary level. For the other subjects students should be left free to choose their optionals according to their needs, interests, age and capacity. Industrial, vocational and technical subjects should be also included in the curriculum, keeping in view the present needs of the nation.

(iv) *Curriculum At the Junior Secondary Level* : General science, social studies, mathematics, agriculture or any fine art or some commercial subject or music or physical exercises for physical development have been accepted as the main subjects of the curriculum at junior secondary level.

(v) *Higher Secondary Level Curriculum* : According to recommendations of the Secondary Education Commission (1952-53) various groups have been favoured. An attempt has been made to make the curriculum multipurpose by emphasizing the inclusion of industrial and vocational subjects and crafts.

4. **Examination and Evaluation** : The prevailing essay type of examination has so many defects. It is not a good measure of academic achievements and development of the students. Though it cannot be abolished altogether, yet some changes and reforms may be introduced into it.

External examination alone is a not a good tool for measuring the success of the students. Internal examinations should also be used for examining the students. The success or failure of a student should be determined on the basis of both these. The sessional work of the whole year should be scrutinised. Monthly and third monthly records of the students should be prepared. Their abilities should be measured in grades. Along with of essay type questions at least 40 per cent of the marks should be assigned to objective tests.

5. **Management and Administration** : Three types of secondary schools are current in India :

(1) Government Schools.

(2) Private or non-government schools.

(3) Schools run by local bodies.

While the Government schools are fully controlled by the governmental machinery, private schools are managed by private managing committees under the supervision of district inspector of schools or some other government officer. The government gives financial aids to all the schools. The school teachers in most of the States in the country are now paid through government treasuries as the local bodies have not been successful in running secondary schools. The government itself controls the education of girls and technical education at the secondary level in many States. Many voluntary organizations are also running girls schools and technical schools. But most of them are in bad shape. Their financial, educational, building and teacher problems are acute. While at some places there are too many of such institutions at other places there are none. Some schools do not fulfil the conditions of recognition laid by the Education Board. Now the government has started interfering with the management of these weak institutions. It has also started appointing teachers for these schools and paying their salaries through the government treasuries.

The administration of the secondary schools is not efficient. Administrative units at central, regional and district level carry on the work of educational administration. There is a Board of Secondary Education in each State for determination of the nature of the curriculum, text-books and for conducting examination. Thus, there is a dual administration over the secondary schools : one by the board of secondary education and the other by the governmental education departments consisting of Director, Deputy Directorate and Inspectionate staff or by private managements. This dual control of the secondary schools lacks of harmony and co-ordination between the officers of the two controlling units. There should be a mutual co-operation between the two for achieving the objectives of secondary education. Only then the administration of secondary schools may be useful.

6. **Finance** : So far there have been more private and voluntary efforts for the expansion of education. The government has tried to establish only one or two model higher secondary schools in each district. The schools run by voluntary organization face the problem of inadequate funds. Their financial resources are insufficient and they look for the government grants. They do not have good school buildings, good teachers and suitable teaching materials. They are not in a position to teach industrial and vocational subjects, as these entail heavier expenditure. In the United States every citizen has to pay an educational cess in proportion to his income. This provides adequate finances for educational purposes. Similarly, in India some educational tax may be levied. Gifts from wealthy persons in favour of schools may be encouraged by exempting the gifted amount from income tax. Huge amount of money is required for the school building, laboratories, reading rooms, libraries, sports materials, workshop, teachers, salaries and teaching materials. Both the government and the public should co-operate in organizing the necessary funds for the schools.

7. **Number of Teachers** : Teachers are the spinal chord of the school. If the teachers are inadequate in number the school cannot function well. Today most schools have few able teachers. Caste and group considerations play the major role at the time of appointment and the question of suitability is thrown to winds. Hence, unsuitable teachers are appointed. Many of the Managing Committees are vindictive against teachers. Strikes and Dharna by teachers have become a common feature in some of the schools. India needs vocationally trained teachers for multipurpose schools. Indian universities and Teachers' Training Colleges are not producing

such teachers. In the absence of suitable teachers the multipurpose schools and vocationalization of education are not succeeding. Specially trained teachers are required for the full implementation of Basic Education. The government should take some positive steps to solve this problem.

8. **Supervision** : Supervision arrangement of the secondary schools is not adequate. The inspectors are busy with their files in their offices. They get little time for supervision and inspection of schools under their charge. The behaviour of inspectors with the teachers is below the norm. They do not consider themselves as co-partners of the teachers in the interest of the all-round development of the students. Their approach should be constructive and helpful in the sacred task of teaching children. Their attitude should be democratic. They should try to solve the difficulties of the teachers in classroom situations and elsewhere. Some refresher course should also be organized for acquainting the inspectors with the latest developments in the field of education.

### Importance of Secondary Education

1. *Adolescence Period* : Secondary stage of education coincides with adolescence period. It is the most crucial period which requires utmost care of the healthy development of the child. It plays a significant role in the development of a well-balanced personality.

2. *Socio-Economic Reconstruction* : Secondary Education plays an important role in training the youth of the country to take an effective part in the social reconstruction and economic development of their country. The social, economic, technical and cultural efficiency of the nation depends on the secondary education. In the post-independent period vocationalisation of secondary education is emphasised. As secondary stage makes the final stage of education for a majority of students, it has to prepare them for various vocations.

3. *Quality Improvement of Education* : Secondary Education determines the quality of education both at the primary and higher stages of education. It provides teachers for primary schools, who can make or mar the standard of primary education. Secondary schools supply students for universities and other centres of higher learning. Thus secondary education is the most important link between the primary and higher stages of education.

## SECONDARY EDUCATION AFTER INDEPENDENCE

The aim and functions of secondary education were disappointing at the time of attainment of independence. It was unable to contribute to the reconstruction of new India. So various education committees and commissions were appointed during the post-independence era for studying the problems of education and recommending suitable measures for bringing about necessary reforms.

### Tarachand Committee (1948)

This Committee was appointed for recommending the reorganisation of secondary education in India with Dr. Tara Chand, the Educational Adviser to the

Government of India, as its Chairman. The following were the major recommendations of the Committee :

1. Secondary schools should be of multipurpose type.
2. Four years of secondary education before admission to the degree course.
3. Pay scales and service conditions of the teachers should be improved.
4. There shall be one examination at the end of the secondary stage; the Universities may, for admission purposes lay down such conditions as they deem fit.
5. All India Council of Education to be set up for co-ordination between the Centre and States.

**University Education Commission (1948-49)**

Although primarily concerned with the University education, it suggested effective steps for implementing secondary education. It pointed out, "Our secondary education remains the weakest link in an educational machinery and need urgent reforms." The following were the important recommendations of the Commission with regard to secondary education :

1. There should be a twelve-year secondary course instead of a ten-year course.
2. An exhaustive list of subjects for general and special education at the secondary stage be given.
3. Liberal grant and better teaching facilities should be given.
4. The lot of the teachers should be improved.

**Secondary Education Commission (1952-53)**

Directed to examine the existing system of secondary education in the country and to suggest suitable measures for the reorganisation and improvement. The Commission expressed its opinion that the secondary education is the vital link in our educational system. It pointed to the following defects in the existing secondary educational system :

1. Education imparted in secondary schools is isolated from the real life. With this education the students cannot participate effectively in social living.
2. It fails to develop self-confidence in students.
3. It is narrow and one-sided. It fails to train the whole personality of students. It gives importance for academic aspects alone.
4. The standard of education is falling day-by-day due to overcrowded classes. This has further undermined the training of character and inculcation of proper discipline.
5. English, as medium of instruction has brought down the standard of achievement of students.

6. The methods of teaching adopted in secondary schools are mechanical and out-moded. They develop cramming and not independent thinking in our students.
7. The secondary education is examination-ridden and is responsible for mechanical and lifeless teaching methods.
8. It has developed a sense of disappointment and job dissatisfaction among teachers.

**Kothari Commission**

According to Education Commission (Kothari Commission) "the single most important thing needed now is to get out the rigidity of the present system. In the rapidly changing world of today one thing is certain that yesterday's educational system will not meet today's and even less, the needs of tomorrow." The Commission pointed out the following major defects in the existing system of education.

(1) Inadequate importance to agriculture.

(2) It is too much academic.

(3) It is not related to national reconstruction.

(4) It encourages disruptive tendencies and caste loyalities.

(5) It does not lay any emphasis on character formation and cultivation of moral and spiritual values.

The Commission recommended that it should be related to the life needs and aspirations of the people, thereby making it a powerful instrument of social, economic and cultural transformation necessary for the realisation of our national goals. This purpose can be achieved by :

(1) Increasing productivity.

(2) Achieving social and national integration.

(3) Accelerating the process of modernisation.

(4) Cultivating social, moral and spiritual values.

**Recommendations of Secondary Education Commission**

(1) There should be multipurpose schools at higher secondary level.

(2) Public schools should continue and State Government should open residential schools in rural areas.

(3) Mother tongue should be the medium of instructions.

(4) A text-book committee should be set up in every State.

(5) Activity methods should be adopted to discourage cramming.

(6) Trained Guidance Officers and Career Masters should be appointed in all secondary schools.

(7) In schools, medical services should be provided.

(8) Teachers of physical education and first-aid training should be appointed.

(9) Number of external examinations should be reduced.

(10) Due credit should be given to internal school tests and cumulative records maintained in schools for every student.

(11) Essay type test should be improved and objective type tests should be included.

(12) Service conditions of teaching personnel should be improved.

(13) A Board of Secondary Education should be constituted in every State.

(14) Playgrounds, buildings, science-equipment and appliances should be provided.

(15) Funds should be provided for library books, art and craft equipment and agricultural farms.

**National Policy on Education (1968)**

The following are the important aspects of National Policy of Education :

(1) Educational opportunities at the secondary level should be extended to all classes of people as it is an effective instrument for bringing about social change and transformation.

(2) Facilities for technical and vocational education should be increased.

(3) Vocational education should conform broadly to the real employment opportunities.

(4) Technical and vocational education should cover large areas such as agriculture, industry, trade and commerce, medicine and public health, home management, arts and crafts, secretarial training, etc.

**Education and the Five-Year Plans**

1. *IVth Five-Year Plan (1969-74).* This Plan made the following provisions:

(1) Development of science education.

(2) Improvement of educational standards.

(3) Starting vocational courses.

(4) Introducing work-experience.

(5) Encouraging girl's education.

(6) Developing school complexes.

(7) Undertaking curriculum and examination reforms.

2. *Vth Five Year Plan (1974-79).* The following were the major provisions in this Plan :

(1) To relate secondary education to the needs of the country.

(2) To bring about qualitative improvement, competent teachers, better

library facilities, better equipment and strengthening educational research.

(3) Expanding facilities for secondary education.

(4) Adopting uniform pattern (10+2+3) throughout the country.

(5) Curriculum reform and introduction of work experience.

(6) Vocationalise education.

(7) Starting of correspondence courses.

(8) To set up Model Comprehensive Secondary Schools.

(9) Developing Science education.

(10) Improving teachers' training.

3. *VIth Five-Year Plan (1978-83).* A sum of Rs. 300 crores was provided for secondary education in this Plan. The following major priorities were fixed :

(1) Emphasis on qualitative improvement and vocationalisation.

(2) Discouraging indiscriminate opening of new secondary schools.

(3) Additional enrolment by 30 lakhs.

(4) Introduction of Socially Useful Productive Work (SUPW), making Science and Mathematics teaching effective, involving students in social service literary programmes and adult education, etc.

(5) Providing facilities for poor talented children to join public schools.

**Expansion of Secondary Education**

Tremendous expansion has been made in secondary education after Independence. This has created many problems such as —

(i) It is unplanned, unsystematic and haphazard in the different regions of the country.

(ii) Inadequate material equipment and teaching personnel.

(iii) Lowering down of standard of education. Kothari Commission has made the following recommendations with regard to the above problems :

(1) To regulate enrolment in twenty years.

(2) Planning for every district and implementing it within 10 years.

(3) Restriction on the number of opening of new schools.

(4) Selected admission.

(5) Vocationalization of secondary education.

(6) Part time education.

(7) Correspondence course.

(8) Expansion of facilities for girls' education, etc.

## SOCIALLY USEFUL PRODUCTIVE WORK (SUPW)

The concept of manual work as a tool of education was recognised long before the advent of formal education. In ancient India education was related to the life of pupils. The dichotomy between education and work did not exist. With the introduction of formal education, bookish education prepared the students for white collared jobs. There was no provision for manual activity in general education.

### Basic Education

Rabindranath Tagore emphasised the role of manual work in imparting all-round education. Mahatma Gandhi insisted that manual and productive work should not only find place in the school curriculum, but also education should centre around it. The educational ideas of Mahatma Gandhi were given practical shape by the Zakir Hussain Committee. Basic education was accepted as the national pattern of education for the elementary stage in 1938.

In 1966, the Kothari Commission suggested the concept of work-experience. Consequently, great emphasis was laid on work-experience in the new 10+2 pattern of education.

### Ishwarbhai Patel Committee (1977)

The Committee pointed out that work-experience is an integral feature of the curriculum, at all stages. The scheme of education, recommended by this Committee has three main components — humanities, science and work (socially useful productive work and community service) together with aesthetic appreciation to illuminate the curriculum.

The National Education Conference held in New Delhi in December 1977 under the Chairmanship of Sriman Narain also recommended that 50 per cent of the total school time ought to be devoted to productive, creative and recreational activities, at least half of which should be focused on Socially Useful Productive Work of various kinds.

Socially Useful Productive Work is purposive, meaningful, manual work resulting in either goods or services which are useful to the community. It is the problem-solving approach which enriches the educational component of the programme. The SUPW should be related to the basic needs of students *viz.*, food, shelter, clothing, health and recreation, community work and social service. It should be predominantly manual. It should either result in some material product or involve children in some form of social service.

The Committee recommended the SUPW should be given the status of a full-fledged subject for the award of certificates at the end of class X.

### Objectives of SUPW

The following are the major objectives of SUPW:

(i) To acquaint children with the world of work and to develop in them a sense of respect for manual workers.

(ii) To develop an awareness of social problems and inculcate in them a positive attitude towards community service.

(iii) To develop in them a desire to be useful members of the society and to contribute their best to the common good.

(iv) To inculcate in them a positive attitude of team-work and socially describable values like self-reliance, dignity of labour, tolerance, co-operation, sympathy and helpfulness.

(v) To lead the children to participate increasingly in productive work.

(vi) To provide opportunities for creative self-expression and for the development of problem-solving abilities.

SUPW is a tool for inculcating Gandhian values, *viz.*, truth, non-violence, self-reliance, dignity of labour, co-operation and classless society, etc.

**Recommendations for SUPW**

The contents of SUPW should be based on the needs of the child, the school and the community. So it has a very flexible curriculum. The problem-solving approach should be adopted. SUPW is 'education in and through' work. It involves effective as well as cognitive and psycho-motor learning.

Schools should set up their own workshops and farms. Provision should gradually be made making proper materials and tools available in time. Provision should also be made for the repair and maintenance of the tools and equipments.

The committee has given the following recommendations for the successful implementation of the programme :

(i) Properly skilled teachers should be appointed.

(ii) There should be provision for the part-time employment of skilled personnel for different activities.

(iii) In-service training programmes should be developed by SCERT and State Institutes of Education.

(iv) Teacher Training Colleges in collaboration with NCERT can produce course materials.

## CO-EDUCATION

**Meaning**

Secondary Education Commission defines co-education as 'the education of boys and girls on a footing of equality in the same institution.' Co-education does not mean just the admission of girls into boys' schools or *vice versa*. Co-education is the education of boys and girls together in the same class of a school. Thus Co-education means education of the children of both the sexes in the same institution with full freedom to mix with each other. Co-educational institutions can play a significant part in turning out good and healthy citizens for our country.

**History**

In the West there was co-education in ancient Greece and Rome. Pestalozzi gave a powerful impetus to co-education. In the U.S.A. practically the entire system of schools is co-educational. There are some instances which show that co-education prevailed in ancient India. But gradually it disappeared because of social and political changes. Because of Purdah system there was no co-education in Muslim period. Even women education was not much favoured. During the British period some parents with progressive attitude started sending their daughters to boys' school. By 1947, 53% of the school going girls were studying in boys' school. After independence, co-education in India was largely for administrative convenience and not for educational advantage.

**Objections to Co-Education at Secondary Stage**

Co-education at secondary stage is beset with various problems as this stage corresponds to the period of adolescence. The objections to co-education at this stage are based on the following grounds :

1. *Physiological* : From physiological point of view there are marked differences between boys and girls during this period. Girls mature more rapidly than boys. They are more susceptible to strain and fatigue. On the other hand, boys have a greater capacity for physical and mental strain. Thus, there can be no uniform programme of physical and mental activities.

2. *Psychological* : The psychological differences are related to the intellectual abilities, emotional development, temperament, and interests. Achievement in examinations shows that there is, by and large, no need for differentiated curricula. There seems to be no appreciable difference in the intellectual capacity of the two sexes. Boys, however, have more bent towards abstract reasoning and mathematics, and girls towards concrete processes.

Greater consideration must, however, be given to the differences in emotional make up and the temperamental qualities. These differences lead to the differences in attitudes and interest. Girls attach greater importance to feelings and sentiments. They have a greater sense of responsibility.

3. *Moral*. Boys and girls attain puberty during this period which is accompanied by deep emotional disturbances. They are extremely susceptible to sex appeal and the morals are exposed to risks.

4. *Disciplinary*. So far as school discipline is concerned, it is claimed that girls exercise a chastening influence on boys who shed their roughness of behaviour and language. Girls gain added dignity. Each sex attempts to appear at its best. In view of the different temperamental and emotional make-up, differential disciplinary treatment would be required for the two sexes. Under a uniform code of discipline, the girls are likely to suffer more.

5. *Sociological*. Fundamentally, the problem of co-education of adolescents is a sociological problem. The women's place in Indian society has been that of the mistress of the home. She has been the conserver of ancient culture and religion.

The emerging social order and awakened political consciousness in India are fast breaking down the social and religious restrictions of ages. The nation expects her women folk to share in the social and cultural inheritance and upsurge.

**Advantages of Co-Education**

(1) It is psychologically very sound. It removes false complexes in both boys and girls.

(2) It is most economical. The country cannot afford to have separate medical, industrial and technical institutions.

(3) It will lead to greater literacy.

(4) Students can study the characteristics of the opposite sex.

(5) It will lead to healthy competition in studies and co-curricular activities.

(6) Psycho-analysts believe that co-education will reduce mental diseases.

(7) In view of the growing demand for general education and lack of separate institutions, co-education is the only solution of the problem.

(8) It will bring about saner attitude for each other. The boys will learn to respect girls and *vice versa*. Better understanding will take place.

**Disadvantages of Co-education**

(1) Whenever freedom is gained all of a sudden, the result is always riot.

(2) Co-education would mean the same type of education for both boys and girls. As Boys and girls are temperamentally different, education must be different from each other.

(3) There are some subjects which cannot be taught together especially Biology and Poetry.

(4) Their vocations in life are different and this points out to the need for totally different types of education for them.

(5) Mixing of sexes at the adolescent stage when sex urge is at its highest pitch, is not advisable.

(6) Co-educational institutions create many problems of discipline.

(7) Emotional disturbances will take place as they are exposed to sex appeal and morals are at risk.

(8) Under a uniform code of conduct and discipline girls are likely to suffer more.

In conclusion it may be said that co-education is desirable at the primary level and at advanced university stage. But it is desirable to have separate schools for boys and girls at secondary level.

**Precautions in Co-education**

Where co-educational schools are unavoidable for some reason or other, the following precautions can be followed to make it successful :

(1) The staff must be composed of both men and women.

(2) In addition to common activities, arrangements should be made for suitable co-curricular activities, suited to girls.

(3) Special amenities should be provided for girls, like retiring rooms, sanitary conveniences and separate playgrounds.

(4) There should be provision for special subjects for girls such as Home Craft, Drawing, Music, House-hold Arithmetic, Dancing, etc.

(5) There should be separate medical facilities for girls.

(6) Co-operative activities should be encouraged instead of competition.

(7) Equal importance should be given to boys and girls.

(8) A lady should be the head of such an institution.

**View of the Education Commission (1964-66)**

As public opinion is generally not in favour of co-education at the secondary stage the following steps may be taken in places where separate schools are not financially feasible :

(1) Women teachers should be appointed.

(2) There should be separate hostels for girls and transport may also be arranged for them.

(3) Special schoolship may be given for girls.

(4) Part-time and vocational education should be developed for girls.

## QUESTIONS FOR EXERCISE

1. Describe the nature of organization and form of secondary education in India. What reforms will you suggest in the same and why?
2. What are the main problems of secondary education? How can the problems of aims and useful curriculum be tackled?
3. How can the administration and finance of secondary education be improved?
4. What is the utility and problem of multipurpose schools?
5. What reforms will you suggest in the current examination system and why?
6. How can the supervision system of secondary education be improved?

# 15

# PROBLEMS OF DIVERSIFICATION OF SECONDARY EDUCATION COURSES

During the British days secondary education was patterned by the Government keeping in view its own administrative necessities. Hence the narrow and one-sided aim of secondary education was as follows :

1. To organize secondary education in such a manner as to produce clerks for carrying out day-to-day routine matters in the office.

2. The students at the secondary level may acquire such a proficiency that they may complete university courses if they so desire.

While the implementation of the above aims helped the British administration in the country, it did irrepairable harm to the nation. With the expansion of secondary education the number of unemployed youths increased and the universities became overcrowded. Secondary curriculum was mainly literary. It lacked vocational, industrial, technical and scientific subjects. The medium of instruction was English. Some Indian languages and optional subjects, too, could be offered. Science was kept in the optional group. The two World Wars had adverse impacts on British. The British government in India became indifferent to the problem of education in the country. Though commissions on education were appointed but their recommendations were never fully implemented. Basic Education Scheme was framed under the guidance of M.K. Gandhi but the government did not implement it fully.

### ACHARYA NARENDRA DEO COMMITTEE, 1939

British government appointed a committee under the chairmanship of Acharya Narendra Deo. It suggested diversification of the secondary school curriculum keeping in view the individual interests of students. It insisted that the curriculum should be practical, useful and realistic to life-situations. It divided the curriculum into the following four groups :

1. Literary group.

2. Scientific group.

3. Constructive group.

4. Aesthetic or Fine Arts group.

## SECONDARY EDUCATION IN INDEPENDENT INDIA

After the Second World War defects of secondary education were realised. The Government of Independent India diverted its attention towards reforms of secondary education. It decided to implement more widely the recommendations of the Acharya Narendra Deo Committee Report. In 1948 the Tarachand Committee was appointed for suggesting reforms in secondary education.

### Tarachand Committee of 1948

It gave the following suggestions :

1. Secondary education should be multilateral.
2. A commission should be appointed to look into the problems of secondary education and suggest reforms.
3. The unilateral secondary schools should not be neglected.

In 1952-53 another Committee was appointed under the chairmanship of Acharya Narendra Deo.

### Acharya Narendra Deo Committee of 1952-53

It gave the following suggestions :

1. Multi-purpose schools should be established for catering to the needs and aptitudes and abilities of various students.
2. Secondary education should be made more usefully making the curriculum more practical.
3. Keeping in view the development of the country provision for technical education should be made in the secondary curriculum.
4. Guidance and psychological bureaus should be opened for psychological tests and guidance of students.

In order to further elaborate the above suggestions the Secondary Education Commission popularly known as Mudaliar Commission, was appointed under the chairmanship of Dr. Mudaliar.

### Mudaliar Commission (1952-53)

It looked into the whole problem of secondary education for the entire country and a gave following recommendations :

1. *Diversification of Courses.* For diversification of courses, the Commission made two main groups — Compulsory subjects and optional subjects. Seven sub-groups were made of the optional subjects. A student could take any sub-group for study according to his interests, needs and abilities.

2. *Compulsory Subjects :*

A. *Language Study.* (1) Regional language or mother tongue and any language allied with a classical language.

(2) Any one of the following languages :

(i) Any classical language.

(ii) Hindi is already offered then any other Indian language.

(iii) Advanced English (for those who have studied only General English earlier).

(iv) Elementary English (for those who will start its study at the secondary stage).

(v) Any foreign language alongwith English.

(vi) Hindi (for those whose mother tongue is not Hindi).

B. (1) Mathematics (2) General Science (3) A general elementary course of Sociology for the first two or three years.

C. *Any one of the following crafts* :

1. Carpentary.
2. Gardening.
3. Printing.
4. Spinning and weaving.
5. Modelling.
6. Workshop experiments.
7. Tailoring.
8. Embroidery.
9. Metal work.

3. *Optional Subjects* : The Commission classified the optional subjects into the following seven groups. A student could chose any three subjects from any group :

(A) *Science Group*

1. Chemistry.
2. Physics.
3. Zoology or Physiology and Hygiene.
4. Mathematics.
5. Geography.

(B) *Humanity Group*

1. Mathematics
2. Home Science
3. Music
4. Geography
5. History

6. Economics
7. Civics
8. One of the languages included from the compulsory subjects or any classical language
9. Psychology or Logic.

(C) *Home Science Group* (for girls students)

1. Home Management and Home Nursing.
2. Home Economics.
3. Maternity and Child Welfare.
4. Nutrition and Cookery.

(D) *Commerce Group*

1. Commercial Geography or Economics and Civics.
2. Commercial Practice.
3. Shorthand and Type writing.
4. Book Keeping.

(E) *Technological Group*

1. Applied Science.
2. Elements of Electrical Engineering.
3. Geometrical Drawing and Applied Mathematics.
4. Elements of Mechanical Engineering.

(F) *Agricultural Group.* Including Subjects relating to agriculture were placed into this.

(G) *Fine Arts Group*

1. Painting.
2. Modelling.
3. Drawing and Engraving.
4. Dance.
5. Music.
6. History of Arts.

## NEED OF DIVERSIFICATION OF COURSES

1. **Solution of the Problem of Unemployment.** Unilateral education is never good because in it the students are compelled to offer only a few prescribed subjects. As the prevailing secondary education did not prepare the youth for any vocation the student is not self-dependent after getting secondary education. In the multi-purpose schools the students will have choices of various types of vocational, commercial, agricultural, fine arts, home science and general science subjects. This

was not possible in an ordinary secondary school. Multipurpose schools make students self-dependent in areas of their own choice. The Secondary Education Commission (1952-53) suggested various subject-groups according to the varying interests of different students. This diversification of courses developed the individual skills of students and goes a long way towards solving the problem of unemployment.

2. **Emphasis on Dignity of Labour :** In the current system of secondary education, a student was not required to do any manual work. He concentrated mainly on mental work. This developed in him an attitude of indifference for any type of manual labour. He thought that a work involving manual labour is below his dignity. The diversification of courses offered the students opportunities for various types of manual work to develop in them an attitude of love for manual work.

3. **Helpful in Earning a Living :** Bookish education does not provide many jobs, it creates unemployment. The secondary school passed youths remain unemployed. They cannot run their own trade or industry, as they have not learnt any trade. Diversification of curriculum offered an opportunity to learn some trade and earn a living after being educated.

4. **A Check on Wastage :** Unilateral education makes many students indifferent to education. They face failures and their time, money and energy are wasted. But when the courses are diversified, the students get varying opportunities of development according to their tastes and aptitudes. It creates interest in them. They devote themselves to the education they are getting according to their interests. Thus there is less wastage of money, time and energy.

5. **Developing an Attitude for Good Citizenship :** By the diversification of courses the student gets an opportunity to obtain knowledge about opportunity to general science and social studies while in the effort to acquire some useful vocational skill. It develops in them good social and moral traits, because they feel that education has made them useful citizens.

6. **Cultural Development :** Cultural development accelerates with the continual development of science and other types of knowledge. Diversification of courses helped the student to acquire a cultural level worthy of a human being. He assimilated in his traditions the technological and scientific knowledge that he acquires. This furthers his cultural advancement.

## USES OF DIVERSIFICATION OF COURSES

1. **Natural Educational Opportunities for Students :** Through diversification the students get opportunities for studying courses according to their interests and capacities. This promotes their natural development. The students feel that they have well utilizing their time, money and energy. They are able to learn the art of some trade or vocation.

2. **Subjects of Study According to Physical and Mental Ability :** Through diversification, the student is able to choose subjects according to his physical and mental ability. This is not possible in unilateral system of education.

3. **Development of Personality :** Diversification of courses provided varied opportunities to students for acquiring various types of useful experiences which may help them in the practical affairs of life. This was helpful in the all-round development of personality, not possible in the unilateral system.

4. **Better Adjustment with the Environment :** Development of science and technology lead to an evitable change in the attitude of the individual. This change demands new modes of adjustment. The diversified courses are prone to provide new opportunities for acquiring new approaches to various life situations. They are helpful in effecting better adjustment with one's environment.

5. **Meeting of Social Obligations :** Diversification of courses enables the students to acquire those skills which may help them to fulfil their social obligation, because these skills will make them such self-dependent citizens who are conscious of their duties and responsibilities.

6. **Preparation of Skilful Workers :** India is a developing country. Several types of skilful workers are needed for many development schemes. The diversification of courses prepares a good background for training these workers.

## QUESTIONS FOR EXERCISE

1. What is diversification of courses? Why is it necessary at the secondary education level?
2. How has the Acharya Narendra Deo Committee of 1952-53 emphasised diversification of courses?
3. How has the Secondary Education Commission of 1952-53 planned to diversify courses at the secondary school level?
4. Discuss the needs and uses of diversification of courses?

# 16

# PROBLEMS OF MULTI-PURPOSE SCHOOLS

Secondary Education Commission (1952-53) emphasised the opening of multi-purpose schools to make secondary education more purposeful and useful for practical affairs in life. The Commission outlined the form of these schools. It suggested compulsory and optional subjects for it. The optional subjects were classified into seven groups.

## IMPORTANCE AND NEED

The system of education as developed by the British Government in India was not useful for the individual and society. After achieving independence, Indian leaders took positive steps for reforms of education, including opening of multi-purpose schools. These schools have been considered important for the following reasons :

1. **Continuation of Basic Education** : At the primary stage the children are generally given Basic education. At the secondary stage this basic education is completely abandoned. The multipurpose schools continue the form and spirit of Basic education further. Various types of industrial, commercial and technical subjects have been included in these schools. Such a secondary school will help the children to further develop the skills that they have acquired at the Basic stage.

2. **Education According to Individual Differences** : The boys and girls seeking admission to secondary schools have varying interests and abilities. Some have aptitude for the study of science others show inclination for humanities or commercial subjects and so on. The multipurpose schools make provision for catering to all these individual differences. Such a provision is not found in the current secondary schools. The students have only limited subjects to study whether they have any interest for the same or not. Thus the multi-purpose schools are more advantageous.

3. **Meeting the Needs of the Adolescent** : As the boys and girls are not sure about their interests and aptitudes during adolescence, they are in great need of guidance, which is not found in the current secondary schools. In the multi-purpose schools many of the psychological and actual needs pertaining to success are met saving the student from wrong selection of subjects. As the students have many options before them they may choose subjects of their own inclinations and interests. This promotes natural development.

4. **Dignity of Labour** : In the existing secondary schools, the students are mainly concerned with mental work. As they have nothing to do with manual work they develop complexes regarding it and consider it below their dignity. In the multi-purpose schools, as the students have to do some sort of manual work in the workshop they become more practical and develop a sense of dignity of labour.

5. **Vocational Self-Dependence** : The prevailing secondary schools, as we have already remarked in the foregoing pages, have added to the growth of the problem of unemployment. When the secondary school passed boys do not get any job and try to seek admission to universities. If they are not admitted, they roam about on streets as social nuisance. But the multi-purpose school passed students have already acquired some vocational skills and they are able to earn their living.

## AIMS AND OBJECTIVES

1. **To achieve Self-dependence** : In the multi-purpose schools some craft has been made compulsory in order to make the student self-dependent for his living.

2. **To Achieve Development According to Individual Differences** : Out of the seven groups of the optional subjects, the student is made free to choose his group according to his interests and aptitudes. Thus his development is assured according to his individual differences.

3. **To Remove the Defects of Unilateral Education :** As the multi-purpose schools provide for multi-lateral education the defects of unilateral education is removed.

4. **To Develop Democratic Citizenship** : The multi-purpose schools provide opportunities for studying general, practical and experimental subjects which develop rational, social and moral virtues.

5. **To Develop Practical and Full Personality** : By giving them useful and practical education the multi-purpose schools make the students self-confident and self-dependent. These schools not only make the students artisans, but help them to become fully develop personalities.

## UTILITY OF MULTI-PURPOSE SCHOOLS

1. **Diversification of courses** : Due to the provision for the study of a number of optional subjects according to the individual differences of students, the multi-purpose schools are much more useful than the existing secondary schools.

2. **Community Spirit** : In the multi-purpose schools children of various classes and castes work together in workshops and laboratories. This feature develops in them a feeling ofbrotherhood and equality. A spirit of co-operation and communal unity is also generated.

3. **No Problems due to Transfer** : There is no difficulty of transfer in these schools, because the courses of all the multi-purpose schools are the same. After transfer a student may select subjects of his own choice in another multipurpose school.

4. **Learning Livlihood :** In multi-purpose schools the student acquires some vocational skill which may help him in later life in earning a living. Thus the problem of unemployment does not come before him.

5. **Dignity of Labour :** The students learn the virtue of dignity of labour in these schools, as they have to do some manual work every day. The students learn some handicrafts, sculpture or some other vocational skill. Vocationally fit for some trade or business they contribute to national prosperity.

6. **Multisided Development of Personality :** Because of the varied courses of study in the multi-purpose schools there is a great opportunity for the all round development of personality. Thus the students are able to acquire many cultural, social and moral traits.

7. **Democratic Citizenship :** These schools work in a democratic atmosphere because of their special features. Hence, they develop virtues of democratic citizenship in the students.

**Development of Multi-purpose Schools**

In India efforts have been made from the year 1954 to open some multi-purpose schools. At first some high schools were converted into multi-purpose schools. About 250 multi-purpose schools were opened during the First Five Year Plan. This number was to be raised to 1150, in the Second Five Year Plan but the target could not be achieved. During the Third Five Year Plan it was decided to meet the target of at least 1,000. During the Fourth and Fifth Plans, the government was not enthusiastic to open many multi-purpose schools. So far the multi-purpose schools have been able to provide for only any two of the seven groups of courses.

**Problems of Multi-purpose Schools**

Following are the problems of multi-purpose schools which have obstructed their growth :

1. **Lack of Training of Teachers** : The multi-purpose schools need teachers well versed in their own subjects and trained in some vocation, sculpture, handicraft or technical subjects. Indian Universities and Teacher's Training Institutions are not preparing such teachers. The multi-purpose schools are not working well due to lack of suitably trained teachers.

2. **Unattractive Pay Scales** : Persons trained in some technical subject are more easily able to get jobs carrying attractive emoluments. Such trained persons are not attracted towards teaching in multi-purpose schools which offer poorer emoluments. Hence, these schools do not get suitable teachers. The condition of privately managed multi-purpose schools is more deplorable, because there the teachers are denied many necessary facilities and are given poorer salaries under pressures exercised by managing committees.

Therefore the emoluments of teachers must be attractive. Teachers should also be given the facilities of residence, medical aid and education of their wards. The government should itself run these multi-purpose schools, unless there are some very efficient and well-managed voluntary organizations coming forward to shoulder the responsibility of running these schools.

3. **Non-availability of Text-books** : Suitable text-books are not available according to the technical and science courses of multi-purpose schools. The existing books are of very poor quality. As most of them are written in English many of them are not useful for most of the students who are not very proficient in English. The government should produce good text-books for multi-purpose schools through its text-book committees. It should also get some good text-books translated into Indian languages. But translated by non-subject persons lack the spirit and soul of the subject. This practice must be discouraged.

4. **Unsuitable Time Table** : Due to the diversified courses and lack of efficient teachers no suitable time-table is prepared in any multi-purpose school. The government should see that a suitable time-table is run in the multi-purpose schools.

5. **Lack of Opening of New Multi-purpose Schools and converting Old Ones** : The Government had planned that some new multi-purpose schools would be opened and some existing secondary schools be converted into multi-purpose models. The government however, did not decide about the places of new ones or about the schools that would be changed into the multi-purpose patterns. During the Second Five Year Plan about 1,000 multi-purpose schools were opened, but becuase of the above mentioned inadequacies they could not be run successfully. In fact, only good schools should be converted. New schools should be opened only at those places where good buildings are available alongwith other facilities. Otherwise, multi-purpose schools will serve no purpose.

6. **Impediments in Working out the Vocational Curriculum** : Diversification of the curriculum and training in practice have been the main attraction of the Multi-purpose schools. For practical teaching suitable workshops and laboratories are necessary which have been difficult to provide in the multi-purpose schools. Because of paucity of funds the government, too, has not taken much interest in it. Under the circumstances, nearby industries should be used as workshops for giving practical experience to the students concerned.

7. **Difficulties of Selecting the Curriculum** : As there are several subjects in the multi-purpose schools, it is difficult to arrange teaching for the various groups of the courses. In the established multi-purpose schools are taught only two groups of courses in each. Thus, the utility of the multi-purpose schools is not fully explored. The All India Board of Secondary Education has prescribed certain groups for some States. But the local needs have been ignored in the assignment. No similarity is found in the prescribed courses and teaching aspects in the multi-purpose schools of the various States. In order to minimise the above difficulties, it is better to teach three groups in each multi-purpose school. There should be similarity in the courses in all the States. The local needs should be duly considered in organizing the teaching aspects in the school so that the local public take interest in them.

8. **Discontent among the Guardians** : The guardians become discontented when their children do not get education according to their interests and needs, and are removed from schools. Some guardians advise their wards to select a particular

group without considering their interests, resulting into failures on the part of the students. There should be guidance clinics for advising the students to choose suitable group of courses.

## QUESTIONS FOR EXERCISE

1. Why have the multi-purpose schools been established? Discuss their need and importance.
2. What are the aims of multi-purpose schools? How far have they been realised?
3. What are the problems of multi-purpose schools? How can they be solved?

# 17

# PROBLEMS OF CURRICULUM CONSTRUCTION

## MEANING OF CURRICULUM

Etymologically the term "Curriculum" is derived from the Latin word 'Currere' which means 'run'. Thus curriculum means 'a course to be run for reaching a certain goal'. In recent years the term curriculum has come to mean all the planned activities and experiences which are available to students under the direction of the school. In the words of Kerney and Cook, "It is a complex of more or less planned or controlled conditions under which students learn to behave and to behave in their various ways. In it, new behaviour may be acquired, present behaviour may be modified, maintained or eliminated; and desirable behaviour may become both persistent and viable." Curriculum includes both the curricular and co-curricular activities. It is the sum total of good learning experiences that the students have in order to achieve the goals of education which determine the direction of these experiences.

## OBJECTIVES OF THE CURRICULUM

(1) To draw out, cultivate, excite and inspire the full development of each student.

(2) To create an atmosphere in which students will learn to think critically and constructively and seek truth and solve problems.

(3) To help students in establishing values through intimate acquaintance with the humanities, the arts, the natural sciences, the social sciences and religion.

(4) To develop the character of students — integrity, honesty, judgement, co-operation, friendliness and goodwill.

(5) To prepare men and women for citizenship in a democratic society where freedom and liberty go hand in hand with law and justice and where responsibility, national and international, is a characteristic of the individual.

(6) To meet the needs not only of more students, but of students with a wide range of ability, aptitudes and interests.

## CURRICULUM AND EDUCATION

Education has to integrate the two processes — the individual process and the social process. In the former sense, it is identical with individual growth and the development of latent power in the child. From the latter point of view, it is identical with socialisation, adjustment to environment and imbibing of culture. Both the processes are integrated.

While education is a process, curriculum is a means to the process. While education is learning, curriculum signifies situations for learning. While education deals with 'how' and 'when' curriculum deals with 'what'. While education is the product curriculum is the plan.

## FLEXIBILITY OF THE CURRICULUM

1. **According to Different Communities** : Curriculum is not rigid and static. It is dynamic and flexible. It changes constantly with the changing needs and ideals of society. In Independent India Curriculum in schools can never remain the same as it used to be in schools during the British regime or in Gurukula in ancient India. Curriculum in elementary and secondary schools in England is not the same as in India, in the U.S.A., in Russia or in Japan. As the demands, ideals and aspirations of different social groups differ widely so curriculum offers a wide contrast.

In India, there are a large number of communities, living in the hilly area, the plain area, the desert area, the plateau area and coastal area — all having their own peculiar individuality, environment, customs and needs. Therefore, the same curriculum cannot be forced upon all, irrespective of their needs and environment. It must differ from locality to locality and from society to society.

2. **According to Individual Capacities** : The learning capacity of children, differs from individual to individual. The activities through which knowledge is expected to be gained, also differ according to the resources of different schools and the characteristics of pupils, studying therein. So the curriculum may also vary from school to school, from grade to grade and even from scholar to scholar. According to modern trends in the eudcational process, the curriculum "can be outlined only in a general way, allowing enough scope for variation within the general framework."

## BASIC PRINCIPLES OF CURRICULUM CONSTRUCTION

The following basic principles of curriculum are recommended by the Secondary Education Commission (1952-53) :

1. **Totality of Experiences** : Curriculum does not mean only the academic subjects traditonally taught in the school, but it includes the totality of experiences that a pupil receives through the manifold activities that go on in the schools, in the classroom, library, laboratory, workshop, playgrounds and in the numerous informal contacts between teacher and pupils.

2. **Variety and Elasticity** : There should be enough variety and elasticity in the curriculum to allow for individual differences and adaptation to individual

needs and interests. Any attempt to force uncongenial subjects and studies on children unfit to take them up, is bound to lead to a sense of frustration and to hinder their normal development.

3. **Related to Community Life** : Curriculum must be vitally and organically related to community life. It should give an important place to productive work which is the backbone of organised human life. The teacher should build up in the minds of the students a lively sense ofbeing an integral part of the local community. The local community should be enabled to realise that the child is a vital and an invaluable part of its life.

4. **Training for Work and Leisure** : The curriculum should be designed to train the students not only for work but also for leisure. A variety of activities, social, aesthetic, sports, etc., should be introduced in the school. This is recommended to make school life pleasant and meaningful for the student here and now. The cultivation of varied interests and different hobbies provides excellent training for leisure, which forms an important and quantitatively large area of every individual's life.

5. **Integration** : The curriculum should not be split up into a number of isolated, uncoordinated, water-tight subjects. Subjects should be inter-related and within each subject, the contents should be envisaged as "broad fields" unit which can be correlated better with life rather than narrow items of information.

## CURRICULUM RECONSTRUCTION IN INDIA

In free India number of attempts were made to renovate and revamp the curriculum to make it suitable to the growing needs, aspirations and demands of a modernising egalitarian society.

### Basic Education 1937

The first major attempt in curriculum reconstruction in India was made in 1937 when Gandhiji propounded the idea of Basic Education. Dr. Zakir Hussain Committee elaborated it in the scheme of studies of Basic Education. After independence the Basic System of education was accepted as the national system of education at the primary stage. The entire instructional programme was to centre round a craft. Besides craft, physical and social environment were also considered to be important factors in the curriculum. Correlation of various subjects was to be achieved through craft and social and physical environment.

### University Education Commission (1949)

In 1948, a year after the attainment of independence, a University Education Commission was set up under the Chairmanship of Dr. S. Radhakrishnan which recommended the adoption of Three-Year degree course and suggested suitable curriculum for this stage, in 1949.

## SECONDARY EDUCATION COMMISSION (1952-53)

With Dr. A. Lakshmanaswamy Mudaliar as the Chairman the Secondary

Education Commission made a faithful analysis of the curriculum, revealed its defects, formulated principles and suggested the needed reform.

**Defects of Present Curriculum**

The following are the main defects of the curriculum according to the Commission :

(i) The present curriculum is narrowly conceived.

(ii) It is bookish and theoretical.

(iii) It is overcrowded, without providing rich and significant contents.

(iv) It makes inadequate provision for practical and other kinds of activities which should reasonably find room in it, if it is to educate the whole of the personality.

(v) It does not cater to the various needs and capacities of the adolescents.

(vi) It is dominated too much by examinations.

(vii) It does not include technical and vocational subjects which are so necessary in training the students to take part in the industrial and economic development of the country.

Thus traditional curriculum is 'narrowly conceived, unpsychologically planned and ineffectively executed'. It leads only to intellectual development at the cost of physical, social, moral, emotional, aesthetic and spiritual development. So it is inadequate, unsatisfactory, uninspring and unscientific.

**Recommendations**

The Secondary Education Commission realised that there was a great need for providing Technical Education in the country. Therefore, it recommended Multi-purpose Schools. It also made recommendations regarding the diversification of the secondary stage in education. A core curriculum at the Higher Secondary stage was also recommended.

1. **Curriculum at the Middle Stage**. After stating the basic principles of curriculum construction, the Secondary Education Commission divided the schools into two main categories. The first category includes Middle Schools, schools which cater generally for the pupils of the age group of 11 to 13. The second category includes High Schools and Higher Secondary, a four-year course. The age-range of pupils in High School will approximately be 14 to 16 and in Higher Secondary School 14 to 17.

The real aim at this stage is "to give the child an appreciation of human achievement in different fields, to widen his outlook and to broaden his sympathies" and not specialisation in any particular branch of learning.

The middle school stage is a continuation of the primary school stage. Since the special function of curriculum at this stage is to introduce the pupils 'in a general way' to certain broad fields of human knowledge and activity, it should include language and literature, social studies, natural science and mathematics. Language will include Mother tongue, Hindi and English.

For the development of the emotional side of human mind, music, art and crafts are recommended. For the proper physical development of pupils, physical education with all its activities, is recommended.

Keeping in view these considerations, the following was suggested as the broad outline of the middle school curriculum :

1. Languages (Regional, National and International).
2. Social Studies.
3. General Studies.
4. Mathematics.
5. Arts and Music.
6. Crafts.
7. Physical Education.

2. **The High School and Higher Secondary School Stages** : At the high school stage, the special abilities and interests of the pupils take a definite form and so a lot of choice should be given to them to choose the subjects from a wide variety. Again at this stage some opportunity for preparing for a vocation to be adopted at the end of the school course should be given. The education will have a vocational bias also. Hence, besides some amount of general education, some training of a technical type which will lead to either an independent vocation or to a specialised course of study at the University, should be imparted. There should be wide choice in the course of technical type, and these should be begun a little later than the beginning of general education course which may be the continuation of the middle school course. The general education course will be the core-curriculum, and the technical courses, formed into groups, will be the Electives.

The Secondary Education Commission gives justification for the inclusion of the following various subjects :

(i) *Mother-tongue and one other language (Hindi or English)* : These are essential to meet the requirements of the pupils for daily communication and inter-state communication.

(ii) *Social Studies and General Sciences* : These are of a general nature with the purpose of explaining the social and physical forces that shape the lives of the people. Craft is to be included for its special importance for the develpment of skill.

(iii) *The Elective Groups* : These are Humanities, Sciences, Technical, Commercial, Agriculture, Fine Arts and Home Science. These seven groups would provide enough scope for full freedom of choice for pupils with different aptitudes. The diversified curriculum will lead to specialised educational courses and vocations in future. It will begin from Class X, and this is the right time for the differentiation of curriculum.

The curriculum as suggested by the Secondary Education Commission was introduced in majority of States, and multipurpose and unipurpose schools were started. High schools were converted at various places into Higher Secondary Schools. The suggested curriculum was introduced with some modification.

As by this time, special abilities and interests of pupils would take definite form the Commission recommended varied courses, with sufficient latitude for choice. The main aim at this stage is to provide suitable scope for the development of special interests of pupils.

As for the majority of pupils this stage is the final and conclusive stage of their education, the curriculum should be vocational-biased, along with providing a reasonable amount of general education. So it would include certain "core" or compulsory subjects common for all, as well as the specialised study of certain optional subjects to be chosen from a very wide range, according to individual aptitude and inclination. Thus curriculum would consist of the following :

A. (i) Mother-tongue and a Regional language or a composite course of the Mother-tongue and a Classical language.

(ii) One other language, to be chosen from among the following :

(a) Hindi (for those whose mother-tongue is not Hindi).

(b) Elementary English (for those who have not studied English in the middle stage).

(c) Advanced English (for those who have studied English in the earlier stage).

(d) A modern Indian language (other than Hindi).

(e) A modern foreign language (other than English).

(f) A classical language.

B. (i) Social Studies — general course (for the first two years only).

(ii) General Science including Mathematics — general course (for the first two years only).

C. One craft, to be chosen from the following list (which may be added to, according to local needs) :

(a) Spinning and Weaving.

(b) Wood work

(c) Metal work.

(d) Gardening.

(e) Tailoring.

(f) Typography.

(g) Workshop practice.

(h) Sewing, Needle-work and Embroidery.

(i) Modelling.

D. Three subjects from one of the following groups :

Group 1. (Humanities) —

(a) A classical language or a third language from A (ii) not already taken.

(b) History

(c) Geography

(d) Elements of Economics and Civics

(e) Elements of Psychology and Logic

(f) Mathematics

(g) Music

(h) Democratic Science.

Group 2. (Sciences) —

(a) Physics

(b) Chemistry

(c) Biology

(d) Geography

(e) Mathematics

(f) 'Elements of Physiology and (Hygiene not to be taken with Biology).

Group 3. (Technical) —

(a) Applied Mathematics Geometrical Drawing

(b) Applied Science

(c) Elements of Mechanical Engineering

(d) Elements of Electrical Engineering.

Group 4. (Commercial) —

(a) Commercial practice

(b) Book-keeping

(c) Commercial Geography or Elements of Economics and Civics

(d) Shorthand and Typewriting.

Group 5. (Agriculture) —

(a) General Agriculture

(b) Animal Husbandry

(c) Horticulture and Gardening

(d) Agricultural Chemistry and Botany.

Group 6. Fine (Arts) —

(a) History of Art

(b) Drawing and Designing

(c) Modelling

(d) Painting

(e) Music

(f) Dancing.

Group 7. (Home Science) —

(a) Home Economics

(b) Nutrition and Cookery

(c) Mother craft and Child care

(d) House-hold Management and House Nursing.

E. Besides the above, a student may take at his option one additional subject from any of the above group, irrespective of whether or not he has chosen his other option from that particular group.

Thus, the Secondary Education Commission's scheme of curriculum was a great improvement upon the other existing schemes. It provided opportunities for meeting the special abilities, interests and aptitudes of pupils. In addition to this the grouping of subjects, offered them a well thoughout compact and integrated programme of studies.

## THE EDUCATION COMMISSION (1964-66)

For the first time in the educational history of the country, the Government of India decided to review the entire educational structure of the country by setting up the Education Commission 1964-66 under the Chairmanship of Dr. D.S. Kothari.

The Kothari Commission made a detailed survey of the curriculum followed in the country. It came to the conclusion that the curriculum was inadequate, outmoded and not properly designed to the needs of the modern times. There was widespread dissatisfaction with the curriculum due to tremendous expansion of knowledge in recent years. There was a good deal of 'Useless Education Lumber' in the school courses. There was 'an urgent need to raise, up-grade and improve 'the school curriculum'.

### Recommendations

(i) School curriculum should be upgraded through research in curriculum development by University Departments of Education, Colleges of Education and other such agencies. Research is also needed in the preparation of text-books and learning materials.

(ii) The teacher should be oriented to the revised curriculum through 'in-service education'.

(iii) The schools should be free to devise the experiment with new curricula suited to their needs.

(iv) The State Boards of School Education should prepare advanced curricula in all subjects and introduce them in a phased manner in schools.

(v) In general or non-vocational school common curricula of general education should be provided for the first 10 years, and diversification of studies and specialisation should begin only at the Higher Secondary Stage. An unified approach should be made to the curriculum synthesising general education with specialised course.

(vi) The standard of attainment should be clearly defined at the end of each sub-stage.

(vii) Science education should be given special importance. "Science and Mathematics", says the Commission, "should be compulsory in the first 10 years of schooling." Science teaching should be linked with agriculture in the rural areas and with technology in the urban areas.

(viii) The study of Mathematics should be emphasised in view of the importance of qualification on the advent of automation in the scientific and industrial revolution.

(ix) Teaching of Social Studies must be made effective for the development of good citizenship and emotional integration. The syllabus in Social Studies must stress the idea of national unity and the unity of man.

(x) The three language formula should be modified, and a new plan presented. It suggested that three languages (Mother tongue, Hindi and English) should be studied from class VIII, but, not on compulsory basis. A classical language also should be introduced on optional basis from Class VIII.

(xi) Emphasis should be laid on 'Work Experience'. Manual work should be emphasised at all the stages. It may take the form of hand work in lower primary, craft in upper primary, workshop training in lower secondary and experience in school workshop, farm or commercial or industrial establishment at the higher secondary stage.

**Suggestions**

In addition to the above recommendations, the following are also suggested :

(i) Programme of Social Service and participation in community developments should be organised at all levels as suited to the different age-groups.

(ii) Labour and Social Service Camps should be run throughout the year and for this purpose, a special organisation to be set up in each district.

(iii) Physical Education should be provided for the physical fitness and efficiency, mental alertness and the development of certain qualities of character. Hence, physical education programme should be re-examined and re-designed.

(iv) Organised attempt should be made for imparting moral education and inculcating spiritual values in schools through direct and indirect methods with the help of the ethical teachings of great religions.

(v) The Government of India should appoint a committee of experts to survey the present situation of art education, and explore all possibilities for its extension and systematic development. Art Departments should be set up in selected University centres to carry out research in art education. A variety of co-curricular activities should be organised to provide pupils an opportunity for creative self-expression.

(vi) The recommendations of the Hansa Metha Committee should be endorsed that there should be no differentiation of curricula on the basis of sex. Home science should be provided as an optional subject but not made compulsory for girls. Larger provision should be made for music and fine arts; and the study of mathematics and science should be encouraged.

(vii) The essential principle of basic education, namely, productive activity, correlation of curriculum with productive activity and environment and contact with local community should guide and shape the educational system at all levels. No single stage of education should be designated as basic education.

## NATIONAL POLICY ON EDUCATION 1968

The Government of India considered the recommendations of Education Commission and adopted a National Policy on Education in 1968 which identified national goals of education. The policy Resolution stated that the educational system must produce young men and women of character and ability committed to national service and development. The following five goals were clearly mentioned :

1. Relating Education to the Needs of the Society.
2. Promotion of National Integration.
3. Equalisation of Educational Opportunity.
4. Linking Education with Productivity and National Development.
5. Acceleration of Social Transformation.

## 10+2+3 PATTERN

1. **National Policy :** A new programme of curriculum development should be undertaken by the adoption of a broadly uniform pattern populary known as 10+2+3 pattern throughout the country. This pattern meant 10 years of general education followed by diversified Higher Secondary Education and then 2 or 3 years of University Education.

2. **NCERT :** In 1975, the NCERT published an "Approach Paper" which outlined the salient features of the proposed model curriculum for classes I to X. There was a nation-wide consultation and ultimately, there was "the curriculum for the 10-year schools."

3. **Ishwar Bhai Patel Committee :** In 1977, the Government of India appointed a Committee known as the Ishwar Bhai Patel Committee to review the working of the new pattern. It suggested certain modifications in the scheme in the

light of its working during the previous years. One of the important recommendations regarding curriculum reconstruction was the introduction of the concept "Socially Useful Productive Work" (SUPW) at the High School stage.

4. **Plus 2 Committee** : In 1977, another committee known as Plus 2 Committee was appointed under the Chairmanship of Dr. Malcolm S. Adiseshiah, the then Vice-Chancellor of University of Madras to review the curriculum of the Plus 2 stage of school education with special reference to vocationalization of education.

5. **National Review Committee** : The following are some of the major recommendations of the National Review Committee :

1. Learning must be based on work either through what the Ishwar Bhai Patel Committee calls Socially Useful Productive Work (SUPW), or through vocationalised course.

2. Vocational course should be in agricultural and related rural occupational areas and in managerial, commercial, health and paramedical vocation.

3. The Higher Secondary Stage should comprise of a General Education Spectrum and a Vocational Spectrum.

4. The curriculum should be so streamlined that the courses lend themselves to imparting instruction in terms of well connected models to enable the students to choose and combine them according to their needs.

5. Semester pattern and credit systems may be introduced in classes XI and XII.

## CURRICULUM OF HIGHER SECONDARY EDUCATION

1. **The General Education Spectrum.** It aims to prepare the students for university education in the arts or science or for professional studies. This is the bridge facet of the Plus 2 stage, the Committee has recommended :

| | *Course* | *Time Distribution* |
|---|---|---|
| (i) | Languages | 15% |
| (ii) | Socially Useful Productive Work | 15% |
| (iii) | Electives (three) | 70% |

It is recognised that this general scheme must be applied with a certain amount of flexibility, allowing individual States and Territories and even individual schools to adopt the courses and distribution of time to local conditions and pedagogic perceptions.

2. **Vocationalised Spectrum of the Higher Secondary School.** It is learning of skill or a range of skills through study of technologies related sciences, and farm or other practical work. Since the content and scope of vocationalization must be in conformity with national goals and the specific needs of the local community at every given point of time the vocationalization of Higher Secondary Education, recommended aims for the next five years at increasing the employment potential of the people through education for self-employment, with emphasis on agricultural

and related occupations including tiny, small, cottage and agro-industries and through preparation for specific competencies in different vocations. The Committee has recommended :

| | Course | Time Allocations |
|---|---|---|
| (i) | Languages | 15% |
| (ii) | General Foundation Course | 15% |
| (iii) | Elective Vocational subjects | 70% |

3. **General Foundation Course.** The objectives of the course are to enable the student :

(i) To become aware of the need for rural development and self-employment;

(ii) To understand the place of agriculture in the national economy;

(iii) To develop skills and managerial abilities to run small scale and cottage industries;

(iv) To gain insight into the problem of unemployment, underemployment and economic backwardness of India.

The General Foundation Course is meant to be taught for 2 years, 4 to 5 hours per week. Part A of the course is common to all vocations. From Part B, may be chosen the unit most related to the particular vocation.

Part A : This includes five heads —

(i) Gandhian concept of education;

(ii) Agriculture in the national economy;

(iii) Rural development;

(iv) Problems of urban slums; and

(v) Health, hygiene and sanitation.

Part B : Any one of the 9 sections to be chosen —

(i) Small scale and cottage industries;

(ii) Enterpreneurship;

(iii) Co-operation and credit facilities;

(iv) Marketing;

(v) Sales Promotion;

(vi) Unemployment, underemployment and manpower utilisation in India;

(vii) Human Relations;

(viii) General exposure to world trends and changes; and

(ix) Environmental protection and development.

4. **Elective Vocational Subjects** : Any one to be selected from among the following groups :

(i) Agricultural and related vocations (15)

(ii) Business and office management (8)

(iii) Para-medical (13)

(iv) Educational service (9)

(v) Local body and other services (4)

(vi) Journalism (2)

(vii) Home science related vocations (6)

(viii) Other general services (7).

## QUESTIONS FOR EXERCISE

1. Discuss the meaning and objectives of curriculum.
2. Describe the recommendations of Secondary Education Commission about Curriculum.

# 18

# PROBLEMS OF TEXT-BOOK NATIONALIZATION

### Utility of Text Books

Among the modern educationists there exists a group which has no faith in the utility of text-books. However, none can deny the importance of text-books. Howsoever efficient the teacher may be, he has to take the help of text-books. Neither the teacher can take the place of text-books nor can text-books replace the teacher. Both have their own importance in the field of education. Following are the main utilities of text-books :

(1) They prescribe the limit ofknowledge which is to be imparted to students. They indicate teacher's field of action.

(2) They place facts and figures before the students in a systematic manner.

(3) They help the student to revise and learn their lessons in an orderly manner.

## HISTORY OF TEXT-BOOKS

### Calcutta Education Press

In India the history of text-books is of recent origin. In ancient and mediaeval periods hand written books were prepared on copper plates or leaves of palm trees. With the invention of paper books began to be written on paper. The number of these books was so small that they were not easily available to students. Hence, oral education was in vogue those days. With the establishment of the rule of East India Company, the Britishers set up a printing press named 'Calcutta Education Press' in 1824. The Wood Charter recommended the publication of text-books. Many books were published in the English, Persian and Sanskrit languages. However, no education commission or committee gave constructive suggestions for the improvement of text-books. After 1910 the Indian leaders certainly raised their voice in favour of education. But they did not pay adequate attention to other important aspects of education except the formulation of a good education policy.

**First Narendra Dev Committee (1938-39)**

With the passage of Government of India Act of 1935 and its implementation in 1937 a beginning of self-government was made at the provincial level. The national leaders paid their attention to text-book problem. The first Acharya Narendra Dev Committee 1938-39 (U.P.) gave suggestions for the improvement of text-books. It suggested that they should be rewritten according to the new requirements and developments. The text-books should be edited by a board constituted by the State government. Writers should be asked to prepare text-books under the guidance of this board.

**Central Advisory Board of Education 1943**

In 1943 the Central Advisory Board of Education suggested that text-books should not be changed before a period of three years. The text-books should be available to the students on a reasonable price. Publishers should not be allowed to exploit students. Only reputed publishers should be allowed to publish books. Eminent writers should be encouraged to write them.

**Second Narendra Dev Committee 1953**

The Second Acharya Narendra Dev Committee in independent India in 1953 examined the problem of text-books and suggested following reforms :

1. Only the headmaster and the teacher be authorised to select text-books.
2. The selected text-books should not be changed before a period of three years.
3. Government should make provision for good book.
4. Ample time should be allowed to writers to prepare text-books.
5. Authors of good text-books should be rewarded.
6. The Government should not take upon themselves the responsibility of printing.

**Mudaliar Commission 1952-53**

The Secondary Education Commission (Mudaliar Commission), 1952-53 criticised the prevailing standard of text-books and stressed the need of their improvement.

**International Party 1954**

Under the aegis of Ford Foundation an international party examined some current text-books in 1954. It suggested that the government should frame rules for the preparation of text-books. The writers and publishers should prepare and publish text-books within the framework of these rules. The government should not take the responsibility of preparation of the text-books upon themselves.

**Kothari Commission 1964-66**

The Kothari Commission 1964-66 examined the question of text-books. It observed that eminent scholars did not take interest in writing text-books. The authorities bungle and commit irregularity in selecting text-books. They suggested some research in this field and the publication of text-book by the government themselves.

## DEFECTS IN THE CURRENT TEXT-BOOKS

1. **Mercenary Motive** : The needs and requirements of students of different classes are not taken into consideration. The writers and publishers show more interest in earning money.

2. **Poor Production** : The production of books is very poor. Paper of very poor quality is used. The cover page is not well bound. Stitching is not good.

3. **Theoretical :** The present text-books do not present a subject in relation to practical life. They place knowledge in an uncoordinated manner before the students. The subject thus becomes uninteresting to the students concerned.

4. **Lack of Attention to Requirements** : The writers of text-books generally do not pay attention to the requirements of the students of the standard for which they prepare text-books. Consequently, the text-books are not suitable.

5. **Absense of National Objectives** : The current text-books lack the objective of national integration and international sentiments.

6. **No Attention to Teaching Methods** : No attention is paid to teaching method while preparing text-books. As a result, the teachers fail to derive much help from them.

7. **Defects of Presentation** : Text-books lack illustrations, drawing and relevant instances. So their utility decreases.

8. **Defects of Printing and Language :** There are many printer's devils and defects in language, because they are prepared hurriedly.

## SUGGESTIONS FOR IMPROVEMENT

1. **Govt. Model Text-Books** : The State Government should publish some text-books. They should have a high standard to serve as models for writers and publishers.

2. **Good Presentation** : There should be suitable drawings, illustrations and examples in the text-books in order to make them interesting to students.

3. **Variety.** There should be at least six or seven text-books on each subject. The headmaster and the teacher should jointly select the most suitable book.

4. **No Pressure in Selection** : No pressure should be exerted on the teachers or others in the selection of text-books.

5. **Attention to National Objectives**: Text-books should not contain undesirable remarks on any society, sect, community or religion. They should help in national integration and generate feeling of internationalism.

6. **Eminent Authors** : Eminent scholars should prepare text-books. They

should be rewarded for good books. Scholars should be invited on national level to write text-books on various subjects.

7. **Co-operation of Union and State Governments** : The Union and the State Governments should co-operate for the preparation of text-books of a high order.

8. **Translations :** High class foreign books should also be got translated into Indian languages. This will make available proper and relevant books. This policy must be followed particularly for books on science and technology.

9. **Revision** : Revised edition of text books should be consistently published. A committee should be formed for this purpose.

10. **Government Publications** : There should be a government institution in each State for the preparation and publication of text-books. This body should publish books of a high order on all subjects but publishers should also have a free hand in the matter.

## ARGUMENTS FOR NATIONALIZATION OF TEXT-BOOKS

1. **To Counter Mercenary Motive** : Indian constitution presents free and compulsory education for children upto the age of 14 years. Efforts are afoot in this direction resulting in an increase in the number of students at all stages of education in each State. The continuously rising number of students has created a big demand for text-books. Many incompetent writers and publishers have appeared in the field to exploit this situation. These authors and publishers have started producing text book of a low order with the sole aim of earning money. Thus, the job of publishing books has declined in standard. This unhealthy atmosphere has to be removed. The government should, therefore, itself publish good text-books for different classes.

2. **Basic Books** : In India Basic education has been accepted as the pattern for primary education. This objective remains unachieved in the absence of good and adequate number of text-books. The government have published some basic education books, but greater efforts have to be made which is only possible through nationalization of text-books.

3. **Research Based** : The Government of India may undertake research work for producing good text-books of a higher order. But the publishers cannot be forced to accept the results of these researches. Therefore, the Central or the State governments should themselves undertake the production of text-books through their nationalization.

4. **Easy** : It is easier for the government to produce ideal text-books because it commands the necessary resources for the same. Hence, nationalization is necessary.

5. **National Objectives** : Text-books can help in achieving national integration and in generating the sense of international goodwill. This can only be properly done only by the government. If left to private publishers, there are chances of it being misused in fanning communalism, sectarianism and regionalism etc. Therefore, nationalization of text-books is necessary for the development of the right type of education.

6. **Reasonable Price** : Through nationalization of text-books good books will be available on reasonable price. This will give relief to guardians.

7. **Free Books** : The government can provide books free of charge to poor and deserving students if the production of text-books is nationalized. This will benefit the poor students and it will cost next to nothing to the government.

8. **Books on Optional Subjects** : Publishers are not inclined to publish books on optional subjects, because there are chances of incurring loss as the number of students offering these subjects is not high. Those who try to publish such books go in for it in a casual way. The nationalization of text-books will make books on optional subjects available to students in adequate number, because the object of government is to serve and not earn money.

9. **Uniformity of Standard** : Nationalization will effect uniformity of standard which is lacking in the text-books published by different publishers. The teachers will find out the prescribed curriculum in nationalized text-book.

10. **Revenue** : The government will also get some revenue by nationalizing books. This income may be well utilised in furthering the cause of education. Evidently, nationalization of text-book is a good and useful scheme.

## NATIONALIZATION OF TEXT-BOOKS IN INDIA

Different policies have been adopted in Indian States about the nationalization of text-books. In some States text-books have been completely nationalized and in some partially nationalized. There are also some States which oppose the policy of nationalization. Following is the present condition on this issue :

1. **Andhra Pradesh** : All books upto primary standard of education have been nationalized.

2. **Tamilnadu** : Text-books have been nationalized but the distribution of books has been left in the hands of private book-sellers.

3. **Kerala** : Text books were nationalized in this State. A committee was formed in 1958-59 to find out whether or not this action was taken to strengthen communist ideology in the State. As committee report confirmed that the action was taken to give a boost to communism, nationalization was withdrawn.

4. **Orissa, Maharashtra and Gujarat** : No special efforts have been made in the direction of nationalisation of text-books.

5. **Bihar** : School text-books have been completely nationalized. The profit derived by the sale of text-books is distributed among the poor students.

6. **Punjab** : School text-books have been fully nationalized.

7. **Uttar Pradesh** : Almost all the text-books on compulsory subjects upto Junior High School standard have been nationalized.

8. **Rajasthan** : A board has been formed for the nationalization of text-books. The members of this board include the deputy secretary of education, a member of board of revenue, secretary of the finance department, director of education, an

officer of administrative service or an officer equivalent in rank to director of education. A Review Board and a High Power Committee have been formed. This work of nationalization is running smoothly under the supervision and guidance of these two bodies. Eminent educationists are the members of the review board. A judge of the Rajasthan High Court and a member of the Rajasthan Public Service Commission are the members of the High Power Committee whose Chairman is also the Chairman of the Nationalization Board of Text-books. The decision of the Review Board are placed before the High Power Committee for final approval.

## PROBLEMS OF NATIONALIZATION OF TEXT-BOOKS

1. **Publicity of Political Ideologies**. There are many political parties in the country. The political party which comes into power may begin to publicise its ideologies through the medium of text-books. This happened in Kerala when the communists were in power. They started publicising their ideology through the medium of text-books. This was a political misuse of nationalized text-books.

2. **No Teacher's Freedom of Selecting Books** : The nationalization of text-book eliminates the choice of the teacher in matters of selection of books. Prior to nationalization he enjoyed the liberty to choose the suitable book out of more than four or five books available in the market. Now, his independent thinking narrows down to one book. The Kothari Commission tackled this question by suggesting that at least three or four books should be nationalized for one subject. This will give the teacher some freedom of choice.

3. **Absense of Different Social Views** : Nationalized text-books are the best medium to convey the knowledge of our social culture to students. But under nationalization only some selected authors write text-books. Consequently, the students do not learn different social views and thought. They get only a partial glimpse of social culture.

4. **Books Not Published in Time** : It has been observed that under nationalization programme the publication of books is considerably delayed. Sometimes due to official red-tapism the books are published after the session has commenced. This harms the education of the students.

5. **Lack of Competitive Spirit among Authors** : Competitive spirit gives birth to better products. Prior to nationalization of text-books many authors were engaged in writing books. They tried to produce better works in order to catch the selectors' eyes. Under the nationalization programme there is no scope for displaying competitive spirit as only some selected authors are entrusted with the job of writing books. This tells upon the quality of text-books.

6. **Printer's Devil and Mistakes in Language** : The aim of nationalization was to provide good, attractive and correct books free from mistakes. Unfortunately, the nationalized books do not display these qualities.

7. **No Proper Distribution of Text Books** : The government generally depends on private book sellers for the distribution of nationalized text-books. The books do not reach the students in time. It will be better if book co-operatives are

opened in schools and the books reach them straight from the government. The government can also use some of their agencies for the distribution of text-books.

8. **Unreasonable Prices of Text-Books** : It was expected that the prices of text-books will come down with their nationalization, but unfortunately the prices have not come down because the government is mostly getting them printed at private printing presses.

## SUGGESTIONS FOR SUCCESS OF NATIONALIZATION

1. **Sufficient Time for Writing** : The authors should be given a period of two years for writing a book. The time of six months or a year is inadequate.

2. **No Profit Motive** : The government should not aim at earning profits in the publication of text-books. This will bring the prices of books down.

3. **Reduction of Cost** : The government should purchase paper for the books straight from the mills. They should have their own establishment for preparing blocks of drawings and pictures. This will help to reduce the cost.

4. **Invitation to New Authors** : The government should invite some new authors every time. This will help in producing books in different styles as also making them interesting. Stress should be laid in adding as many drawings and pictures along with instances as possible.

5. **Research :** The government should set-up a research centre for improving the aesthetic and artistic sense of the text-books. The result of researches should be embodied in the text-books.

6. **Govt. Printing Press** : The government should publish the books in its own press.

7. **Sufficient Emoluments to Authors** : Authors of repute should be invited to write text-books. They should be given decent emoluments and encouragement.

8. **Several Books on One Subject** : Teachers should be given a choice to select their suitable text-books. For this at least four or five text-books should be prescribed for one subject.

## QUESTIONS FOR EXERCISE

1. Describe the merits and demerits of the current text-books.
2. How can text-books be improved in quality and contents?
3. Why is nationalization of text-books necessary? What problems are likely to arise out of nationalization of text-books?
4. Why is the programme for nationalization of text-books not proving a success? Give suggestions for success of the same.

# 19

# PROBLEMS OF PUBLIC SCHOOLS

## Meaning and Nature

Literally, public schools should mean those schools where children from any community or section of the society can get admission and pursue their study without any restriction. Here education should be easily available even to the poorest child. They should be run on democratic principles. But the public schools in India are 'privileged schools' which cater to the educational needs of children from rich and affluent classes. They are costly schools. Children coming from middle class of the society cannot afford to join them. Public schools are situated at secluded places where only rich children can conveniently reach. Public schools have been established by missionaries, industrialists, big businessmen, old taluqdars or persons belonging to landed aristocracy. Rich persons give subscriptions to these institutions with a view to saving the income tax. The public schools charge high fees both directly and indirectly. The management committees of public schools are honeycombed with representatives of affluent sections of the society, no one representing the interests of the poor people. Sometimes scholarship holders of Central or State governments get admission in these schools, but before rich students they suffer from inferiority complex which harms their personality development. Thus public schools in India are not meant for general public, but only for children of well-to-do families.

## PUBLIC SCHOOLS IN ENGLAND

### History

The tradition of opening public schools in England dates back to the later half of the fourteenth century when the oldest public school was opened. In the fifteenth and the sixteenth centuries many other public schools were opened. In the early days, these schools were just like other common schools with the only difference that they functioned without any State aid. The main objective of these public schools was to produce good Christians to become successful social, religious or political leaders. Among the old public schools of England are Winchester — 1382 A.D.; Eaton — 1441 A.D.; St. Paul — 1510. A.D.; Shewsberry — 1552 A.D.; Westminster — 1560 A.D.; Merchant Taylors — 1561 A.D.; Rugby — 1567 A.D.; Harrow —1571 A.D.; Charter House — 1661 A.D.

## Characteristics

In early days the public schools possessed some unique features. The teachers and the headmaster were held in high esteem compared with sages of Gurkulas and Ashrams of ancient India. Even the Lords and the Kings of England respected them. A story goes that Mr. Arnold the headmaster of Rugby did not take off his hat in honour of the emperor although it was against the accepted tradition of England. They were granted complete freedom in determining the educational programmes and in the management of their schools. They were responsible for everything that happened in the schools.

The English public schools laid emphasis on character formation of the students. Almost all the students had to reside in hostels and observe complete discipline. Efforts were made to develop in them the qualities of tolerance, cooperation, devotion to duty, patriotism and religiousness. Many men of destiny, great warriors, politicians, statesmen, administrators, poets and scientists who gave new direction to England have been the products of public schools. Disciplined school life helps the students to progress and occupy high position in their future life. As these schools are financially self-sufficient they do not look towards the State for their finances.

The tradition of public schools in England started in the nineteenth century when a number of public schools were opened on the pattern of the nine old schools. Till then those schools were called public schools where standard of education was satisfactory, where most of the students resided in hostels, showed good results and secured admission in the Oxford or the Cambridge Universities for higher education. Later on those schools were recognized as public school whose headmasters were nominated to 'Head Master Conference'.

These schools had their own special management and educational standard. They maintained special liaison with Oxford and Cambridge Universities. There students got admissions in Cambridge and Oxford universities. Hence, many students try to get admitted in public schools. This created difficulties of admissions in these public schools. As the tuition and other charges were considerably high in these schools it was difficult for poor students to seek admission and pursue studies there. Preference was given to those students whose parents or ancestors had received education there. The standard of education was so high that students were put in preparatory schools before admission to public schools. As a result of this procedure, a student's three or four years time, labour and money were wasted.

At presents there are about 66 public schools in England which enjoy special respect in the society. Their traditions have been highly praised in books on education published from time to time. They have been admired by foreign countries as many distinguished foreigners have received education in these public schools. India's great leader Pandit Jawahar Lal Nehru had received education at Harrow. Students are put in hostels where they are moulded through special training so that they may become fit to act according to schools ideals and discipline. The disciplined and regulated life in the hostel produces good results. The health of the students improve as they develop healthy habits. Special emphasis is laid on timely break-fast and meals, sleep, studies, exercise and sports. The students develop competitive spirit. They try to forge ahead of others in studies and extra-curricular activities, try to get higher position and strive for attracting attention and commanding respect of others. These sentiments and habits help the students to flourish in future life. As the students stay away from the family, they try to compensate this loss through special achievements and by winning affection of others.

### Criticism of Public Schools

With the development of progressive educational ideology the public school tradition has been critized in England. In spite of some modifications made in public schools opened later, their traditions were much far behind the progressive ideology. Dr. L.B. Pekin, a supporter of progressive ideology has gone to the extent of saying that the public schools have nothing worth admiration. Whatever has been written in favour of these schools was penned because the writers considered this writing as respectful.

With the development of democratic traditions some anti-social facts relating to these public schools have come to light. No doubt some persons who glorified these schools attained honour and high position by helping the expansion of British imperialism, but in its background was their social failure and reaction of intellectual and emotional frustration. The barbarous and inhuman crimes committed by these persons for furthering the cause of British imperialism simply showed that the experience of inhuman discipline, dependence, physical torture and suppressed emotions during their stay in hostels produced immense hatred in their heart for fellow human beings. The atmosphere of many public schools was found to be backward, unsocial, narrow and vitiated.

### Reform of Public Schools

The wide criticism of public schools compelled the British people to think about reforming the system. The need to their reform was emphasised in the Education Act (Butler Act) of 1944. Fleming Report criticised public schools and suggested the need of improvement. It was suggested that their doors should be flung open for children of middle class families also who fail to secure admission because of lack of money. At least 25 per cent seats should go to those students who are poor and resourceless. Though the directors of public schools themselves realised the evils and tried to remove them these schools have not yet been able to effect improvement to the desired extent.

## PUBLIC SCHOOLS IN INDIA

After the British Government established a strong foothold in India some children of affluent section of Indian Society started going to British public schools for higher education. These children had to face great hardships due to the standard of education and other matters. Even children of ruling princes and other very rich persons failed to get admission in these schools. Therefore, some ruling princes and other moneyed people thought of opening public schools in India on the pattern of public schools of England. Many princes and wealthy persons donated liberally for this purpose. Teachers and headmasters were invited from England on high emoluments. Like their counterparts in England these school were meant exclusively for affluent section of the society. Their doors remained closed for poor students. The public schools opened in early days were named as 'Chief's Colleges'.

### The Beginning

The idea of public school in India was first born in the mind of Sri S.R. Das a prominent lawyer of Calcutta. He, however, wanted that the children of poor persons should also get admission in the public schools opened in India. In 1929 he formed the 'Indian Public Schools Society' and collected donations to the tune of Rs. 14 lakhs. However, the scheme remained unimplemented due to his untimely demise. It was due to his efforts that the Doon Public School was opened in Dehradun in 1935.

### The Chiefs' Colleges

Chief's colleges were started in India on the pattern of public schools of England. They gave education to the children of ruling princes and rich people. They received aid and grant from the government. During the independence movement of 1930, people raised their voice against these schools. Government grants to these schools was opposed on the ground that the doors of these schools were not open to the children of common people. Therefore, the government had to stop grants. This created financial difficulties for the Chief's colleges. In 1939 the schools held a meeting at Simla and decided to rename these schools as public colleges. It was also decided to introduce residential education and give place to Indian culture in curriculum. It was also decided to set up 'Indian Public School Association'. In 1939 a meeting of headmasters of public schools was held at Gwalior and the Indian Public School Conference was organized, with the headmasters of public schools as the members of this conference. Sir John Sargent, the Educational Commissioner of the Government of India who was present at these meetings, described the opening and development of public schools in India an important achievement. He emphasised the need of development of public school for developing the qualities of leadership in the students. He thought that as Indians will have to administer their country some day or the other they will need leaders for guiding their affairs.

### Indian Public Schools Conference

Despite the setting up of 'Indian Public Schools Conference' many Chiefs colleges did not become its members. The Daly College, Indore, Admission College, Lahore, Bhonsale Military School, Poona, Rajkumar College, Raipur and Rajkumar College, Rajkot declared themselves as public schools. They wanted the support of Indian national Congress for themselves. The headmaster of Rajkumar (Princes) College, Rajpur, Mr. Smith invited Mahatma Gandhi to visit the college though as Mahatma Gandhi did not favour the continuance of public schools he did not accept the invitation. Mr. Smith, however, reiterated his faith in public schools and continued to make efforts to get the support of other national leaders. He pointed out that many leaders did not agree with Gandhi's conception of basic education and he tried to enlist their support.

It is worth noting that most of the Chief's colleges did not accept the membership of the 'Indian Public Schools Conference'. The Principal of Mayo College, Ajmer, Mr. Stow argued that his college belonged to a special class and as such he would not declare it a public school. Many other heads of Chief's Colleges held similar view. In 1940 a meeting of public schools was held at Raipur. It laid down the conditions for becoming members of the Indian Public Schools Conference. It was also decided to make study of Indian languages compulsory in public schools. After this meeting the public schools at Bikaner, Delhi and Ajmer became the members of the Indian Public Schools Conference. Now the Indian Public Schools Conference gained recognition. Hence, some more public schools came into existence at different places, including Yadvendra Public School at Patiala (1948), Birla Public College at Pilani (1944), Maharani Gayatri Devi Public School at Jaipur (1943) and Birla Mandir at Nainital (1947). In 1949 the Ministry of Education of the Central Government took over 'The Lawrence School' at Sanawar and the 'Lawrence School' at Lovedale from the Defence Ministry. However, in 1953 these schools were entrusted to certain committees.

**Controversy over Public Schools**

In 1947 when the country achieved independence it appeared that the future of public schools was dark, because they were considered to be hurdles in the functioning and development of democratic traditions. They were taken as symbols of British imperialism and foreign culture. The presence of English as the medium of instruction and contempt towards Indian culture shown in these schools became a focus of bitterness. However, some people who favoured English in their own selfish and base interest continued to patronise them.

**The Mudaliar Commission**

The Mudaliar Commission of 1952-53 examined Indian public schools and recommended their continuance. It suggested many improvements. It held the view that the public schools helped the development of leadership in children and should be improved instead of closing down. The wave of internationalism also helped these schools, as under the influence of this wave some national leaders emphasised the need of giving important place to the English language. They went out of their way in praising English as they thought that this would bring more money from English speaking countries. This helped the public schools to strengthen their earlier shaking position. Many public schools came up at different places. Today the affluent section of the Indian society considers it a matter of pride and honour to send their children to these public schools.

**The Kothari Commission**

The Kothari Commission of 1964-66, recommended the abolition of public schools. It opined that the existence of public school under a democratic system was undesirable. They are symbols of a privileged class. Those who hold the reins of the administration consider it below their dignity to send their children to common schools. Unless the sons of high dignitaries like the President, Prime Minister, Governors and Ministers will join these common schools, their condition will not improve. In this background that the Kothari Commission recommended the abolition of public schools.

## FAMOUS PUBLIC SCHOOLS IN INDIA

At present there are more than hundred public schools in India. Some Sainik Schools are also considered as public schools. Only half of these schools have accepted the help of 'Indian Public Schools Conference'. Some missionary schools in India are also functioning on the pattern of public schools. Among the more prominent public schools are the following :

(1) Sindhia School, Gwalior.

(2) Daly College, Indore.

(3) Raj Kumar College, Rajkot.

(4) Raj Kumar College, Raipur.

(5) Doon School, Dehradun.

(6) Birla Vidyamandir, Nainital.

(7) Modern School, Delhi.

(8) Yadvendra Public School, Patiala.

(9) Birla Public School, Pilani.

(10) Mayo College, Ajmer.

(11) Shardul Public School, Bikaner.

(12) Maharani Gayatri Devi Girls Public School, Jaipur.

(13) Hyderabad Public School, Hyderabad.

(14) Shivaji Preparatory Military School, Poona.

(15) Lawrence School, Lovedale.

(16) Vikas Vidyalaya, Ranchi.

(17) Lawrence School, Sanovar.

## NATURE OF INDIAN PUBLIC SCHOOLS

### Rules and Regulations

Indian public schools ask for compulsory residence in hostels. The students have to study for six days in a week and every day they have to study for six hours. They have to utilise the remaining time in collective hostel or extra-curricular programmes. Whether in hostel or school or in the field the student is always under the control of the staff. He has to maintain strict discipline. The schools prescribe the time-table for all the 24 hours. A student has to get up early in the morning between 4 to 5 a.m. and remain busy till 8 or 9 p.m. Time is fixed for natural call, bath, meals, studies, sleep and rest.

### Curriculum

Language, Literature, History, Geography, Mathematics, and Science are some of the main subjects included in the curriculum. The education in commerce and agriculture is not encouraged. The student is provided opportunity to master in horse riding, swimming, physical exercise, wrestling and popular hobbies like photography, painting etc. These are controlled or supervised by the teacher. Students of higher classes act as monitor or prefect for the boys of lower classes. They control and supervise the activities of students of lower classes. But this supervision by the monitor or prefect is under the overall supervision of the teacher. The spirit of co-operation, responsibility and competition is developed among students through scouting and volunteer programmes. The students are expected to follow the teachers. The students are divided into many groups called houses. The leadership of houses is entrusted to students. Thus the boys develop the quality of leadership. The atmosphere in houses is like that of the family. The warden of a house takes care of the students like a father. An effort is made to give the hostel a homely atmosphere.

### Resources

Public schools have almost all the resources they need. These schools possess big building, spacious class rooms and hall, library, reading room, laboratory, hostels, games field and auditorium for cultural programmes. They do not take government aid. Their teachers and headmasters get high salaries with residential and boarding facilities. The headmaster has full powers to admit or expel any student and to appoint and promote teachers. Thus the atmosphere of a public school differs from that of common schools. The average expenditure of a student in a public school ranges between four to six thousand rupees per annum. Thus children from poor families cannot afford education in public schools.

### Merits of Indian Public Schools

Some educationists think that these schools help the development of virtues like leadership, co-operation and responsibility. A student gets more opportunity of developing his personality in the free and disciplined atmosphere of a public school. The main emphasis in such a school is on the development of personality along with preparation for examination. As these schools possess ample resources the students and teachers do not find any obstacle in their work. Thus the public schools serve the purpose of an ideal before other schools.

### Demerits of Indian Public Schools

Public schools in India have also been criticised on following grounds:

1. *Against Democratic Ideals* : The main criticism against public schools is that they are against the spirit of democratic ideology.

2. *Expensive* : Public schools are so expensive that only children of millionaires, high officers, big businessmen, industrialists and ministers can afford education in them. Such persons feel it below their dignity to get their children admitted in common secondary schools.

3. *Elitism* : Only those children get education in public schools who come from well-to-do families. Their merits or demerits do not matter. As students spend years in luxury, the habit of living in affluence continues life long, even after leaving the schools. This develops in them the instinct of exploitation and they do not hesitate to exploit anyone to saliate their desire.

4. *Snobbery* : The students of these schools turn out snobs. Their vanity increases. They suffer from superiority complex unmindful of their real worth.

5. *Classism* : Public Schools perpetuate groupism in society to safeguard their class interests. The existence of public schools in a country like India where millions are unable to secure two square meals a day is the mockery of humanity. If the children during their education period cannot realise various basic problems facing the country how can they help the development of the nation. It will be a sheer waste of education.

6. *Vicious Character* : Education in public schools can at best turn out students who are snobs, hypocrites, un-Indian and narrow-minded. They are, at present, producing individuals possessing these vices. They should be closed down as early as possible in the better interest of the country.

## PROBLEMS DUE TO PUBLIC SCHOOLS IN INDIA

1. **Classism :** The public schools in India help the development of a particular class of the society. In these schools the students enjoy all sorts of facilities. When they do not easily get those facilities in the future life, they do not hesitate to acquire them by fair or foul means. They generally develop the tendency of exploiting others. Thus the public schools give birth to a class which is not consistent with the democratic set up cherished in the country.

2. **No Equal Opportunity** : Equal opportunity to every one for his development is one of the basic principle on a democratic set up. Public schools neglect this principle because only children of rich persons can afford education in them. If some brilliant scholarship holder poor boys manage to get admission in these schools they develop a sense of inferiority complex.

3. **Responsible for Poor Conditions of other Common Schools** : The children of privileged section of the society study in these schools. This class controls the finances and the administration in the country. This privileged section of the society, therefore, is not personally interested in the welfare of common schools which have neither big and spacious buildings nor resources to provide libraries, laboratories and other necessary equipments. If the privileged people start sending their children to common schools their condition is bound to improve. As long as the public schools will exist, the condition of common schools will not improve. Thus public school is the cause for poor condition of common schools meant for the general public.

4. **Language Problem** : As English continues to be the medium of instruction in public schools, the boys of these schools have a better command over it. They advocate for the continuance of English. As the English language is still in vogue in offices they easily get government service. Thus the number of protagonists of English increases. In its self-interest this group does not encourage the use of mother tongue in education and government offices. Hence, the problem of language is getting complex every day.

5. **Two Types of Secondary Education** : Secondary education is very important because most of the future citizens study in secondary schools in their important formulative stage of life. Unfortunately Indian secondary schools are ill-equipped and incapable of giving useful education. The public schools, on the other hand, are well equipped. In this way two types of secondary education is current in the country. While the children of rich person receive education in public schools those from the poor section of the society go to common schools. This gives rise to the evil of sectarianism or classism. In a democratic set up when society gets divided into two classes it proves disastrous.

## SUGGESTIONS FOR REFORMS OF INDIAN PUBLIC SCHOOLS

1. **Open** : These schools should be open for the general public. The admission of meritorious students should be ensured in these schools.

2. **Indianized** : They should have Indian background and be based on national culture. They should be discouraged to imitate public schools in England. The medium of instruction should be changed from English to mother-tongue. Either these schools be Indianised or abolished.

3. **Dignity of Labour** : The boys of these schools must be taught the dignity of labour and handicraft or some other suitable craft should be added to the curriculum. The tendency to go in for service should be discouraged.

4. **Less Expensive** : The expenditure of these schools should be substantially reduced to enable poor but deserving boys to get admission in them. These schools should receive grant and aid from Union and the State Governments.

5. **New Nomenclature :** Their names should be changed to Janta Vidyalaya. They should no more be private schools and considered people's property. They should adopt the Indian way of life and take greater interest in Indian educational system, Indian culture and national problems.

6. **Admission on Merit** : Admission in public schools should be based on merit alone. Emphasis should not be given to the knowledge of English at the time of admission. The admission should be open to all. If the selected boy is poor the State should bear all his expenses on education. No attention should be given to regional, communal or sectarian considerations at the time of admission.

7. **No Waste** : There is no harm if superior education is provided in public schools, but waste on show and glamour should not be permitted. They should not have more than necessary resources. Simple living and high thinking should be their motto. All students should enjoy the same facilities.

8. **Parity in Pay Scales** : Parity should be maintained in the pay scales of teachers of secondary schools and teachers of public schools. They can, however, be given residential and boarding facilities so that they can devote more time to their duties.

9. **No State Interference** : Public schools should be kept free of State interference. The headmaster should be allowed to exercise full control over the boys. He should take necessary steps to ensure proper development of students' personality and character. These activities should be within the framework of democratic traditions.

## QUESTIONS FOR EXERCISE

1. Trace the history of public schools in England. How far have their Indian counterparts followed them?
2. Trace the history of public schools in India. Describe their functioning.
3. Describe the merits and demerits of public schools in India. Give suggestions for their reforms.
4. "Public Schools are mockery of democratic traditions in a nation which has opted for democratic set up." Elucidate and comment.

# 20

# PROBLEMS OF STANDARDIZATION IN EDUCATION

## Nature of the Problem

Today every educationist says that the standards of education in India are going down day-to-day. A student has to read a number of subjects in a class, but he misses to obtain the corresponding ability in any subject whatsoever. The standard of an average student has fallen down though the standard of a really brilliant student has not gone down. With the development of knowledge in various disciplines of study his standard has comparatively gone upward. The Kothari Commission (1964-66) opined that the subject-matter of education in the country is not qualitatively and quantitatively appropriate. It does not fulfil the needs of the country. The achievement level of students has gone down. The standard of education has fallen down.

The standard of education generally depends upon the following factors :

1. The aim of education.
2. Qualitative and quantitative standard of the subject-matter.
3. Educational achievement of the students.
4. The behavioural skill.
5. Future expectations of the nation and their fulfilment.

In order to evaluate the standard of education correctly one should remember the following bases :

1. The qualitative and quantitative shape of the general and specific knowledge.
2. The achievement of the general and specific knowledge.
3. Oral or written expression.
4. The practical impact on the whole life.
5. The impact on the social and national life.

What is the nature of the curriculum taught to the students? What are their general and specific achievements? How do the students give expression of their acquired knowledge and experiences? How does the acquired knowledge influence to total life-pattern of the students? How does the personality of the student influence the social and national life? If we find negative answers to these questions, the standard of education in the country has really fallen down.

## CAUSATIVE FACTORS

### Opposite Views

It is said that the mathematics student today is not able to apply his knowledge of mathematics in his daily life. The student of language and literature is not able to speak and write correctly. There is lack of discipline among students. The amicable relationship between the student and teacher is seen no more.

Against these statements some others contend that people overlook the circumstances that are responsible for fall of standards in education. The circumstances and aims of education have changed today. Objectivity is emphasised more than subjectivity. The purpose of education is not only to make the student literate but to educate his total personality.

### Quantity *Vs.* Quality

In the past, only the rich and higher class people could be benefited from education, because they alone could afford it. These higher class and rich people used to become the main bases of the administrative system. But, today attempt is being made to make education available to all. With the growth of population one is finding quantitative explosion in education. But the qualitative improvement has been neglected and there's a fall in standards of education. The government are trying to make education compulsory and free for all the children within 14 years of age group. In this attempt it is not able to provide educational facilities corresponding to a desirable standard.

There has been a great expansion of University education after 1947. The quantitative expansion of university education is responsible for fall of standard of university education. The government policy may be also considered responsible. As all the citizens are entitled for receiving higher education, therefore all types of students get admission in degree colleges and universities. The backward and lower caste people are getting reservations in admission.

### Is there progress?

Some people believe that we have progressed in the standard of education. Formerly, the science subjects were not so much developed as they are today. Because of science education we have progressed a great deal in the various scientific, technological and vocational fields. Civics, political science, sociology and economics have been included in the curriculum for teaching the students' principles of skilful citizenship in a democracy. Formerly, agriculture was not so much developed but now we are almost self-sufficient in food commodities. Formerly, the standard of general knowledge was very low, but today the general knowledge standard of the student is very high.

**Responsibility of the Teacher**

The teacher and his methods of teaching are very much responsible for fall of standard in education. The teacher is either very busy in things which do not pertain to his profession, or he looks lethargic and is not inclined even to do the minimum for which he is paid. His daily routine is not balanced. One finds a tendency of trade unionism in teachers of all categories. They do not take interest in problems pertaining to school, college or university. The students and teachers do not get adequate facilities for investigation and research. They appear to be little interested in finding out solutions to academic and educational issues. Good laboratories, adequate libraries and well equipped workshops are not available. The secondary and primary school teachers are over-burdened and cannot teach any subject properly. The officers in the education department of the government, do not have a sympathetic attitude towards teachers. Their approach is mechanical, fault-finding and not reformative. They are mostly busy in their transfers, distributing favours or awarding punishments. All these causes have led to fall in standards of education.

**Importance of Family**

The family circumstances of students are also responsible for fall of standards in education. Most of the students come from uneducated families. They do not get proper educational atmosphere at home. Their difficulties and doubts are not removed at home. The children of poor families have to devote much time in supplementing the income or accelerating the agricultural products. They start memorising the important elements near the examination. Their major purpose of education is to pass the examination with good marks and obtain the certificate. The teacher, too, prepares his students only for the examination. He is not interested with the development of the various aspects of personality of the student. This situation has led to fall of standards in education.

**Medium of Instruction**

The medium of instruction has also led to fall of standards in education. English has been replaced by the mother tongue but suitable books are not available in the various mother tongues in the country. Most of the teachers are so much overburdened with work that they do not try to produce standard works. They also lack psychological approaches in their methods of work and behaviour with students. Education has become book-centred in place of child-centred. Education has been subordinated to examination. The teacher emphasises only important points of courses for examination. Hence, the student does not get scope for the development of his natural powers. Nor does he take any interest in education. All these features have led to fall of standard in education.

**Committee on Standard of Education (1965)**

In 1965 the Government of India appointed a Committee on Standard of Education for investigating into the causes of falling standards. It accepted the academic achievement of the student as the basis of his qualitative development and drawn attention to the following after studying the behaviours of students :

1. *The Level of Acquired Abilities* : This includes the following two things :

(i) What control does the students have over elements of knowledge, skill, memory, thinking and logical power and judgement?

(ii) What are the levels of the various abilities of the students?

2. *Development in Behaviour* : The behaviour of students was observed for finding out their qualitative development in the following context :

(i) From the point of view of discipline.

(ii) From the point of view of morality.

Thus the evaluation of standard of education was based on achievement and qualitative development. These two things may be expressed in the following way :

(i) How much has the student learnt?

(ii) How successfully can the student express his acquired skill or behaviour?

(iii) To what extent has the student succeeded in making the acquired knowledge and skill a part of his life?

Why is the standard of education falling? What are its causes? How can they be removed? By studying all these things one can find out the standard of education in India.

By studying the achievement level and the qualitative development of average students, it has been found that the educational standard of an average student is falling down and his qualitative development is not satisfactory. The student, the teacher and the guardian alone are not responsible for this situation. There are many more causes for this.

## CAUSES AND REMEDIES OF FALL IN EDUCATIONAL STANDARDS

1. Quantitative expansion in the educated population for meeting the educational needs of the people.
2. Wrong policy of admitting students to educational institutions.
3. The unfavourable condition of teachers.
4. Neglect of primary and secondary education.
5. Unpsychological teaching method.
6. Inappropriate curriculum.
7. Defective examination system.
8. Huge size of classes.
9. Lack of facilities and motivation.

## 1. Quantitative Expansion of Education

The ever growing population of India has necessitated the quantitative expansion of education. As an attempt is being made to give educational facilities to all, therefore, even those children are admitted who are backward in general ability and whose family background is also very low. Because of the rise in number of schools, colleges and universities even those persons have been appointed as teachers who lack the aptitude, motivation and ability for teaching. Many such institutions, schools and degree colleges have been given recognition which do not fulfil the minimum conditions and lack the minimum facilities. The number of students in each class has increased enormously. Even the unfit ones are being given promotion to the next higher classes. According to the constitutional directive for providing equality of educational opportunity, all have been given a chance to get education. This has adversely affected the higher education. Its standard has fallen down because many unworthy and undeserving students have been admitted to colleges and universities.

Having spent much on expansion of education the Government has now expressed its inability to give adequate financial assistance to educational institutions. Consequently, the standard of education has fallen down. Training colleges are giving training to such persons who have no interest, aptitude and ability for teaching. Many of such persons join service in other departments after completing their training. Thus there is huge wastage of money on teacher education. This has contributed to the fall of standards in education.

*Remedies* : A check should be put on huge expansion of education. New institutions should not be opened. The institutions which do not fulfil the conditions of recognition should be either closed down or compelled to fulfil the required conditions. The facilities available in schools, colleges and universities should be further increased. Only the deserving ones should be admitted in colleges and universities. Other students should be diverted to vocational institutions. Only those persons should be admitted for teacher's training who have an interest, aptitude and ability for the same. More teachers should be appointed to facilitate contact between the student and the teacher. This will enable the teacher to find out the interest and ability of a student. The standard of education will ultimately go up.

## 2. Wrong Admission Policy

Though up to the secondary stage each should get an opportunity to receive education, but it is not proper to admit any one in a degree college or university. It brings down the educational standard and also increases the number of unemployed persons. Today the number of students in universities is increasing by about 15 per cent every year. How can India provide university education to such a huge number? Therefore, the government should put a check to the growth of number of university students if standard of university education has to be raised.

*Remedies* : The admission policy should be such that only the deserving ones get admission in educational institutions. Caste, creed and sex differences should not intervene in matters concerning education. The following policy may be adopted for selection :

1. The number to be admitted should be decided according to the facilities available in the institution.
2. Rules should be framed regarding the minimum qualifications required for admission.
3. Each institution should be compelled to follow the rules of admission strictly.
4. An admission test should be taken before the students are given admission.
5. There should be an admission committee in each university, which should formulate rules for admission, based on requirements of the curriculum to be taught in the university. Till such rules are framed, the marks of the previous qualifying examination, socio-economic status and the daily record of the student should be given due weightage in giving admission. Secondary education should be vocationalised so that those not getting admission in colleges and universities may not stay idle and unemployed.

### 3. Unfavourable Conditions

The number of able teachers has not increased corresponding to the rise in number of educational institutions. If the teacher is not able, there will be a fall in educational standards as unsuitable teachers do not inspire students.

*Remedies* : Only those persons should be admitted to teaching professions who have abilities, interest and aptitude for the same. The selection of university teachers should be made on an all India basis. Institutions of international reputation should have teachers of international fame. They should be given residential accommodation and their emoluments should be attractive. If the government thus recognizes the status of teacher, the teacher will be getting recognition from society.

### 4. Neglect of Primary and Secondary Education

As the primary, secondary and university stages of education are inter-related, the neglect of one stage has its inevitably bad impact on the other. Thus neglect of primary education harms secondary education and the neglect of secondary education obstructs the progress of university education. Thus for improvement of university education, there should be quantitative improvement of both primary and secondary education.

*Remedies* : An attempt should be made for bringing in uniformity in the form of primary and secondary education in the country. This may be done by adopting the 10+2+3 system of education. Suitable teachers should be appointed along with giving physical and social facilities for qualitative improvement of primary and secondary education. Upto the tenth class all the subjects should be compulsorily taught to all the children. Certain optionals may be instituted from the eleventh class. Suitable curriculum should be organized keeping in view the regional and national needs. The unfit students should not be given promotion to higher class unless their daily work is satisfactory.

### 5. Unpsychological Teaching Methods

Generally lecture system is followed in Indian schools and colleges. The students remain passive listener in this system. They do not get any opportunity of 'learning by doing'. There is no class interaction between the students and teachers. Teaching remains as a one-way traffic. The students do not develop a power of expression, their curiosity does not develop, their creative instinct is thwarted.

*Remedies.* The teachers should be given training in psychological methods of teaching. The teachers of degree college and universities should get training in methods of teaching. In-service training programme should be instituted for teachers already in service. Refresher courses should be started for acquainting teachers with the latest developments in teaching methods.

### 6. Inappropriate Curriculum

The current curriculum does not prepare the students for facing various problems of life. It is one-sided and inadequate. Vocational subjects and crafts have not been given due place in it. Hence, many aspects of the student's personality remain undeveloped.

*Remedies* : The curriculum should cater to the local, national and individual needs. It should be suitably modified to meet various needs. It should be made useful to life by giving place to vocational subjects.

### 7. Defective Examination System

The University Commission of 1948-49 had suggested that if our educational system needed any reform it was the examination system in the first instance. It is responsible for fall of standards of education. The teaching work has been subordinated to examinations. The teachers pay more attention to that which they consider important for the examination. The evaluation of a student's achievement is made on the basis of one external examination. The internal assessment of the daily work has not been given any place. This has led the student to neglect his studies throughout the whole year. Only at the fag end of the examination period he begins to memorise certain portions on the basis of guess papers which have flooded the markets today. To adopt unfair means and to pressurise examiners for giving higher marks in answer-books have become a common practice today. Objectivity has been sacrificed at the altar of subjectivity. Often a set of ten or twelve questions are given and the student has to attempt any five or six of them for writing essays on them.

*Remedies* : The current system of examination should be reformed by incorporating internal assessment and objective test of the day-to-day work of the student. The essay type questions should be retained, but they should not be made the sole basis for ascertaining the achievement of a student. An examination Committee should be organized in each secondary school, college and university. The teachers should be given part-time or refresher courses for acquainting them with latest developments in standardization of objective tests. The following points may be noted in this connection :

(i) The student should be tested at the understanding level also and not on the memory level alone. Arrangement should be made for testing the student at the reflective level also at the university stage.

(ii) The examination should be based on the total curriculum. It should be both oral and written. The laboratory work should also be given a place in examining a student.

(iii) The question-paper should be divided into three parts — (1) Some essay type questions; (2) Some questions requiring short answers; and (3) Some objective tests.

(iv) The examinee should be required to attempt all the questions. There should be no options. The question-papers should be made in such a way as to have easy questions first followed by more difficult ones. In framing the questions the behavioural terms within the reach of the examinees should be used.

(v) In practical work, the result alone should not be the determining factor for giving marks. The processes, too, should be evaluated through viva-voce test.

### 8. Huge Size of Classes

Due to expansion of education, a class today consists of 60 to 100 students. In some universities the number in a class goes even up to 150 to 200. This makes the personal contact between the teacher and taught impossible. The problems of students remain unsolved. There are not even sufficient chairs and tables for the students to use. Toilet arrangement is extremely poor. All these conditions create discipline problems which vitiate the whole educational atmosphere.

*Remedies.* No class should consist of more than 30 to 40 students. Tutorial system should be encouraged. Suitable teachers should be appointed in large number according to the strength of students in class.

### 9. Lack of Facilities and Motivation

Due to lack of the necessary facilities the atmosphere in an institution is not encouraging. It has led to fall of standard of education. Lack of teachers, laboratories, libraries and workshops in an educational centre appears to be most depressing. It does not motivate the student to attend to their studies. There is no guidance bureau in degree colleges and universities. There is none to give the necessary psychological guidance to a student. Research work is impeded due to lack of library and laboratory facilities. Some institutions do not have even suitable buildings, playgrounds and materials for sports and games.

*Remedies* : Every institution should have suitable buildings, library, laboratory, hostels and playgrounds and the necessary equipments for sports and games. Each educational centre should have a guidance bureau to give the necessary educational and vocational guidance to students.

## QUESTIONS FOR EXERCISE

1. Do you agree that standard of education in India have fallen down ? If so, assign reasons for the same.
2. What do you mean by standard of education? What are its problems?
3. Why has the standard of education in our country gone down? Suggest remedies for removing the causes.

# 21

# LANGUAGE PROBLEM IN INDIA

## Importance of Language

Language symbolizes human development. It is a gift to man as the best living being of the world. Without it, a man is the most superior animal with limited expression. Language is the power of the human race through which he is able to express himself well and understand the expressions of others. On its basis, man utilises the experiences of the past for the present and secures present successes as a basis of future development. As a wonderful discovery of man language has enriched him tremendously. It has saved the world from man using signal sounds like the dumb. Its development is a sign of social and national development. It is a vehicle of human expression. Therefore, the usefulness of an individuals' expression, his influence, his popularity etc. depend on the capacity of the means of expression. The human relations of the space age are not limited to any class, caste, society, nation or continent. Any narrow-mindedness regarding language will only signify the illiberal attitude of a society or nation.

India is a big country in which people of different castes, religions, standards of living, food habits, languages and customs are living. Apart from physical diversities between one region and the other, there are several other kinds of diversities in India. In the Northern region, from Kashmir to Bengal, a vast majority of people have the impact of Aryan culture. In the Deccan peninsula, the influence of Dravidian culture can easily be noticed. The Western part of the country has been influenced by the Aryan culture, but being the gateway of India it has got a mixture of western culture also. Aryans and the Dravidians are the primitive races of India. These two cultures were well developed during the primitive age when civilization had only begun to develop at some places. The developed conditions of country first attracted Turk invaders and subsequently Muslim and European imperialists. These intruders created a number of problems for the coming generation by exerting their influence on the primitive culture in their effort to cut off the developed social structure of this country. The present language problem and the relative difference between various regional groups are the creations of those foreign efforts.

Every class, group, community or people of a region have a particular affinity with their language. It is very natural for the people to become attached to their language sensitiveness, emotional feelings and cultural values. Indians are more influenced by their ancient glory than by their present achievements and consider the old culture as their most important treasure. One of the main reasons for this is faulty presentation of Indian history. Whatever is available in the form of history here is either one-sided or a translation of the works of foreign historians who could not understand the then conditions well.

The language problem in India is not simply academic. Gradually it has taken a political turn. Certain minority parties have given it the form of a national problem in order to earn cheap popularity and fulfilling their vested political ends. Language problem is not peculiar to India, it is found in several other countries. America and some developed nations of Europe also have language problems. But in India it has taken the form of a movement. Riots, loot and arson in the name of language have been resorted to in the past in our country. This is really shameful for any nation. The problem has been enlarged to fulfil group or party interests. People of different regions have been demanding separate States on language basis, forgetting their more important problems. It has lead to mutual ill-will, development plans have been hampered and riots, now and then, have made smooth administration difficult.

## HISTORICAL BACKGROUND

### 1. Under Muslim Rule

With the establishing of Muslim rule in the land a foreign language came into existence for the first time in India. The original language of Muslim rulers converted into Urdu language and was fully installed for government work, but it could not become the medium for inter-provincial communication in spite of government protection. Sanskrit, other native languages (Apbhransh) and Hindi continued to occupy that place. One of the main features of that time regarding language was that the excessive protection and favouritism of rulers to Urdu, created a special attachment towards their own language in people of India and accordingly Indian languages developed more and more.

### 2. Under British Rule

After establishing their empire, the British established schools and colleges for teaching English to Indians for administrative purposes.

(i) *Christian Missionaries* : The Christian Missionaries established educational institutions as a powerful means of propagation of Christian religion. In all such institutions the medium of instruction was English. About the third decade of nineteenth century, the Company Government over India visualised some danger due to growing public awakening in the country. It became clear to them that according to the wishes of Indian people some facilities were necessary in order to rule the country. These facilities also included Indian languages as medium of instruction in English schools and colleges. But Lord Macaulay and Lord Willam Bentinck stood for English as the medium of instruction. The British Government also declared that preference would be given to English knowing people for government posts. Thus English education got more encouragement though this increased the anger of the Indian public against the British Rule.

(ii) *Wood's Despatch 1854* : An amendment was made in the Wood's Despatch of 1854, that English would be the medium of instruction only for brilliant students and all other students would be educated through Indian languages. But due to the disturbances in 1857, that provision could not be implemented and the problem was postponed for about twenty to twenty-five years.

(iii) *Education Commission 1882* : Appointed in 1882 the first Education Commission considered the problem of medium of instruction in English schools in India. It was decided that the medium for Secondary Schools would be English but primary education would be given through Indian languages. In the beginning of twentieth century, the public movement again gained momentum in India and the leaders along with other demands, stressed the demand for making Indian languages as the medium of instruction. The then Governor-General showing his farsightedness accepted the demand for making Indian languages as medium of instruction at the secondary level also, but the decision could not be effectively implemented as English was used in all Governmental work. As such education in Secondary schools continued to be given in English.

(iv) *Calcutta University Commission 1917* : Language movement again led to the appointment of Calcutta University Commission in 1917. It recommended the adoption of Indian languages as medium of instruction upto higher secondary stage. Some English medium schools made regional languages medium of instruction.

(v) *1935 to 1947* : By 1935, regional languages had become medium of instruction in most of the educational institutions. But some important institutions, particularly those run by Christian Missionaries, kept English as the medium. After that till the attainment of Independence, there were some other language changes. The leaders engaged in public movement demanded to make Indian languages as medium of instruction in all types of educational institutions and to adopt the Basic system of education for the primary level. After the Movement of 1942, the British rulers accepted Indian languages as the first compulsory language and English as second compulsory language for secondary education but continued English as medium of instruction for higher education.

**3. In Independent India**

(i) *Dr. Radhakrishnan Commission 1948* : The first education commission, known as Dr. Radhakrishnan Commission, was appointed in 1948 after Independence. It recommended the study of the federal language in the Deonagri Script and that of English and regional language both at secondary and University stages.

(ii) *Secondary Education Commission 1953* : It recommended two-language formula instead of three-language formula recommended by Radhakrishnan Commission. It also recommended that at the State level facilities should be provided for the study of every language spoken in a State. This recommendation further complicated the problem rather than solving it. Regarding language most of the recommendations of this Commission were impracticable. Even before Independence, the provision of study of English as a national language, mother tongue and one additional language was compulsory at the secondary stage and continuing smoothly without any difficulty. After the acceptance of Hindi as a national language, provision could easily be made for the study of national language along with regional languages and English.

(iii) *The Central Advisory Board of Education (1956)* : It recommended the adoption of three-language formula.

(iv) *The Emotional Integration Committee (1961) and Kothari Commission (1966)* : Both these tried to improve the situation through their recommendations but the situation remained out of control. The regions which have been continuing the study of three languages before Independence, now considered it a waste of time and energy of the students. The people of some regions started supporting English for their personal and party interests though they did not have any particular attachment to English.

## NEEDS RELATED TO LANGUAGE

Some of the important needs related to language in India are following :

1. **Mother-tongue should be the Medium of Instruction upto the Secondary Level** : A review of history of education in India upto 1947 reveals that except in institutions run by missionaries and such other institutions, provincial languages had taken the place of medium of instruction in all other secondary schools. The secondary schools with English medium continue as such even today. So the solution that had been offered before Independence exists even today according to the need of the time.

2. **Education in English at the Higher Educational Level** : While admitting retention of English as a medium of instruction at the higher education level will not be in the interest of national development, some people oppose its removal simply for delaying as long as possible. They advance hollow arguments of under-development of Indian languages, lack of terminology in the national language and falling of standard of higher education, if Indian languages are made the medium of education. The other group is in favour of making the national language or regional languages medium of instruction at higher education stage as early as possible. At present, the use of national language and other regional languages in the sphere of higher education is gradually increasing. As languages can develop through their use, the liberal use of the national language and other regional languages at the higher education level will help in overcoming the difficulty of terminology. However, there should neither be undue haste in the removal of English nor should it be unduly retained longer.

3. **Importance of English in Science and Technical Education** : One of the arguments for retaining English at higher stage is that English should be the medium for scientific and technical education. Another argument is that inter-University cooperation and relations, exchange of teacher and students etc.

are important aspects of higher education and only English medium can make these possible. Considering the dearth of scientific and technical books in Indian languages, it will be worthwhile to retain English as medium so long as such books are not prepared or translated in Indian languages. Any haste in this respect will not be in the national interest. Thus the second argument is equally sound. For inter-university relations, it seems necessary that English should be replaced by such language as is easily accessible to the students of all regions. Such a language alone can become the national language. So all the universities should adopt it in place of English. In due course it will replace English at higher scientific and technical education level also. In some States regional languages can also be made medium at the University level, but working knowledge of the national language should be given in order to maintain national values and to make higher scientific and technical education convenient.

4. **Teaching of National Language to Every Child of the Country** : Hindi is the national language of India. According to the Indian Constitution it was to take the place of English within fifteen years. The President had the privilege of declaring the use of Hindi with English for governmental purpose at any time before the prescribed limit. Now as the prescribed time limit has expired any delay in the use of Hindi in Government work is unnecessary. The politicians using the language problem for political manoeuvring know it very well that they cannot ignore the powers of the Union simply for fulfilling their personal or party vested interests or by instigating movement or riots in the name of some regional language. The coming generation will not tolerate the fact that their national estimation is below others because of the narrow-mindedness or selfishness of some people. Provision should be made in every State for teaching general Hindi to the children there so that every person is able to get knowledge of his national language.

5. **Multi-lingual States** : There are several States in India which have multi-lingual regions or groups. Pioneer among them is the Punjab where live Gurumukhi, Hindi and Urdu speaking people. After the division of the State into Punjab and Haryana, most of the Hindi speaking area has been separated in Haryana but the problem of Gurumukhi and Urdu cannot be solved by regional division, because people of both languages live together in every region. In Uttar Pradesh both Hindi and Urdu are spoken simultaneously and there is no special difference between them. It is difficult to distinguish them in daily conversation, daily work as well as even in government use. The only difference is that of the script. Hindi used in district and tehsil offices is nothing but Urdu written in Devnagari Script. Film producers have combined Hindi and Urdu in such a way that Hindi and Urdu words are found in every sentence. Now Urdu literature, too, is being written in Devnagari Script. It is clear that for multi-lingual States like Punjab that a common script or Devnagari Script may be adopted for solving the dispute of several languages. Almost all the languages have their origin in the Sanskrit language. They are considered as different due to the difference in pronunciation and script. There is such a minor difference between Hindi and Bengali language that a basic similarity can easily be noticed in their word-formation, syntax and several letters of script.

Both Assamese and Bengali are spoken in Assam. Assamese is very much near to the Hindi. A Mixture of Hindi and Bhojpuri is spoken in eastern Bihar. Though Assamese script is a mixed form of Hindi and Bengali but the Assamese do not support the idea of making Bengali as the medium of instruction. At present, people of Darjeeling region are opposing the existing language system. People of hill regions of Assam are agitating for giving equal status to their language. Thus language disputes will not end simply by using regional languages in Government work or for education. Academic solution of the language problem is not sufficient. The demand for creating States based on languages will pose a great problem for the Union Government.

## LANGUAGE PROBLEM IN OTHER COUNTRIES

Language problem is not peculiar to India alone. Such problems are found even in such developed countries as U.S.A. and Russia. History of languages bears testimony to the fact that languages values change from time to time. For example, there are two main language groups in Europe, but it has been felt now that the usage of Roman language is increasing and it is reaching those regions where it has never been used. Following examples regarding languages of some nations make it clear that it will be proper to solve the language problem rather than enlarge it. As decisions regarding language in any country cannot be perfect, it is natural that no group can be fully satisfied. But in due course of time, such decisions become convenient for all people speaking the languages.

1. **Germany** : Germany has been divided into two political parts with common language. The study of German language is compulsory for all students. It is also the general medium of instructions. After ten years of age every child has to study one of the languages out of French, Russian or English as a compulsory second language. Generally, there are separate second language regions. This facility of the study of four main European languages is worth following for any nation of the world.

2. **Soviet Russia** : In the Soviet Union, the three language formula has been adopted for solving the language problem. After the Revolution there, it was not an easy task to find a solution to the problem of more than one hundred languages and dialects of sixteen States. Some of the dialects had no regular form. According to the three-language formula, the students have to study the State language, Russian and one foreign language compulsorily. Efforts were made to improve the languages which were incomplete in script or wanting in literature. The language problems of India and Russia are sufficiently similar.

3. **France** : The centre of international activity, though the language of France is the medium of international dealing and rich and complete in itself, but provision exists for the study of more than one language in France. At the secondary level, the study of at least one foreign language German or English is compulsory along with national language. It shows that though the national language may be sufficient for international contacts yet the study of neighbouring languages is necessary in the national interest.

4. **Switzerland** : Among the several languages in this country with a

population of about eight million, the main languages are German, French, Italian and Roman. As individual freedom is most important, here there is no compulsion of national language. Though three-forth of the population here is German speaking but French and English are also taught in the educational institutions. Facilities also exist for the study of Italian and Roman languages. Every person is free to use his own language in public life.

5. **Japan** : A few years ago the national values of Japan were under such a protected cover that any foreign influence could hardly penetrate. Though Japanese language is capable in every respect but today English has been adopted as a second language for international communication. Though the entry-gates of Japan are open for all types of foreign transport and communication, the Japanese are attached to their language as usual but English is also taught along with Japanese at the secondary stage.

## RECOMMENDATIONS OF COMMISSIONS

1. **Mudaliar Commission** : The Mudaliar Commission has given two types of recommendations in report regarding languages. According to the first the following three languages will be taught to the students :

(1) Mother tongue of State language,

(2) English, and

(3) One other Indian language different from mother tongue.

The regions which have Hindi as mother-tongue, should teach a South Indian language and where the mother-tongue is any language other than Hindi, Hindi should be taught as a third language.

According to the second recommendation two-language formula should be adopted :

(1) Mother-tongue or State language,

(2) English or any other Indian language.

It was also recommended in the two language formula that for emotional integration of the country, every child should be taught the other Indian language from class IV or V. This language would be some Indian language of South in Hindi speaking areas and national language Hindi in non-Hindi speaking areas.

2. **B.K. Kher Commission (1955-56)** : In 1955, at the end of five years after the commencement of the constitution, a commission was appointed under the Chairmanship of B.J. Kher which submitted its report in 1956. It is a valuable document for understanding the immensity and complexity of the language problem in India.

A thirty-member committee of Parliament, with the Home Minister of the Union Government as its Chairman examined the recommendations of the Kher Commission. The report of the Committee was submitted to Parliament in 1958. While the Committee expressed the definite opinion that adherence to the constitutional settlement which envisages the replacement of English by Hindi for

Union purposes and by the regional languages for the official requirements of the States is the only safe and practical course to adopt, the approach to the question of final change-over has to be flexible and practical. Thus, the Committee endorsed the recommendations of the official language commission except that it emphasised the necessity for flexibility in the change-over.

*The Official Language Bill, 1963* : This Bill was introduced in Parliament on 13th April 1963. The need for the introduction of the Bill seems to have arisen due to two main reasons: firstly, because Hindi had not grown sufficiently during the last 13 years to be able to replace English after 1965 and secondly, because the existent emotional climate in the country was far from favourable to any such change-over in the near future. This Bill provided the English should continue to be used as associate federal language after 1965 and that ten years later, a parliamentary committee was to be appointed to review the progress made in Hindi.

3. **Radhakrishnan Commission** : This Commission presented suggestions for the teaching of languages on almost all stages of education. Regarding languages the Commission has remained free from all prejuidices of region, State or community. It has recommended three language formula in the field of education as follows :

(i) Every student should be taught three languages at the secondary stage :

(a) Regional or State language,

(b) Union or National Language,

(c) One foreign language, English.

(ii) Higher education should be given both in regional and Union languages. In places where the regional language is other than Hindi, provision should be made for teaching Union Language at the higher stage as well.

(iii) The teaching of English should continue as usual at the secondary and higher stages. There should be no change in English courses due to the recommendations regarding languages. The contact of students with English is necessary for educational development.

(iv) At the higher stage the medium of instruction should be an Indian language but it should not be Sanskrit.

The following recommendations were made developing the languages to be used as medium of instruction :

(i) Devnagari Script should be used for Union Language and it should be developed liberally.

(ii) Every State should make arrangements for the teaching of Union Language both at the secondary and higher stages.

(iii) The books in Science and Technology should be translated in Union language and other Indian languages.

(iv) In preparing the terminology, words of all Indian languages should be included as far as possible.

4. **Kothari Commission**. Appointed in 1964-66, the Kothari Commission proposed some suggestions regarding the language problem in its report, after visiting a number of places and after interviewing students, teachers and parents etc. of all regions and levels. Some improvements have been suggested in this Report while supporting the previous three-language formula. According to it, the language teaching at different stages should have the following form :

(i) Three languages should be taught to students and teaching of four languages should not be compulsory at any stage.

(a) At the lower primary stage, only mother-tongue or State language should be taught.

(b) In higher primary classes, Union language should be taught along with mother-tongue.

(c) At the Junior High School stage, the students should be taught mother-tongue, Union language and one other modern Indian language.

(d) At the higher secondary stage the study of at least two languages should be made compulsory.

(e) There should be no compulsion of languages at the higher stage.

(ii) The study of English would be useful for the students but it should not begin before Class V.

(iii) After the mother-tongue Hindi should be accepted as a second important State-language. Hindi or English should be taught as associate language for three to six years to every student.

(iv) Every State and Union Government at the national level should try for the expansion of Hindi but it should not be imposed on anyone.

(v) Classical languages such as Sanskrit, Persian or Arabic should not be compulsory at any stage. Facilities may be provided for their study as an optional subject in the last year (Class VIII) of Junior High School stage.

(vi) Arrangement should be made to train teachers in language teaching because the progress of the language depends on the ability of teachers.

### Operation of Three-Language Formula

Regarding operation of Three-Language Formula in schools, Kothari Commission has suggested as under :

*Classes I to IV* : The study of one language should be compulsory. It will naturally be the mother tongue.

*Classes V to VII* : The study of the two languages should be obligatory at this stage. First language should be mother tongue and the second language may either be the official language of the Union *i.e.*, Hindi or the associate official language of the Union *i.e.*, English so long as it exists.

*Classes VIII to X* : The study of three languages should be compulsory at this stage and one of these three languages should be the official language of the Union or the associate official language which was not taken up in class V to VII.

*Classes XI to XII* : Two languages should be made compulsory at this stage. The student should be given option to select any two of the three languages studied earlier or any two languages from the groups given ahead :

(i) Modern Indian Languages.

(ii) Modern Foreign Languages.

(iii) Classical Languages — Foreign and Indian.

**Official Languages (Amendment) Bill, 1968**

This bill provided for the continuance of English as the official language and the development of Hindi so that it may become the like language of India and may be adopted as the official language of the country of India when all the States agree to it. The whole of the country was shaken by violence of the language fanatics in almost all the important cities and towns and also by loud dialogues in Parliament. Ultimately the Bill was signed by the President on 10th January 1968 and became an Act. But that does not end the problem as many of the States have not accepted the decision of the Central Government. The Hindi-speaking people do not want that English should be imposed on them and the southerners are in no mood to tolerate the domination of Hindi.

**Ishwar Bhai Patel Committee 1977**

The Committee recommended that in determining the pattern of languages to be taught, the recommendations of the Kothari Commission should be given due consideration and that these recommendations should be used as guidelines in formulating or reformulating any policies on the teaching of the languages.

**The Draft National Policy on Education 1979**

According to this, the three-language formula, will be implemented at the secondary stage. It includes the study of a modern Indian language preferably a South Indian language, in addition to Hindi and English in Hindi-speaking States and of Hindi in addition to regional languages and English in non-Hindi speaking States.

## REMEDIES TO LANGUAGE PROBLEM

On the basis of the recommendations of different Commissions, suggestions of advisory committees and needs of the country, the following remedies may be suggested for solving language problems :

1. **Teaching of Foreign Language :** (i) *English Medium at Higher Stage.* Amongst the foreign languages, the place of English is most important from the point of view of international communication. Indians have been using this language for more than two centuries and it has been occupying the place of Government language for about hundred years. Its percentage is higher in the educated class. For a particular class, this language is more convenient than any other Indian language. But according to the present needs, its study as an associate foreign language would be more worthwhile. In the recent years, most of the books

used at different stages of education have been translated into Hindi and no difficulty has been found in teaching Science subjects upto the University stage in places where the medium of instruction is Hindi. But the knowledge of English is particularly convenient for education in higher Scientific and Technical subjects. Therefore, English should be the medium of instruction at this stage, so long as favourable conditions for its change are not created.

(ii) *English Starting at Class VI* : In the development of Indian education, the utility of English is recognized only at the higher education stage. Hence, its teaching should begin from Class VI so that by the time they reach the University stage the students may gain necessary knowledge of English. As the importance of English in Indian education is recognized as a third useful language, it is unnecessary to start its teaching or use as medium of instruction before the Junior High School stage.

(iii) *No Burden of English* : The courses in English should be so organized that its teaching does not become a burden on students. English is a developed language and its literature is rich. For its thorough knowledge even several decades will not be sufficient. Hence, the aim should be to get a working knowledge of English. At the higher education stage, English will be available as an optional subject for those students who want to offer it. As a compulsory subject, its provision should be general.

2. **Teaching of Indian Languages** : Hindi has been selected as the national language due to some of its qualities and peculiarities. Spoken by a vast majority of the people in India, it is also the language of public communication. Scientifically, its script is the best. In comparison to other Indian languages Hindi is more developed and easy. Working ability in it can be achieved easily and in a minimum possible time. In the present set-up, it has become medium of education in several States. In several other States, its teaching is compulsory. It is taught independently as a second language in some States.

The existence of an Indian language as the Union language is necessary in the interest of the country. Today, persons from different parts of the country are co-operating in the various programmes organized for the execution of different plans. An Indian language is very necessary for their inter-personal communication and contacts and in order to inculcate sociability and community feeling. Hindi is a symbol of national unity because people of two different languages use it in their conversation. It also symbolizes Indian glory and culture as we can see through Hindi programmes on radio. Many Hindi books are being translated in foreign languages. Hence, the teaching of Hindi as first or second language to the people of all regions of the Indian Union is necessary. People speaking other languages can easily learn Hindi. Most of the Indian languages have their origin in the Sanskrit language of which Hindi is a simple form.

**Emotional Integration Committee of 1961**

Organized under the Chairmanship of Dr. Sampurnanand, this Committee has citicised the two language formula while accepting the three language formula. The following suggestions have been made regarding this problem :

1. Provincial (State) languages should be made medium of instruction. Efforts should be made to develop those languages which are fit to be the medium of instruction.

2. People of Hindi speaking areas should learn some South Indian language as a second language.

3. Students of non-Hindi areas should be taught Hindi and English after the primary stage.

4. Some regional languages can also be made medium of instruction at the higher education level. But at present, as inter-university contacts are necessary from the viewpoint of educational development, therefore, medium of instruction in all the Universities should be Hindi or English. It is better to continue English for higher scientific and technical education for the time being.

**Problem of Multi-lingual States**

Uttar Pradesh, Punjab and Assam are the three States where more than one languages are spoken. The following suggestions may be important for solving their language problem :

1. The language spoken by the majority of people should be the State-language and medium of instruction. People speaking other languages should learn it. Education should be given in State-language from the primary classes.

2. States should make arrangements for the teaching of minority language also. In places where there is a good number of students learning a particular language, necessary arrangements for the teaching of that language should be made.

3. In such regions where persons from other regions or States are transferred or settled for the execution of some project or for some administrative arrangements the Union Government or State Governments should establish educational institutions, providing education through the national language. The Indian Government had established English Medium schools in some places connected with its projects. These should gradually be converted into Hindi medium schools. The Union Government should establish model schools of Hindi medium at such places.

**Teaching of Classical Languages**

Some educationists lay special emphasis on the teaching of Sanskrit as a compulsory language as Sanskrit is the symbol of ancient glory of India. It is the origin of almost all the Indian languages. It will maintain our contact with our ancient culture. But too much attachment with the past may hamper our development. Man can make progress only when he continues to move forward. Hence, the following arrangement may seem suitable for the education of Sanskrit and such other classical languages :

1. All ancient classical subjects should be taught independently at the higher education level. Only interested students may study them.

2. The study of these subjects as optional or compulsory subjects does not

appear feasible at the primary or secondary level as it will make the curriculum burdensome. They cannot be included in the three-language formula. In the present arrangement, the teaching of Sanskrit has been included in the syllabus of Hindi. Similarly the teaching of Sanskrit can be included in the syllabus of other languages.

3. At the higher education level some difficulty of previous knowledge may arise while selecting the classical subjects. Their courses may be simplified to make them suitable for the existing situation. The study of these subjects as optional and additional subjects at primary or secondary stages may give the interested students such ability as may enable them to select these subjects as independent (optional) subjects at higher education stage.

4. When the present difficulties regarding the language problem are overcome the teaching of these subjects may be possible as optional at the secondary stage.

## THE PROBLEM OF TEACHERS

The proposals for solving the language problem pose the problem of supply of language teachers in the schools of different regions and States. The following suggestions may be useful in this connection :

1. In the present set-up, people speaking other languages are found in almost all the regions. They are engaged in some Government, non-Government or independent occupations. Union Government or State Governments can train them suitably for the teaching of concerned languages.

2. The difficulty of medium of instruction may arise for teaching of other State languages. The teachers of other languages should have sufficient knowledge of the language of the region concerned so that they may be able to explain the other language to the students. One of the solutions for this may be that the teachers of other languages should be trained in the regional languages for a fixed period in order to increase their knowledge of the regional language which they have gained as a result of their stay in that region.

3. The Union Government may select teachers for different languages. After necessary training, they may be appointed as language directors (guides) in important places of the country. They will train local language teachers and give necessary guidance from time to time.

4. By selecting language-teachers from different regions and by giving them training in other regional languages the Union Government or State Governments may prepare them for the teaching of these languages, by giving them some additional salary.

## QUESTIONS FOR EXERCISE

1. How can the three-language formula be useful for emotional integration? What provisions should be made for its perusal at different levels of education?

2. How is the teaching of English useful in the Indian education? How far it should be delimited for the development of Indian nationalism?
3. What suggestions have been made about language problem by various Commissions on education in India? Give your own opinion for solving this problem.

# 22

# PROBLEMS OF WORK EXPERIENCE IN EDUCATION

## Meaning of Work Experience

Work experience means to obtain experience through work. 'Work experience' is a technique through which 'work' and 'education' are correlated. The 'work' means that activity which is productive. 'Work experience' in education is that activity which develops a tendency for productivity. In India the current system of education is so theoretical that the students seldom get an occasion to learn, things by doing. They are generally passive listeners in the class. The students will be able to learn by their own experiences if more importance is given to 'work' in education. They will not be always dependent upon others' experiences. They will learn many things on self-experience.

India is continuing its old traditional methods of education even now. In vocational education one does not employ the latest technological and scientific methods. Through work experience one may learn use of modern methods in productive activities. One may learn how to bring out productive activities on modern lines. This will ultimately enhance the rate of production in factories, mills and elsewhere.

## Characteristics of Work Experience

While trying to make education production-oriented, one should keep in view the needs of the people. As modernization is not Westernization, work experience methods should be devised in Indian context. Following are the chief characteristics of work experience suitable for Indian conditions :

1. *Development of skill* : Work experience should not be related only with productivity, rather, it should aim at developing a skill for productivity.

2. *Self-experience* : Work experience should give self-experience to students which would satisfy his interests and aptitudes.

3. *Modernization* : As the student has to employ latest technological and scientific methods in work experience it develops a tendency towards modernization. A smooth path is paved for the society for imbibing modern culture.

4. *Self-dependence* : Work experience makes the student self-dependent to a certain extent, as he may earn for himself for a part of his expenses of education.

5. *Vocationalization* : Work experience vocationalizes education.

6. *Community Development* : As work experience makes the educational institution a centre of community development, it meets some needs of the community.

7. *Material Gain* : By education imparted through experience both the student and the school may gain materially through having some products of daily use.

## IMPORTANCE OF WORK EXPERIENCE IN EDUCATION

The Kothari Commission (1964-66) has recommended to make work experience as an integral part of education by emphasising the importance of work experience in education in the following manner :

1. **Making education a part of life** : Introduction of work experience in education is likely to reform our stereotyped educational system. Through this 'education' will become a part of life, as it emphasises learning by doing.

2. **Introducing sense of dignity of labour** : Work experience develops a sense of respect in student for manual labour, as each has to do some labour. This may bridge the gap between the labour and the intellectual class.

3. **Developing community consciousness** : Work experience develops communal unity. The school imparts education according to the needs of the immediate community. This develops close relationship between the school and community. An attempt is made sometime to find out solutions of some community problems through work experience in schools. Thus the school becomes a community centre.

4. **Solving problem of unemployment** : Education based on work experience may solve the problem of unemployment, as the student is able to learn some trade business which makes himself dependent when he completes his education.

5. **Utilizing Natural Resources** : Education based on work experience teaches us to utilize natural resources intelligently.

6. **Contributing to Natural Prosperity** : The student becomes more skilful and may contribute more to the growth of national prosperity through work experience.

## IMPORTANT FACTORS IN WORK EXPERIENCE

The following points should be remembered while employing work experience methods in education :

1. **Work Experience-centred Education** : Work experience cannot be accepted as an independent subject of study. It will have to be integrated with all other subjects of study. It cannot exist by its own. Total education has to be made work experience-centred.

2. **Teaching for Work Experience** : For the success of work experience one will have to make the total atmosphere of the school favourable to it. For this suitable text books will have to be prepared. Teachers will also have to be trained on new lines for this purpose. Teachers' training colleges will have to revise their courses for the preparation of work experience teachers.

3. **According to Stages of Learning** : Work experience method may be freely utilized up to the secondary level of education. Work experience method is not possible at the pre-primary stage, because at this stage the young children lack the necessary co-ordination between the movements of their hands and feet. However, they may be given sensory training which may equip them for some sort of work experience. At the primary stage children may be taught some mechanical activities in order that their hands and feet become suitably trained for using certain implements later at the secondary stage.

## PROBLEMS AND REMEDIES OF WORK EXPERIENCE

1. **The Problem of Determination of Aims**. People assign different aims to work experience. While some take it as a means for creating the trait of productivity, others think that it should develop a capacity for production.

*Remedy* : In fact, the aim of work experience should be dependent on principles of work experience. One does not aim to make the child an artisan by developing in him a capacity for production. Its purpose should be to develop the virtue of productivity in the child. When he develops this virtue in himself, he will himself make production also in due course.

2. **The Problem of Suitable and Trained Teachers and Guides** : Indian training colleges produce teachers to impart theoretical instructions to children. These teachers are unsuitable for giving education based on work experience. It is therefore that our multi-purpose schools have not succeeded. Similarly, our work experienced based education may not succeed in the absence of suitable teachers.

*Remedy* : Keeping in view the implications of work experience we have to prepare such trained teachers and guides who impart education based on work experience. They should establish a close relationship between general education and work experience. Till such trained teachers are available, one should seek co-operation of trained workers from the nearby industries. For making the workshop experience more practicable and meaningful, it is necessary to establish a close relationship between the teachers' training institutions and industries.

3. **Lack of Interest and Motivation for Work Experience** : Education based on work experience requires a close relationship between education and practical work. As 'Work' is more dry and tiring than 'play' it is possible that the child will not take interest and lack motivation in education based on work experience. Under such a situation, he will not be benefited by education through work experience.

*Remedy* : The creative tendency in the child keeps him active. He takes pleasure in satisfying his creative tendency. Therefore, the work experience technique should be introduced through play-way method which is likely to be very interesting to children. The interest and capacity of the child should be taken care of while organizing education through work experience. In order to motivate the child should be acquainted with the benefits of work experience in which he is to be engaged.

4. **The Problem of Incorporation of Work Experience in the Curriculum** : What should be various aspects of work experience? How to plan them? How to incorporate them into the curriculum? The purpose of work experience will remain defeated unless these issues are satisfactorily decided.

*Remedy* : First of all one should decide programmes of work experience according to the mental level, interests and aptitudes of children. Afterwards these should be organized in a logical and psychological manner for incorporation in the curriculum. The various types of activities and works chosen for work experience should be related with local industries or with the needs of the immediate society. This will be a prelude to obtaining co-operation of the local industries.

5. **The Problem of Instruction and Method of Work :** Work experience can be obtained only through doing. Manual labour and social service are necessary for this general education. The objectives of work experience cannot be obtained through lecture method. In this context 'correlation' and 'free' methods may be useful.

*Remedy* : In the correlation method one gives instruction in various subjects around the work experience as a nucleus. The subjects which cannot be taught through the correlation method may be left for the 'free' method. In the 'free' method the student is left free for obtaining experience in the workshop.

6. **The Problem of the Necessary Teaching Materials**. Due to paucity of financial resources it has not been possible to transform secondary schools into multipurpose schools. Therefore, the objectives of vocationalization of education have not been realized. The same problem is faced in relation to work experience. It appears difficult to arrange the necessary materials for work experience in schools and colleges. For the work experience programme is needed a correlated time-table, laboratory, workshop and contact with the local industry. It is really a difficult problem to organize all these.

*Remedy* : Work experience should be related to vocationalization of education which requires organisation of necessary materials, equipments and laboratories, etc. The Central and State Governments should give adequate grant for this purpose. The materials should serve many purposes.

7. **The Problem of Evaluation** : The current system of examination is subjective. It cannot be useful for evaluating the progress of students who have learnt through work experiences. This requires devising objective and rated evaluating devices.

*Remedy* : The productivity of the student should be accepted as the basis of evaluation. This requires practical examination, laboratory experiment and oral and written examination, all taken together. The written examination should be supplemented by some objective tests as well. The daily work of the student be a supplementary device for assessing his merits.

**8. The Unfavourable Attitude of Guardians towards Work Experience** : As the guardians have not fully understood the importance of vocationalization of education, so they do not react favourably against work experience. They do not like to get their wards admitted to those schools where they are required to do manual work. They believe that their wards can get better vocational training without going to schools for it.

*Remedy* : The guardians should be told that the current system of education is creating unemployment because the educated youths who have only theoretical knowledge of things cannot stand on their own legs. Favourable attitude may be created in guardians for work experience. Through exhibition, seminar, lectures, publicity through newspapers and radio etc.

## QUESTIONS FOR EXERCISE

1. What is work experience? Why is it necessary in education? How can it be provided?
2. What are the problems of education in relation to work experience? Suggest measures for their remedies.
3. How can we implement the ideal of work experience in Indian education? Suggest remedies.

# 23

# TECHNICAL AND VOCATIONAL EDUCATION : VOCATIONALIZATION

### Meaning of Technical Education

There are plenty of natural resources in India. Due to lack of adequate technical education, Indians have not yet been able to explore and exploit them fully. With the development of technical education they may be able to explore and exploit them to our best advantage. The student acquires a capacity to earn his living through vocational education. By this capacity he starts production of some kind. For technical education, the trainee has to acquire some specific techniques on the basis of which he may convert raw materials into finished products.

### Aims of Technical and Vocational Education

1. To impart to the trainee fundamental scientific knowledge and skill pertaining to the latest technology. This shall equip him with the latest technology in various areas. This will add to the growth of national prosperity.

2. To give to the trainee a correlated knowledge of general, scientific and special subjects. It must not aim to make him a specialist prematurely.

3. To train even the handicapped individuals in the society in order that they may also usefully adjust themselves in society and may also produce something, if they can.

4. To make the student an expert in a particular field. Even those who have entered a vocation since long and want to equip themselves further in their line or in some allied areas should also benefit by it.

5. To create in the trainee a sense of respect for manual work.

Thus technical and vocational education should be available to all those who need it. It should be of latest nature, comprehensive and useful to life.

### Meaning of Vocationalization

In India, education has little utility to life, as it does not prepare a person for earning a living. Due to this inadequacy the necessity of vocationalization of education has been keenly felt. Vocationalization means that vocational subjects should be given a place in the curriculum of general subjects so that the student becomes competent to earn his living after completing his general education. Vocationalization of education does not intend to make the child a carpenter, an artisan, a weaver, a goldsmith or businessman or producer of some article. It only means to give a self-dependence to the student in life afterwards. Vocationalized education seeks the development of the total personality of the child. Vocationalization, does not mean only to impart vocational education. Vocational education should be organized according to the individual aptitudes of the students. A good vocational capacity may be developed in the child, after ascertaining his various aptitudes and interests. According to the recommendation of the Secondary Education Commission (1952-53) multi-purpose schools established at some places in the country have included the education in various vocational subjects along with education in general subjects. Kothari Commission (1964-66) has emphasised work-experience in education. This type of education will promote the all-sided development of the individual.

## VOCATIONALIZATION OF EDUCATION

Vocational education has been defined by UNESCO as a "comprehensive term embracing those aspects of the educational process involving, in addition to general education, the study of technologies and related sciences and the acquisition of practical skills, attitudes, understandings and knowledge relating to occupations in the various sectors of economic and social life. Such an education would be an integral part of general education and a means of preparing for an occupational field and as aspect of continuing education."

Vocational education is education given to an individual to prepare him for a successful social living by enabling him to realise his own potential within the framework of economic development to which the individual contributes.

Vocationalization means learning of a skill or a range of skills through study of technologies, related sciences or other practical work. Vocationalization of higher secondary education aims at increasing the employment potential of the people through education for self-employment, with emphasis on agricultural and related occupations, including miniature small, cottage and agro industries and through preparation for specific competencies in different vocations.

### Teaching Time Table

The Higher Secondary stream has two spectra — the General Education spectrum and the Vocationalized spectrum. The distribution of time for teaching the General Education spectrum should be :

| | |
|---|---|
| 1. Languages | 15% |
| 2. Socially Useful Productive Work (SUPW) | 15% |
| 3. Electives | 70% |

The allocation of time for vocationalized spectrum should be :

| | |
|---|---|
| 1. Languages | 15% |
| 2. General Education Course | 15% |
| 3. Elective Subjects | 70% |

As mentioned above 70% of the weekly hours of instruction has to be allocated to the teaching of vocational elective subjects. National Review Committee (Adiseshiah Report, 1978) gave the following recommendations :

1. About 50% of these hours should be spent on practical work with certain amount of flexibility.

2. Special attention should be given to the self-employment factor.

3. Vocational education at Higher Secondary stage should not duplicate the training given at Industrial Training Institutes.

4. The main thrust of the proposed vocationalisation is on rural agricultural and related vocations.

5. The course in vocational areas should be drawn up in such a way that the employability of the students will be enhanced.

6. The duration of a vocational course should normally be of two years in the formal system. The courses requiring lesser duration than two years may be pursued through non-formal systems such as part-time and evening courses, correspondence courses etc., and the institutions should be free to offer such courses through non-formal channels.

**Vocational Electives**

1. Agriculture and Related Vocations.
2. Business and Office Management.
3. Para-Medical.
4. Education Sciences.
5. Local Body and other Sciences.
6. Journalism.
7. Home Science and Related Vocation.
8. Other concerned sciences as Commercial Art, Photography, Printing and Lithography, Ceramics, Pottery, Tourist Guides, etc.

**Advantages of Vocationlization**

1. It will help in accelerating the economic growth of the country.
2. It will give a lead to society in the matter of self-employment.
3. It will be a boon to the society as the supply of technical leadership at the grass-root level is enlarged.

4. It will put an end to the mad rush for entrance into Universities, and the consequent deterioration in the standard of education.

**National Review Committee (1978)**

The National Review Committee (1978) has given the following recommendations for making vocationalisation of education successful :

1. There should be no rigid streaming of courses into the General Education and Vocationalised Education spectra. The student should be free to offer either the general education or vocationalized courses or a mix of the two, particularly in relation to the vocational courses as agriculture, and related vocations and other general sciences. There should be in-built elasticity in the choice of the general education or vocationalized subjects.

2. Learning must be based on work. It must be either through the Socially Useful Productive Work (SUPW) or through vocationalised courses.

3. Vocational courses should be provided in agricultural and related rural occupational areas and in managerial, commercial, health and para-medical vocations and not industrial and engineering occupations.

4. Books should be written on a priority basis to suit local conditions and make available to the schools, in order to impart instruction in vocational courses, in agricultural and related subjects.

5. Semester pattern and credit system may also be introduced in higher secondary classes. Suitable steps may be undertaken for the orientation of teachers in this connection.

6. To begin with, teachers with post-graduate qualifications need not be insisted. Persons who have had actual experience of on-the-job may be fruitfully utilised to reach vocational courses. Part-time teachers may also be appointed wherever necessary.

7. Both pre-service and in-service teacher education should be organised, in collaboration with Colleges of Education, SCERTs, NCERT, Agricultural Universities, ICAR etc.

8. A vocational survey of the area-metropolitan, block, taluk, district or State should be undertaken.

9. As little or no vocationalised education facilities are readily available for rural students, all the new schools should be constructed in rural areas and should be adequately equipped.

10. Shift system should be introduced wherever it is feasible.

11. Apprenticeship facilities should be extended to all the students who complete education in vocational streams if they desire to benefit from such training.

12. Vocationally qualified persons should be preferred to graduates and be entitled to the pay scales available to the graduates as long as the job performed are the same or similar.

13. A National Council of Vocational Education should be set up.

14. At the State level, State Councils for Vocational Education be created and should function under the general guidance of the National Council of Vocational Education.

15. The vocationlisation ofEducation must be supported by the local community and other agencies, such as Panchayat, Union, Agricultural Co-operatives, the Small Scale Industries Corporation, Khadi and Village Industry Commission, Local branches of Nationalised and other Banks etc.

## IMPORTANCE OF VOCATIONALIZATION

1. **Sense in Life** : Vocational or general education alone makes the development of the individual one-sided. But while vocationalized education may bring more fullness in life, general education alone leaves an individual unemployed and dependent on others for economic assistance. However, while vocationalized education alone may make a child a skilful worker in some area, it cannot make him a fully developed individual.

2. **Employment** : Vocationalized education gives a capacity to earn ones living. India is facing the problem of unemployment of youths, because she has not yet vocationalized education.

3. **Economic Development of the Society and Nation** : India has enough natural resources. But due to lack of vocational education she could not yet exploit them fully. Consequently, she is behind many other countries in production. Vocationalized education creates the trait of productiveness in the individual. He may learn how to exploit the natural resources intelligently. This may ultimately lead to the economic prosperity of the nation.

4. **Creating a Spirit of Self-dependence** : Vocationalized education creates a spirit of self-dependence in the individual. Through this education he begins to earn even during his school or college career. Thus ultimately he becomes a useful member of the society.

5. **Psychological Tendencies** : An individual may satisfy his instincts of construction and self-display through vocationalized education. Many of his latent interests, may get full play. He acquires some abilities. His talents may be further developed. In vocationalized education, the student is not a passive listener. He becomes an active partner in the very process of his education. He learns by doing things. In order to cater to the varying needs, interests and aptitudes of students, various types of vocations should be incorporated in a vocationalized curriculum.

6. **Dignity of Labour** : As one has to do some manual work for learning some vocational skill in the vocationalized education it develops in him a sense of dignity of labour, not possible in purely general and academic education.

## IMPEDIMENTS IN VOCATIONAL EDUCATION

Hitherto in India all the Committees and Commissions on education have recommended for vocationalization of education. In the countries where education has been vocationalized, there is no acute problem of unemployment or the over-crowding in colleges and universities. The Kothari Commission (1964-66) observed that in India only 9 per cent of the students are able to get education through vocationalized curriculum. In comparison to that in many foreign countries this percentage is very low. The following may be the causes of this low percentage :

1. The Government has not taken up the problem of vocationalization of education with due seriousness.

2. Lack of teachers for imparting instruction according to the vocationalized aspects incorporated in the general curriculum.

3. As Education Department of the Government has not been able to receive guidance for determining the exact nature of the vocationlized curriculum, the vocationlized education programme could not be formulated according to the social and national needs.

4. Due to lack of necessary facilities in schools and training colleges, Laboratories and Workshops have not been satisfactorily organized and the required number of trained teachers is not available.

5. The Universities neglected altogether the programmes pertaining to physical work and social service. These could not get adequate encouragement from schools, colleges and universities.

6. There has been a lack of co-operation between labour, industries and education departments of the Government. No department wholly took the responsibility of vocationalized education on its own.

7. The public remained altogether indifferent to vocationalized education as its utility has not been fully explained to people.

## DEVELOPMENT OF TECHNICAL AND VOCATIONAL EDUCATION IN INDIA

In India the issue of technical and vocational education has already been there since ancient days. With the changes in time, ideas, circumstances and needs of life its shape has been changing. One may understand the technical and vocational education in India in the following two periods :

1. Ancient period; and
2. Modern period.

### 1. Ancient Period

The development of technical and vocational education of the ancient period may be understood in the following periods :

(i) Vedic period.
(ii) Post-Vedic period.
(iii) Buddha period.
(iv) Muslim period.
(v) British period.

(i) *Vedic Period* : Vedas are the oldest literature of the world. One find reference to technical and vocational education in the Rigveda and Atharvaveda. In the Rigveda one finds vivid descriptions of construction of canals, bunds and bridges, vehicles incorporating fast speed and beautiful palaces. Aryurveda is a branch of Atharvaveda. Therein one finds elaborate discussion of medical sciences. In the Vedic literature one finds ample discussion of manufacture of cotton, silken and woollen cloths, agricultural implements and arms and ammunitions.

(ii) *Post-Vedic Period* : During this period the technical and vocational education continued as prevalent in the Vedic age. This is the epic (Ramayana and Mahabharata) period. In the Ramayana, the epic written by Valmiki, one finds frequent references to Rama's journey by Puskpak Viman and construction of bridge for going accross the sea *i.e.* to Lanka, for conquerring Ravana. In the Mahabharata one finds mention of houses made of wax and houses parks of which appear to be having water and other portions dry. The ruins of Mohanjodaro and Harappa remind us of the technical and vocational skills of that period. One finds descriptions of means of fast transport for going from onc place to another. One also finds description of various types of weapons and fire-arms used in wars.

(iii) *Buddhist Period*: During the Buddhist period the Vedic literature was also studied along with the Buddhist religious scriptures. The vocational study of Ayurveda (Science of medicine), Dhanurveda (science of war) and Gandharvaveda (art of music) developed much during this period. The science of medicine, architecture, painting, sculpture, veterinary and chemistry are some of the chief contributions of this period.

(iv) *The Muslim Period* : During this period the art of making various types of silken, woollen and cotton cloths, wood work, architecture, drawing and ornaments developed remarkably. Imperial palaces, mosques, carpets, utencils and embroideries of this period have been of world fame. Vocational education during this period was not organised. The trainees used to learn the art under strict personal control and supervision of the artisans concerned.

(v) *The British Period.* After establishment of the British rule in India, the Britishers engaged themselves in consolidating it. For this purpose, they needed various types of workers. They felt the need of technicians in various areas. As it was very costly to borrow these expert workers from abroad, so they decided to start some technical and vocational colleges :

**1847 to 1902** : In 1847 an Engineering College was started at Roorkee. Afterwards, engineering colleges were started at Calcutta, Madras and Poona. The Wood's Despatch of 1854 emphasized the importance of making Indian education useful to life. By 1902 about 80 technical and vocational schools were established in the country. Lord Curzon took keen interest in expansion of technical and vocational education. He established an agriculture department in each province. He emphasized the need of establishing agricultural colleges. Agriculture was included as a subject for classes VI to X.

**From 1902 to 1921** : During this period also, the Government of India did not pay any attention towards technical and professional education. However, the recommendations of Indian Education Commission were accepted and technical and vocational subjects were included in the curricula of high schools in different provinces.

**From 1921 to 1937** : After the establishment of the dual rule in 1921, demand of the people for technical and vocational education received great momentum. A special Committee under the Chairmanship of Lord Lytton was entrusted this work in order to take a decision in this matter. This committee studied the problems and difficulties of the Indian students studying in foreign countries. It made many suggestions to remove them. The most important suggestion of the Committee was that the technical, vocational and industrial institutions should be established in India. Provision should be made for imparting higher education to Indians in their own country. Following institutions were established in consequence of this recommendation :

1. Harcourt Butler Technological Institute, Kanpur,
2. College of Engineering and Technology, Jadavpur.
3. Government School of Technology, Madras.

In 1937 there were nearly 535 technical, vocational and industrial schools in India.

**From 1937 to 1947** : After 1937, vocational and technical education was expanded with great speed due to the following reasons :

1. Upto the Second World War, the demand of persons with technical education increased.
2. New industries were established in India for the production of war material. Industrial persons having received technical education were required for these industries.
3. The demand of persons having received technical education increased for implementing the post -development schemes prepared by the Central and the Provincial Governments.

In 1941-42 only 264 students were studying in graduate courses of technical education and 22 students in chemical technology respectively.

**2. Modern Period After Independence**

**From 1947 to 1969** : The post-independent period witnessed the tremendous progress in the field of technical and vocational education along with the rapid growth of industrialisation in the country. Earlier, there was the provision of imparting vocational and technical education to only 6,600 students. This number increased to 4,35,796 in the year 1963. Besides this, facilities were also provided to 25,000 students for engineering and technical degree and to 49,000 for diploma in the year 1966.

(i) *First Five Year Plan* : In the First Five Year Plan it was decided to develop Indian Institute of Science, Banglore, to establish 14 colleges of engineering to make provision of teaching of some special vocational subjects and to establish guidance centres for the students receiving professional and technical education. Schemes were prepared for the establishment of industrial, technical and professional schools, conversion of crafts schools into junior technical high schools, establishment of junior multi-purpose schools, development of general secondary schools into technical high schools, giving of proper place to agricultural education in the curriculum, conversion of commercial, vocational and technical schools into colleges and grant of scholarships to the students for receiving higher education in foreign countries. Provision was made for providing more facilities to impart training to the artists and craftsmen and to establish training centres in villages.

(ii) *Second Five Year Plan*. Due to the increasing demand of the technical and vocational workers, a special importance was given to the expansion of vocational and technical education during the Second Five Year Plan. 48 crores of rupees were allotted for technical and vocational education in the Second Five-Year Plan. The Indian Institute of Technology, Kharagpur was developed for graduate and post-graduate studies. Provision was made for the study of graduate courses of 1,200 students and post-graduate and research work for 600 students. The Institute of Science, Banglore was developed for Air and Naval Engineering, Power Engineering, Internal Combustion, Metallurgy and Electrical Research and other types of vocational and technical education.

In the centres already established for vocational and technical education under the First Five-Year Plan, provision was made for the post-graduate course in engineering, technology and research work. Higher institutions of vocational and technical education were established in western, northern, southern regions of the country. Two of such types of institutions were established at Bombay and Kanpur.

Facilities for the education of engineering and technology in Delhi Polytechnic were expanded. Besides this, 9 other institutions of degree stage and 20 institutions of diploma stage were established in other parts of the country. The scheme of training of foremen was implemented with the co-operation of industrial institutions. The number of scholarships were increased from 630 to 800. Some seats were reserved for meritorious students in technical and vocational institutions. Hostels were provided for 13,000 technical students and for 3,300, students of Junior technical schools. Indian School of Science and Applied Geology, Dhanbad was further developed and expanded. Therefore, by the end of the year 1960-61, 57,000 graduates and 6,800 diploma holders in engineering and technical education were made available to the country.

(iii) *Third Five-Year Plan* : It was envisaged that 45,000 graduates and 80,000 diploma holders would be required during the Third Five-Year Plan. A sum of rupees 142 crores was allotted for implementing the programme of the development of the technical and vocational education. During the period of the Third Five Year Plan, the number of students admitted annually in the degree courses was increased by 6,000 by admitting of 5,000 in engineering colleges part-time of correspondence courses. The number of students admitted every year increased from 13,200 in 1961 to 19,200 in 1966. Likewise, the number of students admitted in diploma courses was also increased by 15,000 by admitting 10,000 students in Polytechnic and education of the rest of 5,000 students through part-time or correspondence courses. Thus the number of the students, which was 24,000 at the end of the Second Five-Year Plan increased to 9,000 at the end of the Third Five-Year Plan.

(iv) *Fourth Five-Year Plan* : An additional capacity of 4,000 seats for degree and 3,400 for diploma courses was created during the Fourth Five Year Plan.

(v) *Fifth Five-Year Plan* : Top priority was given to vocational and technical education in the Fifth Plan. The proposed plan outlay for technical education was Rs. 164 crores.

Its aim was to provide technical education to 25,000 students at degree level and 50,000 at diploma level. It was said, in the draft of the plan, "The main stress will continue to be on the consolidation and improvement of the quality of the technical education system".

(vi) *Sixth Five-Year Plan* : The Janta Govt. under the Sixth Five-Year Plan (1978-83) allocated Rs. 150 crores for the expansion of technical and vocational education. In its revised draft the Congress Govt. allocated Rs. 278 crores for its expansion under the sixth Plan.

The following table, shows the progress in the field of higher technical education under the Five-Year Plans in India :

| Year | No. of schools | No. of students | No. of teachers | Exp. (in crore Rs.) |
|---|---|---|---|---|
| 1961-62 | 3,751 | 4,08,443 | 28,657 | 12.80 |
| 1962-63 | 3,846 | 4,24,264 | 29,847 | 13.04 |
| 1963-64 | 4,137 | 4,57,350 | 33,494 | 16.24 |
| 1964-65 | 3,147 | 2,69,096 | 17,380 | 7.39 |
| 1965-66 | 2,755 | 2,47,021 | 17,785 | 7.66 |
| 1966-67 | 2,754 | 2,45,148 | 18,383 | 8.27 |
| 1970-71 | 2,764 | 2,52,412 | 18,745 | 9.32 |
| 1980-81 | 2,972 | 5,16,722 | 18,972 | 13.04 |
| 1985-86 | 3,102 | 8,12,517 | 19,394 | 35.00 |

## THE PROBLEMS OF VOCATIONALIZATION

### The Main Problems

1. *Form and Organization of Education.* What should be the form of vocationalized education and how shall it be determined? These questions are concerned with the form of vocational education.

2. *Organization of the Curriculum.* This includes the problem of how to harmonise the vocational courses with the general courses.

3. *Training of Teachers* : The vocationalized education will require special type of teachers who can impart vocational education along with instruction in general education. It will mean change in the current set-up of teachers' training institutions like the multi-purpose schools. The vocationalization of education will fail in absence of suitable teachers.

4. *Bringing in Changes in the Instructional Procedures* : Vocationalised education requires an integrated teaching procedure in which a certain vocation will have to be accepted as a nucleus and the various subjects will be taught around it in a correlated manner. However, all the subjects of general education cannot be taught in this manner. Only those subjects can be taught which may be correlated with the vocation concerned.

5. *Laboratories and Other Equipments* : Each school will require some workshop, laboratory and other physical facilities and equipments after vocationalization of education. This will mean enough money. But due to want of financial resources even traditional schools lack the required facilities.

6. *Selection of Vocation at the time of Admission of Students* : At the time of admission it is difficult for the student to choose a vocation. His aptitude should be ascertained through aptitude tests. Educational and vocational guidance services should be organized in schools. These services help the students in identifying their aptitudes and interests. Training in a particular vocation may be given accordingly.

7. *Administration and Control*. General education has been under the control of Government education department uptill now. After vocationalization the Government education department alone cannot control education. The co-operation of the departments of industries, agriculture and other ones will be necessary.

## RECOMMENDATIONS OF COMMITTEES AND COMMISSIONS

### Pre-Independence

Committees and Commissions of education were appointed keeping in view the problems arising out of vocationalization of education. These Committees and Commissions have given following suggestions for vocationalization of education.

1. *Indian Education Commission (1882)* : It suggested that vocational subjects should be given due place in the current curriculum. But the government made no effort to implement this suggestion.

2. *Hartog Committee (1929)* : It suggested that after passing the middle school examination a student should be given an opportunity to study industrial and commercial courses.

3. *Sapru Committee (1934)* : It suggested that various types of vocational courses should be taught at high school level.

4. *Basic Education Scheme (1936-37)* : A number of basic schools were opened under this scheme. An attempt was made to teach a number of subjects around a certain craft with the interest of the student.

5. *Abbot-Wood Committee (1937)* : It submitted its report on vocational education. This report emphasised the introduction of vocational courses for removing unemployment.

6. *Sargent Scheme (1944-45)* : It recommended the continuance of the Basic Scheme. It suggested to incorporate local crafts and industries in the curriculum.

**After Independence**

1. **Secondary Education Commission (1952-53)**. It recommended the incorporation of vocational courses in the secondary school curriculum as follows :

(i) Multi-purpose schools should be established. The current secondary schools should be gradually converted into multi-purpose schools. Till then vocational courses should be taught in them according to the varying interests of students. The whole curriculum was sub-divided into seven parts. Every student should study at least one of these parts according to his interest. Each student should study some vocational subject to develop a sense of respect for manual work. The Commission emphasised the need of educational and vocational guidance services in each school.

(ii) Each student should be given an opportunity to do some productive work in the school. The courses should be diversified to make many alternatives available for the students. It will enable each student to choose some manual work according to his interest.

(iii) The student should be given theoretical knowledge and practical training in agriculture. Such vocations as gardening, animal husbandry, veterinary science and bee-keeping etc. may be encouraged in schools. These vocations were considered more useful for rural children. The rural school should function as community centre also.

(iv) Technical education should be provided in secondary schools. The student may choose some technical subject as his hobby. Some industrial tax may also be levied for acquiring some funds for technical education. The Central Government should annually give financial grant to State Governments. A federal board for technical education should be established. Multi-purpose schools should be opened at some places.

2. **University Commission (1948-49)** : It emphasised the need of establishing rural universities for teaching agriculture and allied subjects. It also recommended for making more progressive medical education, teachers' training and education in law.

3. **Kothari Commission (1964-66)** : It emphasised the utility of vocational education and gave the following suggestions :

(a) We have not yet fully emphasised vocational education at the secondary stage. Secondary education must be vocationalized according to the means available to us.

(b) Vocational education should be sub-divided into the following stages according to the curriculum :

(i) *Junior Secondary Stage* : The students who have passed seventh or eighth class should be admitted in Industrial Training Institutes (I.T.I). The admission age should be reduced to 14 years of age. This may also benefit the primary school passed student. Part-time education should be arranged for industrial training to benefit those children who are mostly engaged in domestic work. The students should be given training in agriculture and domestic science.

(ii) *Higher Secondary Stage.* Polytechnical institutions should be established for those students who have passed secondary school classes. Part-time training or Correspondence Courses may also be arranged for such students. In health, commerce, administration and small industries varying courses of six months to three years duration should be instituted.

(iii) Separate Committees and Sub-committees should be organized within the jurisdiction of the Education Department of Government for giving training in their respective vocation. These committees will look after part-time training and correspondence courses in their respective areas. First of all the man-power available for the various vocations should be ascertained. Then the training for the same should be organized. The firms which may absorb the trained hands should also be consulted about the trained hands that they would require.

(iv) The Central Government should give adequate financial assistance to the various States for vocational and technical education. In U.S.A. it was due to the federal assistance that secondary education could be vocationalized. This practice should be adopted in India also.

(v) The current facilities for vocational and technical education should be further extended. The training of workmen should be grouped into two parts : semi-skilled and skilled. The number of vocational and technical institutions should be increased. The private and State trade schools should be encouraged by giving financial help.

(vi) People have no interest in vocational curriculum as they do not understand its utility. Government should try to create interest in the people for vocational and technical training. Vocational courses should be made more interesting. Vocational Guidance Committees should be organized in schools to give psychological vocational guidance to the students.

## PROBLEMS AND REMEDIES OF TECHNICAL AND VOCATIONAL EDUCATION

### 1. The Problem of Qualitative Improvement

Education should be both quantitative and qualitative. While India has made quantitative improvement in technical and vocational education, we have not yet paid adequate attention to its qualitative side. Many technical and vocational institutions are being run in a very bad condition. There are no good workshops, laboratories, libraries and buildings. Well trained teachers are very few.

*Remedy* : Technical and vocational institutions which do not fulfil the minimum conditions should be closed. Those which are well managed and organized should be given adequate financial assistance for organizing good workshops, laboratories and libraries. They should have close relationship with the relevant local industries. The trainees should be sent to these industries to obtain some practical experience.

### 2. The Problem of Creating Favourable Attitude Towards Manual Work

In India, the person engaged in manual work is looked down. A labourer does not enjoy that respect in our society which a teacher, advocate or doctor does. Hence, trainees in technical and vocational institutions do not like to engage themselves in those operations which require manual work. They do not get adequate practical experience. Technical and vocational institutions are not producing good skilled workers. No reform in technical and vocational education will yield the expected result unless this situation is changed.

*Remedy* : Opportunities should be given to students and teachers in schools, colleges and universities for doing various types of creative manual work. Workshops should be organized to give enough practical experience to each trainee. More time should be allowed in the time-table for practical work. It should be corresponding to capacity and interests.

### 3. The Problem of Defective Curriculum

The following defects are found in the curriculum of technical and vocational institutions :

1. It does not fulfil the local needs. For example, in the agriculturally predominant area, agriculture is not given a prominent place in the curriculum.
2. It has lack of productivity.
3. It does not develop in the student a love for manual work.
4. It lacks in variety. It does not have many purposes which should be a special feature of a technical institution.

*Remedy* : It should be estimated as to how many teachers and guides are required for a particular stage of technical and vocational education. The arrangement for the equipment should be made on the basis of this estimate. The teachers and guides should be given attractive salaries and other facilities. The four regional committees established in the country should take the responsibility of doing the needful in this matter.

### 4. The Problem of Medium in the Technical and Vocational Education

The mother tongue has been accepted as the medium of instruction in India upto the secondary stage. After passing this stage, when the student takes admission in some technical institution, he is given the training through English, because good books are not available on the subject in his mother-tongue. This creates a great difficulty for the trainee. He has to devote much time to the study of English at the neglect of the technical subjects. Hence, many capable students are left behind.

*Remedy* : Regional languages should be accepted as the medium of instruction in the technical and vocational institutions. The trainee should not be compelled to acquire proficiency in English, unless he himself insists for the same. Before making regional languages the medium of instruction, it is necessary to produce standard books in regional languages in the various areas of technical and vocational education. The teachers and guides for technical and vocational institutions should be so trained that they may be able to impart the training through the medium of the regional language concerned.

### 5. The Problem of Administration and Control

The Education Ministry of Government of India is not responsible for technical and vocational education in the States of the Union. In States separate departments of the education, at some places two departments together, carry the responsibility for this education. At certain places labour department, industry, or agriculture department is made responsible for this education. At some other place a university is entrusted with its responsibility. This situation has created the problem of administration and control.

*Remedy* : Many problems of technical and vocational education will be automatically solved by solving the problem of its administration and control. The Education Ministry of the Government of India should take up the responsibility of technical and vocational education in the same way as it looks after general education. A Council of technical and vocational education may also be organized for looking after the various implied issues. Suitable persons from various relevant departments may be requested to serve on this Council. The setting up of such a Council should be done both at the Central and State levels . This will bring in a uniformity in administration and control of technical and vocational education.

### 6. The Problem Relating to Research

The Government of India has emphasized the problem of research in technical and vocational education in the various Five Year Plans but we have not yet become self-dependent in this respect and we have still to copy the Western pattern. Process and research styles should be according to our needs in the country. The foreign styles cannot meet our Indian needs. We have not yet succeeded in making such researches on the basis of which we may profitably use our full manpower. In many European countries and in the United States of America, there is a lack of adequate manpower because of the population being thinner. So in place of manpower they use machines as substitutes. But our Indian condition is entirely different from the conditions prevailing in the above foreign lands. As we are still manufacturing such machines which may be used as substitutes for manpower, a major portion of our manpower lies idle and unemployed.

*Remedy* : The research work in the field of technical and vocational education should be carried out according to the needs and conditions in the country. The Government should set up various types of experimental laboratories and research centres. The researchers should be given handsome stipends in order that capable persons may be attracted towards the same.

### 7. The Problem of Post-Technical Education and Training

After getting the training, if the trainee remains unemployed for some time, he forgets all that he has learned in the technical field concerned. And those who are lucky enough to get some employment continue working for years according to the old method that they learnt several years ago. They do not get any chance for acquainting themselves with the latest devices and techniques. They forget even the theoretical aspect of the training that they obtained. In foreign countries an attempt is made to familiarise the old workers with the latest researches, techniques and inventions in their relevant areas. This develops their skills and accelerates the rate of production as well.

*Remedy.* The problem of post-education and training may be solved through any of the following measures :

(i) Correspondence courses.

(ii) Part-time course.

(iii) Close contact with the technical institutions and industries.

(iv) Short-term courses.

(v) Refresher courses.

(i) *The correspondence courses* : These may be organized for those workers who need enough orientation in latest theoretical principles. For in-service workers this is a good device. They already continue their workshop practices. So for 15 or 20 days they may be invited at a certain centre for reorientation.

(ii) *The part-time courses.* These develop the theoretical knowledge and skill of the in-service workers. But the part-time courses may be possible only at some technical institution. Morning or evening classes may be arranged for this purpose.

(iii) *Close contact* : According to the recommendations of the Kothari Commission (1964-66) the training for in-service may be arranged by establishing a close relationship between the technical institution and the concerned industries. This arrangement is likely to benefit both the in-service workers and the trainees.

(iv) *Short term courses* : The in-service workers are invited to attend certain courses for two or three weeks at some technical institution. This programme may be conveniently arranged during the holidays of some relevant industries.

(v) *Refresher courses* : The in-service workers may be trained in latest techniques and devices. This may be arranged at some technical education centre.

### 8. The Problem of Modernization of Technology

Technology has been modernized in U.S.A., U.S.S.R. and other Western countries. Blindly following their method situation has created the following problems in India :

1. By modernization we have begun to understand Westernization. As our needs are different from the Western ones, so we have to modernize the technology according to our Indian needs.

2. The technology dependent upon the invested capital is creating a misunderstanding between the labourers and the owner. The one is the exploiter and the other is the exploited. So a gap is being created between the two.

3. Under the influence of modernization we forget our Indian social values and circumstances. This has an adverse impact on the society.

*Remedy* : No doubt, India should modernize her technologies, but she will have to Indianize them as well according to her own conditions and needs. The technologies should be modernized in such a way as to obtain the maximum production by using the minimum manpower, capital and raw materials. The manpower should be properly utilized and the maximum number of people should get employment. The difference of rich and poor, owner and labourer and the exploiter and the exploited should be eliminated.

### 9. The Problem of Co-ordination Between Training Facilities and Job Opportunities

Through our Five Year Plans India have developed opportunities for technical and vocational education. But the development of these opportunities has created the problems of unemployment of technical hands. At the same time, in some technical areas there were no trained hands.

*Remedy* : An estimate of the manpower needed for the various areas should be made for obtaining a balance and co-ordination between the technical facilities and job opportunities. According to this estimate technical and vocational education should be given to a few selected persons. The technical and vocational institutions should be closely related to the relevant industries, as it is in these industries that the trained hands are to be employed. Its programme should be prepared by the various States according to their own specific needs.

## QUESTIONS FOR EXERCISE

1. Discuss the meaning and importance of vocationalization of education?
2. What have been the causes of slow progress of vocationalization of education in our country? How can we remove them?
3. What have been the recommendations for vocationalization of education given by the Kothari Commission?
4. How has the Secondary Education Commission of 1952-53 tried to solve the problem of vocationalization of education?
5. Give a brief critical account of development of technical and vocational education in India.
6. Describe the development of technical and vocational education in India after independence.
7. Explain the main problems of technical and vocational education in India suggesting remedies.

# 24

# SECULARISM, RELIGIOUS AND MORAL EDUCATION

## DEFINITION OF SECULARISM

1. **Pioneer Definition** : The word 'secularism' was first used in the nineteenth century by George Jacob Holydake. He derived it form the Latin word 'Saeculum' meaning "this present age". He used it in the context of social and ethical values or system. Thus, secularism came to be known as a social and ethical system. The following principles were evolved by Holydake to mark this system :

(i) Primary emphasis on the material and cultural improvement of human beings.

(ii) Respect for and search for all truth, whatever be its source, which can be tested in experience leading to human betterment.

(iii) Concern for this age or world and its improvement.

(iv) An independent rational morality, which does not base itself on faith in divine commandment.

Bradlaugh observed that secularism was hostile to religion and maintained that either secularism or religion should survive.

2. **Western Secularism :**

(i) *Chambers Dictionary* : "The belief that the state, moral, education, etc., should be independent of religion."

(ii) *Oxford Dictionary* : "The doctrine that morality should be based solely in regard to the well-being of mankind in the present life, to the exclusion of all consideration drawn from belief in God."

(iii) *Webster's Dictionary* : "The belief that religion and ecclesiastical affairs should not enter into the functions of the state." The limited sense of the word secularism is often placed in contrast to religion. Thus Webster gives us an alternative definition of secularism — "A system of doctrines and practices that rejects any form of religious faith and worship."

In the deeper sense of the word, secularism is not concerned with what is religious and spiritual, and is surely opposed to everything that is irrational.

3. **Indian Concept of Secularism :** Indian conception of secularism required that there shall be no state religion and the state shall treat all religions equally. In the words of Mahatma Gandhi, "My veneration for other faiths is the same as for my own faith." "We believe in Sarvadharmasamabhava having equal regard for all faiths and creeds."

## CHARACTERISTICS OF SECULAR EDUCATION

Secular education is identified because of the following characteristics :

1. *Moral outlook* : Secular education results in development of moral outlook. It is the foundation for development of character and moral development. It inculcates in students humanity, truthfulness, tolerance, honesty, courtesy, sympathy, spirit of service and sacrifice which form a noble character of man and develop his personality.

2. *Development of wider vision* : Secular education makes a man dynamic and enlightened. It develops in him a wider vision towards life, and he takes interest in social service by sacrificing his selfish motives. Education makes him courageous enough to face the problems of life and solve them to the best of his efforts and intelligence.

3. *Pluralistic outlook* : Secular education leads to the emergence of a healthy pluralist outlook which fosters the growth of science, art, philosophy and even religion. A pluralist outlook is the very essence of democracy.

4. *Democratic values* : Secular education helps man in developing democratic values like liberty, equality, fraternity and co-operative living. True secularism stresses the dignity of the individual and the sacredness of human personality. Secular education helps to establish and incorporate democratic process. Every person is treated as an end and never as a means only.

5. *Cultural development* : Secular education helps in fostering scientific spirit. It releases the individual from the bonds of blind faith. Scientific spirit implies a spirit of free enquiry, a spirit of looking at things objectively and rationally, freedom from an obsession with the past, and a more humble attitude towards one's own history and achievements. Secular education promotes scientific values of rationality, objectivity and open-mindedness. It also promotes humanistic values like tolerance and compassion.

6. *Synthesis of spiritual and material* : Secular education glorifies material needs and promotes reverence for earthly life, without rejecting spiritual values. Secularism is based on fundamental human values. It looks upon science not merely as a means of material progress but as a quest for truth and a search for harmony with nature, it helps to strike a healthy balance between the spiritual and the material.

7. *Humanitarianism* : Secular education leads to humanitarianism. It stands for peace, good-will and understanding. It helps in fostering the brotherhood of

man and the unity of the world. Absence of secular education causes exploitation, corruption, disaster, selfishness, aggression and hatred, chaos and disorder. Betterment of society depends upon secular-based education. It raises man to a high level, it encourages the policy of live and let live. It provides the basis for true humanitarianism. It helps in replacing hatred by love, selfishness by self-sacrifice and violence by non-violence. Secular education leads to happiness, order and contentment in the society by cultivating faith in truth, beauty and goodness.

## EDUCATION FOR SECULARISM IN INDIA

India's present educational system promotes secular attitudes and values through its broad-based aims, curricula, enlightened teachers and appropriate activities, all emphasizing open-mindedness, progressivism, rationality, freedom from bigotry and superstition, and equal respect for all religions. The following traits characterise education for secularism in India.

1. *Secular Aims* : The aims and objectives of such a system are secular. They seek to develop India as a rational, democratic, progressive and modern state. The philosophy of humanism guides such educational objectives. The well being of all the citizens of the country is the goal towards which India's educational energies are directed.

2. *Democratic Organization of Educational Institutions* :The organization of most of Indian educational institutions is based on secular principles. It is necessary to observe secular, democratic, rational criteria in appointments, promotions, admission and all such matters.

3. *Multiple Curricula* : The educational curricula at all levels in India lay special emphasis on the promotion of secular values. Lessons in text-books are free from religious bigotry and prejudice while the good ideas and values emphasised in different religions are presented in appropriate forms. The co-curricular activities aim at promoting harmony and co-operation among different groups and respect for each other's culture in the students. It is not permitted to condemn or unduly praise any one particular religious or cultural system or institution. It is usual practice in all schools, colleges and universities to celebrate fairs, festivals, birth anniversaries, etc., relating to different religions. While imparting moral education equal importance is given to different faiths.

4. *Science Teaching* : Secularism stands for scientific rationalism. It stresses logical thinking and abhors superstitions and irrational things. Therefore, Indian education today puts much emphasis on science teaching. Science is taught in a practical manner at all levels of schooling, so that it might influence the attitudes and values of the pupils. The spirit of science with emphasis on inquiry, experimentation, proof and critical outlook, permeates the teaching of other subjects also.

5. *Enlightened Teachers* : In the education for secularism in India the teachers today are expected to treat pupils in an impartial manner. They eschew all caste, community and class considerations in dealing with students and colleagues. Equal

respect is given to all students and to all religious groups. Every conscientious teacher behaves in a truly democratic and fair manner.

Thus the present Indian secular educational system is trying to create a social climate in the country in which secular values are sought to be promoted effectively and enthusiastically.

## DIFFICULTIES IN SECULAR EDUCATIONAL SYSTEM

In a country like India, in which traditional institutions like religion, caste, untouchability and dowry have been prevailing for thousands of years, the building up of a secular state is a very challenging task. Despite the best intentions of our Constitution makers and great leaders, it is difficult to establish and promote a really functional climate of secularism in India. The main difficulties in secular educational system are as follows :

1. *Traditional bias and narrow outlook* : In our country today denominational schools are allowed to function with a lot of freedom. There are D.A.V. Schools, Jain Schools, Vaish Schools, Ahir Schools, Kayastha Pathshalas, Shia Schools, Catholic Schools, Rajput Schools, etc. In these institutions the children of the respective communities or castes are admitted on preferential basis and also teachers of the same communities are preferred. This creates a serious difficulty in the functioning of Indian education as an integrative and secular force in Indian Society.

2. *Too much emphasis on theoretical learning* : Our educational system presents many things only in theory. Very little effort is made to change the values and attitudes of education. Many highly educated people do not hesitate to demand big dowries. They are too much fastidious about gotras and sub-castes in deciding marriage. They ill-treat women-folk and do not show respect to other religions. The lack of tolerance and courtesy on the part of educated persons towards villagers, women, poor people, minority community members, old people, etc., in buses, trains and at other public places reveals that our present education has failed to change our value system in a desired manner.

3. *Neglect of secular and cultural celebrations* : Schools and colleges observe holidays on the days of important religious fairs, festivals and birthdays. The result is that the students do not get enough opportunities to understand or imbibe secular values.

4. *Neglect of group activities* : Educational institutions do not encourage group activities. Group activities and group methods of teaching and learning are neglected. This is a serious difficulty in the promotion of secular and free values.

## COMMITTEE ON RELIGIOUS AND MORAL EDUCATION (1959)

### Terms of Reference

(i) To examine the desirability and feasibility of making specific provision for the teaching of moral and spiritual values in educational institutions.

(ii) If it is found desirable and feasible to make such provision : (a) to define broadly the content of instruction at various stages of education, and (b) to consider its place in the normal curriculum.

This Committee was appointed with Shri Sri. Prakasa, Governor of Bombay as Chairman.

**What is Religion?**

'Religion' etymologically means something that helps to bind man to man (*religare*, to bind). Broadly speaking every religion can be divided into four parts :

1. *Personality of the Founder* dealing with the greatness and holiness of the founder of the faith.
2. *Genesis* seeking to give an account of the Creator and the Universe created by Him.
3. *Ritual* prescribing some outward forms which the followers adopt and follow.
4. *Ethical code* telling what is right and what is wrong.

While perhaps this can be regarded as generally true of all religions, Hinduism does not completely fit into the above pattern and adds to the intricacies of the problem. The Committee advocated an objective, comparative and sympathetic study of all the important religions of India.

**Moral Values**

Moral values particularly refer to the conduct of man towards man in the various situations in which human beings come together. Moral values should be inculcated from the earliest childhood. Habits, both of mind and body, formed in the early years at home, persist and influence our life afterwards. Good manners are a very important part of moral education.

**Good Manners**

The importance of good manners cannot be overstressed. Good manners will impose proper restraint on us and remove harshness in our words and rudeness in our behaviour. Good manners verily are like the oil that helps to keep the machine of human society running smoothly. Good manners should be sedulously inculcated and teachers must give instruction in this to all students at all times, both by example and by precept.

**Spiritual Values**

Just as moral values affect the relations between man and man, so do spiritual values affect the individual in his relations with himself. The individual is not only a body, he is also a soul. He does not live by bread alone; he wants inner peace and happiness. If he loses all spiritual values, he loses the possibility of being at peace with himself. It is necessary to have some faith in things beyond the flesh, some identification with a purpose greater than oneself in order to achieve this mental equilibrium. It very much depends upon the atmosphere that only good teachers can create. Teachers will help to create and maintain the proper atmosphere in the institutions.

### Patriotism

Among spiritual values, we should also include patriotism. The whole country with all its regions and peoples is seldom envisaged as an organic entity which has to be cherished and served, and whose integrity has to be protected even at the cost of our lives. In the old days, at schools and colleges, students were taught poems that helped them to learn and imbibe patriotic fervour. They were taught books which narrated stories of brave deeds performed in the service of the country. Patriotism should neither be egoistical and chauvinistic nor so limited and narrow as to exclude our duties to humanity. It should foster a burning love for the motherland and an ardent desire for service to one's fellow beings. Anything that helps us to behave properly towards others is of moral value. Anything that takes us out of our self, and inspires us to sacrifice for the good of other for a great cause, is of spiritual value. Any system of education that does not teach us these, is not worth the name. It is necessary that besides patriotism young people should learn during their impressionable years their duties to self, family, neighbours, other human beings and animals.

### Co-curricular Activities

Our educationists have become more conscious of the value of physical education and extra-curricular activities. There is ample scope for the teaching of moral values through such activities. These activities need to be more effectively directed towards the development of character and discipline.

### Major Recommendations

1. *Desirability* : The teaching of moral and spiritual values in educational institutions is desirable and specific provision for doing so is feasible within certain limitations.

2. *Contents* : Education in moral and spiritual value should include a comparative and sympathetic study of the lives and teachings of great religious leaders and at later stages, their ethical systems and philosophies. The inculcation of good manners, social service and true patriotism should be continuously stressed at all stages.

3. *Home* : The faults and drawbacks of our homes both in the matter of their physical orderliness and their psychological atmosphere, should be pointed out through mass media such as leaflets, talks, radio and the cinema, and through voluntary organisations. Instructions should be given as to how these can be removed.

4. *Meditation* : As suggested by the University Education Commission, educational institutions should start work everyday with a few minutes of silent meditation either in the class room or in common hall. There could be some sort of prayer also which need not be addressed to any deity or ask for any favour, but

which may be in the nature of an exhortation for self-discipline and devotion to some ideal. Occasionally in these Assembly Meetings inspiring passages from great literature, religious as well as secular, and pertaining to all important religions and cultures of the world, could be read with profit. Community singing of inspiring songs and hymns can be most effective at the school stage.

5. *Literature* : Suitable books should be prepared for all stages — from primary to university — which should describe briefly in a comparative and sympathetic manner the basic ideas of all religions as well as the essence of the lives and teachings of the great religious leaders, saints, mystics and philosophers. Collections of poems and selected passages from Sanskrit, Persian, English and the regional languages should be made for the use of young people. These publications will teach true wisdom. Books should particularly concentrate on deeds of heroism and self-sacrifice in the cause of the country and in the service of others. Authors should be selected with the greatest care and their manuscripts should be revised in consultation with eminent authors. The entire programme of preparing and distributing such publications should be operated by a central agency set up under the auspices of the union Ministry of Education.

6. *Extra-curricular Activities* : In the course of extra-curricular activities, learned and experienced persons may be invited to deliver lectures on inter-religious understanding. Educational broadcasts and group discussions may be organized to stimulate interest in the study of moral and spiritual values.

7. *Stress on Teaching Virtues* : Special stress should be laid on teaching good manners and promoting the virtues of reverence and courtesy which are badly needed in our society.

8. *Compulsory Physical Training* : Some form of physical training should be compulsory at every stage. This can be graded from clubs and Boy Scouts to Auxiliary and National Cadet Corps. Games and sports should be encouraged and the dignity of manual work and social service to the community should be taught.

## FRAMEWORK OF INSTRUCTION

1. **Elementary stages** : (i) The school assembly should be held for a few minutes in the morning for group singing —

(ii) Simple and interesting stories about the lives and teachings of prophets, saints and religious leaders should be included in the syllabus for language teaching.

(iii) Wherever possible the interest of the child may also be aroused by the use of audio-visual material, especially good quality photographs, filmstrips and coloured reprints showing great works of art and architecture closely connected with the main living religions of the world; such material could be used in the teaching of geography.

(iv) In the school programme, two periods a week should be set aside for moral instruction. In these classes the teacher should relate interesting stories drawn from the great religions of the world and explain broadly their ethical teachings. Dogmas and rituals of religion should be excluded from moral instruction.

(v) Through school programme, the attitude of 'service' and the realization that 'work is worship' should be developed in the child.

(vi) All schemes of physical education and all forms of play in the school should contribute to the building of character and the inculcation of the spirit of true sportsmanship.

2. **Secondary stage** : (i) The morning assembly should observe two minutes' silence followed by readings from the scriptures or great literature of the world or an appropriate address. Community singing should also be encouraged.

(ii) The essential teachings of the great world religions should be studied as part of the curriculum pertaining to social studies and history. Simple texts and stories concerning different religions may be included in the teaching of languages and general reading.

(iii) One hour a week should be assigned to moral instruction. The teacher should encourage the habit of discussion in the class. Apart from this regular class instruction, suitable speakers may be invited to address the students on moral and spiritual values. Joint celebrations may be organized on the occasion of important festivals of all religions. Knowledge and appreciation of religions other than one's own and respect for their Founders, should be encouraged in various ways including essay competitions and declamations.

(iv) Orgnized social service during holidays and outside class hours should be an essential part of extra-curricular activities. Such service should teach the dignity of manual labour, love of humanity, patriotism and self-discipline. Participation in games and sports should be compulsory and physical education, including sex hygiene should be a normal part of school programme.

(v) Qualities of character and behaviour of students should form an essential part of the overall assessment of a student's performance at school.

3. **University stage** : (a) Students should be encouraged to meet in groups for silent meditation in the morning. These meetings should be supervised by the senior staff on a voluntary basis.

(b) A general study of different religions should be an essential part of the general education course in degree classes. In this connection, the following recommendations of the University Education Commission (Radhakrishnan Commission) are commended :

(i) That in the first year of the degree course, lives of the great religious and spiritual leaders like Gautama the Buddha, Confucious, Zoroaster, Socrates, Jesus, Shankara, Ramanuja, Madhva, Mohammad, Kabir, Nanak and Gandhi be taught;

(ii) That in the second year, some selections of a universal character from the scriptures of the world be studied; and

(iii) That in the third year, the central problems of philosophy of religion be considered. Standard works for such studies should be prepared carefully by specialists who have deep knowledge of and sympathy for the religious systems about which they write.

(c) A postgraduate course in comparative religion may be instituted. Due importance should be given to the study of the following subjects in the appropriate Honours and M.A. courses in the fields of Humanities and Social Sciences :

(i) Comparative Religion.

(ii) History of Religions.

(d) A fairly long period of social service should be introduced by all universities. In the organization and conduct of such service, considerable attention should be given to the learning and practice of moral and spiritual values.

The Constitution provides that religious instruction given in institutions under any endowment or trust, should not be interfered with even when such sort of instruction that we have recommended should be imparted in all institutions and if any special religion is particularly taught in some institutions, this should be in addition to what we have proposed. There is no question of conscience involved in this; the instruction proposed is essential for the building of character and the making of proper citizens, and by its very nature it cannot possibly injure the susceptibilities of any religious group. The effective implementation of the suggestions made above will create a proper atmosphere in educational institutions, so that they may train not only technicians or professional experts but also humane and balanced citizens who can contribute to the happiness and well-being of their countrymen and of humanity as a whole.

Many ills that human world of education and human society as a whole is suffering today, are mainly due to the gradual disappearance of the hold of the basic principles of religion on the hearts of the people. The only cure, is in the deliberate inculcation of moral and spiritual values from the earliest years of lives. The edifice of Indian future entirely depends, for its beauty, dignity, utility and stability, on the foundations laid today in the form of the education and training that Indian youths receive.

**Importance of Religion**

The word 'Christos' gave birth to Christianity. 'Christos' means 'bathed in Divine wisdom'. Thus Christianity spreads that Divine wisdom which creates in men the feeling of brotherhood, love, sympathy and tolerance.

Vedic religion is based on Vedas. Veda means knowledge. Hence Vedic knowledge denotes that scientific knowledge which recognizes the absolute supremacy of soul and God and develops the human virtues of peace, non-violence, truth, humanity, love and kindness etc. Thus Religion is the fountain from which flows morality and human virtues. Religion is universal, ever present and all pervading. Hence it must be included in education.

## RELIGIOUS EDUCATION

### Inter-relation of Religion and Education

Both Religion and Education seeks to establish human virtues by promoting all round development of the human being. Hence, both education and religion are inter-related. Some people do not want religion to be included in education, while others argue that religion must get an important place in education.

In India religion has been linked with education since ancient times. According to Dr. Radhakrishnan lack of moral and religious education is the cause of evils and indiscipline growing all over the world. During the Vedic and Buddha periods education remained saturated with religious spirit. People from all over the world came to Indian seats of learning. In European countries movements were launched for linking religion with education, such as Sunday School Movement, the Religious School Movement and the Character Education Movement. As the people in all the corners of the world become convinced that humanity will be free from evils only when education was linked with religion the need of religious education is felt everywhere. Still some people do not want to include religion in education to save their political and economic interests. If religion is taken in its true meaning, education can achieve a revolutionary progress. It can help in the achievement of world-brotherhood, world-peace and world-welfare.

### Arguments Against Religious Education

1. *Impractical* : It is not practicable to include religious education because children of different religions receive education in the same school. If education is based on one particular religion, it will create bad blood, disturb peaceful atmosphere and end the feeling of unity in the school.

2. *Conservatism* : Religious education is based on scriptures. If the students act according to scriptures they will have to observe various formalities. This will lead to conservative atmosphere. A man cannot become virtuous by acquiring religious knowledge alone. He has to shape his conduct accordingly.

3. *Unreal attitude* : The knowledge of virtue and evil, reward and punishment through religious education can lead to misunderstanding and mental tension. Religious education will not be real if confined to the tenets of one religion.

4. *Lack of Suitable Teachers* : It is difficult for a teacher to explain religious knowledge impartially as he may be having faith in one religion. Consequently the students will fail to grasp the deep religious ideas. Analysis of religious dogmas with the help of science will be reasonable but it will injure teacher's own personal faith. Thus, it is difficult to find suitable teachers for imparting religious education.

5. *Inhuman Acts in the Name of Religion* : The purpose of religion is to develop human virtues. However, history is a witness to the fact that inhuman crimes and barbarities have been committed in the name of religion. The emotions of enmity, hatred and violence developed in place of love, kindness, cooperation and sympathy. Such instances can create unreligious ideas in the minds of students

6. *Against Community Consciousness* : An individual develops faith in religion through self-realization which is a personal process. Hence, individual approach is bound to creep in religion which is against the community spirit to be propagated in the schools.

**Arguments in Favour of Religious Education**

1. *The harmonious development of an individual's personality* : It is not possible through physical, mental and intellectual development alone. Spiritual development is also necessary to attain an all round development. Different subjects like history, science, geography etc. display materialistic outlook. Their education helps intellectual development, but it does not create spiritual development. Religious education is necessary for a man's spiritual development. Only it can create all round development of personality.

2. *Curbing Inhuman tendencies* : The cause for world-wide frustration is excessive faith in materialism and lack of faith in spiritualism. Selfishness is the gift of materialism. Hence, religious education is needed to curb inhuman tendencies.

3. *Real Meaning of Religious Education* : Religion should not be tagged with any one faith or following. It should be human religion accepted by all faiths in more or less measure. Hinduism, Islam and Christianity are only faiths and cannot be called religion. Human religion is the real substance in all these faiths. If this is imparted through education, no one will object to it. In the religious education no place should be given to rituals. Only noble human ideals having universal recognition should be taught to make it proper religious education.

4. *Use in Religious Countries* : In countries where religion is a dominant force religious education will be simple, interesting and easily understandable. India is a religion-dominated country. Not taking religion in a narrow sense, the substance of all religions should be consolidated and taught with a liberal outlook.

5. *Need of Co-ordination* : Today scientific researches, scientific reasonings and materialistic outlooks are constantly increasing in progressive nations. But the people throughout the world are crying for peace, while peace is still a far cry and distant vision. The neglect of spiritualism is the main cause for the frustration and unhappiness in the world. The need of the day is that a co-ordination between materialism and spiritualism through the medium of religious education. A hungry nation cannot survive on spiritualism. She must satiate her physical hunger. Similarly a prosperous nation cannot survive on materialism, the hunger of her soul should be satiated with the help of spiritualism. Therefore, universal religious education should be developed.

6. *Human Religion* : Among the persons arguing for religious education, are Sir Syed Ahmad Khan, Tagore, Swami Dayanand, Pandit Madan Mohan Malviya, Mahatma Gandhi, Sri Aurobindo and Annie Besant are some who may be mentioned. In religious education religion is the human religion and not a particular faith.

## EDUCATIONAL RESPONSIBILITIES OF RELIGION

Religion should be interpreted in relation to observance of one's duties. Discharge of one's duty faithfully in this very world is the first obligation under religion. Field of duty is the other name for field of religion. Religion should prepare a man for performance of duties so that after his own development he helps the development of the society. As a man's field of action is pre-determined on the basis of his aptitude, the religion should develop this personal aptitude so that he succeeds in the field of action.

Knowledge (Veda) is the base of religion. Only by attaining knowledge a man gets an insight into religion. The knowledge is acquired through logic, analysis, observation, thinking and change of ideas. Stability of religious-mindedness rests on direct knowledge. Developing faith in religion through reasoning or independent thinking helps in ending superstition, fanaticism and blind faith.

It is the primary duty of schools to help the development of child's character and his moral values. The religious institutions can extend considerable help in this sphere. Religious bodies should take upon themselves the responsibility of character building. They should help the country by producting men of character and morality. Thus, religious education should be introduced in schools in order to help the all-round development of children. Religious institutions should consider it to be their national obligation and fulfil it.

## MORAL EDUCATION

### Objectives of Moral Education

1. *All-round development* : The basic objective of education is to ensure all-round development of human being so that he may achieve higher success in all the walks of life. However, education in the current set up has neglected human qualities like sympathy, kindness, truth, devotion, co-operation, compassion etc. The purpose of moral education is to develop human virtues along with intellectual development.

2. *Formation of Character* : A man's most precious asset is his character. It is even more important than his physical or social stature. The loss of character means the loss of human self. A strong character is the most valuable possession. Moral education is necessary for character formation.

## RELIGIOUS AND MORAL EDUCATION

Religious and moral education go hand in hand. Moral values are the base of every religion as every religion condemns sins, corruption, falsehood and like vices. Religions support truth, non-violence, devotion, compassion, doing good to others and universal brotherhood. Therefore, moral education is linked with human religion based on virtues which are universally accepted.

## MORAL EDUCATION AT DIFFERENT STAGES

1. **Primary Stage** : Particular attention should be paid towards the special

interests and aptitude of children at the primary stage of education. The curriculum should be made attractive and interesting in order to attract students towards extra-curricular programme of moral education. Poetry, stories and songs can be well employed to make moral education interesting.

While determining the curriculum and the teaching method, children's intellectual calibre and ability to grasp the subject at primary stage of education must be kept in mind. The curriculum should be short and simple. The teaching method should be easy, interesting and attractive. Care should be taken in selecting poems, stories and songs to be used as medium for imparting moral education. For example, quoting extracts from Ramayana, the children may be taught obedience to parents, honouring words, brotherly affection and sacrifice. The story of Eklavya from Mahabharat may teach obedience and devotion to the mentor. Similar is the use of many stories which carry messages selected from old books like Veda, Puranas, Panchatantra etc. The character of Ram, Bharat, Shrawan Kumar, Yudhisthir, Prahlad, Dhruva and similar other persons may be described to children. These may serve as good medium for moral education. Good elements should be gathered from all important religions and taught to children so that when they grow up they may possess the spirit of universal brotherhood, tolerance and sacrifice and learn to respect others' views and sentiments.

2. **Secondary Stage** : At the secondary stage the age and the intellectual development reach a state when character formation may be started. The programme of education at this stage should be many-sided so that it may help the student in his future life. The objective at this stage should be to enable students to acquire as much knowledge which may give them confidence to successfully participate in various programmes. The students should be provided with opportunities to do work connected with the welfare of human beings and the society. The help of stories, relevant extracts and suitable instances may be taken for character development.

3. **Higher Stage** : While studying in colleges or universities the students make preparations to enter practical life. The curriculum of moral education should be wide at this stage. A man with good character is imbued with the spirit of humanity and rises above national, social, communal, sectarian, casteism or other such considerations in order to serve the mankind. The student has to rise above all considerations to grasp the essence of all religions and learn the real human religion. Teacher occupies the most important place in moral education. He should himself set example of moral conduct before his students.

## QUESTIONS FOR EXERCISE

1. Define secularism? Discuss characteristics of secular education.
2. Explain education for secularism in India. Point out difficulties in secular educational system.
3. Discuss the report of the Committee on Religious and Moral Education 1959.
4 Describe the framework of Instruction laid down by Committee of Religious and Moral Education (1959).

5. Describe religion in its true perspective. How is it related to education?
6. Describe the importance of religion in human life. Should religious education be given in schools?
7. What can be the true form of religious education? What are the possible hurdles in introducing religious education in schools in India?
8. What role should the religious institutions play in the sphere of education?

# 25

# PHYSICAL EDUCATION

Physical Education is Education through physical activity. It is a judicious blend in the education of body and mind.

### Physical Culture and Physical Education

Physical culture is not Physical Education. Physical culture confines itself to the development of physique only. A muscular body is not the be-all and end-all of Physical Education. Developing the Physique is only one aspect of the total programme of Physical Education. It is a much broader and meaningful term.

### Definition of Physical Education

1. *J.F. Williams.* "Physical education is the sum of man's Physical activities selected as a kind and conducted as to outcomes."

2. *Voltmer and Eislinger.* "Physical Education is that phase of Education which takes place through physical activity."

3. *Dr. J.F. Williams and Dr. C.L. Brownwell.* "Physical Education implies selected physical activities which are conducted with reference to the benefits that may be derived from participation in these activities."

4. *Dr. J.R. Sharman.* "Physical Education is that part of Education which takes place through activities which involve the motor mechanism of the human body and which results in the individuals' formulating behaviour pattern."

5. *Reisner.* "Physical Education or Health Education is education in general, approached from the viewpoints of the necessary physical support to intellectual and moral excellence."

### Physical Education and Physical Training

Physical training is limited in its scope and meaning as it refers to the training aspect of the body. It is regimental in its scope. It enables an individual to gain physical fitness through certain conditioning. It does not contribute to mental and moral development. Physical Education is both modern and scientific. It is all round development through physical activity.

**Education and Physical Education**

Education has been defined as 'a series of experiences which enables one to better understand new experiences'. It is a continuous and lifelong process dealing with the all round development of man. It aims at the development of an integrated and controlled personality. The value of educational efforts is judged by the personality. It helps the individual to adjust himself to the group, to develop right habits of thought and action and to be a constructive member of the society. Physical Education is an integral part of education. "Education without Physical Education is a bottomless vase and Physical Education without Education is a truncated cone." Physical exercises, game and sports, recreative activities and other big muscle activities involving individual and group practices enable one to gain efficiency in action, a sound health, pleasing manners, pleasant character and such other desirable qualities that in turn aids to develop a sound mind. The following are the main objectives :

1. *To develop organic fitness* : Organic fitness means the efficient functioning of the organic systems of the human body. Physical strength and organic vigour can be improved to a large extent by participating in vigorous physical activities.

2. *To develop neuromuscular skills* : The nervous system which controls the behaviour of human beings, is strengthened by proper physical exercises. Neuro-muscular coordination develops through various types of exercises done repeatedly for a long period of time. Neuro-muscular development helps one to perform the daily work with proficiency and develop a well poised body, quick and efficient movement and graceful carrage.

3. *To develop desirable social behaviour* : Man is a social animal. All the important personality traits such as self-control, unselfishness, loyalty, perseverance, control of the emotions, sportsmanship etc., come into play in the games and sports activities of Physical Education. Opportunities for cultivating these traits are available in games situations. The playground is a good laboratory for developing sound character.

4. *To develop the ability to use leisure in wholesome ways* : The machine-age has created more of leisure and people are deprived of creative activities. Leisure time when spent in physical education pays the individual suitably. Recreation during leisure serves as the best tonic as it provides the physical strength and mental balance, and also happiness and joy. Recreation being a part of Physical Education assures pleasure, mirth, joy and happiness to people of all ages, irrespective of their being men or women.

Schools should provide activities to be continued long after school days so that people in old age might engage themselves in some kind of recreational activities to suit their age and strength.

5. *To develop desirable health habits* : Physical Education and Health Education are inter-related. A sound programme of Physical Education contributes to the physical, mental, social and emotional development of the individual. Through Physical Education, good habits such as regular activities, rest, regulated diet, cleanliness of body and clothing can be inculcated.

### Intramural Tournaments in Games and Sports

Life at school is largely desk and book-work muscular inactivity, which tends to produce fatigue, tiresomeness, permanent bad postures and depression. The best remedy for the physically exhausted pupils lies in giving free expression to their limbs through muscular activities to enable them to expend their stored up energies. The best corrective influence is obtained from natural play activities in the form of games and sports.

Every school has playgrounds for playing major games and track and field areas for atheletic practice. These are the necessary components of any school. These should be properly maintained by every educational institution for covering the year long activity programmes in physical education.

## GAMES

Being the natural provision for the overflow of surplus nervous energy, games form a very important part of physical training. The play instinct is the natural method for developing coordination and character. Instincts such as imitation, chasing, fighting and catching make their appearance at different ages and unless the children are allowed to rehearse these primitive impulses by the gratification of the natural desires to play, their development is handicapped.

### Types of Games

Games may be classified into the following categories :

1. Minor games.
2. Major games.
3. Indigenous games.
4. Lead up games.

1. *Minor Games* : Minor games are suitable for young boys and girls. Minor games are of low organisation with less rules, less equipment and less expense. Being purely recreational games they provide a lot of fun frolic and joy. They are well enjoyed by children. They can be conducted in the playfields and also indoors. They can be modified according to convenience. They are played for a shorter duration, on lawns, on sea-shore, on hard courts, on mountain tops and on river beds.

These games are taught at the elementary school level. They are tag games and relay games such as simple tag, couple tag, Rama Ravana, snatching the kerchief, finding the partner, zig zag relay, over ball pass relay, under ball pass relay, jump the stick relay and so on.

Almost every game involves chasing and tagging. Hopping, jumping, skipping, leaping and running are the movements involved in each game and the effect of these exercises are well seen flowing through the muscles. Imitative activities in the form of minor games are totally enjoyed by the children. Most of the activity programmes of the Kindergarten schools, Nursery schools and Elementary schools are nothing but minor games.

2. *Major Games* : Major games are suitable for pupils at High schools and college levels and also for grown up people. These are games of higher organisation with the rules approved by the International Associations. The dimension of the posts and nets, the play equipment, the number of players and substitutes, the duration and extension times are all approved internationally. Each game is played for specific duration on a ground of approved dimensions with markings and equipment as per international specification.

Major games include Football, Volley Ball, Basket Ball, Cricket, Hockey, Badmintion, Tennikoit, Tennis, Khokho, Soft Ball, Kabaddy and Atyapatya. While many of them are played in the open playfields, some of them are played indoors. Women also take part in most of the games. These games require varied skills such as running, dodging, throwing, catching, dribbling, pitching, hitting, spiking, boosting, kicking, heading, trapping, stopping, driving, muffling, bowling etc, with implements or without implements.

Major games give exercise to the grown up muscles of the boys and girls of high schools and College.

3. *Indigenous Games* : Chedu gudu, Kho-Kho, Atya Patya Lazim, Kummi and Kollattam are indigenous games. They are of Indian origin and are native to ones own soil. On occasions like marriage, birth, death, festivals connected with religion and public functions, these games are played with zeal and enthusiasm.

These games find their place in the high school activity programmes.

4. *Lead up Games* : Lead up games are mostly modified and devised for mastering the skills of major games. All the fundamental tactics, skills and stunts are put together to gain practice of major games. For example, the captain ball is a lead up game for Basket Ball. Devised games enable the participants to gain mastery over certain skills and lead up games are usually played repeatedly. Novices and beginners in any game are made to play lead up games in order to master the skills required for any particular game. Each lead up game of any particular major game is so designed that it involves all the finer skills of that particular major game of which it is a lead up one. Lead up games form part of the training programmes in coaching.

**Exercises and Games**

1. *Education values* : Exercise develops health, strength and the power of quick, smooth and easy movements of the muscles but the will of the pupil is not free. There is no continuous play of intelligence, individual or social skill demanding courage, endurance, self-denial, self-reliance and determination.

The characteristics of the games are entirely different. Games keep the participants always active and alive to the situations. They develop keen observation, presence of mind, quick judegement, tenacity, insight into the tactics of the opponents, cool head, ready wit and quick decision.

2. *Nature*. Exercise is of individual or personal nature while game is of social nature. A compulsory participation programme in a high school insists on every one

taking part in all the games extending all facilities or even to specialise any particular game as per the choice of the pupil in addition to the compulsory programme.

3. *Time Table* : Every pupil engages himself in a particular game as per the time table during activity periods. He is at liberty to choose a game of his own choice and specialise it. All the courts, play facilities and equipment for all the games are made accessible for the students to make optimum use of them. This is not so in exercise.

4. *Purposes* : For practical purposes, the games are divided into different skills, and each student is tested twice a year in the skills of the game of his choice and his performance is recorded and marks awarded accordingly. These marks get carried to the total marks in the certificate book along with the other academic subjects. But a failure to secure the minimum in Physical Education does not debar him from getting promoted to the next higher class. This is not so in exercise.

## ATHLETICS

### Nature and Kinds

Sports is a general and comprehensive term. It usually means Athletics. Athletics include the Track and Field events.

They make a widespread appeal. Games and Sports are the two main aspects of Physical Education programmes common to all boys and girls, men and women, old and young. Athletics offer unusual educational opportunities. Every programme of Physical Education provides for the participation of all boys and girls at all school levels in athletic activities suited to their interest and abilities.

Athletics cover a wide range of events which specially deal with the specialisation of natural movements. The most fundamental Skills, Running, Jumping and Throwing, are the basic activities which render one to become a superhuman being through one's performance.

Athletic contribute to the development of skill, strength, stamina, speed, grace endurance and co-ordination. Running fast, jumping high and throwing far are the targets aimed at in athletics. When practised repeatedly each event in athletics, enables the participant to exhibit a surprising performance.

As athletics contribute to the development of health and character, all the events of the track and field (sports) are included in the High School Physical Education syllabus both for practice and for competitions.

### Characteristics of Athletics

1. *Individualistic* : Except the Relay events, all other events in athletics are individualistic in character and the pleasure and values derived from practice and participation are one's and not shared by others. Unlike team games in which specific number of players constitute each team, pupils take part in the athletic events individually and compete with others. The athletic events in sports were practised even during pre-historic periods and are being conducted at intramural levels in schools.

2. *Attractive* : The athletic events are the most attractive, soul stirring and exciting. In the modern Olympics, athletic events are those that attract maximum participation with the spectators in the galleries packed to capacity.

4. *Valuable* : The pleasure and satisfaction that one derives by one's going over the high jump bar or pole-vault an inch more than one's previous performance or in leaping a long jump or in clicking one-tenth of a second faster in Track events or in throwing a little more distance than one's previous throw in shotput, Javeline and discus, are unparalleled in the history of one's athletic career. Every country competes with each other to produce a world renowned athlete of repute who could annex a gold medal in the international Olympic competitions.

5. *Tests* : The High School syllabus in Physical Education includes tests in athletics. Every student is tested in athletic skills twice a year and the marks that he scores gets added to the marks allotted under practicals and entered in the certificate along with the other academic subjects to be considered for promotion to the next higher class.

**Athletic Events**

The following are the events in Track and Field where athletic tests are conducted to measure the progress of individuals, both boys and girls :

| *Track events* | | *Field events* |
|---|---|---|
| 100 metres run | *Jumps* | *Throws* |
| 200 metres run | Long Jump | Shot put throw |
| 400 metres run | High Jump | Discus throw |
| 800 metres run | Hop step and Jump | Javeline throw |
| 1500 metres run | | |
| 110 metres hurdles | (Pentathlon | in five events |
| 400 metres hurdles | Decathlon) | in ten events) |
| 4 × 100 Relay | | |
| 4 × 400 Relay | | |

**Meaning and Objectives**

The above events are the standard events. The events are changed to suit different age groups and sex.

Instead of hammer-throw, cricket ball-throw gets substituted for Juniors and instead 110 metres hurdles, 80 metres is included for girls. Polevault is meant only for boys and not for girls.

## SCHOOL INTRAMURAL TOURNAMENTS

Intramural Tournaments in Games and the Annual athletic competitions in sports form a definite part of the physical education programme of a school under the head, games and sports.

Tournaments and sports mean competitions held for the pupils of the same school within the school compound and not between schools. Intramural programmes form the basis of all games and sports. Sports and games competitions held for the boys and girls of the same school within its compounds are called Intramural competitions. If the competitions are between different schools, they are termed as extramural or inter-school competition.

Physical education activities in Games as per the time table and athletic events are conducted throughout the year and every student takes part in it. Through daily practice, every student gains practice individually. In order to enable the students to assess their own progress and exhibit their prowess, strength and ability in skills, competitions in Games are held right from the beginning of the year classifying them on age-war basis and such competitions are called Intramural competitions or Intramural Tournaments.

Competitions are held in athletics on a particular day which is called as the Annual Sports Day of the school when competitions on the same age-war basis are held in all the athletic events. It is open to all the students of the school, boys and girls; the girls' participation is exclusively separate.

**Organisation and Conduct**

To enable the boys and girls of the school to take part in the games tournaments, they are classified into following categories on age-war basis :

1. Beginners Boys and Girls below 13 years of age.
2. Juniors Boys and Girls between 13 and 15 years of age.
3. Senior Boys and Girls between 15 and 17 years of age.
4. Super Senior Boys and Girls between 17 and above years of age.

Having formed the various classifications of pupils, teams for each games are listed out. The Intramural Committee draws the fixtures announcing the dates and venues. As Director of the Intramural Committee, the Senior Physical Director of the school, elicits the co-operation and service of his assistants and other teachers in addition to the captains of the various games who all are members of the committee.

The tournament committee chalks out a detailed programme of activities covering all the matches for the year. It conducts the tournaments on knock out basis for the various age groups right from the beginning of the year. The tournament's last up to the end of the academic year engaging all the pupils throughout.

Matches in different games are held as per the schedule both in the mornings and in the evenings. As the tournaments are conducted on knock-out basis, the Victor in each game moves to the next round while the Vanquished gets totally eliminated. All the matches are conducted as per the schedule and in adherence to the rules and regulations of the Intramural Committee.

The final winners in each game in each one of the classified groups are declared the champions of that particular game for the year. They are awarded certificates as winners on the Annual Intramural Day.

**Merits of Tournament**

1. *Pleasure* : The pleasures derived by the participants in the Intramural tournaments are long lasting.

2. *Interest* : The tournament affords interest in every one for participation.

3. *Opening* : The tournament serves as an opening for the students to express freely their talents in games.

4. *Opportunity* : The tournament provides an opportunity for the talented players to outshine as heroes and win laurels as champions.

5. *Development* : Through participation in the tournaments, the pupils are able to develop their physical and mental personalities.

6. *Competition* : The tournaments pave way for the development of healthy competitive spirit.

7. *Team Spirit* : Tournaments help the pupils to get familiarised with others, develop friendship, and social contact, obey the laws and regulations implicitly and achieve recognition.

8. *Momentos* : The awards as incentives received as token for participation serve as mementos.

**Incentives to Participation in Games and Sports**

1. *Attraction* : The play fields must be attractive with green and rich shady trees all around.

2. *Size* : The grounds must be exclusively away from the class-rooms and extensive in nature.

3. *Availability* : Playing equipment and play facilities should be made copiously available.

4. *Variety* : Variety of games should be there for the students to choose the games of his choice.

5. *As per rules* : All grounds must be well graded, maintained and marked distinctly with nets tied to fascinate the students to enter for active participation.

6. *Without obstacles* : Ruts, pit-falls, anthills, stumpy grasses and other obstacles should be removed and the ground must be smooth, well rolled, netted and paved. The ground should not be too hard or too soddy.

7. *Equipment* : Balls must be well inflated and the playing equipment should be new and attractive.

8. *Teacher's presence* : The presence of the teacher on the field ensures confidence in the minds of the players.

9. *Freeplay* : Free play and no restriction should be the order of the day in the play fields.

10. *Teacher's participation* : The teacher himself should be an active participant and he should advise every student to turn up for daily practice.

11. *Uniforms and Prizes* : Uniforms should be provided free of cost. Attractive certificates, medals, trophies, utility awards should be presented to the winner and runners up.

12. *Fame* : The names of the champions in athletics and winners in games should find their places on the honour roll, school magazines and newspapers. Their groups and individual photos should adorn the walls of the Pavilion.

## ORGANISATION OF INTER-SCHOOL COMPETITIONS

The Inter-school competitions is an all-school project. It is open to all the schools to participate in these competitions. The successful organisation and conduct of it rests on the fullest co-operation from the Government, the Head Masters, the Physical Education teachers and the pupils.

Different committees should be formed to look after each item and when each committee should attend to its work properly. Competitions are held first between schools at the zonal level. The Zonal winners compete with each other at the district level. All the winners of the different Districts meet together at the Republic Day Sports and Games competitions. District champions at the State level participate in the Inter-State and National Competitions.

The Director of School Education is the *ex-officio* President at the State level, the Chief Educational Officer at the District level and District Educational Officer at the Educational District level.

Each school sends its entries to the Zonal Secretary. At the Zonal level fixtures are drawn and due intimation is given to the schools in the zone supplying them with copies of the fixtures with dates and venues.

With the help of different committees each zone keeps ready with its officials, grounds and materials. The schools report on time as per the schedule and thus the zonal tournaments and sports get conducted and the winners are recorded and sent to the District Secretary who arranges for the conduct of Games and Sports at the District level. The list of winners is forwarded to the Secretary of the Divisions who in turn organises the competitions at his centre and selects the District Champions in sports and games. The District takes part in the Inter District (State level) competitions usually held on the Republic Day of the year.

Rolling Trophies for each game in the Zonal District and Divisional levels are awarded to the Schools that emerge as winners at different levels in Games and Tournaments and the individual players receive winners certificates. Likewise in sports, certificates are issued to the first three places in each event and the individual securing the maximum points is awarded the Individual Championship Cup.

The tournaments for boys and girls conducted separately but on parallel lines.

The Conduct of Tournaments in games and sports is conducted on age-war classification basis.

## Advantages of Inter-School Competitions

1. *Introduction* : Through the organisation and conduct of inter-school competitions, schools come to know each other better.

2. *Assessment* : Each school is able to assess its own standard through its success and failures.

3. *Team Work* : Student participants from different schools get an opportunity to join together with a spirit of comradeship and participate in a friendly manner at a common venue.

4. *Model* : This provides an opportunity to observe better players in action and emulate their styles and technique.

5. *Spirit of Rivalry* : Participation in these competitions, induces a spirit of rivalry to win laurels and bring name to one's institution.

6. *Encouragement* : It serves as a source of encouragement when winners are applauded by the cheering of the spectators while they get up on the Victory stand and receive the awards from the chief guest.

7. *Fighting Spirit* : This induces a spirit to fight till the end and a desire to annex the rolling trophies to the school which they represent, which is a desired quality in every sportsman.

8. *Sportsman Spirit* : Every sportsman gets an opportunity to take defeat sportively.

9. *Character Building* : Obedience to law, taking things easy, forgiving and forbearing shortcomings, viewing failure with a balanced outlook and gentlemanly behaviour both on the field and off the ground are the outcomes of participation in the inter-school competitions.

## Principles for the Selection of Activities

1. *Wide Range* : The Physical Education Programme should provide an ample opportunity for wide range of movements involving big muscles.

2. *Physiological Facts* : The facts related to the growth and development of children should guide in curriculum construction.

3. *Individual Differences* : Provisions should be made in for the differences in physical capacities and abilities which are found among students.

4. *Physical Fitness Needs* : The physical fitness needs to students must be met by the physical education programme.

5. *Play* : The physical education programme should consist predominantly of natural play activities.

6. *Psychological* : The activities should be selected in the light of the psychological age characteristics of the child as well as physiological.

7. *Emotional* : Activities which are valuable in arousing and expressing emotions should be choosen.

8. *Progress* : In the selection of activities provision should be made for some progress.

9. *Sufficient Duration* : In the selection of activities, sufficient time should be provided so that the skills may be learned reasonably well.

10. *Seasonal Drives* : Select activities which meet the seasonal drives of the students.

11. *Variety* : The activities should include a variety of items that may suit the individual needs and interests.

12. *Rich Possibilities* : Activities which are rich in possibilities for the training of the mind and body of the individuals should be included in the programme.

13. *Value* : Activities should be such that they carry over values throughout life.

14. *Interest and Age* : Activities that could suit the interest and age of both the sexes should find their places in the daily programme.

**Activities Suitable to Age groups**

The programme of activities and time allotment should be well balanced to create interest and to ensure progress at all age levels irrespective of sex difference :

1. Pre-school stage — below 5 years of age.
2. Elementary school stage — 5-10 years of age.
3. Middle school stage — 10-13 years of age.
4. High school level — 13-17 years of age.
5. College level — 17-24 years of age.
6. Adults level — above 24 years of age.

1. *Pre-School Stage (Below 5 Years)* : All kinds of natural activities like kicking, pulling, pushing, running, using balls, wooden blocks and cubes, playing in sand, hide, and seek etc., provide them great pleasure. They do not mind the time and are even prepared to play in hot Sun.

2. *Elementary School (5-10 Years)* : Running, chasing, climbing, dodging and activities involving these traits are commonly indulged in by children of this age. Rhythmic activities, imitation, folk dance, story plays, stunts, dramatic activities etc., are liked by them. They are fond of relay races, athletic games of low organisation and games using implements and balls. Apparatus like sea-saws, Jungle Jim, swings, slides, ladders etc. satisfy them most. Stunts and self-testing activities are mostly liked by children of this group.

3. *Middle School Stage (10-13 Years)* : The growth is rather rapid at this age. They form into groups and gangs and co-operative spirit increases. They like to play team games. Better endurance and neuromuscular co-ordination are noticed. Competitions are of attraction to them and they associate themselves, in activities, such as Marching, Rhythmics, Calisthenics, apparatus work, games involving skills, lead-up games, recreational games etc.

The programme of activities for girls should be separate and they should be segregated from the boys. Lead up games, relay races, minor games, folk dances, Rhythmic activities, Lazeme, Kummi, Kolattam are the activities quite suited for girls at this age level.

4. *High School Level (13-17 Years)* : The activities such as swimming and hiking, Major games such as Foot Ball, Basket Ball, Volley Ball, Hockey, Cricket, Tennis, Badmintion, Soft Ball and Indigenous games and such as kho-kho, kabaddi and track and field athletics provide interest to this group.

5. *College Level (17-24 Years)* : Sports, acrobatics, stunts, endurance activities, team games, weight lifting, boxing, wrestling etc., satisfy him most and he is even prepared to take risks. Facilities must be amply provided for more individualistic type of events such as tennis, golf, archery, squash, swimming, riding etc.

6. *Adult Level (Above 24 Years)* : Activities such as asanas, swimming, boating, bicycling, hiking, walking, running and games such a golf, tennis, billiards, badminton can be profitably pursued at this stage with advantage. These activities not only provide pleasure and recreation but also help in maintaining and promoting physical fitness.

## QUESTIONS FOR EXERCISE

1. Physical education and education are inseparable like the two sides of a coin. Explain.
2. Explain in detail the manifold objectives of physical education.
3. "Life without recreation proves to be dull and drab. Games and sports provide the necessary recreation from cradle to grave." Explain.
4. "Games and sports are as old as life itself." Elucidate.
5. "Games not only help in building physical health but also for a sound mind wholesome character." Explain.
6. Bring out the significance of intramural competition in sports and games.
7. Explain how the inter-school competitions in sports and games are being organised annually at District level.

# 26

# HEALTH EDUCATION

## Definition of Health

Health is a state of complete physical, mental and social well being. It is the quality of life which enables the individual to live most and serve best.

The strength of any nation depends on the health of its citizens and likewise their happiness also depends purely on their health. Thus both the strength and happiness are the direct outcomes of good health.

## Physical Education and Health Education

Physical education and Health education are not synonymous. Physical education is education through activities compressing of physical fitness, games, sports and a number of other activities involving the big muscles of the body. Health is only one of the objectives of physical education. Physical education is a meaningful activity that contributes to the health of the participants.

Physiology, Anatomy, Hygiene, First Aid, Safety Education and many other subjects are closely connected with each other. All of them centre round the subject of health. Hence, every child should be made to gain as much knowledge as possible to enable it to understand and maintain its own health. A comprehensive knowledge of health habits and health attitudes is necessary to every child. A wide knowledge on individual, family and community health and hygiene is also necessary. The correct principles of living are imparted through health education. The principled way of living guarantees a healthy life which provides the maximum happiness. A person with good health habits gains confidence and stands prepared to serve the community. If every one follows the principles of health education and if his attitudes are wholesome, the nation as a whole can enjoy the happiness of life producing successive generations possessing vigour and vitality.

Therefore, Health Education programme should form part of the general education programme of the school. It consists of three important phases : (1) Health Instruction. (2) Health service. (3) Health supervision.

1. *Health instruction* : It gives intelligent and essential information about personal and community health.

2. *Health service* : It consists of Medical inspection and follow-up work.

3. *Health supervision* : It attempts to regulate the environment and the educational procedure so that pupils' health will be ensured.

**1. Health instruction**

According to D.K. Barce 'Health instruction is that organisation of learning experiences directed towards the development of favourable health knowledge, attitude and practices'. Health instruction in school include an elementary knowledge of diseases, the causes of diseases, the preventive methods and treatment, personal cleanliness, community hygiene, care of the most important organs of the body such as ear, nose, throat, eyes and hair, first aid, diet and the evil effects of intoxicants.

Teachers must conduct regular morning health inspection of pupils. They must recognise the signs and symptoms of various childhood aliments so that they can detect such conditions easily and take necessary steps to help the child and also to isolate him if necessary. The class-rooms, the play-fields, hostels, and hostel mess may be inspected every now and then. Prizes and awards may be awarded to the group of students who maintain cleanliness. Every one should learn to obey the laws of health, hygiene and sanitation.

**2. Health Service**

A health service programme for schools, consists of the medical examination of pupils, protection from communicable diseases, first-aid services; correction of postural defects and follow-up work.

Medical examination with the necessary follow-up work forms the essence of health service.

All the school children must be medically examined at least three or four times during the period of education leading to the end of high school. Special and doubtful cases must be examined more frequently. The physical education teacher should be able to detect cases which are to be referred to the doctor.

**3. Health Supervision**

Health supervision guarantees the cleanliness and hygienic conditions of the school and play-fields. The environmental conditions of the school should assure a congenial atmosphere. Every hour of his stay in the school be conducive to the development of health habits. The authorities of the school should provide the following to make the school site and play area attractive. Green and shady trees, meadows and lawns, class-rooms with proper ventilation and seating arrangements, play-fields with painted posts and with uniform surface, galleries and drinking water taps.

The common needs are :

1. Food and eating
2. Elimination of body wastes.
3. Exercise and play.

4. Sleep, rest and recreation.
5. Needs of the — i. Eyes
   ii. Ear
   iii. Nose
   iv. Throat
   v. Teeth
   vi. Skin.
6. Posture.
7. Illness and diseases.
8. Accidents and injuries.
9. Emotional adjustments.
10. Sex adjustment.

1. *Food and Eating.* Children should be educated to understand the value of food and nutrition. Educational programme must emphasise on greater consumption of the protective foods on greater caloric intake. The diet should contain the following things — carbohydartes, proteins, fats and minerals. Each of this contributes to health as follows :

(i) Carbohydrates and fats give ready energy.
(ii) Proteins are for building up of the body and for repair work.
(iii) Minerals and Vitamins are for growth and for protecting us from sickness.

Food requirements are calculated as per energy calories :

(i) Carbohydrates give 4 calories per each gram.
(ii) Proteins give 4 calories per each gram.
(iii) Fat gives 9 calories per each gram.

Vitamins and minerals do not give energy but they are required for protecting our body from diseases.

A balanced diet gives all the above factors of food in proper proportions to give energy, to aid growth, to do repair work and to protect from illness as per age, sex and occupation of the person.

For an adult, normal food should give 3000 calories of heat from 500 grams of carbohydrates, 100 grams of protein and 100 grams of fat.

2. *Elimination of Body Wastes.* Waste products of the body including products of metabolism and unused food materials, must be removed regularly through the organs of elimination, including the lungs, skin, kidneys and inter issues.

3. *Exercise and Play.* Exercise is one of the most fundamental needs of human beings. Muscle tone is improved through exercise, which influences posture, the

process of elimination and the development of strength and endurance. Opportunities for healthful exercises should be provided compulsorily.

4. *Sleep, Rest and Relaxation*. In accordance with the requirements of children of different age groups, work, rest, relaxation and sleep are commonly the daily routines. Strenuous work should be followed with rest to relieve fatigue. During rest time recreation should find its place. These three should be followed with a long and sound sleep.

5. *Care of the Ears, Eyes, Nose, Throat, Teeth and Skin*. Large number of children are victims of handicapping defects, that lower physical efficiency and cause poor emotional and scholastic adjustments.

6. *Posture*. Defective posture causes incapacity for normal work. Defects of bones, muscles and joints are common amongst children. They are called orthopaedic defects. Proper attention should be shown in removing the causes. Children should be given guidance in the corrective work programme classes. Medical guidance should be made available.

7. *Illness and Diseases.* Disabiling illness and diseases interfere with the growth of the children. Acute conditions may cause disabilities. Frequent causes of illness are cold, accidents, digestive disorders, sore throat, middle ear infection and ear ache. Communicable diseases take a heavy toll in illness and death among school children despite an expanding use of modern drugs and wide application of preventive measures.

School should arrange for teaching and taking measures for prevention and control such as immunization programmes, school sanitation and hygenic living practice.

8. *Accidents and Injuries*. Many lives are needlessly lost and many people incapacitated because of accidents and injuries. Bodily injury may cause crippling, emotional and social maladjustments, sickness and even death. School building accidents are quite common. School ground accidents are mostly due to unorganised activities. Safety education should necessarily form part of educational curriculum. Each school should study the accident situations and determine the most apparent need of the locality. Children should be given training in First Aid.

9. *Emotional Adjustments*. Every child has certain emotional needs such as the need for affection: to be like others; and to be comfortable. Life is a series of adjustments to meet these basic needs. When the adjustment is too difficult, emotional disturbances and behaviour problems arise. Anxieties and timid frustrations make the child aggressive or conversely he withdraws from people and situations.

Many emotional problems can be carefully studied by the classroom teachers and solved by seeking psychiatric help.

10. *Sex Education.* A fundamental need of every child is to be well adjusted sexually. He should have good personal sex habit and should have wholesome relations with his age level, both with the members of his own sex and with those of the opposite sex.

## SAFETY EDUCATION

### Importance of Safety Education

Safety Education forms an integral part of Health Education. In the modern civilized world, though man has been able to conquer space and time, he has not conquered risks and dangers to life. Electricity has become an unavoidable necessity in providing convenience and comforts, though the slightest carelessness in dabling with it costs life. Thus safety education has to be taught to children. They should be trained to avert and avoid risks and dangers instead of inviting them through carelessness.

1. *Safty at School.* Safety, like health, is the responsibility of the school as a whole. As every child spends almost the whole day time in the school, safety should be ensured at all places in the school.

Classrooms, drinking water, sports, bath rooms, lavatories, urinals and all the surrounding areas inside the school compound should be safe. To ensure safety, all places should be free from obstructions.

Fire extinguishers are to be fixed to the walls at places where fire can break out or where there are inflammable substances.

Areas outside the classroom building should be kept clean. Shrubs and heaps of wastages should be removed periodically as they would prove to be the abodes of reptiles and other poisonous creatures.

It is not safe to keep any electric contrivance uncovered. As such livewire hanging anywhere, uncovered switches, and broken parts of electrical installations exposed anywhere are tempting ones for the children to meddle with. Therefore, immediate attention may be given in rectifying and restoping them to order.

2. *Safety at Play Fields.* There is a close relationship between safety education and physical education. Every activity in physical education should be taught according to the safety standards. All equipment should be inspected periodically for safety as safety forms an integral part of a sound physical education programme.

The relationship between Physical Education and Safety Education is reciprocal. While Physical Education contributes to safety, Safety Education is necessary under varying situations during physical activities. Safety Education forms part of modern physical education. The physical education teacher is put to the necessity of stressing safety factors to the participants when they indulge in activities.

First-aid facilities should be made available as close to the playfield as possible. The service of a physician should be available to the players particularly during activity hours.

3. *Safety at Home.* As children are under the care of their parents at home, it is the duty of every parent to look after their safety. They have to educate them to gain sufficient knowledge to keep themselves safe at all times. No child should be prevented from playing. Growing muscles need exercise and besides this pleasure, mirth, happiness and jubilation in the company of play mates is unparalleled. The parents should see that they are safe from the menace of accidents.

Bleeding, bruises, dislocation, tearing and teasing of muscles and skin, breakage of bones, heavy haemorrhage and several other complications take place in their children for want of carefulness of the parents. 'A stich in time saves nine, 'Prevention is better than cure' are to be remembered by every parents. What is safe is to be practised and what is unsafe is to be avoided.

## QUESTIONS FOR EXERCISE

1. When Health is lost everything is lost. Explain.
2. What are the common school health problems?
3. What are the fundamental needs of the body?
4. Sanitation plays a major role in school organisation. Explain.
5. As a classroom teacher what are the physical defects which you can detect in children?
6. As a classroom teacher what precautionary steps would you take to avoid accidents in the classroom?

27

# PROBLEMS OF HIGHER EDUCATION

## Historical Review

World's first Universities were founded in India. Taxila, Nalanda, Varanasi and Kancheepuram were centres of higher learning which attracted many diligent students from abroad. During Muslim rule, Madarsas imparted higher learning. Universities in the modern sense were established by the British. Wood's Despatch (1854) recommended the establishment of Universities. In 1857 Calcutta, Bombay and Madras Universities came into existence with the faculties of Arts, Law, Medicine and Engineering.

## The Indian Education Commission (1882)

The Hunter Commission made following important suggestions regarding higher education in India :

1. Slow and gradual withdrawal of Government support to higher education.
2. Provision of ordinary and special grants to colleges.
3. Institution of alternative courses in larger colleges.
4. Regulation of tuition and special fees.
5. New scholarship regulations.
6. Special textbooks for moral instructions.
7. Lectures on citizenship.

## Indian University Commission (1902)

This Commission recommended legislation to protect University autonomy and promote educational standards and discipline. On the basis of its recommendations, Indian Universities Act was enacted in 1904. The Government of India Resolution (1913) stressed the need for research in Universities. Though England dispensed with the system of afflicting colleges it was found unavoidable in India.

## Calcutta Universities Commission (1917)

In India there were more than 200 colleges before the First World War. Higher education needed restructuring and modernisation. The Calcutta Education Commission (1917) was asked to examine the state of higher education in the country. It made following important recommendations :

1. New Universities should be residential in character.
2. Pass and Honours courses should be started.
3. Inter-University Boards should be established.
4. Technical and Technological courses should be started to suit local needs.
5. Physical education should be encouraged.

The Annamalai University, Unitary and Residential in nature, was founded in 1929.

**University Education Commission (1948-49)**

Headed by Dr. Radhakrishnan University Education Commission was instituted to report on the conditions of Indian Universities and offer suggestions to revitalise it. The report has given the following objectives for higher education :

1. India is rich in natural resources and human potential. University should educate and train students to bring these two resources together and raise our living standards.
2. Universities should produce leaders with intellectual analysis and imaginative insight.
3. Intellectual adventure should be promoted.
4. Life has meaning. An integrated way of life leads to human betterment.
5. No amount of factual information would make ordinary men into 'educated' men, unless something awakened in them, an innate ability to lead a higher life.
6. Higher education should promote a new social order based on democracy, justice, liberty, equality and fraternity.

**The Education Commission (1964-66)**

The Kothari Commission made a few radical recommendations, including the New Pattern of Education (10+2+3). Accordingly many States shed the Pre-University Course. The Commission redefined the ideals of higher education as follows :

1. Seeking knowledge within the framework of truth, using traditional knowledge in new circumstances.
2. Developing leadership in every sphere of life.
3. Giving educated and trained man-power to society.
4. Promoting social justice.
5. Inculcating right values.

6. Reduction of social and cultural disparities.
7. Developing national sentiments.
8. Introduction of adult education programmes.

**National Policy on Higher Education (1979)**

In 1979 the Parliament of India approved the National Policy on Education giving new guidelines about higher education :

1. Higher education should play a vital role in national development.
2. Unchecked growth of institutions of higher education without adequate facilities will endanger quality.
3. Alternative strategies like correspondence courses, part time courses and own time studies should be explored.
4. Quality of post-graducate education should be improved.
5. Linkages with the society should be strengthened through extension programmes.
6. Autonomous colleges should strive to become centres of excellence.

**National Enrolment Policy**

The national enrolment policy was evolved to copé up with the rush for higher education. The Policy states :

1. Regulation of admission in order of merit, keeping in view, the intake capacity of each department or college without affecting the standards.
2. Checking the establishment of new Universities and Colleges except in backward areas where also it may be considered only after a survey of its educational needs.
3. Vocationalisation of the secondary level of education and its impact on University admission.
4. Restructuring of courses of study at the first degree level.
5. Provision of facilities for greater enrolment through correspondence courses.
6. Equalisation of educational opportunities for weaker sections of the society.

**Defects of the Prevalent System of Higher Education**

1. *Quality* Versus *Quantity* : There are about four million students in our Universities and Colleges. The demand for higher education is due to the socio-economic transformation that is taking place in the country. The Indian economy has neither the resources to expand higher education at the present rate nor the capacity to absorb the large number of graduates in gainful employment. A kind of Iron Law of Educational Growth whose logic is very simple, 'universalisation of elementary education leading to generalisation of secondary and the latter to a

corresponding growth of higher education' is evident. There is a lot of criticism about the deplorable fall in the intellectual standards of the Universities. So, the developmental strategy must cover man's hopes, aspirations and welfare.

2. *Faculty in Competence* : The volume of knowledge doubles every ten years. New skills and knowledge are required to be an upto date. Unlike in the West, the contribution of our Universities to Science, Arts or Literature is very meagre. Research facilities do not exist in many colleges. University teachers do very little research work; college teachers do even less. Many teachers are content with their present qualifications and record. Only a few voice their views on academic or national problems.

3. *Wastage* : Failure rate in Indian Universities is as high as 50%. Time, money and effort are needlessly wasted because of the 'open door policy'. In U.K. the wastage rate is only 14%. Educational guidance is not provided to the candidates.

4. *Student Activism* : Youth is a restless period in life. Owing to social, psychological, emotional and economic reasons the student unrest is on the increase in India. Very often, it takes violent and ugly turns. Students rarely involve themselves in ideological disputes. Most of their agitations stem from petty, personal grievances — real or imaginary.

5. *Imbalances* : 70% of Indian study humanities and social sciences; only 30% study physical science and related faculties. Colleges within the same University area have unequal standards.

6. *Intellectual Slavery* : In India the colonial heritage has stifled the spirit of independent inquiry. Scholars readily subscribe to official views and hesitate to voice their dissents. Indian academicians are overeager to imitate foreign systems and models. Most professors are reconciled to the position of well paid employees. A college teacher is rarely absorbed in a University department. Distance is carefully maintained and aloofness is encouraged between the University and a College affiliated to it.

7. *Medium of Instruction* : Gandhiji and Tagore championed the introduction of Indian languages as the medium of instruction at all levels. English medium is supposed to have denationalising effect. Lectures are delivered in faulty English. Students have more difficulty with English than with the subject matter. In this futile struggle Indian Universities waste their talents. The elite favour and the continuance of English warn that regional loyalties will undermine fellow feeling and may lead to balkanisation of India. Until Hindi becomes familiar in all parts of India, the teaching of English cannot be given up.

8. *Irrelevance* : Higher education is not linked to manpower needs of the country. The courses offered are obsolete. Vested interests block progressive reforms. Indian universities are pale limitations of those which existed in nineteenth century England. Imaginative and socially rewarding courses are not planned and introduced. Practical and applied courses to regenerate Rural India and emancipate the underprivileged are seriously lacking. If there is more co-operation from the industrialists and agriculturists, the University can successfully complete its social obligations.

9. *Uneconomical* : Cost benefit considerations are ignored. Educational policy makers are more optimistic than the most optimistic forecasters. Expansion targets are never fulfilled. Every college and University should examine (i) whether it is utilising the available resources to the maximum extent possible, and (ii) whether the quality of its output can withstand the rigorous of the competitive world.

10. *Faculty Examinations* : The present system of examinations is inconsistent and arbitrary. It only tests the memory of the student and it ignores the slow but thoughtful learner. Marks in examination are not true indicators of a student's mastery of his subject. In the words of University Education Commission (1948-49), "If we are to suggest one single reform in the University education, it should be that of examinations. The crippling effect of examinations on the quality of work in higher education is so great that examinations reform has become crucial to all progress and has to go hand in hand with the improvement in teaching."

## HIGHER EDUCATION FOR WOMEN

In recent years, the education of women has come to be regarded as a critical input for national development and a key factory in the transformation of character and value system and in the mobilisation of human resources.

S.N.D.T. Women's University, Bombay was founded in 1951. Recently a Women's University was founded at Kodaikanal in Tamil Nadu. Following are the comparative figures to understand the progress of women's education in India :

TABLE 1

**Colleges Exclusively for Women**

| Year | Number |
|---|---|
| 1971-72 | 430 |
| 1975-76 | 528 |
| 1980-81 | 609 |

Enrolment of girls in higher education is increasing. One-sixth of the students are girls as is clear from the following table :

TABLE 2

**Enrolment of Women Students**

| | 1950-51 | 1960-61 | 1980-81 |
|---|---|---|---|
| Total enrolment in higher education (in thousands) | 40 | 150 | 749 |
| No. of women students (per hundred men) | 14 | 21 | 27 |

TABLE 3

**Facultywise Enrolement of Women Students** (per cent)

| Faculty | 1970-71 | 1980-81 |
|---|---|---|
| Commerce | 3.1 | 15.9 |
| Agriculture | 0.5 | 3.3 |
| Veterinary Science | 0.7 | 3.3 |
| Medicine | 2.9 | 24.4 |
| Law | 3.7 | 6.9 |
| Education | 36.5 | 47.3 |

Educated girls prefer teaching, nursing and medicine to other professional courses.

TABLE 4

**Women Teachers** (Per cent)

| Different Levels | The total teaching staff |
|---|---|
| Primary School | 26 |
| Middle School | 37 |
| Secondary School | 30 |
| Collegiate Level | 15 |

## AUTONOMOUS COLLEGES

In India, Universities enjoy autonomous status. Governmental interference in their administration and academic activities is not usually allowed. On the basis of the recommendations of the Education Commission (1964-66), reputed colleges with necessary pre-requisites were given autonomy to frame their own curriculum, evaluation methods and admission policies with the co-operation of the concerned Universities. However, the autonomous colleges are accused of neglecting social justice and catering only to the elitist classes. Teachers complain of victimisation and students grumble about favouritism. Periodical assessment of the scheme is necessary to make the experiment a success. A democratisation should be the pre-condition for giving the special status. There are 10 autonomous colleges in the country including the engineering colleges and one college of education. Excepting one engineering and two Arts and Science colleges, all the others are in Tamil Nadu.

## UNIVERSITY GRANTS COMMISSION (U.G.C.)

The University Education Commission of 1948 recommended the constitution of the U.G.C. for providing funds for the Universities of India and for co-ordination of standards in the Universities. Even though there was an Advisory Committee functioning in 1945, it had no funds of its own. So the Radhakrishnan Commission recommended an expert body to be constituted. In pursuance of their recommendations, a non-statutory University Grants Commission was constituted in 1952 to consider the financial needs of the Universities for discharging their responsibilities. With more pressure on the Government of India by Vice-Chancellors and State Education Ministers for forming a statutory authority, the University Grants Commission Bill was introduced in the Parliament by the Government of India in the year 1954. With the passing of the University Grants Commission Act in 1956, the University Grants Commission became a statutory authority.

According to U.G.C. Act of 1956, the Commission will consist of 9 members to be appointed by the Central Government of which three will be from among the Vice-Chancellors, two from officers of the Central Government and the remaining from among persons who are educationists of repute or who have academic distinction. Now, in addition to a full-time Chairman, there is a full-time Vice-Chariman and the total number of the members of the Commission is increased to 12 as amended in the year 1966. Each member holds office for a period of 6 years. A Secretary is to be appointed by the Commission as well as the others in the secretariat. The orders and decisions are to be signed by the Chairman and authenticated by the Secreatry.

**Functions**

*The University Grants Commission may —*

1. inquire into the financial needs of the universities;
2. allocate and disburse grants to central universities for their maintenance and development;
3. allocate and disburse grants to other universities;
4. recommend to any university the measures necessary for the improvement of university education and advise the universities upon the action to be taken for the purpose of implementing the recommendations;
5. advise the Central Government or any State Government on the allocation of any grants to university for any general or specific purpose out of the consolidated Fund of the State;
6. advise any authority, if such advice is asked for, on the establishment of a new university or any proposals connected with the expansion of the activities of any university;
7. advise the Central Government or any State Government or University on any question which may be referred to the Commission by them;
8. collect information on all such matters relating to university education in India and other countries as it thinks fit and make the same available to any university;
9. require a university to furnish with such information as may be needed relating to the financial position of the university or the studies in the

various branches of learning undertaken by the University, together with all rules and regulations relating to standard of teaching and examination in that University in respect of each branch of learning;

10. perform such other functions as may be prescribed or as may be deemed necessary by the Commission for advancing the cause of higher education in India or may be incidental or conducive to the discharge of the above functions.

## CONTINUING EDUCATION

Life styles are changing and civilization is becoming more complex. People should be helped to learn from their own places at the time suitable for them and to equip themselves to adjust to changed conditions. Continuing education should provide the adult learners education according to their needs. It is a learner-oriented activity and not a syllabus-oriented activity. Courses include environmental protection, population education, nutrition education, science for the masses etc., 17 universities were offering part-time and own-time education in 1980-81.

**Recommendations of Education Commission (1964-66)**

1. Educational institutions of all types and grades should be encouraged and helped to throw open their doors outside the regular working hours to provide such courses of instruction as they can to those who are desirous of receiving education. A parallel part-time system of education should be created to provide adults with opportunities for taking the same diplomas and degrees as students in schools and colleges.

2. Educational institutions should give the lead in organizing *ad hoc* courses which will help people understand and solve their problems and acquire wider knowledge and experience.

3. Further education should be provided for workers for improving their knowledge and skills, widening their horizon in life, inculcating in them a sense of responsibility towards their profession and improving their careers. Special part-time and sandwhich courses should be offered for them which would lead them step by step to higher courses.

4. Special institutions such as those run by the Central Social Welfare Board for Adult Women and the Vidyapeeths in Mysore State should be established. The existing institutions should be frequently reviewed in order to enable them to be of service to the rural community.

## CORRESPONDENCE COURSES

The University of Delhi started B.A. correspondence course in 1962. Now 22 universities and one institution with 'deemed university' status are offering correspondence courses. B.A., M.A., B.Ed., M.Ed., LL.B., B.Com., and even M.B.A. degrees are offered through correspondence courses. These courses are usually supplemented by Radio and T.V. Programmes, Audio-cassettes and contact seminars.

**Benefitting Persons**

Correspondence course is benefitting more than a million students all over India. It is a boon to (i) students who had to discontinue their formal education owing to pecuniary and other circumstances, (ii) students in geographically remote areas, (iii) students who had to discontinue their education because of lack of aptitude and motivation but who later on become motivated, (iv) students who cannot get a seat or do not wish to join a regular college or university department, although they have the necessary qualifications to pursue higher education, and (v) individuals who look upon education as a life-time activity and may either like to refresh their knowledge in an existing discipline or to acquire knowledge in a new area.

**Suggestions for Improvement**

1. Widespread organization of correspondence courses should be organised. In order to bring education to those who are unable even to attend part-time courses.

2. Students taking correspondence courses should be provided opportunities to meet the teachers occasionally. They should be given the status of recognized students and where possible be attached to some colleges in order to enable them to make use of the library and other facilities.

3. Correspondence courses should be supported by well co-ordinated radio and television programmes.

4. Correspondence courses should not be confined to preparing students for the university degrees but should also provide agricultural, industrial and other workers such special courses of instruction as would help them to improve production.

5. Correspondence courses should be made available for those who desire to enrich their lives by studying subjects of cultural and aesthetic value.

6. Correspondence courses should be developed for the teacher in schools to keep them abreast with knowledge as well as with new methods and techniques of teaching.

7. The Ministry of Education in collaboration with other Ministries should establish a National Council of Home Studies, for the purpose of accreditation and evaluation of agencies which provide correspondence courses, identification of the areas in which different types of correspondence courses would be of benefit, promote creation of such courses through proper agencies, and conducting evaluation and research.

8. Opportunity to take examinations conducted by the Secondary Education Board and Universities in the country should be made available to those who wish to work on their own without any assistance.

## OPEN UNIVERSITY

The Open University in the U.K. started functioning in Janunary 1971. It became popular in a short time. Cost per student was much less. The teaching methods include correspondence courses, radio, listening, reproduction of taped material discussion and personal contacts in its regional offices. For science students, a special kit has been devised to enable them to conduct experiments in their own places. A person may get even Ph.D. through this programme. There are compulsory contact sessions. Systems Approach is used — men, money and materials are put to maximum use. 'Distance learning' is just a part of this comprehensive scheme.

Mysore and Madurai Kamaraj Universities have started Open Universities. People above a certain age may appear directly to many degree examinations. Foundation courses are a must to those who have no basic qualification.

## RESEARCH

Jawahar Lal Nehru said : "A University stands for humanism, for tolerance, for reason, for the adventure of ideas and the search for truth." Universities should devote more attention to research. Unfortunately Indian universities do not have the distinction for outstanding inventions and discoveries. Research should be an integral part of post-graduate courses. In 1979-80, Indian universities turned out 5076 Ph.Ds. of whom 4092 were from Arts and Science faculties. Centres of Advanced studies in 10 universities provide Research Facilities in Humanities and 31 University departments offer facilities for Research in Science subjects. All of them get liberal assistance from the University Grants Commission.

## UNIVERSITY FINANCES

Kothari Commission made the following recommendations in this connection:

1. The State Governments should place adequate financial resources at the disposal of Universities and simplify rules and procedures for operating them.
2. The UGC should be enabled to give both development and maintenance grants to State Universities.
3. There should be some reasonable sharing of developments expenditure on Universities between the UGC and State Government.
4. The UGC should take steps to resolve problems faced by some Universities on account of the non-payment of grants on committed expenditure by State Governments.
5. The system of grant-in-aid from the State Governments should be reorganized on the basis of a suitable system of block grants.
6. The finance of Universities should be placed on a sound footing on the basis of advice given by the UGC to the State Governments and the Universities after periodical review.
7. Universities should be immune from direct Governmental intervention and also from direct public accountability.

## TYPES OF UNIVERSITIES

Education comes under the concurrent list. It is the joint responsibility of both the Central and State Governments :

1. *Centrally administered universities* : These include the Banaras Hindu University, Aligarh Muslim University, Delhi University, Vishwa Bharathi University and Jawaharlal Nehru University, Hyderabad University and North Eastern Hill University. All the other universities are administered by their respective States. State Governors act as Chancellors of these Universities.

2. *Affiliating type* : Here teaching particularly at the undergraduate level is carried on in the affiliating colleges. University prescribes the syllabus, conducts examinations and awards degrees.

3. *Unitary universities* : These are encouraged by the U.G.C., teaching is carried on by the university departments. Every unitary university serves only a limited area.

4. *Residential universities* : There are a few residential universities where residential facilities are provided to all the full time students.

5. *Federal universities* : These are a group of constituent colleges or higher departments of study each of which may have autonomous status or not.

6. *Deemed universities* : These enjoy the status of universities. They are unitary in character. Indian Institute of Science, Bangalore was accorded this status in 1958. There are now 22 deemed universities and institutions of national importance with an enrolment of over 3 lakhs.

## EDUCATION AND EMPLOYMENT

Following suggestions may be made to remedy this situation :

There is large scale of unemployment and underemployment among educated persons in India. The unemployed and temporarily out of job youth, are frustrated in the absence of social insurance. It creates social problems like racketing in jobs, late marriages, cult of violence etc. Educated unemployed is a reflection on the weakness of our economic policy. Indian Universities turn out more graduates than our economy can immediately absorb. Following suggestions may be made to remedy this situation :

1. Higher education should be planned to meet the needs of the agricultural and industrial sectors.

2. Job-oriented courses and applied sciences may be introduced in Arts and Science colleges.

3. Technical institutes, professional education after higher secondary education and providing work experience to all students may help to solve the problem.

4. Education which promotes self-reliance, initiative and originality is the need of the hour. It alone can prove the skills and confidence necessary for self-employment.

5. Career guidance may be offered at all terminal points in the system.
6. Degree should not be insisted upon for clerical posts.

## UNIVERSITIES IN INDIA

| **A. Affiliating Type** | | *Year of Establishment* |
|---|---|---|
| 1. | Agra University, Agra | 1926 |
| 2. | Andhra University, Waltair | 1925 |
| 3. | Awadh University, Faizabad | 1975 |
| 4. | Awadesh Pratap Singh University, Rewa, Madhya Pradesh | 1968 |
| 5. | Bangalore University, Bangalore | 1964 |
| 6. | Berhampur University, Berhampur | 1966 |
| 7. | Bhagalpur University, Bhagalpur | 1960 |
| 8. | Bharathiar University, Coimbatore | 1982 |
| 9. | Bhopal University, Bhopal | 1970 |
| 10. | Bharathidasan University, Tiruchirappalli | 1982 |
| 11. | Bihar University, Muzzafarpur | 1952 |
| 12. | Bhavnagar University, Bhavnagar | 1981 |
| 13. | Bundelkand University, Jhansi | 1975 |
| 14. | Burdwan University, Burdwan | 1959 |
| 15. | Calcutta University, Calcutta | 1857 |
| 16. | Calicut University, Calicut | 1968 |
| 17. | Dibrugarh University, Dibrugarh | 1965 |
| 18. | Garhwal University, Srinagar, U.P. | 1973 |
| 19. | Gauhati University, Gauhati | 1947 |
| 20. | Gorakhpur University, Gorakhpur | 1956 |
| 21. | Gujarat University, Ahmedabad | 1949 |
| 22. | Gujarat Ayruveda University, Jamnagar | 1965 |
| 23. | Gulbarga University, Gulbarga | 1980 |
| 24. | Gurunanak Dev University, Amritsar | 1969 |
| 25. | Himachal Pradesh University, Simla | 1970 |
| 26. | Indira Kala Sangeet, Viswavidyalaya Khairagarh, Madhya Pradesh | 1956 |
| 27. | Jabalpur University, Jabalpur | 1956 |
| 28. | Jagannath Sanskrit Viswavidyalaya, Bhubaneswar | 1978 |
| 29. | Jadhavpur University, Calcutta | 1955 |

30. Jammu University, Jammu 1969
31. Jiwaji University, Gwalior 1963
32. Kalyan University, Kalyan 1960
33. Kameshwar Singh Darbhanga Sanskrit Viswavidyalaya, Darbhanga 1960
34. Kakatiya University, Warangal 1980
35. Kanpur University, Kanpur 1965
36. Karnataka University, Dharwar 1950
37. Kashmir University, Srinagar 1948
38. Kerala University, Trivandrum 1937
39. Kumaon University, Nainital 1973
40. Kurukshetra University, Kurukshetra 1956
41. Lalit Narain Mithila University, Darbhanga 1972
42. Madras University, Madras 1857
43. Madurai Kamaraj University, Madurai 1965
44. Magadh University, Bodh Gaya 1962
45. Marathawada University, Aaurangabad 1958
46. Manipur University, Imphal 1977
47. Meerut University, Meerut 1965
48. Mangalore University, Mangalore 1977
49. Mysore University, Mysore 1926
50. Maharishi Dayanand University, Rohtak, 1976
51. Nagpur University, Nagpur 1923
52. North Bengal University, Darjeeling 1962
53. Nagarjun University, Guntur 1975
54. Osmania University, Hyderabad 1928
55. Punjab University, Chandigarh 1947
56. Poona University, Pune 1948
57. Punjabi University, Patiala 1962
58. Rabindra Bharathi University, Calcutta, 1962
59. Rajasthan University, Jaipur 1946
60. Ranchi University, Ranchi 1960
61. Ravishankar University, Raipur 1963
62. Rohelkhand University, Bareli 1975
63. Sambalpur University, Sambalpur 1966

| | | |
|---|---|---|
| 64. | Sampoornanand Sanskrit Viswavidyalaya, Varanasi | 1958 |
| 65. | Sardar Patel University, Vallabh Vidanagar | 1955 |
| 66. | Saugar University, Saugar | 1946 |
| 67. | Saurashtra University, Saurashtra | 1965 |
| 68. | Shivaji University, Kolhapur | 1965 |
| 69. | Shreemathi Nathibhai Damoday Thakersey Women's University, Bombay | 1949 |
| 70. | South Gujarat University, Surat | 1966 |
| 71. | Sri Venkateswara University, Tirupathi | 1952 |
| 72. | Shri Krishnadevaraya University, Anantapur | 1980 |
| 73. | Udaipur University, Udaipur | 1962 |
| 74. | Utkal University, Bhubaneshwar | 1943 |
| 75. | Vikram University, Ujjain | 1957 |

**B. Unitary Type**

| | | |
|---|---|---|
| 1. | Allahabad University, Allahabad | 1887 |
| 2. | Annamalai University, Annamalainagar | 1929 |
| 3. | Jodhpur University, Jodhpur | 1962 |
| 4. | Kasi Vidyapeeth, Varanasi | 1974 |
| 5. | Lucknow University, Lucknow | 1921 |
| 6. | M.S. University, Baroda | 1949 |
| 7. | Patna University, Patna | 1917 |
| 8. | Tamil University, Thanjavur | 1980 |
| 9. | Vidyasagar University, Calcutta | 1980 |
| 10. | Mother Teresa Women University, Kodaikanal | 1984 |

**FEDERAL**

| | | |
|---|---|---|
| 1. | Bombay University, Bombay | 1857 |
| 2. | Indore University, Indore | 1963 |

**CENTRAL UNIVERSITIES**

| | | |
|---|---|---|
| 1. | Aligarh Muslim University, Aligarh | 1920 |
| 2. | Banaras Hindu University, Varanasi | 1915 |
| 3. | Delhi University, Delhi | 1922 |
| 4. | Hyderabad University, Hyderabad | 1974 |
| 5. | Jawaharlal Nehru University, New Delhi | 1966 |
| 6. | North Eastern Hill University, Shillong | 1973 |

7. Viswa Bharati University, Shantiniketan 1951

**C. Technological and Agricultural Universities**

1. Andhra Pradesh Agricultural University, Hyderabad 1963
2. Anna University of Technology, Madras 1975
3. Assam Agricultural University, Jorhat 1968
4. Bidhanachandra Krishi Viswavidyalaya, West Bengal 1974
5. Birsa Agricultural University, Ranchi 1981
6. Chandrasekhar Azad University of Agriculture and Technology, Kanpur 1974
7. Cochin University, Cochin 1971
8. G.B. Pant University of Agriculture and Technology, Nainital 1958
9. Gujarat Agricultural University, Ahmedabad 1972
10. Himachal Pradesh Krishi Viswavidyalaya, Palampur 1979
11. Haryana Agricultural University, Hissar 1970
12. Jawaharlal Nehru Krishi Viswavidyalaya, Jabalpur 1964
13. Jawaharlal Nehru Technological Institute, Hyderabad 1972
14. Kerala Agricultural University, Trichur 1971
15. Konkan Krishi Vidyapeeth, Dapoli 1972
16. Mahatma Phule Krishi Vidyapeeth, Ahamednagar 1967
17. Marathwada Krishi Vidyapeeth, Parbhani 1972
18. Narenda Deo University of Agriculture and Technology, Faizabad 1974
19. Orissa University of Agriculture and Technology, Bhubaneshwar 1961
20. Punjab Rao Agricultural University, Akola 1969
21. Rajendra Agricultural University, Patna 1970
22. Punjab Agricultural University, Ludhiana 1961
23. Roorkee University, Roorkee 1948
24. Tamilnadu Agricultural University, Coimbatore 1971
25. University of Agricultural Sciences, Bangalore 1963

**D. Institutions of National Importance and the Deemed Universities**

1. Birla Institute of Technology and Science, Pilani
2. Central Institute of English and Foreign Languages, Hyderabad
3. Dayalbagh Educational Institute, Agra
4. Gandhigram Rural Institute, Gandhigram, Madurai

5. Gujarat Vidyapith, Ahmedabad
6. Gurukul Kangri Viswavidyalaya, Hardwar
7. Indian Agricultural Research Institute, New Delhi
8. Indian Institute of Science, Bangalore
9. Indian School of Mines, Dhanbad.
10. Jamia Millia Islamia, New Delhi.
11. School of Planning and Architecture, New Delhi.
12. Shri Sathya Sai Institute of Higher Learning, Anantapur.
13. Tata Institute of Social Sciences, Bombay.
14. All India Institute of Medical Sciences, New Delhi.
15. Dakshina Bharat Hindi Prachar Sabha, Hyderabad.
16. Indian Institute of Technology, Powai, Bombay
17. Indian Institute of Technology, Kanpur.
18. Indian Institute of Technology, New Delhi.
19. Indian Institute of Technology, Madras.
20. Indian Institute of Technology, Kharagpur
21. Indian Statistical Institute, Calcutta.
22. Post-graduate Institute of Medical Education and Research, Chandigarh.

## RECOMMENDATIONS ON UNIVERSITY EDUCATION

### A. University Education Commission (1948-49)

1. The importance of the teacher and his responsibility should be recognised.

2. Only suitable teachers should be selected.

3. Minimum requirement for admission to the university courses should be successful completion of 12 years of study.

4. Maximum number in Arts and Science Colleges should be restricted to 1500 and in the universities to 3000.

5. There should not be any prescribed text-books for any courses of study.

6. Laboratories should be improved.

7. Education should be well balanced, general education is preferable to narrow specialisation.

8. Admission to Ph.D. courses should be made with care and should be on an all India basis.

9. D. Litt and D.Sc., degrees should be awarded for published work of outstanding quality.

10. New professional courses should be introduced to accelerate the process of industrialisation, technological changes and human relations.

11. Tenets of all major religions should be taught.

12. English should be studied in order to keep in touch with the living stream of ever growing knowledge (Library language).

13. Three languages (mother tongue, federal language and English) should be studied.

14. A university degree should not be required for Government administrative service. Special examinations for recruitment to services may be organised.

15. Standards for success should be uniform 40% for a pass in third class, 55 to 69% for a second class and 70% and above for a first class.

16. Admissions should be based on merit.

17. Nutritious noon-meal should be provided at reasonable cost.

18. Communal hostels should be abolished.

19. An Advisory Board of Student Welfare should be constituted; a Dean to look after the students may be appointed.

**B. Education Commission (1964-66)**

1. Universities should promote national consciousness.

2. Colleges which have a consistent high standard may be given autonomous status.

3. Mother tongue may be introduced as medium of instruction at the undergraduate level.

4. Classroom teaching should relate to essentials.

5. Guidance and counselling services should be provided.

6. Cultural values should be inculcated.

7. Educational standards should be improved.

8. Admissions should be restricted to the facilities available.

9. By 1986 one-third of the students should be enrolled in part-time courses.

10. Unplanned expansion of higher education should be stopped. U.G.C. should regulate future expansion.

11. Area studies should be instituted in select universities.

12. Education of girls and weaker sections of society should be encouraged.

13. Inter-University Boards should co-ordinate the programmes of the universities.

14. University Departments should be given autonomous status of the universities.

15. Vice-Chancellors should be scholars or educationists.

16. A university court, to frame laws, policies and regulation may be constituted.

17. Research should be encouraged. Schools of Excellence should be started by the universities.

18. A National Academy of Education should be set up.

19. Joint councils with representatives of the faculty and students should be set up to promote discipline.

20. College students should be involved in working with the community and particularly in spreading education.

## THE ROLE OF THE UNIVERSITY SYSTEM (FROM THE UGC REPORT)

The University system has important responsibilities to the society as a whole as well as to the educational system itself. A modern university has to undertake following functions :

1. Inculcate and promote basic human values and the capacity to choose between alternate value systems.
2. Preserve and foster our great cultural traditions and blend them with essential elements from other cultures and peoples.
3. Promote a rational outlook and scientific temper.
4. Enrich the Indian languages and promote their use as important means of communication, national development and unity.
5. Promote the development of the total personality of the students and inculcate in them a commitment to society through involvement in national service programme.
6. Act as an objective critic of society and assist in the formulation of national objectives and programmes of their realization.
7. Promote commitment to the pursuit of excellence.
8. Promote the development of science and technology and of an indigenous capability to apply it effectively with special emphasis on national problems; and above all.
9. Contribute to the improvement of entire educational system so as to subserve the community.

## ADMISSION TO HIGHER EDUCATION

The policy to be adopted about admission should consist of the following :

1. Adoption of measures which will reduce pressures on the University system, such as effective vocationalisation at the secondary stage, delinking most of the jobs from degrees, and changing the present recruitment policies which virtually make a degree a minimum qualification for any good job.

2. Exercising great restraint in the establishment of new institutions which should not be set-up except in backward areas unless their need is clearly established on sound academic considerations and adequate resources in terms of men, materials and money are available.

3. Planning the location of new institutions very carefully and rationalising that of the existing ones of the extent possible.

4. Adopting a policy of selective admissions to full-till institutions of higher education at first degree and post-graduate level on the basis of merit with reservation of at least half the seats for to weaker students to pursue their studies on a whole time basis ensuring to them the full cost of their education through appropriate bursaries, for which funds may be raised from public and private bodies.

5. Providing facilities for expansion of higher education through channels of non-formal education such as correspondence courses.

6. Opening Board and University examinations to private candidates and encourage self-study.

## SYLLABI AT UNDERGRADUATE STAGE

1. A set of foundation courses which are designed to create an awareness of areas such as Indian History and Culture; History of the freedom struggle in India and other parts of the world; Social and economic life in India including the role of Science and Technology in development; alternative value systems and societies based thereon; Cultures of Asia and Africa (selected countries) and Gandhian thought.

2. A set of Core Courses which will give the student an opportunity to acquire a broad familiarity with some chosen disciplines including a study of one or more of them in depth.

3. Some Applied Studies, projects, field activity which will form an integral activity of the course and will be carried out in the final year.

4. Involvement in a programme of National or Social Service for the first two years.

## POST-GRADUATE EDUCATION AND RESEARCH

1. Every institution providing post-graduate instruction must have competent staff actively engaged in research and adequate research facilities in terms of laboratory equipment and research journals.
2. At present about 50 per cent of post-graduate students and about 11 per cent of research students are studying in colleges. While a few colleges have outstanding research and teaching departments, most of them are poorly equipped for post-graduate instruction. Their situation should be reviewed in terms of the norms established by the University Grants Commission, and those having the potentiality of coming up to the norms within a few years should be assisted to do so as soon as possible while the others should discontinue post-graduate instruction in the interest of standards.
3. With the rapid increase in the number of universities, there is a need to

ensure that all the University Departments, themselves satisfy the norms as viable units of teaching and research.

4. While inter-disciplinary courses should be introduced at the under-graduate level also, special efforts must be made in this regard at the post-graduate and research level.
5. Individuals, groups and departments in universities and colleges should be supported, on merits, in carrying out high quality research. Special encouragement should be given to collaborative research efforts by a group, drawn from one or more departments on the basis of pooled resources.
6. High quality experimental research demands the development of indigenous instrumentaion capability and culture. Efforts in this direction should be encouraged through support of research and the creation of university instrumentation and service centres and regional instrumentation centres.
7. While universities will continue to be involved in fundamental research, application-oriented research, especially in collaboration with national laboratories and industries should be specially encouraged in universities. Both fundamental and applied research require the highest intellectual qualities.
8. The universities have to go outside the four walls of the classroom and get involved in a participatory understanding of some of the societal problems. Such research programmes should be encouraged as contribute to social developments, especially to rural development.
9. While fostering knowledge of science and technology at the highest theoretical level and spreading it in the rural areas there is a growing need to develop technology relevant to emergent national needs. This requires appropriate interaction between the institutions of higher learning and the productive processes and organs of society.

## AUTONOMOUS COLLEGES

Autonomy for a college implies that the college and its teachers assume full responsibility and accountability for the academic programmes they provide, for the content and quality of teaching, and for the admission and assessment of their students. This will make it possible for institutions of higher education to become communities of teachers and students engaged in an agreed and mutual satisfactory joint pursuit of truth and excellence. The terms and the conditions of service for teachers prescribed by the Government and the University Grants Commission would continue to apply to these institutions. The concept of autonomous colleges requires an institution to be continously subjected to periodic reviews. It should be liable to lose its recognition if the conditions of higher academic excellence as well as its contribution to society are not maintained at the expected level. Each institution shall seek its identity in its own unique fashion, consistent with its local situation and the academic perspectives of the local community.

## PROBLEMS OF UNIVERSITY EDUCATION

### 1. Problem due to Government Control

All the universities in India are dependent on government grants. On the recommendations of the University Grants Commission the Central Government sanctions grants to the State and Central Universities. Thus both the Central and State governments are responsible for financing universities. This gives scope to both the Centre and State to interfere in university affiairs. The government controls the university in the following manner :

(i) *Final Approval by Chancellor* : The Governor of the State is the Chancellor of the university. For the Central universities the President is the visitor. This is a hinderance in the autonomy of the university. The Regulations passed by the Executive Council or the Senate are finally approved by the Chancellor. If the chancellor does not agree the same may be cancelled.

(ii) *Vice-Chancellor's Appointment* : The Vice-Chancellor's appointment is controlled by the Governor. The Chancellor may appoint a Vice-Chancellor under political pressure of the ruling party. Consequently, the Vice-Chancellor is always afraid of the Chancellor. Thus indirectly, the Vice-Chancellor becomes responsible to the ruling party, thus the autonomy of the university is infringed.

(iii) *Govt. Representatives* : Some members of the Executive Council are representatives of the government. They do not co-operate with the Executive Council if it seeks to frame some rules and regulations within the jurisdiction of its autonomy.

(iv) *Govt. Repression* : When the atmosphere of the University becomes tense because of students problem, the government interferes through its P.A.C. who terrorise the teachers and students. Sometimes the university is closed for months.

(v) *Strict Govt. Control* : As the university has to function within the direct or indirect control of the government, many small and big matters become pending because the government instructions are awaited for the same. These instructions are strictly according to the government rules, even when they adversely affect the university functioning.

(vi) *Powers and Justification Determined by the Govt.* : According to the Indian Constitution universty education is a responsibility of the State. For their existence universities depend upon government grants. Hence, their powers and regulations are determined by the government. The legislatures of the States decide about the powers and jurisdiction of the universities. Even the opening of a university depends upon the resolution passed by the State Legislature.

(vii) *Dependence on Central Govt.* : The State government is responsible for the development of primary and secondary education, a major portion of its grant is spent over primary and secondary education. Therefore, it is not able to spend much on university education and the university has to depend upon the Central Government for financial support. Many of the university schemes in the State are not started unless sufficient grant is sanctioned by the Centre. Thus the universities are practically under the control of the Central Government.

In view of the above problems it is necessary to think over the question of relationship between the government and universities and also about the nature of autonomy of the university. In fact, the government should not interfere in the internal affairs of the university. The university should be left free to do anything in the interest of raising the academic standards. It should be given the necessary grants without any string attached. Its files must not remain pending in the government secretariat. The Chancellor should grant his approval to any plan or scheme or regulation submitted by the university, provided the same fulfil the objectives for which the university is established. Ministers and members of the legislature should not exert any pressure on the university for getting anything done. Party policies, nepotism and casteism should be discouraged. The Vice-Chancellor should be selected on merits and not on the basis of party politics. Retired government officer should not be appointed Vice-Chancellors as they are generally tools in the hands of the government. The person appointed as a Vice-Chancellor should be an educationist, a good administrator and a person above the board. He should be able to think for the university and initiate and execute without any fear of any one, how influential he may be.

The university must get timely financial aid and the government should also see that this aid is properly utilized. Unworthy persons must not be appointed anywhere for any university work. The university should develop the spirit of democratic attitudes and behaviour and strengthen the bonds of national integrity. If this spirit is violated, the government may interfere in the best interests of higher education.

Universities and degree colleges should function under a free environment so that the main work of teaching, study, guidance and research does not suffer. They should be free from casteism, groupism, regionalism, conspiracy and party politics.

### 3. Financial Problems

Universities and degree colleges have many items demanding heavy expenditures, though their source of income is quite poor. Students' fees and donations, the chief sources of income, do not meet even half of the expenses. Due to increase in the number of private candidates, the number of regular students have gone down resulting into loss of revenue to the university.

The University Commission of 1948-49 suggested that through the University Grants Commission the government should give financial aid to universities and degree colleges for implementing the U.G.C. grades for teachers, for study-leave, Provident Fund, libraries, laboratories, building, construction of hostels and teachers' residences, pension, development of means for teaching and research, technological and vocational education, and for implementing the scheme of three year degree courses.

The concerned institutions should be timely informed about the kind and amount of grant to be given. This will help them in planning their schemes and programmes. Besides some permanent recurring grant there should be some grants to meet contingencies. In the State of Uttar Pradesh the government has taken the full responsibility for paying salaries to teachers. 80 p.c. of students' fees are deposited in the government treasuries.

**4. Problem of Students Admission**

In spite of the increase in number of universities and colleges the number of students seeking admission has increased so much that all of them cannot be admitted. Hence, new regulations have been made for permitting to appear as private candidates in examinations. After obtaining university education only a few get some service, while the rest remain unemployed. Neither has the university education created in them a spirit of self-dependence nor have they acquired vocational skill for earning a living. Thus, universities and degree colleges are increasing the number of unemployed persons. Hence, only the persons having the aptitude and ability to benefit from university education should be permitted to go to university. The rest should be encouraged to take some other worthwhile pursuits or diverted to obtaining some vocational skills for becoming economically self-dependent. This may be possible if vocational education is made compulsory at the secondary stage. This will also solve the problem of unemployment at least partially.

There should be scientific objective and national policy regarding admission of students to universities and colleges. Those who cannot benefit from university education should be diverted to take up some fruitful pursuits which may add to the national prosperity. It will be a sheer national waste of time, energy and money if all are given admission to universities without selection.

**5. The Problem of University Curriculum**

After independence in India an attempt has been made to infuse the spirit of nationalism, internationalism and national integration among students at all levels — primary, secondary and university. Hence, necessary improvements have been made in the courses at all these stages. However, these courses still suffer from the following inadequacies at the university and college level of education :

(i) *Few Subjects* : As only a few subjects of study are available in the degree colleges, the students do not get subjects corresponding to their interests and abilities.

(ii) *Lack of Guidance* : There is no provision to measure the relative traits of the students in order to guide them to more suitable pursuits. Hence, guidance bureaus should be instituted in each degree college and university for helping the students to choose subjects according to their interests and abilities.

(iii) *Lack of Vocational Education* : Vocational subjects should be given due place in the curriculum so that the desirous students may acquire some vocational skill by the end of university education. This may help them to stand upon their own legs after receiving university education.

(iv) *Lack of Wide-based Curriculum* : Social and natural sciences should be given a wider place in the university curriculum. This is necessary to acquaint the students with the latest developments in the field of arts and sciences. This will broaden their outlook.

(v) *Lack of Integration* : The various subjects in the curriculum should be integrated as far as possible. Thus, interdisciplinary approach is necessary for liberalising the students.

(vi) *Lack of Practical Knowledge* : Even in specialised courses, an attempt should be made to acquaint the students with the rudiments of some other subjects which are generally related with the common-day human affairs.

### 6. The Problem of Medium of Instruction

Upto 1960 in India the medium of university education has been generally English. But afterwards a demand came from the student community to make the regional language the medium of university education. This demand has been met fully at the under-graduate level and partially at the post-graduate level. However, in some universities regional language has been accepted as the medium at the post-graduate level as well. But the pro-English spirit is still alive and the students using regional language as the medium are looked down upon by most of the teachers. This has retarded the growth of Indian languages in the various parts of the country. English still remains the chief medium of instruction in institutions of higher learning where vocational and technological and medical courses are taught. Suitable text-books of high standard should be produced in Indian languages before the same are accepted as the media of instruction. The government should invite suitable subject-persons to write good text-books on various subjects or to produce good translations of standard works. In this area as well, nepotism and favourtism play the major role in the selection of prospective writers. The chosen writers should know the subject as well as the language. But in each and every discipline of study translations of standard works have been made by persons who do not have command over the language nor did they learn the subject.

### 7. Problems of Teaching

The standard of teaching in universities and degree colleges has fallen down to a deplorable degree. In each and every department in a university or degree college, there are some teachers who seldom teach. They come only to collect their mails to show their faces to the office clerks who mark them present. Some teachers usually go late to the class by 15 or 20 minute and leave the class usually before the period is over. Some other teachers talk in the class about everything else except the subject which they are to teach. Some teachers are politician-teachers, busy in numbering votes in their favour or in favour of their candidates or proposals in some meetings. Many teachers take much pleasure in back biting and in black-mailing other teachers. Others appear to be more interested in gathering favours from the Heads or the Vice-Chancellor. There is much tussle among teachers over obtaining examinerships. Under these tragic situations the sacred task of teaching and research has been thrown to winds. Some heads of departments take special pleasure in tyrannising some and in favouring others. Some heads of departments try to add feathers to their clumsy caps on the basis of research works done by their junior colleagues and research scholars.

**8. Problems of Examination system**

The current system of examination has been criticized in various ways. Its main purpose is to obtain divisions in examinations. Many students regard using unfair means as their birth right. If some teachers happen to set the examination papers they choose to teach only that portion which they have included in the question-paper. The teachers are terriorised and sometimes even assaulted in the examination halls.

For doing away with and evils of the examination system the University Commission (1948-49) has recommeded that there should be fortnightly, monthly, quarterly and half yearly examinations and the marks of all these examinations should be added to the division to be finally awarded on the basis of an annual examination. The student's day-to-day work should also be evaluated while deciding the final division to be given to a student. The question-paper should be framed under the supervision of an examination committee constituted by responsible teachers of great repute. The question-paper should have some objective items also.

**9. The Problem of Social Service**

To fulfil some social purposes is one of the objectives of university education. The universities should give training to students to make them able to render some social service. In U.S.A. every student at the graduate level is required to do some social service. This creates a spirit of social service among the students and develops traits of healthy citizenship. Some opportunities should be created in the form of social service in the university. These include recreational programmes, extension lecture, dramas, exhibitions, cleaning and health programme etc. Now National Social Service Programmes have been started in the universities as well as in the affiliated colleges. The government allocates crores of rupees in every Five Year Plan for National Social Service Programmes. N.S.S. should be made compulsory for each university and degree college student.

**10. Expensive University Education**

The University education in India is getting very expensive. In spite of their suitability for higher education the poor students are deprived of higher education because it is too expensive. In U.S.A. part-time courses and adult education schemes have been instituted for helping poor students who can earn a part of their expenses while getting higher education. The State universities and colleges charge nominal fees from the resident students of their own State. Thus higher education is brought within the reach of many students. The university also tries to give part-time employment to the students. Some such kind of arrangement is necessary in India also so that the poor students may not be deprived of the opportunity to get higher education.

**11. Problems of Affiliation of Colleges**

As universities alone cannot fulfil the needs of higher education, some degree colleges have been opened and affiliated to a university on fulfilment of certain prescribed conditions. These degree colleges teach courses prescribed by the university. The teachers of these colleges are appointed by the experts appointed by the university. College examinations are also conducted by the university. In some states the Government has constituted a Commission for Higher Education for appointment of degree college teachers. In degree colleges the standard of work is generally lower than that in the university. Independent research works are done only in very few degree colleges. The degree colleges have to look towards the universities for guidance in many academic matters. They generally duplicate in a poorer manner the work that the universities are doing. The degree colleges do not meet the local requirements. Many degree colleges are run on commercial lines. Other colleges offer illegal gratification to some persons in power for getting their work done in the university. Many bogus and false papers are submitted at the time of submitting application for affiliation. Unscrupulus persons help these delinquent colleges to lower the standard of higher education. The university authorities must see that such proposed colleges are not granted affiliation and the delinquent ones are disaffiliated.

### 12. Problem of Research Work

One of the prime duties of a university is to do research work of high standard. Before independence satisfactory facilities were not available for research in universities. But now State and Central Governments are keen about higher order of research in various areas of study. They are giving crores of rupees to various universities for this purpose. However, there are very few research works of international standard having done by universities. Most of teachers and students in universities are very enthusiastic for high order of research. Their main aim is to help getting the doctorate degree anyhow. Though a research degree is awarded but the thesis which fetches it is seldom an original piece of research of a high standard. Hence, it never sees the light of day and ever remains in the bound thesis itself. Hence, good laboratories, workshops and libraries should be established wherever needed. Research facilities should be available to worthy researchers. The supervisors should have a missionary zeal to help the students. They must not require the research scholars to attend to their (supervisor's) domestic affairs. Supervisors who are dishonest to their research-scholars must give up their bad habits in the best interests of high order of research.

### 13. The Problems Concerning the Registrar

The Registrar occupies a special position in the administration of a university in India. He is one of those officers who are most overworked. He goes to his office early and returns home late. His major job is to sign documents and various types of papers. He answers a number of telephones and studies files. However, he enjoys a good salary and much power. He moves the whole administrative machinery of the university. He has to record, observe and listen. He has to make arrangements for admission, examination and convocation. In an affiliating university, the registrar has to receive a number of Principals and teachers and students of degree colleges affiliated to the university. Sometimes he is gheraoed by student-leaders for change of date of examination and other things about which he is helpless. He is assisted by a number of Deputy Registrars, Assistant Registrars and a host of Office Superintendents and other assistants, but each one of these officials, high or low, have their power over which the Registrar has little control. Hence, in any reform of university education, Registrar's position and office has to be seriously considered. If he happens to be a strong, honest and sincere person, everything will go on well with the university. If he is otherwise, he becomes a centre of all sorts of politics, cliques, groupism, nepotism, favouritism, casteism and other evils. Certain Registrars had become so vicious and malicious in their approach and method of work that the U.P. Government has made the post of the Registrar transferable within the State since 1976. A Registrar should be selected after great care and scrutiny. He should be a person of high academic merit and experienced in university work and administration and a person above the board.

## QUESTIONS FOR EXERCISE

1. Explain the present problem of universities? Suggest measures for reforms of university education.
2. Discuss any two problems of university education.
3. Should the university enjoy full autonomy? Give reasons.
4. Discuss the internal problems of a university. How can they be resolved?
5. How does a Registrar of a university occupy a pivotal position in the university administration? Suggest measures for making his functioning smooth.

# 28

# TEACHER EDUCATION AND TEACHER'S TRAINING

## HISTORY OF TEACHER EDUCATION

1. **Ancient period** : In the ancient period sometimes so many students came to a teacher that he could not fulfil his responsibilities towards them. Hence, he used to seek the assistance of meritorious students of higher classes called 'pattacharya' who assisted their teacher (Guru) in teaching. If the teacher sometimes went away, he used to entrust the whole work of teaching and school to such students.

As in the monitorial system in this system meritorious students of the same class and some students of the higher classes assisted the teacher in the performance of teaching and other allied works. After having been thus trained these students used to become efficient teachers and school organisers.

2. **Muslim period** : As the chief aim of Muslim rulers in India was to propagate their religion it was very difficult for them to have any idea of teacher education.

3. **British Period** : (i) *Early Beginning* : In this period, the educational Boards of Bombay, Madras and Calcutta for the first time felt the need of teacher education. They established a few training centres where the teachers of primary schools were imparted training. The Native Education Society of Bombay trained 25 teachers and sent them to different parts of the province so that the standard of teaching in the primary school might be raised. In 1812, Calcutta School Society was established at Calcutta which made provision for the training of the teachers on the basis of monitorial system. East India Company started giving Rs. 500 monthly aid since 1825. Training School for the training of the teachers was founded at Madras in 1825, in order to encourage the work of the society, in accordance with the suggestions of Munro, the then Governor of Madras.

(ii) *Wood's Despatch* : Wood's Despatch of 1854 mentioned "We desire to see the establishment, with as little delay as possible of training schools and classes for masters in each Presidency in India."

(iii) *From 1859 to 1882* : Lord Stanley mentioned in his Despatch that a special attention should be devoted to the training of the teachers. After the transfer of the power it was not possible for the British administrators posted in India to ignore or disregard the orders of the Secretary for State of India. Hence, they worked with enthusiasm for the establishment of training schools for the teachers of primary schools. As a result of their efforts many Training Schools were established in each province by the year 1882. In 1882 there were 7 Training Schools for men and 2 for women. The number of students studying in these schools was 553. In Madhya Pradesh technical schools were 43 for men and 1 for women. The number of students studying in these schools was 118.

Normal School system was started in Bengal in 1862. According to this system the teachers of the native schools or their relations were sent to Normal Schools. In 1874 Campbell, the Governor of the Province, prepared a new scheme for the training of the teachers. Consequently, 46 Normal schools were established at the cost of Rs. 1,64,000.

In Madras, there were 32 training schools with 927 students. Provision of the training of the teachers of primary school was made in other provinces also. In 1802, there were 106 Normal schools in the whole of India and 3,886 men and women were being trained in those schools with an annual expenditure of Rs. 4 lacs.

(iv) *Regular System of Teacher Education* : In India regular system of teacher education was started in accordance with the recommendations of the Indian Education Commission, 1882. Hence, by the end of 19th century, there were Training Colleges at Madras, Lahore, Allahabad, Kursang, Rajahmundri and Jabalpur and 50 Training Schools in the whole country.

(v) *Government Resolution of Education Policy, 1904* : Lord Curzon devoted sufficient attention towards education and training of the teachers. The Government Resolution of Educational Policy of 1904, made the following recommendations :

1. Provision should be made for higher training of able and experienced teachers for the Indian Educational Service.
2. The importance of the equipment of the Training colleges is almost equal as that of General college.
3. The training period for the graduates should be only one year. Thereafter they should be granted degree by the University. The knowledge of teaching method and practical training should also be included in the curriculum. The training period for the non-graduates should be two years.
4. Theoretical training and practical training should be mutually connected with each other. There should be a practising school connectd with each Training College.
5. Training colleges should be connected with ordinary schools so that the teachers may apply the methods learned in the Training colleges.

(vi) *The Government Resolution on Educational Policy* : The Government Resolution on Educational Policy of 1913 declared : "Under modern system of education, no teacher should be allowed to teach without certificate that he is qualified to do so."

(vii) *Calcutta University Commission* : The Calcutta University Commission (1916-17) made the following recommendations : (1) The number of trained teachers should be increased; (2) Research work in education should be encouraged; (3) A demonstration school should be attached with each Training college so that practical work may be done in it; (4) The subject of education should be included in the curriculum of B. A. and Intermediate classes; (5) Education Department should be established in Calcutta and Dacca Universities.

(viii) *Hartog Committee of 1929* : The Hartog Committee recommended the following: (1) Education standard of the teachers should be raised; (2) Training period should be extended; (3) Able teachers should be appointed in training institutions and their number should be increased; (4) Provision of refresher courses should be made from time to time for the teachers of primary schools; (5) In order to attract able persons in the teaching profession the conditions of teachers should be improved and made attractive.

(ix) *Training institutions* : In 1947, there were following three types of institutions for teachers training in India :

(1) *Normal schools.* For teachers of Primary schools.

(2) *Secondary training schools.* For the teachers of middle schools.

(3) *Training colleges.* For teachers of High schools.

4. **Training Facilities in Free India** : Facilities of teachers training have been expanded in the post-independent period. Suggestions given by the University Education Commission, 1949, Secondary Education Commission, 1953 and Kothari Commission, (1964-65) have been implemented by the Government. These suggestions are as follows.

(i) *University Education Commission (1948-49)*

1. The curriculum of training institutions should be reformed. Importance should be given to the practice of teaching in schools instead of bookish knowledge.
2. While evaluating the work of the students, special attention should be given to their success in teaching work.
3. Only suitable schools should be selected for practice of teaching.
4. Most of the teachers of the training schools should have sufficient experience of teaching in schools.

(ii) *Secondary Education Commission (1952-53)*

1. Training schools should be of two types — (a) Schools for those students who have completed secondary education; (b) Schools for the guardians.
2. Teacher-student should be trained in more than one teaching method.
3. Provision should be made for Refresher Courses, Short Intensive

Courses on special subjects and practical training in workshop in the training schools.

4. No fees should be charged from the teacher-students of the training schools.

**Expansion of Teacher Education**

| Description | 1950-51 | 1960-61 | 1979-80 | 1980-81 | 1985-86 |
|---|---|---|---|---|---|
| Number of Training Schools | 782 | 1,138 | 859 | 897 | 959 |
| Number of Training Colleges | 53 | 478 | 501 | 1500 | 1,598 |
| **Trained Teachers** : | | | | | |
| (i) Primary Schools (Percentage) | 58.8 | 64.1 | 86.8 | 87.4 | 95.7 |
| (ii) Middle Schools (Percentage) | 53.3 | 66.5 | 88.9 | 89.4 | 94.4 |
| (iii) High/H.S. Schools | 1,26,504 | 2,96,305 | 8,59,359 | 9,02,332 | 1,12,732 |

**Certificates Confered by Some States**

| Name of the place | Training period | Name of certificate |
|---|---|---|
| Bombay | 1 year | T.D. |
| Bombay | 1 year | S.T.D. |
| Baroda | 1 year | T.D. |
| Gujrat | 1 year | T.D. |
| Karnataka | 1 year | T.D. |
| Poona | 1 year | T.D. |
| Nagpur | 2 year | Dip.T. |
| Sagar | 2 year | Dip.T. |
| Bihar | 2 year | C.T. |
| Madras | 2 year | T.S.L. |
| Mysore | 1 year | T.C. |
| Orissa | 2 year | C.T. |
| Uttar Pradesh | 2 year | J.T.C. |
| Calcutta | 1 year | L.T. |

## CHANGING ROLE OF THE TEACHER

In the words of Prof. Humayun Kabir. "Teachers are literally the arbiters of a nation's destiny. It may sound a truism, but it still needs to be stressed that the teacher is the key to any educational, reconstruction.'' Teacher's influence is everlasting. He shapes the destiny of future citizens. The Secondary Education Commission (1952) rightly points out ''we are convinced that the most important factor in the contemplated educational reconstruction, is the teacher—his personal qualities, his educational qualifications, his professional training and the place that he occupies in the school as well in the community.'' The teacher occupies a very important place in society because he brings about the transfer of the intellectual tradition from one generation to the next. He maintains the level of technological skill and keeps the light of civilisation burning bright. ''He is expected to help in the silent social revolution that is taking place in the country. His duty does not end in the classroom with his students. He owes a duty to the society and the nation. He should be abreast of the developments in the country and the world. He should be able to constantly adjust his methods and approach to suit the changing times.

## TEACHER COMPETENCIES

A competent teacher is expected to possess following qualities :

1. He should be educated in the literal spirit of learning so that he may make his contribution as an individual and a citizen.
2. He should be competent to represent the education profession and his subject-matter field in the school and in the community.
3. He should be thoroughly grounded in the theory and practice of his subject-matter and have knowledge and skills necessary for teaching theory and practice in an integrated manner.
4. He should be able to contrive and use a variety of effective teaching learning procedures.
5. He should be able to develop and use instructional materials including audio-visual aids.
6. He should be able to select and organize subject-matter for instructional purposes.
7. He should be able to use a variety of methods to evaluate pupil progress and the effectiveness of his own teaching.
8. He should be capable of organising, supervising and participating in co-curricular activities.
9. He should be able to select and use appropriate equipment and determine supply needs.
10. He should be able to function effectively in the guidance programme of the school.
11. He should be capable of functioning effectively as a teacher as evidenced by actual classroom performance.
12. He should be interested in continued growth through participation in professional associations, community activities, in-service education, research and experiment.

**Suggestions of Kothari Commission on Teacher Education**

1. Universities should have teaching and research departments in education.
2. The status of Training Colleges should be equal to Arts and Science Colleges.
3. Education should be introduced as an elective subject in the pre- and post-degree courses.
4. The period of training for matriculates should be two years and for graduates and post-graduates one year.
5. Part-time courses should be introduced to remove the backlog of untrained teachers.
6. State Boards of Education should be established to regulate teacher education.
7. Barriers between the training programmes of teachers of general subjects and special subjects should be abolished.
8. The number of working days in teacher training institutions should be raised to 230.
9. Every teacher should be given in-service training once in five years.
10. U.G.C. should help in maintaining the standards of teacher education.
11. Facilities should be provided for the professional growth of teachers.
12. To promote excellence in education, schools of education may be started in selected universities.
13. Isolation of the teacher training institutions from the universities as well as from school education system should be removed.
14. Dynamic methods of teaching should be practised in teacher training institutions.

**Objectives of Teacher Education**

1. To develop Gandhian values of education such as non-violence, truthfulness, self-discipline, self-reliance and dignity of labour.
2. To perceive his role as an agent of social change in the community.
3. To perceive his role not only as a leader of the children but also that of a guide to the community.
4. To act as a liaison between the school and the community and employ suitable ways and means for integrating community life and resources with school work.
5. To help in the conservation of environmental resources and preservation of historical monuments and other cultural heritage.
6. To possess warm and positive attitude towards children and their academic, socio-emotional and personal problems, and skills to guide and counsel them.

7. To develop an understanding of the objectives of school education in the Indian context and awareness of the role of the school in achieving the goals of building up a democractic, secular and socialistic society.
8. To develop understanding, interests, attitudes and skills which would enable him to foster all-round growth and development of the children under his care.
9. To develop competence to teach on the basis of the accepted principles of learning and teaching.
10. To develop communication, and psycho-motor skills and abilities conducive to human relations for interacting with the children in order to promote learnings inside and outside the classroom.
11. To keep abreast of the latest knowledge of the subject-matter he is teaching and the techniques teaching the same.
12. To undertake action research and investigatory projects.

**Objectives of Teacher Education for the Primary Stage**

1. To possess competence in the first and the second language, mathematics, and in the topics of natural and social sciences related to environmental studies.
2. To develop skills is identifying selecting and organising learning experiences for teaching the above subjects in formal and non-formal situations.
3. To possess sufficient theoretical and practical knowledge of health, physical and recreational activities, work-experience, art and music, and skills for conducting these activities.
4. To develop understandings of psychological principles underlying growth and development of the children of the age group 6+ to 14+.
5. To acquire theoretical and practical knowledge about childhood education, including integrated teaching.
6. To develop understandings of major learning principles which help in promoting cognitive, psychomotor and attitudinal learnings.
7. To understand the role of the home, the peer group and community in shaping the personality of the child, and help develop and amicable home school relationship for mutual benefit.
8. To conduct simple action research.
9. To understand the role of school and of the teacher in changing society.

**Objectives of Secondary Teacher Education**

1. To possess competence to teach subjects of his specialisation on the basis of accepted principles of learning and teaching in the context of the new school curriculum.

2. To develop skills, understandings, interests and attitudes which would enable him to foster all round growth and development of the children under his care.
3. To possess sufficient theoretical and practical knowledge of health and physical education, games and recreational activities and experience.
4. To develop skills in making use of educational technology in teaching academic and/or vocational subjects.
5. To understand the bio-psycho-social needs of the adolescent and the problems arising out of their non-fulfilment; develop skills in guiding and counselling the adolescent in solving his personal and academic problems.
6. To undertake investigatory project, action research and experimental projects both in education and specialised subject areas.
7. To understand the role of the school and the teachers in changing society.

**Structure of the one Year (Two Semesters) B.Ed. Programme**

| Area | Weightage | Suggested Courses |
|---|---|---|
| 1. Pedagogical Theory | 20% | (i) Teacher and Education in the Emerging Indian Society.<br>(ii) Educational Psychology.<br>(iii) Special Courses according to the needs and facilities available. |
| 2. Working with the Community | 20% | (iv) Work situations in the school and Community. |
| 3. Content-*cum*-Methodology and practice teaching, including related practical work | 60% | (v) Core Training Programme Package (10%)<br>(vi) Special Training Programme Package—Package I. Life Sciences/ Physical Sciences/Social Sciences/ Languages/Mathematics (20%)<br>(vii) Special Training Programme package II. Work Experience (10%)<br>(viii) Special Training Programme III. Health, Physical Education, Games and Recreational Activities (10%)<br>(ix) Related practical work (10%) |

**Objective of Higher Secondary Course**

1. To develop competence to teach the subject of his specialisation on the basis of accepted principles of learning and teaching and knowledge of

the subject by striving to keep in touch with the latest developments in both the subject and methodology of teaching.

2. To deveop an understanding of the aims and objectives of education in general, and of higher education in particular in the Indian background, to promote awareness of the role of education and of the teacher in building up a democratic, secular and socialistic society.
3. To develop skill cognitive and psychomotor — for teaching academic and/or vocational subjects by providing appropriate learning experiences.
4. To develop skills in making use of the educational technology in teaching academic and/or vocational subject.
5. To understand the bio-psycho-social needs of the adolescent and the problems arising out of their non-fulfilment; develop skills in guiding and counselling the adolescent in solving his personal and academic problems.
6. To undertake investigatory projects, action research and cxperimental projects both in education and specialised subject areas.
7. To understnad the role of school and the teachers in changing the society.

**Structure of Teacher Education (One Year — Two Semesters) For Higher Secondary Level**

| Area | Weightage Stream | Academic Stream | Vocational |
|---|---|---|---|
| 1 | 2 | 3 | 4 |
| 1. Pedagogical Theory | 30% | (i) Teacher and Education in the Emerging Indian society.<br>(ii) Educational Psychology<br>(iii) Psychology of Adolescence<br>(iv) Special courses as per the needs and facilities available. | Same as in Col 3. |
| 2. Working with the community | 20% | (v) Work education related to the course | |
| 3. Content-*cum* Methodology and Practice, Teaching, including Related practical work. | 50% | (vi) Core Training Programme Package (10%)<br>(vii) Special Training Programme Package I : Special Subject (20%) | Special Training Programme Main vocation. |

| 1 | 2 | 3 | 4 |
|---|---|---|---|
| | | (viii) Special Training Programme Package II (inclusive of content) : Any one vocation, preferably related to his Subject.<br>or<br>Special Training Programme Package I or II (10%) | Special Secondary Training Programme Package III |
| | | (ix) Related practical work (10%) | Related practical work. |

## IN-SERVICE EDUCATION

Most of the Colleges of Education offer only pre-service training. Only a few Colleges of Education have Extension Departments which organise short term courses or workshops for the benefit of teachers in-service. Every teacher should continuously update his knowledge. It should be possible for the State to give him facilities through periodical seminars, orientation courses, workshops and refresher courses. There is a communication gap between the academicians in-charge of educational planning and teachers who have to make these schemes successful. The Secondary Education Commission has aptly remarked : "However excellent the programme of teacher training may be it does not by itself produce an excellent teacher. It can only engender the knowledge, skill and attitudes which will enable the teacher, to begin his task with a reasonable degree of confidence and with the minimum amount of experience. Increased efficiency will come through experience critically analysed and through individual and group efforts in improvement."

Stresseing the need for providing in-service training to all teachers, the Education Commission recommended :

1. A large scale and co-ordinated programme of in-service education for teachers should be organised by universities, training institutions and teachers' organisations for teachers at all levels. The target should be that every teacher will receive at least two or three mohths in-service education in every five years of his service.
2. The programme of Summer Institutes for in-service education of secondary school teachers should be extended with follow up and active collaboration among the agencies concerned.

Each College of Education may specialise in one or two subjects. Through its Extension Department it may organise necessary short-term courses for secondary and higher secondary school teachers in the area with the co-operation of the Department of School Education. This shall arrest the falling standards in school education. NCERT is providing financial assistance to State Councils of Educational Research and Training/State Institutes of Education to conduct workshops, refresher courses introduction courses etc. These programmes have brought secondary and higher secondary school teachers and the Colleges of Education closer and have resulted in the revision of teachers preparation courses.

## INTER-DISCIPLINARY APPROACH IN TEACHER EDUCATION

To break the isolation of teacher education, the Education Commission stated. "Our first suggestion is that education should be brought into the main stream of the academic life of the universities. In India, the general trend has been to indentify education with pedagogy. It has been brought mostly in training institutions and is studied only by those who decide to enter teaching profession, after such a decision has been made. In the educationally advanced countries, however, education had developed considerably as a social science and a separate academic discipline.

The realization that education is an instrument of change social, political and economic is having far reaching implications, not only for education as an intellectual discipline of great scientific and philosophic import, but for other disciplines as well. It is also worth noting that philosophers as social scientists have begun to give special attention to education as an important part in their fields of study. We therefore, recommend that in view of the increasing scope and importance, "education should be recognised as a social science or an independent discipline."

Education develops as an independent discipline by its own right. It enriches itself by adapting the fields of Engineering, Biology, Economics etc. Many University teachers have come forward to acquaint themselves with the theories, practices and researches in education. Kurukshetra University attempted interdisciplinary approach in 1960 by introducing a three year degree course in education. Four year integrated B.Sc. (Ed.) and B.A. (Ed.) and two-year M.A. (Ed.) and M.Sc. (Ed.) courses are offered by the Regional Colleges of Education at Mysore, Ajmere, Bhopal and Bhubaneshwar.

### Aims of Regional Colleges of Education

1. Achieve excellence through inter-disciplinary approach;
2. Improve professional competence through organized learning experiences;
3. Master the subject with professional preparation.
4. Integrate the subjects in the curriculum, co-curricular activities and team work by subject specialists and experts in education.
5. Thorough grasp of educational theories, practices and problems and capacity to analyse and judge educational issues as the course offers ample time and adequate facilities.

### Objective of the Regional Colleges

1. To develop and provide a programme of teacher education for the

secondary schools and to prepare teachers of technical subjects, Science, Crafts, Agriculture, Commerce, English, Home Science and Fine Arts.

2. To prove in-service programmes and field services for the teachers, supervisors and administrators concerned with the secondary schools in the region in which it is located.
3. To develop and provide post-graduate courses for training teacher-educators and specialists in selected areas.
4. To organise and develop a demonstration school.
5. To undertake pilot studies and research projects in the methods of teaching in relation to the secondary schools.
6. To prepare and disseminate instructional materials for secondary schools in critical areas.
7. To collaborate with other institutions in initiating and promoting improved methods and practices, to function as a cleaning house in this regard and generally to provide leadership.
8. To become Regional Centres of the National Institute of Education and disseminate the message of NIE in the region.
9. To provide all kinds of consultancy services to the State Departments of Education and collaborate with all agencies of education.
10. To clear the backlog of untrained teachers through all kinds of emergency measures.

## PROBLEMS OF TEACHER EDUCATION

1. *Untrained Teachers* : To cope with the expansion of secondary education untrained graduates had to be appointed. Many primary school teachers and specialist teachers who acquired a degree after private study also needed B.Ed. degree for their promotion. When the +2 course was started there was dearth of trained post-graduates to teach many subjects, particularly science subjects. To clear the backlog of untrained teachers, the Regional Colleges offer summer-*cum*-contact courses which maintain good standards. Several universities also offer correspondence-*cum*-contact courses for post-graduates and working teachers. Annamalai University is a pioneer in this area.

2. *Lack of Professional Status* : Though teachers education is a training for the 'noblest profession', however, Colleges of Education are not treated on par with other professional institutions like medical, engineering or law colleges. They are not even treated on par with Arts or Science colleges in many States.

3. *Drop-outs* : At least 10% of the trainees discontinue the B.Ed. course in the middle. Many women teachers leave their jobs after marriage.

4. *Limited Student Strength* : Many Colleges of Education admit only about 100 students every year. The Kothari Commission opines that at least 200 students may be admitted to make the colleges effective and economically viable. In the

primary teacher training institutes the student strength may be raised to 240. The additional intake is necessary to reduce per capita expenditure and also to utilise to a greater extent the resources and man-power in the institution.

5. *Outmoded Curriculum* : There is very little interaction between the teacher training institutions and the school in the area. The teacher education curriculum is blind to the changes taking place in the school education. Periodical revision and updating of the teacher education courses are necessary. To meet the changing classroom atmosphere teachers need a great deal of skill, understanding of individual differences and resourcesfulness.

6. *No Special Training for Teacher-Educators* : Teacher-educators are not required to have special qualification or training. Some advanced courses in Curriculum Development, Educational Technology, Teacher Education etc., may be provided in addition to M.Ed.

7. *Lack of Funds* : Colleges of Education lack the facilites needed to train post-graduate teachers for higher secondary schools which have an advanced syllabi compared to the pre-university course. Some improvements have taken place to wherever SCERT and Colleges/Institutes of Education are under the control of a single officer.

8. *Isolation* : Teacher Education Colleges lack synchronisation with other Colleges of Education, co-ordination with colleges of general education, co-operation from secondary and higher secondary schools in the area. They face all alienation from the University. Colleges of Education should try to break this spell, through their extension programmes. Only a few colleges have Extension Departments. As N.S.S. has not been extended to Colleges of Education, so very little contact exists with the local community. Policy on Education (1967) states "the training of school teachers should be brought within the broad stream of university life and the isolation of training institutions from the schools should be ended. Schools of education should be established in universities. Each State should prepare and implement, on a priority basis, a plan for the expansion and improvement of teacher education at all stages."

9. *Internship* : About six weeks of practice teaching or internship under an experienced guide teacher is prescribed. This system is not as rigorous as it should be. The student-teacher is seldom exposed to modern communication techniques.

10. *Imbalances* : Due to faulty admission policy more language and humanities teachers are trained than the actual need, leading to sectoral unemployment. If preference is given to youths coming from rural areas the dearth of teachers in village schools can be overcome.

11. *Drawbacks in the Present System of Teacher Education* : The Education Commission (1964-66) has identified the following drawbacks in the present system of Teacher Education :

(i) The training institutions have remained isolated from the main stream of academic life of the university, as well as from the daily problems of the school.

(ii) The quality of training institutions is poor.

(iii) Teacher educators, in many cases, are not very competent.

(iv) Vitality and realism are lacking in the curriculum. Only traditional courses are offered. Choices are limited.

(v) Teaching practice is carried on as a matter of routine.

(vi) Bright students are not attracted to the training institutions.

(vii) Student teachers lack motivation. Teaching is the last resort of the unemployed.

(viii) Student-teacher ratio is high.

12. *Status of Teachers Profession* : A profession should have the following characteristics to deserve that name :

(1) strong motivation on the part of its practitioner;

(2) sense of solidarity, responsibility and mutual support;

(3) systematised technical knowledge.

Viewed against this criteria teaching has not yet emerged as a full-fledged profession in the real sense. While Medical Council of India, and Bar Council of India maintain unity and guard the interests of their respective professions. Teachers are yet to come under a single professionally motivated organisation which may take up the following functions as suggested by the Education Commission :

1. Securing individually and collectively their rightful status — social, economic and political.
2. Safeguarding their professional interests such as security of service, promotions etc.
3. Promoting professional growth of teachers through in-service education.
4. Effecting suitable changes in the educational system to meet the changing socio-economic context.
5. Establishing faculty-wise associations to promote effective teaching.
6. Evolving a code of conduct for teachers.

## CODE OF CONDUCT FOR TEACHERS

1. No teacher shall speak or act in a way which may bring discredit or disgrace to the profession.
2. No teacher shall ask or accept the students' support to further his personal and professional interests.
3. No teacher shall violate the accepted behaviour patterns towards the students entrusted to his case.
4. No teacher shall incite communal or linguistic passions in the students for any reason whatsoever.

5. No teacher shall talk in public or write, defaming his colleagues and superiors.
6. Every teacher shall strive to maintain the nobility and integrity of the profession.
7. Every teacher shall seek only legal and civilised means to get redressal for his grievance.
8. Every teacher shall strive to be worthy of the great faith reposed in him by our culture.
9. Every teacher shall try to serve the people to the utmost of his capacity.
10. Every teacher shall refrain from undertaking non-academic activities and joining political agitations.

## QUESTION FOR EXERCISE

1. Trace the history of the progress of teacher education in India with special reference to attempts made in the direction after Independence.

# 29

# PROBLEMS OF EVALUATION AND EXAMINATION

The aim and object of education is the comprehensive, overall development of the child. This development and progress is gradual. Hence, it is essential to examine the child at regular intervals to find out the extent to which he has progressed. In the school, students study a number of subjects. To test one in respect of these subjects from time to time is essential as it makes clear the success with which he is studying and understanding them. It is the examination that makes possible for one to know the child's achievement in terms of ability learning these subjects. Hence, in almost all schools some mode of examining all that is taught to them, is prevalent.

## PRESENT SYSTEM OF EXAMINATION

Under the present system of examinations in this country, all the students are put in a single hall, at the end of each session, and answer books are distributed to each of them. At the appointed time, the question papers are distributed to them, following which during the space of two or three hours the student is expected to answer a required number of questions. Finally, the answer books are gathered and sent to an examiner whose appointment in that capacity is previously confirmed. Sometimes, the examiner is other than the person who sets the examination paper. If the student's attempt in the answer books is considered worthy of being awarded 33 per cent marks by the examiner, he is deemed to have passed the said examination. The individual who does not succeed is compelled to spend another session in the same class.

## DEFECTS OF THE PRESENT EXAMINATION SYSTEM

There is hardly any need to point out that the existing examination scheme is not conducive to the proper development of children. The following are some of its shortcomings, that have been time and again pointed out by various educationists and commissions appointed for the purpose :

1. *Student does not study through the whole year* : For the present examination system the student is not compelled to exert himself through the entire session, but

achieves competency for it by labouring only through the last few weeks before the examination. In this manner, the student does not attain in any real ability or capacity even though he passes the examination. He forgets a lesson just as soon or as rapidly as he learns it. During the first two or three months of the session, it is a rare student who is seen at his desk. In this manner from the educational viewpoint, a major portion of a student's time is completely wasted.

2. *Studying from question-answer books and key books* : In the present context, a student's ability is gauged from the scores he obtains in the examinations. And for obtaining good marks in the examinations there is no need to wander into a maze of extensive reading and comprehensive knowledge. In every examination paper, the student is required to do four to five questions out of nine or ten that are set. The consequence is that even without having gone through more than one-third of the course prescribed for study, the average student finds three or four questions that he is in a position to answer. And four to ten pages of writing are considered adequate in answer to each question.

3. *Fear of examination* : In the modern examination system, the examination is taken at the end of the session with the result that the student is fearfully conscious of the examination of right through the session.

4. *Success in examination a matter of luck* : In the way examinations are conducted at present, success is more a matter of luck than anything else. His entire future is to be decided in two or three hours. No matter what skill a student has gained in his subject through constant labour during the entire session, his effort is completely wasted if for some reason or the other he fails to exhibit his skill in these three hours. Some students fail to attend the examination through some contingency such as illness during the examination period, or an accident or any other human involvement. On the other hand, even though they are in a position to attend the examination they fail to give their best performance. The only consequence in such a case is that their whole year's effort is wasted.

5. *Mechanical method* : In this way, the existing system of education is a machine in which conclusions are reached, no importance being attached to the human elements involved. Hence, people have devised new methods of succeeding in the mechanical set-up. Some students do not bother to put in more than a few week's effort for the examinations, during which they do nothing more than make a cursory study of guess papers and question-answer books. As a result, they are in a position to come to grips with the paper, even though there is no element of mastery involved. And in subjects in which the question paper outdoes expectation, and unexpected questions crop, the contingency is overcome by fraternizing with the examiner and having their marks surreptitiously increased. And in the case of such a success in any examination, it is only natural for the individual to be devoid of any skill whatsoever in the subject in which he has passed the examination.

6. *Defects concerning evaluation of answer books* : Under the present system of examination, a student's achievement in any subject is measured by the marks that he obtains during the examination. Hence, his fortune depends upon the

evaluation of his effort in the answer book. Such a method is susceptible to numerous faults :

(i) If the teacher's mental condition is disturbed, he does not evaluate the answer books correctly. What most often occurs is that the few copies in the bundle sent to him are examined with due care, but as he gradually tires and reaches the stage of growing exhaustion, the subsequent copies are gone through as a matter of necessity and duty.

(ii) It is only too apparent that all copies are not examined from the same standpoint or standard. Of course, different examiners would award differing marks to the same copy, but even if the same examiner is asked to examine the same copy, it is quite likely that he will award it different marks on different occasions.

(iii) The maximum number of marks that any student may be awarded depends upon the examiner's mental tendency.

(iv) It often happens, that due to very great variety of causes, the examiner has very little time at his disposal to examine the copies.

(v) Many of the examiners are completely prejudice or biased in their thinking, having only most incomplete knowledge of their respective subjects. Secondly, some teachers even fail to understand the actual implications of the question asked in the question paper. It is only to be expected in such circumstances, that there is no justice done to the student.

7. *Long examination period* : The present examination system allows the period of examination to spread over a very considerable period of at least a month. It is often seen that students get some weeks between two individual examination dates. Such a long period of inactivity has the worst effect upon the student's attitude towards the examination as it tends to lull him towards the seriousness of the matter. Secondly, the provision of time periods between various papers is not at all proportionate. He gets no more than a few hours between two papers while between another two he has a few days at his disposal. Evidently, the opportunity available for the preparation of each subject is unequal.

8. *Wrong Objective* : The present aim of examination is to obtain marks in order to get a degree, not the desire to gain skill in any subject. Hence, the main attention in any examination is concentrated upon getting good marks so that one can have proof of one's ability or skill. There are innumerable methods of obtaining an adequate number of marks in the examination though all of them are not proper.

9. *Defects of the essay system* : Under the existing scheme of examination, the student is required to answer each question in the form of an essay, with the result that the educational system has acquired all the defects inherent in the essay type examination. In this method the students pay much greater attention to learning answers to questions than to understanding the subject and delving deep into it. In the examination hall, they do no more than reproduce these learned and remembered answers on the answer books. Once the examination is over, the facts learned for

it are as expeditiously forgotten, since once they have been put in the answer book, they no longer possess any importance for the student. One natural outcome of this method is that even though the student may have done exceptionally well in the examination, he is more or less blank on all the subjects that he has made a pretence of studying.

## SUGGESTIONS FOR IMPROVEMENT

Many thinkers, educationists and education commissions have pointed out the above defects in the existing scheme of examinations in this country, but there are many difficulties that hinder the complete replacement of it. The main difficulty is financial besides which the extremely large number of candidates makes it difficult to evolve a different examination system for them. Hence, the practicable solution is to maintain the existing scheme of things and make efforts to effect definite improvements. Main suggestions in this respect are the following :

1. *Certificates should not be required for services* : If the tradition of requiring certificates for various jobs and services is given up, and individuals are separately tested for qualities that the job requires, then, people will give up the race for obtaining certificates and degrees, and turn their attention to development of qualities required in the professions of their choice. It must, of course, be kept in mind that this method is not practicable in all professions nevertheless, it should be used in as many as admit of its use.

2. *Improvement in the evaluation of answer books* : The method and system of examining and evaluating answer books should be improved. The remuneration of evaluating copies should be enough to induce the examiner to attend to them himself, and to do his work efficiently and well. The time allowed to the examiner of evaluating the answer books should be sufficient to allow him to work in peace, so that no haphazard work results from hurry or strain. There should be a definite standard of reference concerning the answers of different questions. Every examiner should be required to send copies that he is to examine as samples so that his standard of judgement can be measured, and he should be requested to evaluate the remaining copies similarly.

3. *Terminal or monthly examination* : Nevertheless, student's knowledge of his subject cannot be properly gauged once in a year in a sitting of only three hours. For this it is essential that the teacher should examine the students in the class every fifteen days or a month in the subject-matter that he has taught till then. The results should be announced on the basis of these monthly tests as well as the annual examination. This 'method will compel the students to spread their labour over the whole year.

4. *Examination in other aspects of development* : The aim of education is not only to impart information but to achieve the complete development of the individual. It is the only information that is examined in the present examinations. Hence, it is essential that the child's physical, emotional and social development also be examined, even through the marks obtained therein may not be made the reason for detaining him if he fails. Yet, these marks will help in advising and

improving him. If the children understand that it is essential for them to pass in these respects also, they themselves will try harder to improve themselves.

5. *Re-examination.* Examinees, who, for one or the other legitimate reason such as disease, accident, etc., fail to take their examination at the regular time, should be given a chance to be examined once the reason for their abstaining from the regular examination has been confirmed. Their efforts during the entire year should not be allowed to waste.

6. *Discouragement to rote learning.* Questions in the examination papers should be such as discourage the practice of rote learning but encourage the expression of the student's skill in the subject.

7. *Change in questions* : Questions should vary radically from year to year so that the practice of basing preparation and guess papers on questions asked in previous years and then rote learning answers to them is discouraged and ultimately discarded.

8. *Covering Entire Course* : Questions in the paper should cover every aspect of the curriculum even if more than one questions are given and the solution of one is required. Such methods will induce the students to study all that is prescribed rather than making a selection from it.

9. *Paper Scheme* : During the period of examinations, the distribution of papers should be equitable and proportionate, the normal period of inactivity not stretching over more than one or two days. Only one paper should be set for one day.

10. *Sufficient Number of Examiners* : The number of examiners should be considerably increased so that all of them can conveniently judge a smaller number of copies in the period of one or two weeks provided them for the purpose.

11. *Punishment for Wrong Practices* : Strict measures should be adopted for punishing all wrong practices in examinations or obtaining certificates.

12. *Responsibility of Teaching* : Finally, the fundamental fact that must be pointed out is that the improvements in the existing scheme of examinations depend upon the teachers themselves. It is for them to encourage the students in their classes to attain high degree of skill and efficiency in the subject rather than to prepare them for the examinations. In educational institutions, the principal and teachers can specially attend to this aspect of the matter. Cooperation between teachers and the various examining bodies can help to improve the system of examinations.

## COMMITTEE ON EXAMINATIONS (1971)

The Committee was appointed by the Chairman of the Central Advisory Board of Education to examine the prevailing conditions regarding examinations and to make recommendations to counteract malpractices. Union Education Minister was the Chairman of the Committee. The Committee invited opinions of those concerned with examinations by issuing a questionnaire.

**Recommendations**

1. *Legislation* : The State and Central Governments should immediately take suitable measures to get amending Legislation passed in the relevant laws pertaining to the following matters :

(i) Empowering the board/university to grant autonomous status to well-established institutions.

(ii) Empowering the examining authorities to check students and prohibit those with weapons from entering the examination halls.

(iii) Making the assembly of persons within a certain distance from an examination hall a cognizable offence.

(iv) Making the indulgence in malpractices by employees and authorities of the universities/boards a cognizable offence.

(v) Empowering the examining authorities to take out risk insurance for the invigilators and examiners.

(vi) Making the assault on an examiner or an invigilator or other person connected with examination, a cognizable offence.

2. *Conduct of examinations* : (i) Paper-setters should be appointed at least six months prior to the commencement of a public examination and they should be given at least eight weeks to draft questions. The papers should be finalized at a meeting of the paper-setters.

(ii) Where the number of candidates in public examination is very large, there should be decentralization with separate examinations for each group of 10,000 school students or 1,000 college students.

(iii) A public examination should be conducted in the institution in which the students study. The majority of the invigilators and superintendents should be drawn from the institution concerned.

(iv) Admission to the centre of a public examination should be through one main entrance. Only *bona fide* candidates with identity cards should be admitted in the examination centre after thorough checking.

(v) Model answers should always be prepared and supplied by the paper-setters.

(vi) Copies of the question-papers set should be made available to the teachers in the schools and colleges on the day of the examination but after it is over, so that the teachers could comment on the paper to the authorities quickly.

(vii) The method of spot evaluation at a central place to which all the examiners are called, should be adopted.

(viii) The result should be declared subject-wise and furnished in the form of grades. The 'raw' marks given by the examiners should never be made available.

(ix) Subject-wise passing should be introduced and the public examination certificate should be given to the candidates passing in the minimum number of subjects.

(x) The certificate issued by an examining authority should have two columns, *viz.*, one giving the result of public examination and the other giving the result of the internal assessment by the teachers.

(xi) For the awarding of prizes and scholarships to a candidate who stands first in an examination or in a subject, a separate test should be conducted and admission to the same limited to those who secure the highest grade in the public examination.

(xii) There should not be too many public examinations. There should be one at the end of the upper primary/middle school stage, another at the end of the secondary stage and the third at the first degree stage. All others should be internal assessments only.

3. *Use of examination results.* (i) Recruitment to the services should be made on the basis of tests/examinations conducted by the Public Service Commissions and the maximum age for appointment for clerical posts be reduced to 29 years.

(ii) Admission to colleges including professional colleges should be on the basis of an entrance test conducted specifically for assessing the aptitude of a student for a particular course. Eligibility to appear at these tests should be determined by the results of the public examination.

4. *Budgeting for education :* In future, both the Central and State Governments should earmark funds separately for guidance and studies and research on examinations.

5. *Research* : There should be continued study and research on examinations, both at the State and Central levels and in the boards/ universities in a coordinated manner. Necessary funds for the same should be provided on a priority basis.

6. *Novel ideas* : Novel ideas for the organization and conduct of public examinations should be encouraged.

## QUESTIONS FOR EXERCISE

1. Give a critical evaluation of the prevalent system of examination for the assessment of educational attainment. What reforms may be suggested?
2. Discuss the recommendations of Committee on Examination (1971).

# 30

# STUDENT UNREST AND INDISCIPLINE

## STUDENT UNREST

The phenomenon of student unrest started in India with the agitation of 1905 led by Calcutta and Dacca students to oppose the partition of Bengal. This marked student involvement in agitations. As a part of national struggle it was encouraged by all political parties and welcomed by the public. Therefore, since then the student's participation in national political movement in India increased at every stage particularly in Quit India Movement in 1942. Most of the national leaders were students during the period of national struggle. They left the colleges and the universities to participate in National Movement at the call of their beloved leaders M. K Gandhi, J. L Nehru and B. G. Tilak, etc.

### Student Unrest in the World

Students' involvement in politics is nothing new. In Germany, Russia and France a large number of students participated in political activities in the 19th century. In 20th century the student activities in South Korea were effective in changing the iron regime of Syghman Rhee. In Japan the students demonstrated against Prime Minister Kishi. In Indonesia and Vietnam the students protested against U. S. interference. In England and America one occasionally witnesses student demonstration against expansion of nuclear weapons. Peace marches are a usual scene. A large number of students in Afghanistan were fighting as guerillas against Russians. In Dacca students have several times strongly demonstrated on national issues. In U. S. S. R., however, the phenomenon of disturbed campus is not traceable. On the other hand, in almost all the other countries of the world one finds students' participation in demonstrations, strikes, processions and mass meetings.

### Role of Political Parties in India

In India by the participation in national struggle the students learned agitation methods of protest and realized the power of student unity. After the country achieved independence this experience was utilized to highlight students' sentiments on local, regional, national and even international issues. Since the political parties were in the habit of using students as the youth power in political agitations, most of the political parties encouraged students organisations on political basis. Thus, while B. H. U. has been dominated by rightist students, J. N. U. is the centre of leftist activities. Congress-I, B. J. P., and D. M. K all the political parties have been maintaining their student wings since independence in India. Therefore, it is quite understandable that the disturbed campus is not a temporary phenomenon. Disturbance is only a symptom, a fruit whose roots are being nourished by all the political parties.

### Growth of Youth Power

This, however, does not mean that the students have themselves no political consciousness and that whatever they do is at the instigation of the political parties. Leadership is a phenomenon which is nourished and grown in institutions of higher learning everywhere. This is necessary for the growth of youth leadership in the country. This is most welcome though when it takes wrong turns it becomes a headache to the government and the people alike. In recent years several universities have witnessed growth of student power. In most of the universities the students unions have their own buildings, budget extending to thousands of rupees and all the paraphernalia of a political party. During the period of elections the whole campus and even the city is on siege. All types of methods of propaganda are utilized. Vote catching devices are practised even more shrewdly as compared to the techniques of general elections. Propaganda material worth lakhs of rupees is utilized. Posters come up on all the walls of the city. Hundreds of vehicles of all types are utilized. Money flows from the capitalists and the political parties. And when the winners celebrate they are blessed by the national leaders belonging to the political parties to which they owe allegiance.

### The Modus Operandi

After the leaders are elected, they take stock of the situation local, regional and national. If the issues are not pointed enough, even the flimsiest issue is taken up for starting agitation. It is not because there is something to do that the political activities go on but because the leaders have to justify their election and to show their presence that issues are created. This, however, does not mean that all the activities are baseless. Some student activities have undoubtedly cleaned the campus, made the teachers more responsible and kept the administration awake. From time to time the student leaders do the cathartic function of unveiling the mask from the face of the administrators and powerful teacher-politicians to show them in their true colours. This service is of high importance.

## PHENOMENON OF INDISCIPLINE

Indiscipline is the initial symptom as well as result of a disturbed campus. While discipline is the adherence to rules and regulations, indiscipline is their contravention. According to the report on the problem of student indiscipline in India in 1960 presented by the committee appointed by the U. G. C. to investigate student indiscipline, "Indiscipline is a mass moral turpitude and collective defiance of authority and the use of techniques in seeking redress of real or imagined grievances which are not appropriate for students to use." This definition was formulated after a close study of the disturbed campus. The acts of indiscipline noted by the committee involved discourtesy to teachers, misbehaviour towards women students, student riots, damaging college building; disruption of the normal life of society, squatting on train lines, stopping and burning the buses, physical violence against this or that individual and group and a host of other activities resulting into disruption of the educational process, growth of violence and general elimination of peace and order. These acts of indiscipline start on any issue and led by the student leaders followed by thousands of enthusiastic students. The committee called these techniques inappropriate. This is far from convincing since it suffers from the dual standard, allowing the use of these techniques to political leaders and disallowing them to students. This double standard is far from convincing to the student leaders.

**Multisided Phenomenon**

Thus the phenomenon of the disturbed campus is multisided. Physically, it may be seen in acts of violence, damages to property, impediments in the normal working of the educational institutions, mass meetings, hunger strikes, agitations, processions, etc. The psychological aspect, however, is more important. This is made of power-mongering on the part of the leaders and frustration among the students. So many lapses on the part of the government administrators result in a sense of frustration on the part of the students. One of the most glaring factor creating frustration is the phenomenon of educated unemployment. The student leaders on the other hand are constantly on the look out to take an issue to show their power to the student community on the one hand and to the administrator, the government and the public on the other. It is notable that it is from the ranks of these student leaders that some of the most famous national leaders in India have grown. Their example serves to encourage the ambitions of every student leader. By taking up an issue he makes promises to the student community and exercises pressure by threats and coercion upon the administrative authorities.

**Psychological Factors**

In brief the following psychological factors work at the root of the phenomenon of disturbed campus :

1. *Loss of faith in the aim of education* : As more and more students become disillusioned about the goals of education in the colleges and universities, they withdraw from studies and involve themselves in union activities.

2. *Loss of faith in the means* : Even if the goals sought by educational institutions may be sound, loss of faith in the means of education may result into frustration. This may be concerning any part of the educational machinery such as admissions, appointment of teachers, discipline among teachers, time-table, curricula, methods of teaching, rules of discipline, rules concerning hostels, efficiency of the general administration and finally the mode and validity of examination and evaluation methods. It is a truism that in India at present all these aspects of education are full of problems which do not appear to be solved in near future.

3. *Lack of internalisation of values and attitudes* : It is well known that without teacher's involvement in the process of education, no betterment in educational institutions is possible. This involvement, however, requires several conditions. If so many teachers are known to be having side jobs, running tuition shops, doing insurance business or things like that, they can hardly have any involvement with teaching in the educational institutions. This involvement requires more conscientiousness among teachers. The teachers themselves should be free from politics before asking the students to do so. If the teacher unions are functioning like labour unions how can they suggest anything different to the student unions. The repressive techniques of the research guides can only help to increase frustration rather than any real creative work among the research students. But while the teachers know that there is no necessary correlation between teaching methods and evaluation techniques their enthusiasm in teaching cannot be maintained, unless the teacher-management relationship, the teacher-principal and the teacher-student relationship is improved. The involvement of the teachers is not possible if the teacher-taught ratio is beyond a certain proportion. No educational institution can remain undisturbed without solving this problem. Therefore, the values and attitudes demanded from the students should be first created among the teachers. And before asking for involvement on the part of teachers, suitable conditions for its natural growth must be created.

## SOCIOLOGICAL FACTORS

In *The Sociology of Education in India,* NCERT (1967), Mr. S. H. Asthana and Suma Chitnis have analysed the phenomenon of the Disturbed Campus under two heads as follows :

### (A) THE EDUCATIONAL SYSTEM, ITS GOALS, FAILURE AND INDISCIPLINE

1. **Goals of education :** The minimum goal of education is training for earning a livelihood. The maximum goal of education is socialization, diffusion of knowledge, values, attitudes and norms of relationships, required for playing adult roles in society. In a healthy system of education both these goals must be realized.

2. **Failures of educational system** : The above mentioned goals have not been realized. The growing number of educated unemployment clearly shows failure of our educational system to provide livelihood. During British regime even a matric fail could find a job. Now persons with post-graduate degree are unemployed in a great number. And this number is constantly growing, this failure may be attributed to the following causes :

(i) *No accurate assessment of manpower needs* : As there is no accurate assessment of manpower needs there is no correlation between the number of educated persons growing every year and the number of employment opportunities. Expansion in education has been more rapid than generation of job opportunities.

(ii) *Prejudices* : Caste, region, language, religion and nationality have been the basis of appointment in non-government and even government agencies. Therefore, the organization failed to provide livelihood on the basis of merit.

(iii) *Irrelevance of Education to Occupations* : A general criticism of the present educational system is about irrelevance to occupations other than white-colar jobs. The values created by academic education do not create initiative and necessary qualities of character such as national integration, equality, patriotism, democratic attitude to life, etc.

(iv) *Lack of national integration* : Casteism, communalism, and parochial tendencies arc fast disintegrating Indian society. Far from eliminating these tendencies, the education sometimes, encourages them. For example, in most of the colleges and universities linguism, regionalism and casteism are rather the rule than exception. Communalism, though not much rampant, may also be seen particularly in the educational institutions organised and run by a particular community. Unless national integration is maintained the conflict among various groups of students and teachers is inevitable.

(v) *Absence of democratic values.* It is an irony that the student unions which were primarily established to fulfil the demands of democratization of education have themselves become source of the disturbed campus. Equality may be declared in policy but it is not properly practised. Liberty takes the form of indiscipline and rowdy behaviour. Fraternity is conspicuous by its absence. In the words of H. S. Asthana and Summa Chitnis, "Democracy, to many, is voicing an opinion insisting on one's right, student unions give an excellent exercise in these qualities. But the more important concept of democracy as a partnership of free men, united in the common purpose of national development, does not emerge."

3. **Examples of Teaching** : Unfortunately the examples of academic fraternity set by the teaching community is far from encouraging this value among the students. Most of the university departments in every residential university exhibit cut-throat factionism among teachers. This factionism sometimes goes to the extent of teacher's activities against the research students and disciples of rival colleagues. Every university department has become a den of favouritism, in-fighting, casteism, communalism, regionalism, hatred and jealousies. In this atmosphere no youth can learn democratic values. Team work is a phenomenon unknown to Indian scholars. While in the West most of the valuable academic advancement has been achieved through team work, in India hardly a group of scholars can see eye to eye on any problem. Seminars exhibit leg pulling and personal aggrandisement, vain show and mannerism rather than any solid contribution to knowledge. Lectures are organized to oblige friends. Examinerships are exchanged. Ph. D. degrees are distributed on clique basis. Appointments are made on the basis of personal favour. In the face of such a low level of character and behaviour among *gurus*, it is small wonder that the new generation learns that opportunism, nepotism-politicking, wire pulling, back-biting, cut-throat competitions and ruthlessness are the values and traits required for progress in life. It has been rightly lamented by Asthana and Chitnis, "The academic community between teachers and administrators swings between the two extremes of callous flouting of authority and a subservience that smothers self-respect. A mood of lethargy and pessimism prevails."

### (B) NORMS, SANCTIONS, VALUES AND ATTITUDES

1. **Change in Norms** : Formerly, it was the norm in education that the teachers were respected. According to Indian philosophy of education academic achievements are correlative to respect toward teachers. This norm has now been reversed since education is linked with payment of fees. The modern students have barely any respect towards their teachers, the idea of serving the teacher is beyond their comprehension. This discourages the teachers to give their best to the student. The modern teacher is stimulated by the challenge he faces in the class. The old teacher was encouraged to give his best because of his love and sentiment of service, dedication and sacrifice for the academic cause. Thus, the norms both on the part of teacher and the taught have been reversed.

2. **Change in Sanctions** : Formerly, the teacher's attempts to maintain discipline was sanctioned by the administration, the community and even by the students themselves. Even corporal punishment was appreciated. Today attempts to discipline the students do not receive sanction from the community and the students. The administration is helpless against the strength of the student unions. It is a common feature in the universities that rustication of rowdy student leaders is opposed by student unions tooth and nail. It sparks off protests, strikes and even violence. The students turn a deaf ear to the teachers, the Principal and the Vice-Chancellor. The parents do not approve punishment any more. Corporal punishment is opposed by the parents.

The most important sanction to discipline in education comes from social ethos. Formerly, the social ethos emphasized reverence for elders. The children were asked to obey their parents and teachers. Today the emphasis is on freedom — freedom to think, freedom to act, freedom to react and even freedom to all kinds of indiscipline. In almost every sphere of life today the only value is self-regard or selfishness. In the absence of the sanction of the social ethos discipline cannot be created in educational institutions.

3. **Change in Values and Attitudes** : Indian society was formerly authoritarian. In the wake of democratic values authoritarianism has been substituted by liberty. Not only in the field of education but in marriage and family modern boys and girls do as they like. The age of marriage is growing, making norm of twenty to twenty-five for girls and twenty-five to thirty for boys. Till then boy and girls stay in universities and colleges. Therefore, they learn all types of individual ways of behaviour and conduct. They are not governed either by parents or by teachers. The media, the film, literature, radio, television and everything else are laying emphasis upon personal choice irrespective of what it means to others. Therefore, the values of equality and fraternity have been often set back by liberty. In fact, of the three democratic values, fraternity is the proper basis for equality and liberty. Liberty, on the other hand, cannot be the basis of equality and fraternity. Unfortunately, the modern youth lays emphasis upon liberty as the highest value. Therefore, there is no wonder that he is only concerned with self.

4. **One-sided Value System** : In Indian axiology *Dharma* was the highest value while *Artha* and *Kama* were subordinate to it. *Moksha* was the ideal of life. This was an integral value system. It has now been substituted by a one-sided value system of *Artha* or *Kama* as the only values to be cherished. According to Indian wisdom while *Artha* and *Kama* are provided by destiny and *Dharma* and *Moksha* are actively pursued. The history of culture in different human societies has shown that mammon worship leads to cultural degeneration and final deface. This is the inevitable result of the present day culture. The emphasis is rather on smartness than culture, mannerism than character, general knowledge than scholarship. Therefore, mediocrity is the rule and excellence is exception. Scholarship, simplicity and hardwork are no more necessary values. Not excellence but success is the goal. Not *Dharma* but *Artha* and *Kama* are the aims to be achieved. The modern student aims at enjoyment. The emphasis is on fashion, excitement, novelty, speed and enjoyment. Heterosexual relationships are gradually breaking all norms of decency and restraint. Student politics knows no level. All means are adopted for self-aggrandisement. The techniques taught by M. K. Gandhi are being used in educational campus all over India for achievement of goals which are far from decency, discipline and even student welfare.

## YOUTH UNREST IN INDIA

### Nature and Meaning

The analysis of disturbed campus in India shows several features. While some of it is revolt against oppression most of it may be termed indiscipline. While some of it may be attributed to exuberance of young, most of it is delinquency, vandalism and even crime. While some of it aims at general welfare of student commodity, most of it is for the calculated benefit of a clique of student leaders. While some of it may genuinely represent uprising of Indian youth, most of it is due to the inroad of political parties into campus. Most of the union activities are guided not even by the union leaders but by their political mentors outside the campus. While some of the budget of the student unions is covered by contributions from the student, most of it is met by secret donations from political parties and vested interests. Therefore, it goes without saying that the disturbed campus requires corrective measures.

Basically the disturbed campus in India is the result of youth unrest. Youth unrest in India is a phenomenon exhibiting moral perplexity, lack of ideal educators, defective system of education, political gangsterism, groupism among educators, repressive policies of the state, social disorganization, absence of teacher-parent relationships and finally, the psychological defects of character. An analysis of these causes of youth unrest in India will pave the path to the means of curing them.

### Causes of Youth Unrest

1. *Moral perplexity* : The youth of today is in a dilemma because he does not know what is right and what is wrong. Most of the teachers express such completely

contradictory opinions on moral problems that the educand is confused. On the one hand, he finds very strong arguments being advanced for a materialistic philosophy by some teachers, while other educators are found supporting the cause of idealism with equally valid arguments. The confusion is made worse by the differing opinions on the subject of religion also. Some educators are devout religionists while others are complete atheists. On the one side are the educators who believe in the ancient ideal of abstinence as the sole means of developing character. On the other, one finds more liberal educators who believe that the casual mixing of sexes and social intercourse, etc., are the most important formative influences in character development. They argue that sex is natural and there is no need for any restraint. It is only something natural that the educand should be stupefied and left completely adrift when he is faced with such contradictory alternatives. Consequently, he finds it difficult if not impossible, to act according to any rational principle. He has no choice but to do as he likes, and one finds that his more animal tendencies are being manifested in the form of indiscipline.

2. *Lack of ideal educators* : Most of the youth forming part of the existing educational structure are completely lacking in ideals. Some of the causes are often insufferable working conditions, nepotism and favouritism in appointments, absence of any social prestige, etc. But, whatever the causes, it cannot be doubted that the majority of teachers at the primary and secondary level of education are individuals without ideals and principles . In fact, many of them are morally degenerate and there is little cause for surprise if indiscipline among educated persons increases when they are guided by such individuals. But, it must also be remembered that the government is also very much to be blamed for this situation. Fairly recently, the staff at the primary level in U. P. went on strike to support its demands for increase in pay. It was argued by the educators that the government could not expect good teaching at the salary it offered to the educator. The government countered this with the suggestion that it wanted the educands taught 3 R's, not ideals. If the government itself exhibits such lack of concern towards the fundamental principles which guide civilized life, it can blame only itself for the difficult situation created in the country by increasing indiscipline.

3. *Defective system of education* : After India had won her independence, a series of committees and commissions have criticised the existing system of education and pointed out its defects. In spite of this the system continues till today. It was introduced by the East India Company with a view to producing qualified clerical staff. There has been no change for the better, in fact, there has only been a steady erosion of standards. Corruption at all levels is not rampant but accepted as another fact of life. Accepting bribes to give better marks, co-operating with another educator to give better marks to his candidate, favouritism in the evaluation of doctoral research, these are some of the common practices. In fact, one can sum up the entire situation by saying that now there appears to be no correlation between hard work and study, writing the correct answers in the examination answer books and getting good marks. There is, therefore, no occasion for surprise if one finds that the educand's only aim is to secure degree by fair means or foul. Apart from the system of examination, the education system is further eroded by such defects

as an impractical teacher-taught ratio in the classroom, absence of extra-curricular programmes, the prescription of sub-standard text-books, etc. It is only manifesting one's ignorance if one imagines that indiscipline can be removed when the education system is so beset with defects.

4. *Political gangsterism* : Most of the colleges and universities in the country have become nothing more than hotbeds of political gangsterism and polemic. Most of the students unions are dominated by stooges of some political parties, and they are concerned only with achieving their own ends by using the students unions. Such influences not only lead to gangsterism in the institutions, they also create the possibility of misusing the students for political ends. One finds that during elections, political parties become even more active in their efforts to woo the educands to their side. There is no denying that political parties have played a sufficiently destructive role in bringing about indiscipline and the consequent problems although it would be unfair to imply that political interference is the sole cause.

5. *Grouping among educators* : If an individual takes it upon himself to attend the functions and gatherings of teacher's unions of some institution on three or four occasions, he will soon arrive at the conclusion that the groupism found among teachers perhaps exceeds that which is found among the members of any other professional group. Students are not only aware of this groupism, but they are deliberately made aware of this, because in many cases they are directed by one group to observe the activities of the other group of educators and to report it to the first. Thus, the educand becomes conscious of existing rivalry between the various groups among his educators. All this has a very detrimental effect on the educand's mind, because he feels that such activity must be justified.

6. *Repressive policies of the state* : Clashes between the students and police have become a regular feature in almost every state. One hears of many incidents in which the police thrashed the students, carried out a baton charge, entered the college campuses, destroyed property, attacked students inside the college, even resorted to firing and killing students. Lack of discipline among the students cannot be compared to revolution and rioting, and it should not be treated as such. At the root of it there are some causes which have to be understood and then eradicated. Adoption of a repressive policy only adds fuel to the fire, and ultimately this fire spreads from one part of the country to another, unit! it engulfs most of the country.

7. *Social disorganisation* : Social disorganization is a condition in which the organization, control and mutual co-operation that normally exists between various social institutions and committees deteriorates and practically ceases to exist. This kind of disorganization leads to the disorganization of such fundamental institutions as marriage and finally, ultimately leading to personal disorganisation. Indiscipline is just one instance of this kind of disorganization. Hence, one cause of the indiscipline found among students today is the general disorganisation of society.

8.·*Absence of teacher-parent relationship* : In a more normal situation, the absence of relationship and contact between teachers and parents is another cause of indiscipline. Both the teacher and the parent are unaware of the difficulties of each other, and thus they blame each other for the defects of the students without making any effort to improve the student. In fact, the responsibility for the student's indiscipline must be equally divided between the student, the parent and the teacher, but mutual cooperation and contact between the latter two can solve this problem to a great extreme.

9. *Psychological causes* : At its root, indiscipline is a psychological defect of character. Among its more prominent causes are abnormalities concerning sex, inferiority and superiority complexes, feeling of insecurity, absence of any aim, etc. All these factors contribute to the frustration of the educand, which is converted into violence. This violence is manifested in the facts of indiscipline which are universally condemned. The responsibility for giving rise to such psychological symptoms rests upon bad and morally degenerate films and literature, lack of character among the educators, social class distinctions, absence of any normal relations between girls and boys in the college, neglect of moral education, etc.

The most important factor among those outlined above is the defective nature of the system of education, because all other causes have their origin in the basic shortcoming. The existing system of education cannot do with some small changes. It needs to be completely overhauled, in fact, scrapped and replaced by a different system altogether. It should be made to conform to the cultural characteristics of the nation, education should be imparted through the medium of the national language, and it must incorporate better working conditions for the educator, and a more efficacious and reliable system of examination.

## SUGGESTIONS FOR REMEDIES

The means of curing youth tension can be inferred from the foregoing account of its causes. The following suggestions have been made in this regard :

1. *Improvement in the teacher's conditions* : This comprehends increase in salary, better conditions of work, more just and impartial selections and appointments, reasonable prospects of advancement, etc. If these conditions are met, the educators will be able to live satisfactory lives, and thus they will be encouraged to impart some idealism to their educands.

2. *Presentation of right ideals by the educators* : Since almost all educands imitate their educators both consciously and unconsciously, it is necessary that the educators must present the correct ideal in every sphere of conduct.

3. *Improvements in the system of education* : As far as possible the defects in the system of education pointed out by various committees and commissions should be removed immediately.

4. *Preventing political influence in schools* : No political party should be given the chance to penetrate into schools and college life.

5. *Control of unwarranted state interference* : More often than not, the Vice-Chancellors appointed to the universities are appointed on any consideration except that of merit. These appointments are made by the government, and hence,

are illustrations of undue state interference in education. It is undesirable for the state to interfere in the working of education in this manner.

6. *Protection of the independence of educational institutions* : Of the many incidents of violence and destruction by the students in the recent past, many were inspired by the entry of the police into college compounds, either without the permission or in violation of the express command of the college authorities. All educationists agree that no government employee has the right to enter the premises of the educational institutions without the permission of the Principal. If this rule is not violated it would be easier to prevent manifestations of youth unrest, from becoming violent and destructive.

7. *Contact between educators and parents* : Another method of curbing youth unrest is to encourage contact between educators and parents so that they can meet and discuss the problems of educands and thus remove the causes leading to indiscipline.

8. *Moral education* : Most thinkers agree that absence of moral education is responsible for youth unrest and character defects of the educands. In any case moral education will definitely curb indiscipline.

9. *Creation of proper atmosphere in colleges* : The psychological factors at the root of youth unrest can be eliminated by creating the proper atmosphere in schools. As far as possible, the atmosphere should resemble that of a large family in which the relations between boys, girls, educators, students, etc., would be morally and psychologically healthy.

Youth unrest is a complex problem having its social, political and psychological aspects. In order to remove it, these aspects must be understood and the cooperation of educators, parents and state must be used to solve this problem.

## IMPROVEMENT OF STUDENT UNION

The role of student leaders in campus is not negative. Student unions cannot run on the pattern of labour unions. Instead of aiming at students' unity and demand of students' rights, they should rather aim at furthering the cause of education and strengthening teacher-taught relationship. This, however, requires a periodical survey of the needs and demands of the students by the government and the administration and prompt remedy to them. Restriction on admission of black listed students is a necessary condition for checking indiscipline of the campus. The following suggestions may be advanced for the better organization of student unions.

1. *Student's participation in management* : In the college government by managing committees the student leaders may be given representation in the managing committees so that they may get their demands directly fulfilled without any confrontation with the Principal.

2. *Limitation on expenses* : There should be restriction and proper auditing of budget of student unions. If evidence for spending much beyond it becomes dear, enquiry should be made into the extra source of income.

3. *Restriction on activities in public* : The activities of students unions should be confined within the campus. They should be restrained to do anything in the city.

4. *No permission for litigation* : All the controversies concerning students should be decided by the Principal, the Vice-Chancellor or the district administration. At no time the students union may be permitted to go to court for pressing its demand.

5. *Proper permission for activities.* The students union is governed by campus rules. They should give prior information and seek sanction for every activity from the Principal in the college and the Vice-Chancellor in the university. Activities should be organized not only by prior information but prior sanction.

6. *Correlation of manpower needs and educational planning* : This point has been repeatedly emphasized by every education commission. Education planning includes educational guidance. Manpower planning depends on vocational guidance. Vocationalisation of higher education is necessary for practical use of educational facilities. Job efficiency should be the criteria for organization of courses, method of evaluation and modes of instruction.

7. *Better teacher-taught relationships* : Peace on the campus depends on proper teacher-taught relationships. This requires satisfaction and involvement of the teachers as well as the taught. This depends upon proper policies concerning admission, curriculum, methods of teaching, administration, evaluation, appointments and general facilities.

8. *Better socialisation* : This requires elimination of parochialism, casteism, communalism, linguism, regionalism and factions from the campus. On the other hand, national integration should be propagated by all means.

In the end it should be remembered that some sort of disturbance is a part of the normal life in the campus. It is only when indiscipline crosses limits that action should be taken. Prevention is always better than cure. This is particularly true in the case of educational campus.

## REPORT ON STUDENT INDISCIPLINE 1960

The Committee to give this report was appointed to study the whole problem of indiscipline among the students of universities and colleges and to suggest suitable remedies.

### Major Recommendations

1. Students should be admitted to the university after careful selection. Admission to the universities and colleges should be made strictly with reference to qualifications and merit.

2. Every effort should be made by universities to raise the minimum age of entry from +16 to +17.

3. No college should ordinarily be allowed to have more than 1,000 students, so that opportunities for organised community life can be developed.

4. Universities and colleges should take appropriate steps to bring about

increasingly close touch between teachers and pupils so as to secure a full impact of the mature teacher's personally on the not yet mature students.

5. The salary of a lecturer in a college or university should be similar to that of a Class I Government servant in the Government of India or the State Government.

6. There should be a very careful selection of teachers. In addition to their academic qualifications, it is necessary to see that the men and women recruited to the profession are persons of the highest integrity and of sound character.

7. It is difficult to reconcile teaching and active participation in politics and such a combination of interests should be avoided to the maximum extent.

8. It should be a strictly honoured code amongst our public men not to allow any corrupting influence from outside to enter into the universities and colleges.

9. The Vice-Chancellor should be selected for his eminence in the academic and educational world.

10. The proportion of students living in the hostels and other units of residence under the control of universities and colleges should be greatly increased. Care should, however, be taken to investigate into students' grievances at the earliest stage possible with maximum sympathy.

11. The formation and development of students' unions in universities and colleges may be usefully encouraged.

12. Steps may be taken to provide vocational and moral guidance in the colleges and universities by trained and sympathetic persons.

## THE KOTHARI COMMISSION (1964-66)

The Kothari Commission has remarked that the responsibility for the problem of students' unrest falls on the shoulders of parents, guardians, teachers and some political parties. Hence, if any adequate measure has to be adopted to solve the problem of students' unrest the Government should try to seek co-operation of all these members of the society. The programmes of education should be made more adequate. The standard of services offered, to the students in hostels, libraries and on the campus should be improved. The Kothari Commission has placed the responsibility of students' unrest on our current educational system. In the opinion of the Commission, Students' welfare services should be an essential part of any programme of education. The Commission has mentioned the following services as essential for the students :

1. *Health Services* : These should be organized at each educational centre.

2. *Guidance and Counselling Services* : These are necessary in the context of the various curricular offerings. So there should be a guidance bureau at each educational centre.

3. *Adjustment of New Students* : At the beginning of each academic session a number of new students are admitted in a school, college or university. Certain

programmes should be organized with the co-operation of senior students for adjustment of these new entrants. Through these programmes the new students should be well acquainted with the various activities on the campus, the rules and regulations about library, hostel, games, freeship and examinations etc.

4. *Students' Union* : The formation of Students' Union should be encouraged. It should inculcate a sense of discipline, self-control and hard creative work among students.

5. *Hostel* : Good hostels in adequate number should be organized in every college and university. The hostel should provide the minimum comforts pertaining to daily life, regular nutrition, games and reading rooms.

## THE TRIGUN SEN COMMITTEE (1965-67)

In 1965-67 the Government of India appointed a Committee under the Chairmanship of Trigun Sen for suggesting measures for the solution of students' problems. This Committee suggested the following measures :

1. The students should be encouraged to participate in the various programmes of universities and colleges.
2. Small hostels should be established in place of big hostels, not more than 50 or 60 students should be kept in a hostel.
3. Suitable and learned teachers of good character should be appointed in universities.
4. There should be a guidance bureau for advising students.
5. Political parties should not interfere in the affairs of universities.
6. Education should be job-oriented, the students should be able to stand on their own legs after having received education.

## CONFERENCE OF STUDENTS' REPRESENTATIVES IN 1969

With the co-operation of Ministry of Education, Government of India and the University Grants Commission a conference of representatives of students was organized from May 23 to 25, 1969. This conference recommended the following things for the welfare of students :

1. To participate in the various programmes of the university.
2. To reform the examination system and the curricular offerings.
3. To correlate education with employment.
4. The membership of N.C.C. should be made voluntary.
5. Each university should have a students' union.

## THE GAJENDRA GADKAR COMMITTEE OF 1971

The University Grants Commission established a Committee in 1971 under Dr. Gajendra Gadkar, the Vice-Chancellor of the University of Bombay for suggesting measures for the solution of students' problems. Following are some of its main recommendations :

1. The students should be given representation in various committees of a university.
2. The admission policy should be approved by the public concerned.
3. Students should not participate in meetings of the Academic Council, because they are not yet mature.
4. Each university should have a students' union.
5. Each hostel should be well organized and equipped with all the daily necessities of life and there should be social and cultural activities in it.
6. No university should have more than 30 affiliated colleges.
7. Some autonomous colleges should be established for lightening the burden of the university.

## QUESTIONS FOR EXERCISE

1. Write short note on Student Unrest.
2. Analyse the phenomenon of indiscipline. What factors are involved in disturbed campus?
3. Discuss the causes of youth unrest in India. Suggest remedies.
4. What suggestions may be given to cure youth unrest in India? Give suggestions for improvement of the working of students' unions.
5. Suggest measures to improve students' unions.
6. Write short note on Report on Student Indiscipline, 1960.

# 31

# POLITICAL IMPACT ON EDUCATION

In the history of most of the countries, the rulers took the help of educational systems to consolidate their positions because citizens and the society reflect the impact of education. They develop according to the pattern of education. Consequently, the pattern of education has to be changed for changing the values and traditions of a particular society or for the formation of a new society. Political principles and dogmas are given strength through education. Due to this reason Napoleon changed the then prevailing educational pattern in France soon after destroying the Republic. The lessons were revised and those preaching loyalty to monarch were taught so that the future citizens developed faith and loyalty to the monarch. Whenever there occurred a political upheaval, the educational pattern also changed.

## Pre-Independence Political Impact

The Britishers came to India as businessmen, but gradually they became rulers. By and by, their empire gained strength. Educational system in India also underwent a change according to their political principles. The political impact on education in pre-independence India may be studied by dividing it into following different periods.

1. **From 1600 to 1833** : The political impact of British rule on Indian education starts from the year 1765. Though Englishmen came to India with the sole object of doing trade but after some time English missionaries started their religious activities. This condition continued till 1765 when political power had not come in their hands. After achieving political power, the East India Company started encouraging education. In 1780, Warren Hastings established the Calcutta Madrasa in order to gain the co-operation of Muslims. In pursuance of the similar policy, Jonathan Duncan opened the Banaras Sanskrit College in 1791. Till then Englishmen gave some attention only to the expansion of Indian education. The pattern and organization of eduction almost remained immune from their influence, because till then their political standing had not become firm. Much of sub-continent of India had not come under their domination. In such a condition, introduction of a new system of education could have proved fatal to their political interests. Hence, no change occurred in the traditional Indian educational system till 1833.

2. **From 1833 to 1853** : So far only some intereference was made by the state in the Indian education system, but no definite policy of education could be laid due to the controversy between the protagonists of Western and oriental education. In 1834 this controversy was resolved on Lord Macaulay's entry in the field and English system of education was introduced in place of Indian system of education in order to provide a permanent footing to British rule in India. For safeguarding the political interests of his country in India Lord Macaulay made it clear in his Minute that by introducing English and putting an end to the education of Sanskrit, Arabic and Persian, a new class of Indians would be created which had the impact of English culture and was loyal to the British Government. Thus, with the object of ruling over India, Englishmen gave a death blow to Indian system of education, its culture and literature by replacing them with English system of education, its culture and literature.

In pursuance of the above policy, the East India Company directed the Madras Government in 1830 to provide English education to that influential section of Indian population that commanded respect in society. Thus, the Britishers, in order to consolidate their position and for laying a strong foundation for their empire, destroyed the Indian system of education which was available to the common man by replacing it with English education. The patronage afforded to English made Indians indifferent towards their culture, civilization and literature. The Britishers knew that for strengthening their empire and for tightening the shackles of bondage, it was necessary that Indian culture should first be destroyed. This would never allow Indians to stand against the British empire since it would kill the spirit of independence in them and they would remain faithful and loyal to the English rule.

Lord Hardinge announced that in government services preference would be given to those who had received English education. Consequently, the object of education became limited to finding jobs only and English education made rapid strides. Besides learning English, the Indian public also came to love and respect the Western civilization and culture. The country's old system of education became almost a dead system.

3. **From 1853 to 1882** : English missionaries played an important role in popularising and publicising English education in India. But the religious bias in the education imparted by missionaries created apprehensions in the minds of Indians. Besides, the policy of repression adopted by Britishers in 1857 for crushing the revolt hurt the feelings of Indians. Consequently, once again Indians became conscious of their old civilization, culture and education and developed love for the same. They engaged themselves in the task of bringing back their old culture, society and education system. This process of rethinking was redirected towards Indianization of education.

4. **From 1882 to 1905** : (i) *Secondary Education*. By this time, the Indian public had become conscious of its educational rights. The Government appointed the Indian Education Commission to meet the public demand. It recommended that the Government should bear the expenditure on primary education and the local

bodies should control it. The Commission also submitted outlines of the secondary and higher education. But motivated by their self-interest the English Government did not accept the recommendations in toto. While it handed over the control of primary education to local bodies it did not agree to finance and afford protection. The secondary education institutions started receiving grants because the Government needed persons having completed secondary education to meet the requirements of government services. Thus, the foreign rulers agreed to it simply because of the political interests. Consequently, the secondary education developed considerably due to individual efforts.

(ii) *Higher Education*. Higher education was also influenced by this rapid development of secondary education. The Britishers adopted the policy of divide and rule. They provided special educational facilities to Muslims and arrayed them against Hindus. Pakistan is a living example of this policy. The Englishmen also tried to put this very policy in practice in relation to Harijans also, but fortunately Mahatma Gandhi, saw through the game of Britishers and did not allow it to succeed. As such, Harijans remained the part and parcel of Hindus.

(iii) *Lord Curzon's Rule*. The year 1899 marked the advent of Lord Curzon, as the Viceroy of India. He was a great scholar and his name will ever be remembered in the history of the development of education in India. He set up the Indian University Commission in order to encourage higher education. He encouraged the study of Indian languages by accepting the mother tongue of the pupil as their medium of instruction at the primary stage. Thus under the protection of Lord Curzon started the era of all-round development of Indian education. Useful and practical subjects like science and agriculture were introduced.

5. **From 1905 to 1921** : (i) *Movement Against Partition of Bengal*. Revolutionary changes occurred in the Indian political horizon in 1905. The British Government partitioned Bengal into two parts. Not only the people of Bengal, but the entire Indian community rose in protest. Established in 1885, the Indian National Congress started a nation-wide movement. Although the movement affected the entire sub-continent, yet its effect was particularly felt in Bengal. The main aims of the movement were : (1) expansion of national education; (2) to achieve independence; (3) popularizing Indian made goods; and (4) boycott of foreign goods.

The movement took a serious turn in Bengal. In order to check the students from participating in the movement, restrictions were imposed on their entry in schools, besides stopping their scholarships and school grants. The students were threatened with expulsion, but before this step could be taken the students themselves boycotted the foreign education.

(ii) *National Education Committee*. As the responsibility of imparting education to nationalist students fell on the public leaders, a National Education Committee was formed under the chairmanship of Sri Guru Das Bannerji to open national educational institutions in Bengal. The Committee opened a number of national high schools and colleges.

(iii) *National Institutions* : Emphasising the need of national education at the

Nagpur Session of the All India Congress, Mahatma Gandhi called upon the people to open more national educational institutions in the country. Inspired by his exhortation, the students of Aligarh University passed a resolution demanding the nationalization of the university. As the British Government punished those students who demanded nationalization with expulsion, Jamia Milia Islamia was opened in Aligarh to provide national education to these students. Now this institution is in Delhi. Bengal National University was opened in Bengal and a number of Vidyapeeths were opened in Bihar, Banaras (Kashi), Gujarat and Maharashtra. The Maharashtra Vidyapeeth was named after the great nationalist leader Bal Gangadhar Tilak.

(iv) *British efforts* : This action of setting up national institutions surprised the Britishers who were compelled to introduce changes in the then educational pattern. The Government appointed the Calcutta University Commission and opened seven major universities. In 1913, the Government published a resolution on educational policy. Having been influenced by the liberal educational policy of Baroda ruler and the Bill presented by Gopal Krishna Gokhale for making primary education compulsory, the Government made the primary education compulsory in some prominent provinces in 1920.

6. **From 1921 to 1937** : (i) *Govt. of India Acts 1919 and 1937.* The system of administration underwent a change in 1921. According to the Act of 1919 and the introduction of dyarchy, the Indians got an opportunity to participate in the administration. Consequently, commercial and vocational education got an opportunity to prosper. Besides, some arrangements were made for adult education and for the teaching of engineering, law, agriculture, medical science, commerce, science and veterinary subjects. Thus educational progress continued till 1937. This pace of progress gathered momentum by the implementation of Government of India Act of 1937.

Differences between the British Government and Indians arose on the question of Indian's participation in the Second World War and the Congress ministries tendered resignations. After the end of the War, Congress ministries came in office in eight provinces. Sri Jawaharlal Nehru became a member of the Viceroy's executive council. Thus the influence of Indians was felt at the centre, as well as in the provinces. The Central Advisory Board of Education was re-established and the Centre laid emphasis on the development of every part of education. The responsibility of educating Indians fell on Indians themselves. Programmes of women education, adult education and Harijan education were started and changes were introduced in the policy of primary education. Three types of primary education was under the consideration of the Government. Of this, the basic education pattern as recommended by Mahatma Gandhi was adopted and it made good progress. It was contemplated to transform all primary schools into 'Basic Primary Schools'.

**Impact on Education Under British Rule**

1. The old Indian system vanished. The Indians lost knowledge of Indian languages and literature as medium of instruction was English.

2. Materialism increased with the introduction of English system of education which had no place for religious education.
3. Illiteracy reigned supreme in India as facilities for universal education did not exist.
4. The English system of education gave new inspiration to Indians as a result of which national educational institutions were opened.

**Political Impact After Independence**

India attained independence on August 15, 1947 after a lot of sacrifice by the countrymen. A Republican Democratic Constitution was introduced in January 1950. As visualised in the Constitution the image of future India differed from her picture during bondage.

The Constitution provided to every citizen freedom of thought, expression, worship and religion. Equality irrespective of caste and creed and equal opportunities for advancement in life were guaranteed to every individual by the Constitution. The Constitution also guaranteed equal social, economical and political justice to every citizen. This provision was made for a society based on a socialistic pattern, which completely differed from the one that existed in dependent India. Fundamental rights were provided under the Constitution. Greater facilities relating to education and services were given to the minorities and backward sections. Although Indian Constitution was prepared on the basis of Constitutions of U.S.A., France, England, Germany etc., yet it differs from the Constitutions of other countries. Protection of every individual's rights and provision of all possible facilities for his progress is the special feature of Indian Constitution.

The politics in India took a new turn after the adoption of the Constitution. Revolutionary changes occurred in the sphere of education. It is the responsibility of education to acquaint people with their fundamental rights and duties. Education makes them efficient citizens.

Revolutionary changes in the political set-up necessitated reorientation of education. The leaders and the educationists of the country pondered over the question as to how changes should be brought into education in order to make it suitable for a society based on socialistic pattern and how the social and national ambitions should be fulfilled. As such, following changes in various aspects of education were introduced in a planned manner for reorganizing and making it more useful :

1. *Nationalization of Education* : In developed nations like England and France etc., private institutions occupy an important place in the educational set-up, while the conditions of such institutions is in a deplorable state in India. During Indian renaissance, private institutions were opened in a large number, but these schools failed to organize education properly due to bad financial conditions. They could not achieve the proposed educational targets during the early period of independence. Therefore, it was decided to adopt the policy of nationalization of education for improving their condition.

2. *Education for Everyone* : According to the Constitution India is a secular and democratic welfare State whose success depends on the co-operation and contribution of every individual. Hence, it is necessary for every Indian to receive such an education that may not only acquaint him with his rights and responsibilities but also inspire him to discharge his obligations faithfully and honestly so that he may become a worthy citizen of India and lead the country consistently on the road to progress. Keeping in view this aim, primary education has been made compulsory and free under the old pattern of primary education and Basic education so that the individual becomes self-supporting and makes his contribution towards the progress of the country.

3. *Co-curricular Activities* : During pre-independence era the aim of education was simply to turn out clerks. This position has now changed. The objective of education now is the all round development of an individual's personality. Along with the intellectual development, co-curricular activities are being provided in the schools for their physical and social development.

4. *Reorganization of Curriculum* : Since independence the development of the country has become the responsibility of Indians. More and more Trained persons in the sphere of commerce, arts and technical subjects are needed for the execution of programmes and schemes relating to the country's development. This has necessitated the inclusion of various subjects in the curriculum of secondary schools so that the boys and girls may get an opportunity to pursue the study of subjects in accordance with their tastes and aptitudes, besides fulfilling the needs of the country.

5. *Changes in the School Atmosphere* : In the changed political conditions of independent India the atmosphere that prevailed in schools during the pre-independence era could not prove of any utility. Therefore, educationists found it necessary to change the atmosphere of the schools. They tried to give it a creative shape so that the students may also get an opportunity for their self-expression and developing their creative instincts beside acquiring bookish knowledge. This would enable students to maintain discipline and achieve a position of honour in the society. In order to achieve this objective some provisions have been made for vocational education in numerous schools. Basic and polytechnic schools have been opened.

6. *Opening of Multi-purpose Schools* : Prior to independence there was an uniformity in the curricula of schools of the same grade and there were few prescribed subjects which had to be studied compulsorily. Thus the natural tastes and aptitudes of students were neglected and the study of prescribed curriculum was forced upon them. The prescribed course did not have any organic relation with the basic requirements of life nor did it serve the interests of society. In order to remove these defects, steps are now being taken to convert some secondary schools into muti-purpose schools. Institutions are being started where students may study subjects of their choice and make the best use of their talents and energy. Efforts are being made to enable students to acquire proficiency in some vocational subjects so that they may get an incentive for their all-round development.

7. *Creativeness in the Curriculum* : If only bookish knowledge, in a set form, is made available to him there remains no opportunity for the development of creative talents in a student. The burden of bookish knowledge retards the development of emotions, aptitudes and tender instincts and his basic development is checked. Stress is now being laid on the opening of more and more secondary schools in order to remove these defects and to provide full opportunity to the student for his all-round development. This step would help in the growth of a student's creative instincts. Every effort is being made to give to the school atmosphere.

8. *Opening of People's Colleges* : As the majority of Indians live in rural areas provision has been made for opening Janta Colleges (People's Colleges) to provide training in leadership to the local public. Provision has been made for acquainting the students of these colleges with the country's Constitution, besides the study of Indian literature, history and social sciences. In addition to the civic education, the students are also required to study the current economic, social and other problems.

9. *Adult Education* : Illiteracy increased by leaps and bounds during British rule in India. This happened because religious education diminished and general education remained confined to higher sections of the society during bondage. Illiteracy ruled supreme in rural areas and people could get education only in cities. The leaders realised the need and importance of education for awakening the people. Whenever there was an opportunity for spreading education, the leaders availed it. But after the attainment of freedom, the need of adult education was keenly felt for conducting properly the affairs of the State. A welfare democracy could only function successfully when the general public possesses the ability to take a proper and wise decision. In its absence the situation becomes dangerous. Hence, it became the responsibility of the State and every Indian to help the cause of adult education so that every Indian could contribute his best for the all-round development of the country. A vast scheme of adult education has been implemented.

10. *Schools as Community Centres* : Schools occupy an important place in the society. In the socialization of human beings, the family occupies the first place, the school comes next. The schools are organized by the society for inspiring men to protect social traditions, its values and originalities and help society in its march towards progress. Thus, the school is that representative institution of society through which we can see its every aspect. Schools may be called the mirror of the society. If the school does not possess this quality, it cannot prove useful for the society. The effect of political change on the community in India necessitated change in schools. Keeping in view the interests of the community, the Government of India, decided to make every school a centre of community activities.

11. *Democratic Shape of Education* : During dependence, education was limited mostly to the well-to-do class. The general public could not benefit from it. But with the change in the political set-up, the old restrictions on the entry in some schools, based on religion, caste, creed and sex have been removed in order to make education available for every one. Efforts are being made to educate backward and depressed classes by providing them monetary help and other facilities. The poor

but meritorious students are being granted scholarships so that they may pursue their studies.

12. *Youth Welfare Schemes* : Youths have a vital role to play in the progress and development of country. The progress and prosperity of the society and the nation rests on them. Keeping in view these basic truths, the Government of India have started a youth welfare plan for conducting various youth welfare activities. Under this scheme, provision has been made for grants and other financial help to youth welfare associations. Grants are given for organizing youth functions, holding camps and for undertaking educational tours of historical places.

13. *Character Building and Moral Education* : It has become necessary to introduce moral education for establishing a society based on socialistic pattern as visualised in Constitution. Consequently, a special committee was formed to make this possible. The Central Educational Advisory Board has honoured the recommendations of this committee. It has ordered some changes in the text-books in accordance with the Committee's recommendations.

14. *Physical Education* : A healthy mind lives in a healthy body. So the aim of education should not be confined only to a child's intellectual or mental development. Its aim is the all-round development of child's personality. To achieve this object physical education has been made compulsory in all the educational institutions since independence and a number of physical education centres have been opened under the All India Sports Council and Rajkumari Sports Training Scheme. Sports councils have been set up in every State. The Government of India's National Physical Education and Entertainment Scheme has also been implemented. In U.P. the schemes relating to physical and military education such as N.C.C., P.E.G. and A.C.C. have been successfully implemented. A new scheme of physical education was prepared under the Third Plan. The Kunzru Committee was formed for examining the physical education organizations in States. Thus, since the attainment of independence, physical education has made rapid strides in India.

15. *Development of National Language* : After the dawn of independence the question of choosing the national language came before the leaders as a number of languages were current in India. In order to maintain unity and ensure progress, Mahatma Gandhi suggested Hindustani as the national language, but it was Hindi language that was chosen as the national language. Since Hindi language has been given the status of national language, the Government of India are making efforts for its development. Various committees have been formed. New dictionaries and lists of technical terms are being prepared through them. Words commonly used in various Government offices are being translated into Hindi. New words are being coined and necessary changes are being effected in typing machines. Institutions and committees connected with the development work of the national language are given grants and financial help.

## QUESTIONS FOR EXERCISE

1. What has been the impact on education of political condition in India during the British rule?
2. How have the problems of education in India changed after the attainment of political independence in 1947? Explain with examples.

# 32

# SOCIAL AND ECONOMIC IMPACT ON EDUCATION

## Society and the Individual

Society and human beings are inseparable. A man needs society for his existence and for developing his personality just as human body needs air for its existence. It is true that man is born with some inherent qualities such as the power to feel the pangs of thirst, pleasure and pain etc., but it is equally true that the development of these inherent qualities is possible only in the society. The man creates society, the motivating force behind which is his desire to live in company with others. The society may be called a group of individuals living together in particular geographical environment with some accepted principles of common behaviour.

## Changing Nature of Society

The shape and size of a society is based on the conduct of its members. It is because of this characteristic that a student of social science once remarked that the society is a structure based on man's social conduct. Man's social behaviour is influenced by external factors. This influence succeeds in changing the pattern of society. It is because of this that nature of the society goes on changing rapidly. This may be observed if we look at the conditions of ten years back. We shall find that the nature of the society has changed in many respects during the decade.

## Social Change and Education

Experts in social sciences differ about the reasons and factors of social change. Some hold the clash of economic interests responsible for changes in the society, while others opine that changes in technology bring social changes.

Geographical conditions shape the pattern of society. As the geographical conditions differ from place to place, human societies also differ in their shape and form. Hence, human community organized itself in different types of organizations. Although in the modern scientific age, every facility is available to human organizations for establishing contact with each other, yet they differ in their values, conventions, traditions and codes of conduct. These factors differentiate one society from the other and play an important part in the formation of societies. When these factors change, the society, too, undergoes a change. Men's socialization is not possible in the absence of society and without being socialized, the man cannot become a social being. Through a society only he acquires the knowledge and experience of various things. A society does not allow its members to do some things. Those who violate the social code of conduct are punished. By observing the code of conduct prescribed and recognized by the society, a man earns respect and honour in the society. Due to this fear and favour a man tries to act according to the code of conduct recognized by the society. He observes the rules of various organizations and principles guiding his future years are formed accordingly. Hence, the social institutions occupy an important place in the socialization of man.

In the socialization of man family occupies the first place as a social institution. Next comes the school. When he comes out of the surroundings of his family and enters the school the child finds difference in the values recognized by the family and those by the school, because children from different families observing different values come in schools. They try to establish harmony in their behaviour towards each other and the school tries to socialize the student in such a manner as to make him useful member of society. Sometimes a wide difference appears in the child's home and school atmosphere. This happens when a change occurs in the society or else the need to bring change is felt. The examples of nations like Germany, France and England may be cited in this context. The history of education in France reveals that teachers in that country not only acted as mentors only but also held the position of social leaders. In order to consolidate their administration the rulers of these countries first effected a change in the educational system. Education played a vital role in the progress of Japan. Thus education is the most important factor in the rise or fall of a nation.

## EDUCATION SYSTEM AND ECONOMIC CHANGES

Marx, the well-known scholar of social science, went to the extent of saying that it was the economic change that brought about changes in the society. Technology and industrialization are also instrumental in bringing about changes in economic structure. These factors change the economic policies and set up a new society. In order to know a person we must acquire an insight into his work, nature of his work and the way in which he does his work. It will then be easily possible to know the nature of the man and his aptitude. His thinking and philosophy of life must bear the impact of his work. His financial condition, too, will be according to his work. The education system will be best on the financial condition of the man and in accordance with the ideologies of the society to which he belongs. Schools are the instruments of education. There are social institutions where, besides teaching of ideals and values of the concerned society, efforts are also made to widen the road to progress. The policies of education are laid down by the higher ups and foremost persons of the society, keeping in view the interests of the society for its smooth functioning. Economic co-operation in the society plays a vital role in the functioning of educational system. If the society is financially well off, the education will be of a high standard and well-organized. On the contrary, if the economic condition of the society was poor it would result in low educational standards. For example, the Reform Act of 1867 was passed and primary education

was made compulsory in 1870 as the result of industrialization in England, which brought about changes in the economic conditions.

Political revolution, too, brings about wholesale changes in the economic set up. Its effects are reflected in the educational sphere. For example, after the Russian Revolution, communist rule was established in that country. Thereafter books were published in 111 languages in accordance with the communist ideologies, that is for the fulfilment of every individual's needs and for making education available to everyone and for encouraging the development of all regional languages. As a result of commendable efforts made in Russia for the eradication of illiteracy only 10 per cent persons remained illiterate in 1941. This progress of education in Russia was the result of a change in her fiscal policies. Consequently, it may be said that educational, economic and social set-ups in a country are inter-dependent.

## IMPACT OF SOCIAL AND ECONOMIC SET-UP IN INDIA

To examine as to how far educational set-up in India is influenced by its social and economic set-ups, the changes that have occurred in the educational set-up in the country should be divided into various periods. This will include time from the beginning of the 19th century to the year of independence. From the political point of view this period may be termed as the British period and the period after independence as the free India period. The British period may be sub-divided into the first half of the 19th century, second half of the 19th century and the first half of the 20th century.

### Education During the First Half of the 19th Century

1. *Social Transformation* : The British rule was fully established in India by the end of the first half of the nineteenth century. The rulers tried to change the ideologies of Indian people in order to give a permanent footing to the British rule. The British policy aimed to replace the Indian culture, tradition and social and moral values by the English civilization, traditions and values. This could make the Indians loyal and respectful to Britishers. The Englishmen first tried to bring in disrepute the religion that controlled the society. Missionaries opened a number of schools for spreading Christianity. Those Indians who joined these missionary schools were given various types of factilities. In contrast, the financial position of Indian schools was not good. They could not afford to give facilities to students. In addition to facilities, the students who passed out of these missionary schools were given preference in government service with attractive salaries. Consequently, they were able to command greater respect in the society. This accelerated the pace of social transformation.

(ii) *Economic Transformation* : The Englishmen entered India as traders. They continued to trade and earn profit for a considerable period. Later on when power came into their hands their trade policies also underwent a change. This increased their profits manifold and turned this prosperous country into a poverty stricken one. Being in power Britishers purchased Indian raw goods at the lowest rates and sold their finished products by dictating prices. The Indians had to purchase their products in utter helplessness. Indian industries were destroyed. The country was made a market for European goods. Hence, the economic condition of Indians deteriorated and became deplorable. The Indian people went on suffering humiliations out of sheer helplessness. They became poorer and poorer.

(iii) *Impact on Educational Set-up* : The interference of missionaries in the social life of the Indian people had its evil effects. The traditional basic educational system began to deteriorate. India had already become a poor country, its industries were paralysed and its agriculture completely disorganized. Service remained the only source to sustain life. The prevailing Indian education system was not such as to help the students in procuring service. The educational set-up in missionary schools, on the contrary, suited students who aimed at getting service.

**Education during the second half of the 19th Century**

(i) *Social Transformation* : After coming into contact with the Western civilization the Indians began to look down upon evil social practices like bigamy, *sati*, untouchability, child marriage and infanticide etc. Fortunately, the Indian National Congress was formed in the year 1885. It did commendable work in the sphere of social uplift. A weekly paper entitled "Indian Social Reformer" started its publication in the year 1890. Besides, other social organizations, like Arya Samaj, Brahmo Samaj, Dharma Samaj and others started doing commendable work in the sphere of social reform. Crusade against caste system and untouchability and work of Harijan uplift also helped in the setting up of new factories, railway system and hotels. Mahatma Gandhi made really praise-worthy contribution in the uplift of untouchables. These efforts of social leaders to remove evil social practices received the co-operation of the government also. A number of Acts were passed. Thus major changes took place in the social set-up.

(ii) *Changes in the Economic Set-up* : Industries play a prominent part in the economic development of a country. The main factor responsible for the poverty of India has been the crippling of its industry and trade. British economic and trade policies were mainly responsible for giving a death blow to the Indian industries and trades. There was no dearth of raw materials and minerals in India. But the hostile British policies kept Indians away from utilizing them. The English rulers created circumstances in which Indians had to depend upon others. Agriculture became their main occupation. They produced raw materials while Englishmen filled their coffers out of the profits derived from the purchase of raw materials at cheap prices and by the sale of finished products at their dictated rates.

The American Civil War which broke out in the year 1861, proved inspiring to Indian textile industry. Textile mills were opened in the country. In addition, iron, steel and cement industries were established. In the history of India this period may be called a period of great economic changes and the age of industrial development.

(iii) *Impact on Education* : The above mentioned economic and social changes made a deep impact on the educational set-up. Social changes gave birth to national consciousness and love for the nation. Education developed as the medium of fulfilling the people's and leader's ambitions of new national reconstruction. Changes took place in the educational system. Public leaders opened institutions throughout India at various stages for the eradication of illiteracy. Financial aid was secured from the Government for this purpose.

The Indian Education Commission was set up in 1882 to reorganize education on proper lines. The local bodies were made responsible for the management and expansion of primary education. They were given the right of levying taxes for educational purposes. The demand for education increased and changes in the economic pattern gave birth to industrialization. Besides the opening of secondary schools, industrial and commercial subjects got place in the curriculum.

The social and economic changes during the first years of the nineteenth century attracted government attention. Colleges for higher studies were set up in 1857 in Madras, Calcutta and Bombay. The foundation of Punjab University was laid in the year 1882. Private individuals inspired with national sentiments also contributed towards the expansion of education. The Central Hindu College, Varanasi, Ferguson College, Poona and Dayanand Anglo-Vedic College, Lahore, were founded.

Due to the efforts of social leaders and various social organizations the old social structure of the Indian society had changed considerably. The feeling of untouchability was considerably reduced due to movements for the uplift of the untouchables. Religious intolerance and the problem of casteism, had been removed to a large extent. Harijans got the right of admission in all educational institutions. Industrialization greatly helped to solve these problems.

Indian education recorded an all-round progress during this period. Women education started due to the efforts of social reformers like Ishwar Chandra Vidyasagar, Bairamji Malabari, Agarkar and Mahadev Govind Ranade etc. As the people's outlook had changed by now, the public, too, joined hands in this noble work.

## EDUCATION DURING THE FIRST HALF OF THE 20TH CENTURY

### Social Changes

In the first half of the nineteenth century the efforts made to widen the path of social progress had changed the entire Indian social structure by the first half of the twentieth century. During this period stress was laid on eradication of untouchability, Harijan uplift, expansion of education, eradication of casteism, social narrow-mindedness and evil social practices. The committees and organizations (given on p. 338) did praiseworthy work in this sphere.

Dr. B.R. Ambedkar, M.C. Raja and Mahatma Gandhi rendered great service to the cause of Harijan uplift and eradication of untouchability. The women also became conscious of their rights. In 1917 they made representation to Mr. Montague, the then Secretary of State for India and demanded their fundamental rights. In 1923 they got the right to vote in the elections for the Provincial and the Central legislatures. The All India Women's Conference of 1926 demanded the expansion of women education. Sarda Act of 1930 made an attempt to stop the evil practice of child marriage. Thus, the structure of Indian society considerably changed during the first half of the twentieth century.

**Particulars of Organizations and Committees**

| Name of Committee | Organizer's Name | Year of establish-ment | Main Objective |
|---|---|---|---|
| 1. Bharat Sevak Samaj | Sri Gopal Krishna Gokhale | 1905 | Eradication of untouchability. |
| 2. Servants of India Society | Sri Gopal Krishna Gokhale | 1905 | Service of the Motherland. |
| 3. Depressed class mission | Sri Vithal Ram Shinde | 1906 | Harijan Uplift. |
| 4. Social Service League | Sri Narain Malhar Joshi | 1911 | Raising the standard of living of the public. |
| 5. Sewa Samiti | Sri Hridaya Nath Kunzru | 1914 | Development of health, education and sanitation. |
| 6. Sewa Samiti Boy Scout Association | Sri Shri Ram Vajpayee | 1914 | Development of health, education and sanitation. |
| 7. Mahila Bhartiya | Smt. Dorothy Jinrajdas | 1917 | Achievement and protection of fundamental rights of women. |

**Economic Changes**

Though there was no dearth of raw materials in India, but the control and commercial policies of the British rulers did not allow the Indian trade and industry to prosper. Raw materials were exported to England and in its place finished goods were imported. Imports were also started from industrially developed countries like Germany and Japan. Even ordinary things of every day life like needles, watches, buttons, knives etc. were imported.

In 1914 imports stopped as the First World War broke out. The government acquired the industries for the production of war materials. Factories were established for producing things like matches, sugar, iron, steel, textile, papers etc. Industrial development made progress. It received further impetus when the Second World War broke out. With the improvement in economic condition and the growth of industries, migration to urban areas started. People's outlook underwent a change.

**Impact on Education**

Due to the above mentioned social and economic changes that took place in the second half of the nineteenth century efforts were made to make education available to every individual. Industrial subjects were included in the curriculum of secondary schools. English language continued to be the medium of instruction. The pattern of education remained almost similar to that practised in English schools. Only urban population could benefit from this progress of education. Since social and economic changes did not make its impact on villages, yet the rural people benefited by the industrialization and consequent urbanization. During this period educational expansion took place at all the following stages of education :

1. *Primary Education* : For making primary education compulsory Sri Gokhale introduced a Bill in the Central Legislature in the year 1911. Inspired by the noble sentiments behind the Bill many provinces introduced compulsory primary education. During 1937-39, the Congress ministries made commendable efforts. A new pattern of primary education was introduced based on Mahatma Gandhi's Basic Education Scheme.

2. *Secondary Education* : Indian languages replaced English as medium of education. Stress was laid on the teaching of agriculture along with vocational and technical education.

3. *Higher Education* : As the Indian business community had become rich every one appeared to be anxious for the progress and development of the country. As many as 16 new universities were set up and older ones were reorganized with the help and co-operation of the public and businessmen.

4. *Women's Education* : The social status of women had improved. Education was available to women at all the stages. In order to meet the high demand of educated persons service facilities were extended to educated women also during the war period. This encouraged more and more girls who started joining schools in larger numbers. S.N.D.T. Indian Women's University was established in Poona in 1916.

5. *Harijan Education* : Harijans did not enjoy the facility of admissions in schools. But as a result of social and economic changes and by the coming into power of the Congress ministries all their demands were met, they were given scholarships, stipends and other types of facilities. To improve their social status, preference was given to them in service. Seats were also reserved for them in legislatures and Government services.

6. *Vocational Education* : The demand for vocational and technical education grew stronger as a result of change in social and economic conditions. Although the alien government did not pay adequate attention to this demand but the impact of the Second World War proved beneficial in this respect. Some progress was made. Schools were opened which taught medical science, law, animal husbandry, arts and crafts, commerce, agriculture and subjects related to engineering. All India Council of Technical Education was set up in 1946 for the development of technical education.

7. *Adult Education* : The illiterate persons developed a desire for education as the result of industrialization. Consequently, some efforts were made to remove illiteracy through literacy campaigns and in 1937 a well planned scheme of adult education was implemented.

## IMPACT OF POST-INDEPENDENCE CHANGES ON EDUCATION

### Social Changes

India achieved independence on August 15, 1947. The social structure of the society underwent changes with the change in the political set-up. On January 26, 1950 a new Constitution was adopted. It provided equality, social freedom and freedom of religion and worship to every citizen. India was made a secular State. Casteism and sectarianism began to lose its grip over the people. The State took over citizen's social security. Five Year Plans were launched to improve the social and economic condition and for achieving the fundamental objectives laid down in the Constitution. Efforts were made to establish a welfare state and provide equal social status and opportunities to every one. An unprecedented change about the social structure came in the outlook of the people.

### Economic Changes

Before the attainment of freedom the economic policies of Britishers were not in the interest of the country. They favoured their own interests. With the change in the political set-up changes occurred in the economic sphere as well. Five Year Plans were launched for the all-round development of the country. In accordance with the accepted Constitution, a socialistic economic policy was adopted. It aimed at providing economic freedom to every section and individual of the society. In pursuance of this policy, the economic aspects of the Five Year Plans were so framed as to bring the standard of living of every citizen to a satisfactory level. It also aimed to keep the economic development in accordance with the social development. Efforts were made to shape production, consumption, distribution and other economic factors to achieve financial developments and economic parity between individuals, to bridge the gulf between the rich and the poor sections of the society. This required to bring a change in the outlook of the people for which education was the only medium. Therefore, major changes were introduced at different stages of education.

### Impact on Educational Set-up

Education is the only medium for achieving benefit by the developments and the changes in the society. Consequently, following important changes had to be made in the educational system in India in post-Independence period :

1. *Primary Education* : For the eradication of illiteracy and for providing every individual an opportunity to acquire the qualities of a good citizen, primary education was made free and compulsory. It was given the shape of basic education so that every student may learn a vocation and be able to earn his living and contribute to the economic development of the country.

2. *Secondary Education* : In 1952 the Secondary Education Commission was appointed to suggest ways and means to make secondary education compatible with the changed economic and social conditions of the country. On its recommendations some multi-purpose schools were started and curriculum was diversified. It was expected to effect an all-round development in student's personality by providing him opportunity to choose and study subjects of his liking.

3. *Higher Education* : In the Five Year Plans emphasis has been laid on the development of industries in order to improve the economic condition in the country. Changes were introduced in the curriculum of universities for turning out efficient scientists and engineers. More importance was attached to the study of science. Changes were also introduced in the general education for the all-round development of students.

4. *Technical Education* : The economic policies underwent a rapid change in the country after independence. Having experienced the need of efficient and trained workers, technical and vocational subjects were included in the curriculum. The estimate of the number of workers needed was based on the Five Year Plans.

5. *Women Education* : After independence, women were given equal rights with men in the new structure of the Indian society. Consequently, as we have remarked in the foregoing pages, many other facilities, besides co-education, were provided for their education.

6. *Rural Education* : Indian people living in rural areas were always looked down upon during the foreign rule. After independence, they were given their due place in the new social structure. Degree colleges, training centres and institutions of higher education were opened in rural areas also.

7. *Health and Medical Education* : According to the Indian Constitution the State is responsible for protecting and looking after the health of the citizen. This led to the opening of new medical colleges and hospitals.

Institutions imparting higher education in the subjects of fine arts and handicrafts besides those teaching vocational, commercial and technical subjects, were started for the all-round development of the country. The government made provisions for special financial assistance, scholarships and stipends in order to bring harijans, untouchables, depressed and backward class people on equal status with others. The States also made praiseworthy efforts for education of disabled, deaf and dumb persons. Thus the government made all possible efforts to achieve the objective of bringing social and economic equality.

## QUESTIONS FOR EXERCISE

1. How do social and economic conditions influence education in a country? Illustrate from examples, prevailing in India during the nineteenth century.
2. How did education influence in India during the twentieth century by its social and economic conditions? Explain with examples.
3. How have new problems of education emerged in India due to the changed social and economic conditions after independence? Suggest remedies.

33

# TECHNOLOGICAL IMPACT ON EDUCATION

Modern age is the age of science and technology. Today we receive news from every corner of the world through radio and television. We are controlling the nature and deriving benefits thereby. After conquering the moon man is trying to reach other planets. In view of the new inventions and their utility for the society, it has become necessary to include the subjects of technology in the curriculum and give them their due importance.

**Importance of Technological Education**

Science and technology have been responsible for the development of various countries. The U.S.A., the most powerful nation of the world, has a well-organized education of science and technology. Despite the presence of capital, raw material and minerals necessary for the progress of a country, progress is not possible unless it possesses technological resources to turn the raw materials into finished products. Ancient India was one of the most powerful nations in the world. The reason for her prosperity was her comparatively advanced technological knowledge and resources. On the contrary, although minerals and raw materials were available in the country during the period of foreign rule, yet in the absence of technological resources full benefits could not be derived. Cloth was manufactured in foreign countries out of the cotton produced in India while the Indians had to purchase it. Thus Indians paid the cost of exporting raw materials, manufacturing expenses and profits to sellers of the products of their own raw materials in the shape of price, because technology had deteriorated in India during the foreign rule. Foreigners' policy of making India their market drained out its wealth continuously for decades. Due to this uninterrupted outlet of Indian wealth during the alien rule India became extremely poor. Despite Five Year Plans, Indian economy continues causing worry. The low standards in the sphere of science and technology are responsible for our dependence on imports. Hence, the Government of independent India laid particular stress on the education of science and technology.

**History of Technological Education**

In ancient days, India did not lag behind in the sphere of technology. It is necessary to glance through the history of technology in India to understand the reasons that led the country to poverty.

1. *Ancient India* : It is clear from the descriptions in the Vedas that Indian ancient culture was on the peak during those days. There were many kinds of

commercial federations or guilds in the country. Every federation practised its separate trade. The training of the trade and its technological knowledge descended from the father to the son and from the teacher to pupil. The main technical subjects in those days were dyeing, manufacture of cotton and woollen cloths and embroidery, manufacturer of horse-driven vehicles, metal wares, leather work, earthen wares and arms-manufacture.

Thus, for a considerable period technical knowledge continued in this shape. Afterwards castes came into existence on the basis of technical trades. For example, those who manufactured gold ornaments came to be known as Swarnakars. Technology in India continued to progress till the Rajput period under the patronage of commercial communities.

2. *Muslim Period* : Muslim invasion gave a severe blow to India but no particular change occurred in its economic condition with the settling down of Muslims in the country because Muslims did not establish their rule with the intention of taking away Indian wealth for enriching Arabia while the Britishers adopted the policy of removing Indian wealth to England. Muslim rulers accepted India as their country. They used its wealth for its development and their own comforts as is clear from the beautiful specimens of fine arts of the Mughal period.

The pattern of technical education during this period almost remained similar to that in the ancient period, but its pace gathered momentum due to State patronage. Fine arts made good progress as Mughal emperors needed luxurious goods. The production and trade of cotton cloths were exported from India to Burma, Malaya and Uttamasha sub-continent. Silk production and trade was also in a good condition. Ships and Gun-powder were manufactured. Kalins, Muslin and Kimkhawab were produced. Things of daily use of Mughal emperors like wine-cups, inkpots, pen holders, etc., bear testimony to the highest type of artistic work of period. Tajmahal is still an unparallel feat of engineering of that time.

3. *British Period* : Englishmen came to India not to rule only but to carry on trade. They first time opened their factory at Masulipattam in 1611. Even when they got an opportunity to rule India, they never accepted India as their home. They kept it only as a market for English goods and exploited their political and other powers for developing their trades. As a result of this policy the Indian technology did not receive State patronage but faced State's hostile and destructive attitude. The Britishers destroyed the Indian trade of cotton cloth. They imposed tax on domestic handlooms, and enhanced the taxation rate so high that people had to give up this vocation. Indian cotton was exported and in its place cloth manufactured in Manschester was imported. Thus the Englishmen took away the profits on Indian raw materials. The Indians had to pay freight from India to England and back on goods prepared from their own products. Indian technology almost reached its death-point. Englishmen even destroyed the salt trade of India.

However, even during the British regime some efforts were made for development. It is convenient to divide the period between the year 1800 and 1947 into four parts to study the progress and efforts made during the British regime :

(i) *Technology From 1800 to 1902* : The period between the years 1800 to 1882 is regarded as the period of industrial revolution in England. England made desperate efforts for her industrial growth. This home policy of industrial development of England did not prove of any help to India as the Britishers wanted to carry the wealth of India to their own country.

The Famine Commission of 1877 recommended the rehabilitation of Indian technology in its report. The missionaries opened some technical institutions where the training in crafts like carpentry and smithy was given to those students who accepted Christianity as their religion. Thus it remained confined to handicrafts only. These schools were not technical or industrial schools.

By this time, the Indian National Congress sent proposals to the Government for opening technical and industrial institutions. But the alien Government was not prepared to sacrifice her interests by accepting these resolutions. Hence, despite Indian leaders' ceaseless efforts, only 80 technical or industrial schools could be opened in India till the year 1902. Only a few of them were worth their names.

(ii) *Technology from 1902 to 1911* : According to the recommendations of Indian Education Commission of 1882 the Government during this period allowed the inclusion of technical and vocational subjects in the curriculum of High School.

(iii) *Technology from 1921 to 1937* : In this short span of 17 years the Government agreed to grant scholarships to those few students who pursued technical education though the amount of scholarship was not sufficient to cover the expenses of those students who had to go overseas for studies. Moreover, the number of scholarships was so small that a large number of students had to go without them. During the period between 1905 and 1917 only 113 scholarships were given by the Government. Appointed for examining the progress of Indian industries the Morrison Committee of 1917 recommended in its report that preference in the award of scholarships be given to those students who were receiving training in industries like paper, pencil, mining, pottery, matches, glass, sugar, textile and tanning etc. The Government however, did not pay any attention to this recommendation.

Some years later, dyarchy was introduced in the Indian administration. On getting this opportunity Indians again raised their voice for technical training. The Government was urged to set up schools for imparting higher technical and industrial training in India. The Government responded to this demand. A Committee under the chairmanship of Lord Lytton was appointed to report on the Indian educational set-up. On the recommendation of this Committee three institutions were opened for imparting technological and engineering and technical education namely, College of Engineering and Technology, Jadavpur, Government School of Technology, Madras, and Harcourt Butler Technological Institute, Kanpur. In addition in 1937 there existed 532 such institutions.

(iv) *Technology from 1937 to 1947* : The period from 1937 to 1947 may be called the period of India's technological advancement. Due to the Second World War the demand of technical hands shot up not only in India but in the whole world. Scientific inventions occupied a high place during this period. Every nation was busy in exploiting its resources to conquer others. Different types of bombs, gases and aircrafts were used for destructive purposes during the war. Under these conditions, it became necessary for technologically backward countries like India to arrange for technological training of their people. It became all the more necessary to produce men with technological, industrial and technical knowledge for the implementation of India's development plans. But in view of the needs of the country whatever progress has been made in the sphere of technological education during these years was insufficient.

## TECHNOLOGICAL EDUCATION IN INDEPENDENT INDIA

At the dawn of freedom, the economic condition of India was pitiable. The Britishers policy of exploitation, the Second World War, partition of the country and communal disturbances had hit her hard. But the outlook of the people had changed. The responsibility of developing the country rested on people's shoulders. Natural resources needed for the development of a country already existed in India. The problem that faced the country was the exploitation of the natural wealth with the help of science and technology. As the country was technologically backward, it was difficult to exploit the natural wealth. It was necessary to improve the techniques of production because the older techniques became out of date. The backwardness of the country in the sphere of technology was keenly felt and emphasis was laid on the technological education and improvement. The result of scientific researches made in other countries and also the results of their practical applications promised good results when applied with suitable modifications according to the special conditions of the country.

### Technological Impact on Education

After independence India took the road of all-round development through her Five Year Plans. Schools and colleges for imparting education in technological, industrial and engineering subjects were started for raising technologists, engineers and technicians required for implementing various development plans. By the end of the year 1952 arrangements were made for the education of 12,700 students in technology. This figure was only 6,600 in the year 1947. As many as 149 multi-purpose diploma courses and 89 degree colleges were started by the year 1958-59. These schools could take in 19,400 students in the diploma course and 11,100 in the degree one. A need for expansion and increase in the number of these institutions was still being felt for the implementation for the future Five Year Plans. It was, therefore, aimed to raise 25,000 students with diploma course and 13,000 holding degrees by the end of Second Five Year Plan.

The only way of development of India was through the successful implementation of its Five Year Plans. As such, sources helping in its implementation were developed. The Union Government opened 8 engineering and 28 multi-purpose institutions. In addition, an engineering college was opened at Delhi. Thus the Union Government made arrangements for imparting education to 4,024 students in diploma courses and 2,035 in degree courses. Efforts were also made for the expansion of existing institutions. Arrangements were made in 1957-58 for additional 2,096 students in degree and 3,399 in diploma courses. In 1958-59 in order to increase the above number of students still further steps were taken for undertaking expansion in 19 colleges and 41 multi-purpose schools. This resulted in educational facilities for additional 35,400 students at the diploma courses level and 2,568 at the degree one.

Private institutions and organizations also made valuable contributions. The Government appreciated their efforts and gave them financial assistance.

Particular attention was given for the training of teachers of technological and technical schools. The demands of better pay and service facilities of these teachers was given a sympathetic consideration. The Planning Commission requested the Union Government to provide for the money to be spent on teachers for a period of five years.

The Union Government had a large hand in the financial affairs of these schools. Half of the expenditure of institutions imparting education upto degree courses and the entire expenditure of institutions providing post-degree education and carrying research work is today borne by the Union Government. The Union Government also extends financial assistance in the expansion of technological and technical institutions.

### 1. First Five Year Plan

The First Five Year Plan occupies an important place in the development of India. It was the first step towards the reconstruction of the country. It sought to find resources for the prosperity and development of the country to raise the edifice of Ram Rajya of Gandhiji's dream. Hence, it was necessary to lay particular emphasis on the education of reconstruction technology, engineering, technical and vocational education. Hence, the expansion of these types of institutions was undertaken and many other new schools and institutions were opened. As many as 14 colleges were established. The Indian Institute of Science, Bangalore was fully developed and made more useful. The standard of education of the already existing industrial, engineering and technical institutions was raised. The Union Government made provision for scholarships for study abroad for acquiring higher engineering education. The most significant step of this period was the provision of teaching of agriculture in schools. A new scheme for rural uplift was implemented. Arrangements were made for imparting technical, vocational and technological education to rural public through the opening of training centres in rural areas. The traditional artisans were given training facilities at these centres. During First Plan Rs. 23 crores were spent on technological education.

### 2. Second Plan

An amount of Rs. 48 crores was provided for technological education in the Second Plan. It was estimated that the progress would be twice as much as had been achieved in the First Plan. Besides continuing the institutions opened in the First Plan, it was also decided to start new institutions and undertake expansion of the existing ones. Following are the most important institutions that were further developed during this plan :

(i) *Indian Institute of Science, Bangalore* : It was expanded and extended during the First Plan. Arrangements were made for conducting researches in mining and electrical engineering and to provide higher education in the Air Force and Navy Engineering, power and internal combustion.

(ii) *Indian School of Science and Applied Geology* : Technological education was imparted in the subjects of mining and metallurgy at this institution situated in Dhanbad. It was expanded in the Second Plan period. More training facilities were provided.

(iii) *Multi-purpose Institution, Delhi* : This polytechnic institute of Delhi was developed to meet the growing demand of technologists and engineering. Its technological and technical wings were expanded to provide training to more students.

(iv) *Indian Institute of Technology, Kharagpur*. It provides training of higher order in many subjects. In the Second Plan it was further extended to provide graduate and post-graduate training and research.

Besides extension in the above institutions, the standard of technological education was raised in numerous colleges. Technological institutions providing graduate and post-graduate training and institutes for printing technology were established at Bombay and Kanpur. The number of scholarships and stipends were increased. Provision for hostel accommodation was made.

Thus efforts were made during the Second Plan for the development of technological education by continuing the programmes started in the First Plan and for meeting the growing demand of technologists. It was estimated that 5,700 trained graduates and 6,800 diploma holders were made available every year for taking up various development works in the country.

**Development in Technological Education during 1949-50 to 1981-82**

In the year 1949-50, there were 81 institutions with an enrolment of 5,900 students. In 1981-82 the number of schools rose to over 200 with an enrolment of 20,000. Similarly the number of degree colleges in 1949-50 was 53 with an enrolment of 4,120. The enrolment for 1981-82 was over 20,000.

Indian technology is receiving help from foreign countries also. The Institute of Indian Technology of Madras has received considerable assistance from Western Germany. Three more institutions of this standard have been opened in the country. By 1981-82 more than 30 engineering colleges and 80 multi-purpose institutions have been set up. Through them training for diploma and degree course is given to 50,000 and 20,000 students, respectively.

In order to encourage students to study technology, the Union Ministry of Scientific Research has made provision for 'Efficiency and Resources' Scholarships.

## QUESTIONS FOR EXERCISE

1. What was the condition of technical education in India before independence? Give reasons.
2. Sketch the development of technological education in India after independence. What are its particular problems? Suggest remedies.

34

# INDIANIZATION OF EDUCATION : IMPORTANT EXPERIMENTS

## The Meaning of Indianization

Indianization does not mean to accept everything Indian in utter disregard of all that is good and acceptable elsewhere. The term 'Indianization' implies to accept whatever is good in India and to enrich it further with the help of better elements found elsewhere. This enriching however, does not mean imposition of foreign elements. The foreign elements may be accepted, if good. But this acceptance should be in Indian context and manner. Thus Indianization seeks to make Indian people conscious of the greatness of India, her culture and the necessity of enriching it for making it fuller and greater. Indianization may also imply the generation of a national spirit and responsibility for the upliftment of the country as a whole. Indianization does not mean a tilt towards any particular community or religion of the land. Indianization refers to all the sects, religions and people gracing the land.

Indianization should imply creating of love in the Indian people for their own culture, literature, languages, religions, national flag, songs and language, great men of the land and great national values. All those who have respect for all these are part and parcel of Indian national life. The national spirit of Indianization is normal attitude of all those who have any regard and love for their motherland and its high traditions. It has no reference to any particular religion, language or political faith.

## INDIANIZATION IN EDUCATION

### Meaning

Indianization in education means planning education in such a way as to meet all the aspirations and necessities of Indian people. Indians should always try to adjust their educational system in terms of their ever-developing needs and goals. Indianization of education means that education should acquaint Indian people with the ever-abiding greatness of the essentials of Indian culture. After the achievement of independence in 1947, Indians have become conscious of this necessity. Indian planners of education have consistently endeavoured to bring education nearer to the cultural soil of the land. They have tried to plan education for meeting the needs of the day.

**Tendencies in Indianization**

The following tendencies may be noticed as Indianization of educational efforts :

1. *Incorporation of ancient in modern* : In the tendency to incorporate the basic elements of ancient Indian education in modern Indian system of education, educationists are emphasising the necessity of contact between the teacher and the taught, good hostel life of the students, the ideal of self-control and discipline on the part of the students which have been some of the examplary essentials of ancient Indian education.

2. *Modernization* : In order that education may meet the ever-developing needs and aspirations of the people, our educational planners are trying to develop such a system as to make all the knowledge and skills which modern sciences and other disciplines have made available to our students. It is rightly felt that this attempt will ultimately bring the country in the comity of progressive nations of the world.

3. *Basic Education* : Experiments in Basic education have been a glaring example of attempts to Indianize education. Mahatma Gandhi propounded Basic scheme in 1937. Now it has been accepted in some modified form as a national policy of primary education. It consists of the following elements :

(i) The child as the centre of education.

(ii) Learning by doing.

(iii) To engage the child in some productive work.

(iv) Some handicraft as the nucleus of education.

(v) To develop in the child a love for manual labour.

(vi) Mother-tongue as the medium of instruction.

(vii) Teaching of various subjects in a correlated manner around the chosen basic handicraft.

(viii) Both the teacher and taught imbibing the attitude of truth and non-violence.

(ix) Both the teacher and the children working for social progress.

Basic education has been a revolutionary step towards Indianization of education. It has not succeeded because of its many inherent weaknesses.

4. *Commission and Committees* : The Radhakrishnan University Commission (1948-49), the Mudaliar Commission on Secondary Education (1952-53) and the Acharya Narendra Deo Committees on Reorganization of Secondary Education of 1939 and 152-53 of the U.P. Government have been only the attempts of our Governments to Indianize and modernize education.

5. *The Kothari Commission of 1964-66* : It has been another revolutionary step to Indianize and modernize education at all the levels — primary, secondary,

university, vocational and professional education. It has rightly viewed education as a national development. Following is the basic spirit of its main recommendations :

(i) Education should develop social, moral and spiritual values.

(ii) Democratic values should be developed through education.

(iii) The speed of production can be accelerated only through education.

(iv) The objectives of modernization of the country can be obtained only through education.

(v) Social and national unity may be developed through education.

6. *National Education Policy of 1968* : On the basis of recommendations of the Kothari Commission, Indian Government declared a national policy of education which is indicative of efforts towards Indianization of education leading towards the goal of Indianization.

It sought to bring the education nearer to the life of the people in general through the following :

(i) Making qualitative improvement of education at all levels.

(ii) Developing new social and moral values.

(iii) Trying to develop opportunities for education.

(iv) Paying special attention to the study of science and handicrafts at all the levels of education.

The Government of India decided to proceed according to the following principles in the field of education.

1. To make education free and compulsory for the first fourteen years of age.

2. To effect increase in the salary and allowances of teachers and to give them a place of honour in society. The Central University Board of Education and the University Grants Commission have jointly tried to raise the emoluments of the teacher of all the levels in the country. They have also been given wider facilities.

3. To encourage the development of all the Indian languages included in the schedule for effecting improvement in the life of the people, help has been given for the development of all the Indian languages, literatures and culture. Special efforts have also been made for the study of English and other foreign languages.

4. To encourage students to participate in national services and work-experiences.

5. To provide equitable opportunities for education in the various areas — hilly, sea-coast and forest areas.

6. To give special educational opportunities to the children of tribal areas and scheduled castes.

7. To give special opportunities for the education of talents of gifted and handicapped children.

8. To give special importance to education and research in science. This has been considered necessary for the national growth and prosperity.

9. To give education in agriculture and industries in order to make the country self-sufficient as far as possible.

10. To encourage production of standard works with a view to develop arts, sciences and literature, it is decided to reward authors of standard original works.

11. To reform the defective examination system.

12. To spread secondary education in the areas where it has not gone and to provide technical and vocational education at the secondary level.

13. Objectives for University Education :

(i) To develop technical and vocational education at this stage.

(ii) To organize laboratories, libraries and other equipments.

(iii) To be careful in the opening of new Universities.

(iv) To effect improvement in the post-graduate courses, research and training.

(v) To establish some independent research centres within the control of universities.

(vi) To provide opportunities for part-time education and correspondence courses.

(vii) To spread literacy and adult education.

(viii) To give facilities to students for sports and games.

(ix) To give adequate attention to the education of children of minorities.

(x) To reorganize a uniform system of education for the whole country.

(xi) To introduce the 10+2+3 system of education in the country.

In fact, we have to admit that a consensus is still to be developed regarding the actual form of Indianization of education. However, the foregoing account explicitly indicates that our national Government and leaders are striving towards Indianization of education.

## IMPORTANT EXPERIMENTS IN INDIAN EDUCATION

After having been subjected to long political and social tyranny under the foreign rulers, a desire to break the shackles of bondage was born in Indians which brought forth the revolt of 1857. This revolt, did not succeed owing to inexperience and lack of universal support. However, while the Britishers succeeded in crushing the Indians physically, yet they could not change the India's mental defiance. The revolution was crushed but the sparks continued to emanate and the fire of revolution remained burning in the hearts of Indians. One of the sparks that emanated from this fire was that of educational revolution. Men in position made efforts to start educational centres that followed the education pattern of Vedic and Buddhist era and were also in keeping with the pattern followed by the other progressive nations of the world. It was decided to impart education of nationalism, co-operation and social unity, besides various other subjects. It aimed at creating in the students love for the country, for society, for independence and for human beings and boycott foreign language, foreign dress, communalism and untouchability. Some such institutions were founded that did not have any interests in the Government financial help and its educational policy. Among these were the Viswa-Bharati, Vanasthali Vidyapeeth, Gurukul Kangri, Jamia Milia, Aurobindo Ashram, S.N.D.T. University, Vidya Bhavan, Udaipur etc. Although these institutions had people's inner sympathy, they did not receive their solid and open support because of the Government's wrath. But with the appearance of Mahatma Gandhi on the political horizon of the country and also of a number of political parties, these institutions received encouragement. The courageous among the public also gave their full support and co-operation to them. During the British rule these institutions continued their struggle for life in the hope of a better future atmosphere and started developing after the country achieved freedom.

## 1. VISWA BHARTI UNIVERSITY (SHANTINIKETAN)

### Ideological Background

The English system of education aimed at strengthening the British rule in India. It produced a class which adopted the English dress, language and culture. All this was disliked by another section of Indians. Rabindranath Tagore disliked the English schools and its education system. He considered that English system of education is opposed to Indian traditions and far away from reality. English pattern of education had not the quality of establishing co-ordination and educating the soul, heart and mind of an Indian. No spiritual relation was possible between the teacher and the taught. Hence, Tagore cherished an ideal educational centre where the education could be conducted in accordance with the Indian traditions. Tagore was a poet of Nature and had faith in the educational system of ancient Vedic period — the Ashram system and the pattern adopted in the universities of Nalanda and Taxila.

### Establishment

Tagore's father Maharshi Devendranath Tagore was an ardent follower of Brahmo Samaj. He established an Ashram at Bolepur, a place nearly 100 miles away from the crowded city of Calcutta. He built here a temple and laid out a garden. Here he spent his time in prayer and worship. This place was so charming and natural in atmosphere that Maharshi Devendranath Tagore found himself in absolute peace whenever he went there. On account of this sentimental reason he named it as Shanti Niketan, *i.e.*, an abode of peace. Rabindranath Tagore saw this Ashram for the first time at the age of eleven years. He found in his father's Ashram established for God's worship an ideal place for running an educational centre. He was so much enamoured by the atmosphere of this place that he converted it into an educational centre as soon as he got an opportunity to do so.

### Methods of Teaching

When Rabindranath attained youth he had to spend his time at Shanti Niketan for looking after the affairs of his Zamindari. He had to visit the neighbouring villagers. He got an opportunity to know the villagers, their sorrows and comforts; their education and other affairs. Everywhere he found shortage and poverty. This created in him a desire to work for villagers' uplift and welfare. With the consent of his father, he opened an independent school in 1901 with no control of the Government or the education code. The rules and the pattern of education of this school were based on Tagore's own ideas. In the beginning he had only five students and he himself was their teacher. The contact between the teacher and the taught, their dresses and every other thing aimed at acquiring knowledge. Tagore was totally against teaching subjects without the will of the students. He gave total freedom to his students in pursuing studies according to their tastes and aptitudes. His sole job was to give proper guidance to the students and create in them a desire for acquiring knowledge.

### Finance and Administration

Gradually as the number of students increased the financial problems arose. Tagore met the expenditure of the school from his personal earnings, a major part of royalties from his books and money from awards. In 1922 when the number of students considerably increased, the problem arose about opening new departments, setting out the programmes and framing of rules. Tagore named the institution as Viswa Bharati Vidyapeeth and laid down its object. In order to facilitate teaching, several departments were opened and each was given the name of Bhavan (school). Its main departments were Shiksha Bhavan, Kala Bhavan, Vidya Bhavan, Sangeet Bhavan, Shilp Bhavan, China Bhavan and Sri Niketan.

### Various Departments

1. *Shiksha Bhavan* : In this department general education and general knowledge is taught which is compulsory for students.

2. *Kala Bhavan* : It includes constructive work relating to arts and making different kinds of pictures.

3. *Vidya Bhavan* : Under this department comes the study of ancient, modern and other languages, literature and philosophy, *i.e.* the study of Sanskrit, Pali, Hindi, Bengali, Urdu languages and literature of Vedic, Buddhist and Gupta period; foreign languages like Arabic, Persian etc. and researchers relating to them.

4. *Sangeet Bhavan* : Under this is taught music (vocal and instrumental), dance and acting.

5. *Shilp Bhavan* : Under this department come constructive works relating to various arts and crafts.

6. *China Bhavan* : Under this department the students are taught the Chinese languages, its literature and the culture and civilization of China. Chinese students are taught Indian culture, Sanskrit language and literature.

7. *Sri Niketan* : Under this department subjects relating to society are taught, besides, traditional Indian industries like agriculture, animal husbandry, village industries and village uplift work. Students are also expected to do research work. They are encouraged to develop contact with other sections of the society. Sri Niketan has been divided into two departments. Under the first department come village industries and village organizations with their problems relating to finances, society, public welfare and health etc. The students are acquainted with these problems and taught how to remedy them. The second is the Department of Cottage Industries. Under it the students are encouraged to learn and develop cottage industries. They are asked to chalk out programmes for their expansion. They are taught various home industries like utensil making, carpentry, book-binding, spinning, weaving, tailoring, embroidery, tannery etc.

**Aims of Education**

The aim of education imparted at Viswa-Bharati University is to give a practical shape to those high ideals of Tagore which represent the highest in education of the East and West. Tagore had immense faith in the Buddhist education as reflected in the education of eastern countries like China and Japan. Due to his visit to Europe and America he was also influenced by the independent education system prevailing in those countries. There, instead of burdening the students with conventional education, the boys are encouraged to acquire knowledge and develop the instinct of inquisitiveness and learning. This factor dominated the educational policy of Viswa-Bharati. Tagore gave more importance to national and foreign literature, society and philosophy as compared to any other particular subject.

**Aims of education at Viswa-Bharati**

1. To make Viswa-Bharati a unit of human education where the educational system be patterned as to contain every good aspect of other progressive nations of the world so that it may become capable of removing differences between nations, races, communities and sects and establish international and inter-social harmony.
2. To study various mental tendencies with different angles and to make comparative analysis of various ways of realizing truth.
3. To make efforts in order to establish co-ordination between the culture, civilization and philosophy of western countries and those of India.
4. To establish in the world one cultural unit and peace through the exchange of mutual thoughts between Eastern and Western countries.
5. To study the basis of culture of all Eastern countries in order to bring a basic unity between them.
6. To study thoughts, ideologies and philosophy of different communities, sects and religions in order to make Viswa-Bharati an educational centre of civilization, culture and traditions.
7. To enable Viswa-Bharati to make education available to every one

irrespective of caste and religion and to observe strict impartiality in the selection of students, teachers and workers.

**Programmes of Viswa-Bharati**

The Viswa-Bharati University has been founded in open natural surroundings. Very good hostel arrangements have been made for students. Major portion of education having been based on thinking, longer periods are not provided for classroom study, as is done in other schools. Educational programmes apply both to the schools and the hostel. Indian traditions are followed in fixing times for breakfast, lunch and rest. The daily routine of the school starts at 4.30 in the morning and finishes at 9 in the night. Community study and teaching take place between 6.30 a.m. and 10.30 a.m. in the morning and 2 p.m. to 4 p.m. in the afternoon. Every one has to get up at 4.30 a.m. and is allowed time upto 6.15 for toilets, cleaning their rooms, exercise, bath and prayers. After that there are lectures till 10.30 a.m. The time between 10.30 a.m. to 1.p.m. is fixed for taking food and rest. From 1 p.m. to 2 p.m. the boys are allowed personal study. From 2 p.m. to 4 p.m. again there are lectures. The time between 4 p.m. to 5 p.m. is fixed for toilets, cleaning of rooms and breakfast. From 5 p.m. to 6 p.m. the students are required to attend games and sports and other health building activities. All students and teachers sit under trees and enjoy lectures which are generally interesting. The time after 6.p.m. is for taking food and rest.

**Shri Niketan : Village Organization**

In the programmes of Shri Niketan is included an exhaustive programme of village industries and organisation. Subjects, relating to village development and village industries, such as, agriculture, animal husbandry, cottage industries and village welfare are included in it. It seeks to bring students in contact with village life, to understand their problems and extend their co-operation in solving them. The students go to villages, study their problems, discuss them amongst themselves to find out their solutions and then again go to villages to tell the village people about necessary guidance. They also move in villages to observe the effect of their advice and guidance. Research work is conducted in this university on village problems. In addition to the above, there are many other minor works relating to village welfare, such as village sanitation and hygiene, encouraging villagers to do all their work with their own hands, developing the social and co-operative spirit amongst them, and how to sell them on good prices, to tell them simple and necessary things of animal husbandry, to educate them and to create in them a community consciousness. For executing the above programmes training camps are held in villages, where the village people are given training in various village industries, handicrafts, home and cottage industries, agricultural methods and animal husbandry, first aid, elementary features of first aid and sanitation, scouting, games and sports, physical exercises and drama, etc.

Under the village development and village organization scheme come the agriculture and animal husbandry departments where the breeds of cattle are improved. The neighbouring village people are allowed to get benefit by this work.

The dairy of this department provides pure milk, butter and ghee to Shanti Niketan. Under the agriculture department farming is done through improved and scientific method and guidance in this respect is given to villagers. They are encouraged to adopt modern methods of agriculture. Village youths are also trained.

In the year 1951 the Union Government recognized the Viswa-Bharati University and started giving financial assistance. Since then it has become a Central university.

## 2. GURUKUL EDUCATION

Swami Dayanand founded the Arya Samaj in order to free the Indian society and the country from slavery and for the rehabilitation of Aryan civilization and culture. He pointed out the need for the Gurukul education system in order to free the society from the English pattern of education and its inherent defects. Gurukul literally means the family of the teacher. Gurukul education means that type of educational system where the pupil establishes a permanent relation with his teacher, becomes a part of his family and acquires knowledge from him. Gurukul education represents India's ancient educational system and is based on the Ashram system. It was established at Kangri, Hardwar, Dehradun, Sasni, Baroda and at some other places by the local branches of Arya Pratinidhi Sabha.

Swami Dayanand made a detailed analysis of the defects and virtues of the English education. The English system of education went against Indian culture and traditions. Its biggest defect was that it made Indians followers of Western culture. Dayananda considered the study of India's old language and culture as necessary for every Indian so that he may know the glorious past of India's culture and civilization and also study Vedas that symbolized the country's past glorious achievements. There was no originality in the Sanskrit institutions of Dayanand's time. The character of teachers did not possess that much of sacrifice and devotion which was necessary and was found in the Gurus of ancient India. These Sanskrit schools only taught Sanskrit. The number of students in these Sanskrit schools was very low.

Keeping in view the changed conditions of the country, Swami Dayanand Saraswati implemented a reformed ancient Gurukul system of education. A student after attaining a certain age may live in Gurukul till he completed his education. During the period of his residence in Gurukul, the student was expected to consider Gurukul as his own home and Guru as his father. He was to lead a simple and hard life observing perfect celebacy. The teachers were expected to watch the education of every individual student, love him, shower affection over him and be impartial towards him. Uniformity was to be observed in the living standard and food of students. More emphasis was to be laid on building character and health. Education was to be imparted in natural surroundings away from the din and bustle of the cities. Separate education was recommended for boys and girls. Character, health building and discipline were emphasised more than literary education in the case of girls also. This was a co-ordination between the ancient and the modern, the Indian and the Western. The syllabi included teaching of astronomy, history, geography and science alongwith that of Sanskrit, Hindi and English languages. Study and teaching of Vedas was an important part of the curriculum. Development of Ayurved and provision of research were also some of the features of the Gurukul system as recommended by Swami Dayanand.

**Gurukul Kangri, Hardwar**

The biggest Gurukul in India, a central university today, consists of more than 2,000 students at present. It was established in 1902 by the Arya Pratinidhi Sabha, Punjab and founded by Swami Shardhha Nand, the most notable amongst Swami Dayanand's disciples. In 1924 it was transferred from Hardwar to Kangri, a place nearby. Boys between the age of six and eight years are admitted in this institution and they go back to their homes after completing 14 years of education. Students may also stay for two years more to acquire the degree of 'Vidya Vachaspati'. Education in this institution follows the lines advocated by Swami Dayanand. The students in Gurukul live like students of ancient Gurukul Ashrams of India. They have to lead a life of simplicity, hard work and celibacy upto the age of 25 years. They have to perform regularly religious rites like Yagna, Sandhya, Prayers, Havan etc. Students are encouraged to become religious minded. There is a very big laboratory for teaching and carrying on research in Ayurveda. The medicines prepared here sell all over the country.

Gurukul has many branches. Education upto secondary stage is imparted at Kurukshetra. Girls are educated under the control of Gurukul at Mahila Mahavidyalaya, Dehradun. The students, have to learn their lessons and read them out the next day before the teacher. They are promoted on the basis of annual report. More importance is given to health and physical exercises in programmes outside the class-room. Education is free. The expenditure is met by the Punjab Arya Pratinidhi Sabha and through Central Government grants. Examinations are held as in other residential universities.

A Gurukul for men was founded in 1902 at Sikandrabad and later transferred to Vrindaban. It is managed by the U.P. Arya Pratinidhi Sabha. The programmes and arrangements at this Gurukul are like the one at Kangri.

Two other Gurukuls for girls worth mentioning are Kanya Gurukul, Sasni (U.P.) and Arya Kanya Mahavidyalaya, Baroda. They also follow the programmes laid for other Gurukuls at Kangri and Vrindaban. In the Gurukuls for girls mostly subjects relating to arts are taught, besides general education. Rules regarding conduct and control are also compulsory for girls as is the case with boys.

## 3. SRI AUROBINDO ASHRAM (PONDICHERRY)

**Objectives**

The Ashram was founded at Pondicherry in the year 1910 by saint Sri Aurobindo to practise Yoga and Sadhana. Here a family of eight Sadhaks started living. The main aim of Aurobindo's Sadhana was 'complete Yoga' and 'complete education'. The programme under this aim was to chalk out a line for the achievement of 'world welfare' through the study and deep thinking of ancient

Indian philosophy of life and spiritualism to awaken in the man enlightenment, power and consciousness through 'sadhana' and Yoga truth to develop the instinct of devotion to God and deep thinking so that man may conquer his 'self' and may rise to become one with God. 'Complete education' also aims at studying the spiritualism and philosophy of life of Indians and non-Indians as it existed at various times and stages striking a balance between them and making the Ashram an international education centre. Sri Aurobindo had more faith in spiritualism. He believed that the development of man's inherent powers was the main aim of education.

**Development**

In Sri Aurobindo Ashram, persons of all ages, caste and religion who were influenced by Aurobindo's philosophy started living like one family. In 1920 there came a French lady to this Ashram now known as 'The Mother'. With her co-operation and efforts, the Ashram expanded considerably. Its name spread far and wide and people from Western countries came and joined it. Till 1942, this Ashram remained a centre of spiritualism and Sadhana. New persons came and started living like a family in the open atmosphere of this Ashram. They were completely free. They lived in buildings built at distances and observed a prescribed code of conduct. Provisions in the Ashram existed for meeting the needs of Ashramites. People observed the tradition of doing their work with their own hands.

**Ashram School**

As many members of the Ashram lived with their families, a primary school was founded in 1943 for the education of children living in the Ashram. In this school the children were acquainted with the spiritualism of Aurobindo besides general education. In the beginning there were only 32 students in this school. In course of time other children of Pondicherry influenced by the objectives of the Ashram also started joining the school. As a result of an increase in the strength of the students the institution expanded and its education was increased. English, French and German were taught. Provisions were made for the study of various subjects relating to literature, science and art. All the teachers of this school belong to Ashram families. They are not paid any salary. According to Ashram tradition their family expenses are met by the Ashram.

Examinations are not held in this institution. Its educational standards are neither recognized by any educational council nor by any university. The students are promoted to higher class on the basis of annual report and conduct. However, the Education Departments of India and France have recognized the higher secondary education of this Ashram as equivalent to their secondary education standard for appearing in some examinations. Those students who want to appear in the equivalent examinations have been provided the facility of studying other subjects prescribed for the examination. Unlike other institutions there exist no hostel facilities in the Ashram, as the children either belong to Ashram families or to those in the neighbourhood. However, if any particular student needs hostel accommodation some arrangements are made for him by the Ashram management.

Alongwith the general knowledge and education of other subjects the students are encouraged to develop their individuality to develop collectively and cultivate the tendency of independent living. Nursery education system is provided for small children. Students are divided into different sections for teaching purposes. The classification of students is done on the basis of standard of knowledge, capacity and aptitude and the medium of instruction.

**Sri Aurobindo International University Centre**

After the death of Sri Aurobindo in 1950 the Aurobindo International University was founded with the object of the study of spiritualism, Yoga, mathematics, philosophy and social science, etc. Its objects were to achieve co-ordination between Western and the oriental education and to develop mutual good relations. It is the bigger form of Ashram school and is open to people of every religion, race, nationality, sect and caste. The education at this Ashram which represents the ideas of Sri Aurobindo is an experiment wherein efforts are made to co-ordinate the ancient and the modern, the Western and the oriental educational systems.

## 4. JAMIA MILIA ISLAMIA

In the year 1920 Jamia Milia Islamia was founded at Aligarh by prominent Muslim leaders with the object of extending co-operation to national movement and establishing Hindu-Muslim unity. It also aimed to put in practice Mahatma Gandhi's ideas regarding education. Dr. Ansari and Hakim Ajmal Khan were more prominent among these Muslims. Through their ceaseless efforts this institution was transferred from Aligarh to Delhi, the centre of political activities. This institution sought to provide Muslims an educational system based on religious background for establishing unity among them. It aimed at developing in them the spirit of nationalism to raise them above narrow communalism and conservatism and bring them to consider themselves as a part of the nation, co-operation in the national struggle for independence and welfare of the country; living in harmony with the followers of other religions and contributing in creating an atmosphere of peace and plenty in the country.

In 1928 the management of Jamia Milia Islamia was handed over to its staff. The teachers and other office-holders formed a council named 'Anjumane Talime Mille' for managing education. All the members of this council took a vow to work on a fixed minimum salary of Rs. 150 for the next 20 years and not to demand any increment in their salaries. In 1938 the name of the council was changed to Jamia Milia Islamia Council and got registered according to law. Since then, this institution has continued to march on the road to progress. In the sphere of Basic and Adult education its programmes have proved a success. It consists of the following :

1. *Residential Primary School* : This primary school is based on Wardha Scheme of Basic Education wherein efforts are made for the development of a child's creative and artistic faculties, besides developing personal relationship between the teacher and the taught. In this school besides general education,

students are required to practise physical labour through handicrafts, mechanical work and gardening. A poultry farm, sweets-cum-fruit shop, a bank and a book and stationery shop have been provided in this school.

2. *Residential Multi-purpose High School* : The students of this school receive general education to training in advanced type of manual labour, *e.g.* radio repair and other not very complicated machines, tailoring, carpentry etc. For displaying the products of students there is a section named 'Delhi Museum'.

3. *Residential College :* In this institution, the boys are given practical training in social education, public works, agriculture etc. Facilities to students are available for the study of social and arts subjects. The students of social science go to neighbouring villages to do social education work. They develop and establish contacts with village people.

4. *Training Institute for Teachers*.: This institute imparts training to teachers in accordance with the principles of Basic education at the lower and higher stage. Successful student-teachers are awarded certificates or diplomas.

5. *Institute of Rural Economics and Sociology* : Studies and researches on village society and village problems are carried out in this institute. Successful students are awarded post-graduate degrees.

6. *Institute of Rural Education* : Research work on basic education in rural areas is conducted in this institute. Discussions are held and programmes chalked out for the guidance, direction, control, curriculum, teaching methods, books, arts and crafts etc. of rural basic schools. Evaluation of products made is also undertaken.

7. *Children's Brotherhood* : Under this come the activities of creating suitable atmosphere and provision of facilities for games, sports and other extra-curricular activities of children. This institute also carries out the programmes of public children welfare schemes.

8. *Other Sections* : There is an institute for producing books on history and political science for secondary and higher secondary schools. Maktab Jamia Limited prepares and publishes text books for all standards in Jamia Milia. The Institute of Art Education trains art teachers for all standards. The Institute of Adult Education prepares programmes, literature and books for adult education centre. By the collective co-operation of all these institutes, Jamia Milia makes its contribution in the Basic, adult and rural education in the country.

## 5. VIDYA BHAVAN SOCIETY, UDAIPUR

Managed by Vidya Bhavan Committee, Vidya Bhavan, Udaipur is an independent educational institution in Rajasthan. In it exist arrangements for all stages of education from primary to higher. Dr. Mohan Singh Mehta established it in the shape of a small institution in 1931. During the last 65 years it has made tremendous progress. The original institution established by Dr. Mehta included a junior secondary school comprising of two separate nursery and primary sections and a higher secondary school for secondary and college education. In addition, today there is a higher basic school on the pattern of Wardha the scheme that makes programmes and undertakes education expansion work in rural areas. There is also an institute for teachers training where teachers for secondary education are trained for B.Ed. and M.Ed. degrees. Arrangements also exist for research and Ph.D. affiliated to the Rajasthan University. There is also a special social service training course and an institute of handicraft under which teachers are trained in different types of handicrafts.

The main aim of Vidya Bhavan is to undertake social service, social reform, village development through the medium of special programmes of this institution and work for public consciousness. For the purposes, Dr. Mehta established a small institution which made tremendous progress within a span of a few years and is a big institution now. Experiments and research work are conducted there throughout the year. At present, this institution gets financial assistance from the Union Government and also enjoys its patronage and protection. It is a successful experiment in social service and rural development through the media of education. The students and teachers are encouraged to develop social outlook. It has made commendable contribution in the sphere of expansion of basic education.

## 6. S. N. D. T. WOMEN'S UNIVERSITY, POONA

Srimati Nathibai Damodar Thackersey University named after the name of the mother of a prominent Bombay businessman Sri Thackersey who rendered considerable financial assistance to it. This institution was founded by Professor Karve. The object behind opening this institution in the beginning was to give protection to Hindu widows, to control their natural urges and instincts through education and to afford them opportunity to make proper use of their time. After some time, on the suggestion and co-operation of the local public, a school for girls was started in the premises of this institution and few years after a secondary school was opened.

This institution was established in the shape of an independent school. The curricula at all the stages of education were based on the ideas and thinking of Professor Karve. It provides for women's education for primary and secondary teacher's training. Having felt the need of higher education for women, graduate and post-graduate classes were introduced in 1916 and it was declared an independent university. The Government recognized this university in 1951. Girl's schools controlled by this university are today spread all over the Maharashtra and Gujarat States. Women's colleges affiliated to it have been opened in prominent cities like Bombay, Ahmedabad, Baroda, Poona, etc.

### Aims and Objectives

Professor Karve held the view that education should meet the requirements of one's future life. As the responsibilities and duties of men and women differed in their social life, the subjects of education and programmes should also differ in their cases. The educational programmes and subjects for a girl's education should help her in becoming a successful wife, efficient housewife and a capable mother. Therefore, while prescribing the curriculum for girls, priority was given to such subjects which helped in the development of good womanly qualities in them.

**Form and Administration**

This university is the examining, controlling and regulation making body for its affiliated schools and colleges. It has been recognized by the Government. It makes arrangements for higher secondary education and teachers' training for all standards. It prescribes the curriculum and programmes relating to women's education and gives certificates, diplomas and degrees for all kinds of education and training. It is a successful experiment in the sphere of women's education for developing in women their natural qualities.

## 7. VANASTHALI VIDYAPEETH, RAJASTHAN

Sri Hiralal Shastri, a social worker of Rajasthan founded Vanasthali Vidyapeeth, an Ashram at a place 45 miles away from Jaipur city, was surrounded with illiterate and poor villagers. Sri Shastri made his Ashram a centre for social service and carried on his activities of social service and social reforms from there. In order to perpetuate the memory of his beloved daughter who died at this Ashram he opened a girls' school in the Ashram. This school rapidly developed. In 1942 higher classes were introduced in this school and it was baptised as Vanasthali Vidyapeeth. After the country attained freedom every possible help was extended to this institution. Despite curriculum, programmes, standard of education being similar to other institution it is recognized as a successful experiment in the sphere of women's education because of special emphasis laid on student's health, conduct, simplicity, thrift, social and national outlook, irrespective of caste, creed and religion.

Nearly 1000 girls are receiving education in different classes in this Vidyapeeth. Education upto M.A standard is available here. Arrangements for education and training exist from the pre-primary to the university standard. The education from intermediate to M.A. is under the control of Rajasthan University. There is also a provision for three years' secondary education as prescribed by the Union Government. Multi-purpose curriculum is included at the secondary stage of education with a two years' course. Provision of child education exists at the pre-primary stage. General education is prescribed from primary classes to class eight.

Vanasthali Vidyapeeth is exclusively for girls. Despite the curriculum and subjects being of a general nature efforts are made to inculcate in girls an Indian outlook, high ideals and co-operative spirit, courage and enthusiasm. Training in horse riding and use of arms is also imparted. Education, in this institution has five objectives : morality, development of intellect, development of artistic talents, development of cultural and social outlook and development of healthy body. In addition, girls are taught to develop a spirit of nationalism, dignity of labour, co-operation in social and public work, respect of their duties and responsibilities towards the society, love for nation, love for society and taking part in all kinds of social service programmes. All possible freedom needed to a girl is given during the education here. The atmosphere of the school is Ashram-like. Special emphasis is laid on the study of arts subjects.

## QUESTIONS FOR EXERCISE

1. What is the meaning of Indianization of education? What efforts have been made towards the realization of this goal in any country ?
2. How can we Indianize our education and why? Give your constructive suggestions on this issue.
3. Discuss the objectives and functioning of the Viswa-Bharati University.
4. How does the Gurukul Kangri of Hardwar maintain the tradition of the Gurukuls of Ancient India? Explain with examples.
5. Describe the purposes and working of the Sri Aurobindo Ashram, Pondicherry.
6. Describe the objectives and functioning of Jamia Milia Islamia, Delhi.
7. How is the Vidya Bhavan institution different from other institutions in the country? Give examples.
8. Write short notes on — (i) S.N.D.T. Women's University, Poona and (ii) Vanasthali Vidyapeeth, Rajasthan.

# 35

# EDUCATION FOR NATIONAL AND EMOTIONAL INTEGRATION

National and emotional integration is of paramount importance for the security of the country in a nation like India where one finds people with different religions, castes, creeds and languages. While variety enriches and helps the development of a country, misguided and unscrupulous hands sometimes misuse it to threaten the very existence of the nation. India is passing through a difficult phase at present. The country is plagued by the evils of linguism, communalism, sectarianism, provincialism, regionalism and some other evils. Unscrupulous peole are sacrificing national interest for individual or regional interest. In order to establish true democracy we have to ensure that there is unity in diversity and that diversity does not get an upper hand to strike at the very root of the national existence. The demand for lingual States, border disputes, occasional communal riots, Urdu controversy etc., indicate that the nation is not proceeding on the right path of national and emotional integration.

The political parties have not proved of any help in the achievement of national and emotional integration. On the contrary, they have vitiated the atmosphere by their groupism and unprincipled alliances. They have placed their own interests above the national interests. The nation has yet to cover many milestones in the direction of national and emotional integration.

## UNITY IN INDIA

1. **Political Unity** : Unity in diversity has remained a significant feature of the Indian sub-continent since time immemorial. Our great ancestors established places of pilgrimage in all the four corners of the country in order to achieve cultural integration throughout the country and increase contact between the people of different regions. Thus Badrinath, Kedarnath, Rameshwaram, Dwarika and Jagannathpuri are the most important centres of pilgrimage established with this point of view. The people of east go to west and *vice versa*. People of South go to North and those of North to South. This provides the people of India an excellent opportunity for visiting other parts of their country, exchange ideas and be familiar with various cultures.

Hindu religion has called Indian rivers sacred whether they may be flowing in

North to South or East to West. Ganga, Yamuna, Gomati, Krishna, Kaveri, Godavari, Narmada, Bramhaputra are some of the many rivers considered sacred and a dip in them is prescribed in the religion. Various mountains and hills, too, have been given places of honour by Hindu religion. Many important towns situated at different places have been recognised as places of pilgrimage and centres of culture. Evidently, great sons of India always tried to bind the people of the country in one cultural link.

The sentiment of cultural unity inspired great social and religious leaders to instil in the people a uniform feeling of common citizenship. Due to this feeling of common citizenship whenever the leaders raised their voice for any cause the entire country from North to South and from East to West stood as one person. It was this feeling that united the people of different faiths and ideologies behind the banner of Indian National Congress. The unity which the people of India displayed during the struggle for independence was real. The revolt of 1857 is a brilliant example of people's unity. Dandi March, Salt Satyagraha and Quit India Movements are instances of unity of Indian people which sent a wave of fear in the heart of British rulers. After independence the people of this country demonstrated examplary unity at the time of Chinese aggression in 1962 and Wars with Pakistan in 1965 and 1971. We need to keep the torch of political and national unity lighted forever. We should not allow fissiparous tendencies to take the upper hand.

2. **Emotional Unity** : Emotional unity is a pre-requisite for achieving national unity. The people must first realise that one has to subordinate his individual, social, his community and religious interests to the national interest. Unity cannot be achieved unless these interests are considered secondary to national interest. The people will have to be explained that India has remained one country geographically and historically and has enjoyed a glorious culture of which she can be proud. Any one who visits the Himalayas in the North, the Bay of Bengal in the East, the Kutchha region in West and Cape Comorin in the South is overtaken with a wave of emotion. He is filled with devotion to the country. Similar feelings overtake us when we stand at the banks of great rivers like Ganga, Yamuna, Gomati, Kaveri, Godavari, Narmada, Bramhaputra etc. The sacred water of these river takes our minds back to those days when saints and scholars had been adding new chapters to our cultural history. The mountains and the valleys, the rivers and the springs are the places where Indian culture was born and attained glorious heights. The sages and the seers of ancient India made forests and mountain caves their abode and developed a culture. We have to strengthen this emotional unity for which education is a powerful instrument. It is the duty of our creative artists, poets and scholars to popularize our natural flora and fauna in a manner that every Indian starts taking pride in them. Only education can achieve this goal.

3. **Social Unity** : The Indian society is divided into many sections based on religious, sectarian and financial considerations. This has divided the society into different sections. Sectional interest creates bad blood between different sections of the society. It harms the feeling of brotherhood. This state of affairs is deplorable. It creates obstacle in the path of social and national integration. In order to achieve

national unity it is necessary to bring different sections of the society close to each other.

Community programmes should be organized and people of all shades of life should be invited to participate in these programmes. It should be made clear to all that the community's interests are safe only when national interest is safe and consequently community's interest must remain subordinate to national interest. Indians will have to give up communalism, casteism and religionalism for the sake of achieving social unity. The national interest should be given the prime importance. The slogan should be national interest first and everything else afterwards. This has been the secret of the success of European nations and the U.S.A. In the U.S.S.R. there are numerous languages and sections of society, but the people there give first place to national interest which has enabled them to achieve national unity.

Due to their narrow outlook and self-interest some political parties in India have encouraged fissiparous tendencies like regionalism, communalism, casteism and linguism. Their actions have created obstacles in the way of achieving national unity. In the elections they try to secure votes by exploiting the religious, sectarian and regional sentiments. Almost all parties select candidates on these considerations. This tendency goes entirely against the national unity. It should be curbed before it takes an alarming shape.

4. **Economic Unity** : Disparity in the income of the people is very glaring in India. It has proved a big hurdle in the economic unity of the people. In the same town some are multi-millionaires and some cannot afford even two square meals a day in order to keep their body and soul together. The economic disparity will have to be removed at all cost if we want national unity. The minorities and backward classes will have to be given preferential treatment in matters of education, residence and State services. National integration will receive a big boost if these classes are happy and satisfied.

5. **National Language** : The issue of national language has become a very delicate problem in India. Hindi in Devanagari script has been accepted as the national language under the Constitution. It was to replace English in 1965 but unfortunately language riots broke out in Calcutta and South. In view of these riots the Government have adopted the policy of go slow in respect of the national language. We should wait till the non-Hindi speaking population is in a receptive mood to accept Hindi. We have to explain to the people living in the Southern States that we cannot retain a foreign language as national language. The sooner this is done the better it is for the national unity and the people. The English language is a symbol of slavery though it has its own merits and cannot be completely overlooked. It is also necessary, rather a must, for international contact and advanced and specialized technical and science subjects. However, we cannot afford to neglect our national language which is Hindi in Devanagari script. We will have to adopt and recognize it and make persistent and persusive efforts for its recognition by the non-Hindi areas when convenient to them. These efforts should continue till the entire country accepts Hindi as the national language. But we

should be careful in not pressurising any one and forcing Hindi on those who are yet not mentally prepared for it. In the long run pressure tactics do more harm than good to the cause of national unity.

## EDUCATION FOR NATIONAL INTEGRATION

Education is the most powerful medium for the achievement of national and emotional integration in India. It provides the necessary inspiration. All those who are concerned with education should keep in mind that we have to achieve national and emotional integration through the education of masses. The theme of national and emotional integration should remain at the top in deciding upon the curricula, in the teaching process, in educational centres and programmes, in the appointment of teachers, in the preparation of text-books and in all other educational activities. Such policies should be formulated and implemented as strengthen the cause of national and emotional integration and discourage fissiparous tendencies.

National and emotional integration needs top priority in the present national and international conditions. We need to be ever vigilant on this issue and achieve the goal as early as possible.

## EFFORTS AT INCREASING EMOTIONAL INTEGRATION

It was this question of integration which inspired the Central Education Ministry in 1961 to organise a committee for integration under the chairmanship of Dr. Sampurnanand. This campaign to increase integration had the solid foundation of belief in the principle of unity in diversity. All that is needed is that the younger generation should be educated in this direction through various kinds of programmes. Speaking at the inauguration of the Indian Integration Committee, Sri K L. Shrimali explained the significance of education and commented that if we want to generate a national consciousness in our people, we will have to plan our education accordingly. Education must be so designed as to encourage each participant to think of himself as a responsible part of the Indian nation. Education must take upon itself the responsibility of awakening the younger generation to the truth that, despite obvious external differences, all Indians are the same, emotionally.

Keeping in mind the objective outlined above, the Integration Committee gave following suggestions:

1. **Reorganisation of Syllabi** : In order to reorganise and reshape the syllabi of colleges and universities to accord with the needs of the nation, the committee made the following suggestions:

(i) At the primary stage, stress should be laid upon nationalistic stories, poems, songs, etc.

(ii) At the secondary stage in addition to the other subjects being taught, special attention should be given to the study of national literature, social studies, moral and religious guidance and extra-curricular activities.

(iii) At the university level, the syllabi should include the various social sciences, languages, literatures, cultures and arts. Teachers and students should be given facilities to travel to various parts of the country.

2. **Encouragement to extra-curricular activities** : Besides imparting formal knowledge to the students, the teachers must provide them with the opportunity to take part in such extra-curricular activities which are important from the standpoint of emotional integration. Besides, such programmes must also represent the entire nation. Such programmes help in the development of 'we' feeling, a feeling of unity and sympathy. One example of such programmes is the Inter-University cultural festivals, in which teachers and students participate from all parts of the country.

3. **Improvement of text-books** : It is desirable that text-books on various subjects, and especially on history, should be amended and improved. They should be designed to encourage a sense of emotional unity with people living in other parts of the country. This will also help to check the growth of communal feelings. But it should also be remembered that such amendments should not be made at the cost of truth because such violence to truth is not necessary. That the country is one is an undeniable truth. What is required is an expression of this truth.

4. **Improvements concerning language and script** : In this connection the Committee on Emotional Integration made the following recommendations:

(i) The use of the Roman script should be permitted to increase knowledge of Hindi in certain areas.

(ii) International numerals should be used in every part of the country.

(iii) Arrangements should be made to teach the Devanagri script where it is not known.

(iv) Hindi text-books should also be provided in the regional scripts. Dictionaries using both Hindi and the regional languages should also be prepared.

(v) At the university level, study of Hindi and English literatures should be encouraged so that integration is encouraged and divisive forces checked.

(vi) The rights of the minorities should be protected in formulating a language policy.

In addition to the above list of suggestions, the Committee for Emotional Integration also made certain other suggestions. In schools the daily programme should be started after a community prayer and a ten minute talk, either by the principal or by some respected person, on some subject which may encourage emotional integration. Another way of encouraging emotional integration is to organise a mass meeting of the school once a year and asking the students to take an oath to increase emotional integration. Besides, all subjects and activities likely to lower awareness of differences should be encouraged. In this manner it is possible to create a climate in which all people feel that they are members of one nation. On the negative side, all efforts must be made to destroy all elements which tend to obstruct the growth of emotional integration.

## SUGGESTIONS FOR IMPROVING EMOTIONAL INTEGRATION

Apart from the suggestions outlined above, education can be used in the following suggested ways for improving integration in the country :

1. **Development of an All India Language** : The first condition for increasing emotional integration in the country is that an All India language should be evolved. Hindi is the only language capable of performing this role. Hence, it is desirable that knowledge of this language be made compulsory for every citizen. Government should extend every facility for developing Hindi literature. The development of a national language will not prejudice the interests of regional languages. They should be allowed to pursue their own course. But all communications between the Centre and the States should be conducted in the All-India language. Applicants for administrative jobs in the government should be required to know Hindi, although they may be allowed to take the examination in their regional language.

2. **An All India education policy** : Education is the most effective tool for spreading emotional and national integration. For this reason emotional educational plan should be devised. This plan should aim at providing child with knowledge of the ideas of great men, poets, elders, religious thinkers, etc. Text-books should be prepared under the supervision of the Central Government and provided by it, so that the younger generation may be brought up in an atmosphere of nationalistic fervour. Rules for the appointment of teachers, their pay scales and their conditions of working should be common all over the country. The same syllabi should be applicable to all institutions in the country at the primary, secondary and university levels. All-India organisations like the N. C. C., Scouting, Girl Guides, etc., should be given appropriate encouragement. University education should be through the medium of the national language, even if the students are permitted to answer questions in their mother tongues. In this manner, the objective of national unity or integration can be achieved by evolving an All-India educational plan.

3. **Programmes for increasing national unity** : Many kinds of programmes can be devised for increasing national unity. For example, the cinema can be used to spread the feeling of national unity. Radio and television can also be used equally effectively. All-India competitions and meetings can be organised in various parts of the country to increase national unity. Such programmes help people living in different parts of the country to meet residents of other parts and learn through ideas and understand them. These facilities should be made more common and delegations and tours encouraged. During the last few years special trains made up of farmers of different areas, students and members of Parliament toured the entire country. This helped the cause of national integration. Other programmes similar to these can be organised.

4. **Development of inter-cultural understanding** : In all the programmes outlined above, inter-cultural understanding will be promoted. This helps people to achieve liberality of attitudes to other cultures, an essential precondition of national unity in a country in which there are many cultures.

5. **Role of teachers** : Success of most of these programmes for increasing national unity depends upon teachers. As long as the teachers themselves do not rise above their petty narrow-mindedness and create ideals, there is little hope of the students developing any emotional unity. Hence, it is desirable that national consciousness should first be stirred in the students. For this, teachers from various

parts of the country should be encouraged to meet each other. This can be done through the All-India Teachers' Organisation. Even otherwise, most of the problems may be solved through exchange of ideas. At the same time, a national consciousness will awaken in them. Yet, attention must be paid to reselling the development of a class consciousness among the teachers. The government can make a positive contribution in this direction by organisation of lectures from time to time and distributing literature of this kind.

6. **Governmental efforts** : Governmental effort is essential for bringing success to all the projects outlined above, because without official blessing, there is little that education can achieve. This cannot be doubted because there are many agencies which are working against the development of emotional integration. So long as the government fails to check agencies which encourage linguism, communalism, religious bigotry and other disruptive forces, education will not be able to achieve the goal. One of the first steps in this direction is control over destructive political parties. In every part of the country laws should be enacted to prevent any individual from giving expression to linguism, communalism, casteism, untouchability, etc. This should be followed up by a strict application of these laws.

## COMMITTEE ON EMOTIONAL INTEGRATION (1961)

### Introduction

At the Conference of the Education Ministers held in November 1960, the importance of the role of education in counteracting divisive trends and in fostering unity was stressed. The Conference recommended that a Committee be set up to study the problem and to suggest positive educational measures for promoting integration. This was followed by the appointment of the committee in May 1961 by the Ministry of Education under the chairmanship of Dr. Sampurnanand.

### Terms of Reference

(a) To study the role of education in considering and promoting the processes of emotional integration in national life and to examine the operation of tendencies which come in the way of their development; and

(b) In the light of such study, to advise on the positive educational programmes for youth in general and students in schools and colleges in particular, to strengthen in them the processes of emotional integration.

### Role of Education

Education can play a vital role in strengthening emotional integration. It is felt that education should not only aim at imparting knowledge but should develop all aspects of a student's personality. It should broaden the outlook, foster a feeling of oneness and nationalism and a spirit of sacrifice and tolerance so that narrow group interests are submerged in the larger interests of the country.

### Recommendations

1. *Re-orientation of the curriculum* : The school and college curriculum should be re-oriented to suit the needs of a secular State :

(i) At the primary stage the importance of stories, poems, folklore and teaching of social studies, national anthem and other national songs, has been emphasized.

(ii) At the secondary stage the curriculum should include among other things, the study of language and literature, social studies, moral and religious instruction and co-curricular activities.

(iii) At the university level the study of different social sciences, languages and literature, culture and art and also the exchange of teachers and students have been recommended.

2. *Co-curricular activities* : It is felt that participation in co-curricular activities helps in the growth of a well-balanced and well-adjusted personality. It creates a group feeling of oneness and brotherhood, broadens the outlook and develops a catholicity of spirit and tolerance which are necessary for good citizenship. These activities include common observance and celebration of festivals and events of national importance, sports, educational excursions, towns and picnics, military training like the NCC, ACC, scouts and guides, student camps, debates, symposia, dramatics and youth festivals. The use of audio-visual aids like films, pictures, radio and TV has also been recommended.

3. *Special stress on the teaching of social studies* : The teaching of social studies has been recommended at all levels *i.e.* the primary, secondary and university stages. This would impart knowledge of the geographical, historical and cultural background of the country and of the world as a whole.

4. *Textbooks* : Textbooks should be re-oriented and improved.

5. *Language and script* : (i) The use of the roman script may be permitted in certain areas for an interim period to enable persons to improve their acquaintance with Hindi.

(ii) Throughout India the international numerals must be used.

(iii) To reduce the burden of three scripts Hindi may be learnt in the non-Hindi areas in the regional script.

(iv) To popularize the study of Hindi in non-Hindi speaking areas a beginning may be made with the publication of Hindi books in the Roman script and the compilation of simple dictionaries in Hindi — other languages, also in the Roman script.

(v) Hindi books may be published in the regional script and the compilation of regional language — Hindi dictionaries should be encouraged.

(vi) At the high school stage Hindi must be taught in the Devanagari script, keeping in view the constitutional provision.

(vii) The two link languages — Hindi and English — should be effectively taught at university level so that conditions of emotional and intellectual isolation are not created.

(viii) It is necessary to ensure that in implementing any language policy the rights of minorities are adequately protected.

6. *Uniform for school children* : It is desirable to have a uniform for school children; one common uniform for the whole India is not necessary; schools may have their own preference in regard to colour and pattern.

7. *Singing of national anthem* : Children should be taught to sing the national anthem in unison and behave in a disciplined way when it is sung. They should be taught the meaning of the verses.

8. *Reverence for the national flag* : Students should be told the history of the national flag and taught at the very earliest stage to show reverence to the national flag.

9. *Celebrations of national days* : National days — January 26, August 15 and October 2 — should be celebrated in schools with the full participation of the teachers, the students and the community.

10. *Special talks on the unity and oneness of the country* : Special meetings of the school assembly should be held from time to time and the speakers speak to the children on topics dealing with the unity and oneness of the country.

11. *Taking pledge* : Students may be asked to repeat a pledge twice a year dedicating themselves to the service of their countrymen. A draft of such a pledge in English is given below:

"India is my country, all Indians are my brothers and sisters.

"I love my country, and I am proud of its rich and varied heritage. I shall always strive to be worthy of it.

"I shall give my parents, teachers and all elders respect and treat everyone with courtesy. I shall be kind to animals. To my country and my people, I pledge my devotion. In their well-being and prosperity alone lies my happiness."

12. *Open-air dramas* : Open-air dramas may be staged four times a year by every school. At least one play should be based upon a theme derived from the classics or from the history of ancient India. In predominant Hindu areas there should be some plays dealing with non-Hindu lives and *vice versa*.

13. *Student's exchange and tours* : Such tours should be conducted from one State to another. The inter-State visits, if properly organized, should do much to acquaint both teachers and children with different parts of the country. A network of youth hostels should be set up by all the States in selected places.

14. *School Improvement* : Students should be associated with the cleanliness of the school premises. This would not only increase their pride in it, and loyalty to the school but would also help in improving the school for future students.

15. *Admission* : Admissions to schools, colleges and other educational institutions should not be given on the basis of caste but on the basis of means and merits.

16. *Recognition of institutions* : Recognition should not be given to institutions where divisive tendencies are encouraged.

17. *Freeship and scholarships* : These should be awarded only on the basis of means and merit.

18. *No domiciliary restrictions* : Domiciliary restrictions in regard to migration of students between one State and other should be removed.

19. *Suitable hand-books for teachers* : Suitable hand-books for teachers in the social studies and languages should be published.

20. *All-India award* : An annual all-India award for the best general essay on different States in India should be instituted.

21. *Educational and travel documentaries* : Educational and travel documentaries with particular emphasis on various aspects of Indian scenery, flora and fauna, on various development and reconstruction programmes should be produced for use in schools and these should form a regular feature of the schools.

22. *School projects* : Schools may conduct several projects which improve their general knowledge of the country. For instance 'Know Your Country' project can be undertaken during which children may share in the collection of information about a State in the Indian Union other than their own.

23. *Exchange of professors* : Distinguished professors should also be deputed periodically to different universities so that a large range of students can benefit from their experience.

24. *All India Youth Council :* An all-India youth council should be set up to coordinate all the youth programmes taken up by the Central and State Governments and also to help various agencies to extend their efforts.

25. *Teachers* : The Union Ministry of Education should implement a scheme providing for a national minimum scale of salaries for teachers in the primary, middle and secondary schools.

26. *A Pay Revision Committee* : A Pay Revision Committee consisting of representatives from the Planning Commission, the Ministers of Education and Finance and representatives from the teaching profession, should be immediately set up to work out the full financial implications and operative details of implementing the scheme for a national minimum scale of salaries for teachers with the help of a sub-committee at State levels, if necessary. This work should be completed as expeditiously as possible.

## QUESTIONS FOR EXERCISE

1. Describe the role of education in achieving the goal of national and emotional integration.
2. What are those fissiparous tendencies and elements that create obstacles in the path of national integration? How can education overcome these hurdles? Explain.
3. Describe the recommendation of Committee on Emotional Integration (1961).

# 36

# EDUCATION FOR INTERNATIONAL AND INTER-CULTURAL UNDERSTANDING

## NEED FOR AN INTERNATIONAL ATTITUDE IN EDUCATION

Inernationalism implies the awareness of all human beings as members of a single human society, irrespective of national boundaries and other differences. The modern period has seen a remarkable transformation of the means of transport and communications, the tremendous spreading of education, the notable increase in the mutual contact between citizens of the world. As a consequence the world has shrunk in size, which in itself has led to local problems influencing areas and peoples far removed. For example, it is now being recognised that the excessive increase in poverty in any one part of the world is almost certain to affect the economic conditions of other countries as well. If peace and prosperity are to be created in one country, it becomes necessary to create good living conditions all over the world. Now that man has set foot on the moon, there is an increasing demand for international understanding. Besides, the two world wars of the century have enforced the useful lesson that, in this age of nuclear weapons, the people of the world have to live and die together. Communist and non-communist countries both feel that they cannot hope to maintain their status in the world, unless they make efforts to spread their ideology in other countries. The failure of the League of Nations depressed the desire for internationalism. For this reason its successor, the United Nations, is aiming at cooperation not merely in the field of politics but also in the economic, educational and cultural spheres. UNESCO, one specialized body of the U. N. O., is dedicated to the spread of international understanding through the medium of education in every part of the world.

## INTERNATIONALISM IN MODERN INDIAN EDUCATION

Modern educational philosophers in India have supported the notion of internationalism for a specific and unique reason. This attitude is based on the philosophy of the ancient Upanishads which taught that God lives as soul in the bodies of all human beings, irrespective of differences of race, nation, area, sex, etc. Vedanta philosophy provides the strong foundation for it. Sri Aurobindo was a staunch internationalist, in spite of his very emphatic expression of nationalism. He expressed the opinion that, just as the ideal nation is one in which the individual's freedom and perfection is harmonized with the development and organisation of society, the freedom and development of an international society should be harmonized with the development and perfection of humanity in its entirety.

Of the many modern thinkers, Rabindranath Tagore expressed such vehement support for internationalism that people misunderstood him and took him to be opposed to nationalism. His creation, Shanti Niketan, is the concrete manifestation of the international attitude in education. Dr. Radhakrishnan, the Chairman of the Indian Universities Commission drew attention to the need for an international attitude in education. He expressed regret at the failure of the current educational system to propagate feelings of internationalism and universal brotherhood. An educational system should be such that it may create a new generation of individuals who believe that all human beings are brothers and that differences of caste, region, community or nation have no significance. True education leads to internationalism. Dr. Radhakrishnan commented that we must make efforts for the unity of the world. We should try to create a new generation which has faith in the nobility of intellectual life, in purity, in a feeling of brotherhood towards humanity, in love and peace. There should be no national educational plan which proves an obstacle in the growth and spread of this feeling. In fact, there is no opposition between nationalism and internationalism, but if it becomes necessary to make comparisons, both Rabindranath Tagore and Dr. Radhakrishnan incline towards internationalism. Education must aim at making every man and woman a citizen of the world, by developing within each one such thinking, concentration, insight and intellectuality or spirituality that they can perform useful roles in life. Peace in the world can be expected only when this ideal is pursued by education in every country. These ideas of Dr. Radhakrishnan have found echoes in every part of the world, and there is consensus of opinion among educationists everywhere that training men and women in internationalism through education is the only way of avoiding a Third World War.

## PROPAGATION OF INTERNATIONALISM BY UNESCO

The role of UNESCO in spreading internationalism is notable. This body is special organ of the U.N.O. dedicated to the spread of international understanding. It has been said in its constitution that "since wars begin in the minds of men, it is in the minds of men that the defence of peace must be constructed." The breadth of its scope can be judged from its name, the United Nations Education, Scientific and Cultural Organization. In order to achieve its goal of spreading international understanding, it performs the following functions:

1. This organization transmits knowledge of the literature, art, science, etc., of one nation to all other nations.

2. It also provides many opportunities to thinkers, scientists, teachers and artists to meet each other and exchange ideas and put forward creative plans for promoting world peace and justice. Efforts are made to prevent the people from being influenced too much by narrow parochial thinking.

3. UNESCO also seeks to improve the mutual relations between various nations and remove fear, suspicion and lack of confidence between them.

4. Considerable financial aid is given by UNESCO to improve the teaching facilities in backward and exploited countries.

5. UNESCO also provides guidance in modifying texts prescribed in various syllabi in order to make the books more internationally-oriented. The organisation does its best to root out illiteracy and lack of education from the poor countries.

6. In order to promote international understanding, UNESCO provides facilities to students and teachers to visit abroad and to exchange views and also gain experience in international living.

7. It also organises art and literature exhibitions at the international level to promote feelings of love and friendship.

8. Research is also encouraged by UNESCO, for it provides financial help and other facilities to researchers.

It is evident from the varied functions of UNESCO that the organisation is particularly aiming at creating an international feeling in education but this objective cannot be achieved by UNESCO alone. For this it will be necessary to make proper arrangements for education in many countries.

## SYNTHESIS OF THE NATIONAL AND INTERNATIONAL POINTS OF VIEW

Here it is essential to understand how the national and international standpoints can be synthesized and reconciled with each other. Nationalistic feeling attaches the greatest importance to the nation's interests. Inspired by such feelings individuals are even willing to lay down their lives in order to protect the honour of their nations. It is only by awakening such feelings that many nations have gathered so much military power and have attempted to extend their own frontiers. But, if carefully examined, it will be seen that this is a distorted form of nationalism. In its best form nationalism does not oppose internationalism. It has helped various nations to collect power in their hands in order to throw off the yoke of a foreign nation. Nationalism has played a vital role in throwing out colonialism. But despite these great advantages and positive qualities, nationalism underwent a change and became colonialism itself. As a result of the nationalistic feelings, people focused their eye on their own country and lost interest in anything other than their own sectarian interests. Just as any interest turns into an ism by becoming narrow and thus harms the more liberal interests, in the same way, this narrow-minded nationalism has become an obstacle in the development of internationalism. It is this nationalism which inspired many nations of Europe to establish big colonies in Africa and Asia. Later, Germany and Italy became jealous of the English and French colonies, a feeling which manifested itself in the First and Second World Wars. After the First World War, an international organisation known as the League of Nations was established, but it came to a premature end due to the narrow nationalism of its members. It was the precursor of the United Nations Organisation which came into being after the second experience of a global conflict. Despite the lessons learnt earlier, many nations continue to constitute a very grave threat to international peace because of their own interests. One concrete example of this is South Africa which continues to exercise its policy of apartheid, despite the many warnings given by the U.N.O. It is now universally felt that it is only the distorted form of nationalism which hinders the growth of internationalism.

On the other hand, healthy nationalism is a boon to internationalism. As has already been pointed out, it is only nationalism which has inspired many nations to throw off foreign rule. It is nationalism which has helped even the smallest nations of the world to raise their hands and stand proudly by the side of their mightier brothers. In fact, nationalism can be used or misused by human beings. The two international wars of the present century should be sufficient to teach human beings that there is need for balance and synthesis between nationalism and internationalism. There is a parallel to be drawn here. Individuals sacrifice the interests of family, race, town, etc., for the benefit of the nation, because they realise that these also gain when the nation gains. In the same way, national interests can be allied with international goals. National interests can be restricted for this, and it cannot be questioned that progress of isolated groups also depends very much upon the progress of the world as a whole. This fact must be realized first of all by the rich, powerful and the prosperous nations, because on them lies the onus of the world's development. In fact, it is the realization of their responsibility which is persuading the rich nations to extend a helping hand to their poor neighbours, but when some political strings are attached to the aid given, it defeats the purpose of encouraging internationalism. It must be remembered that there would be no international feeling in the absence of a national one, for it is the latter which inspires the former. No nation should become an obstacle to the progress of another nation in trying to achieve greater prosperity for itself. Secondly, progressive nations must help the underdeveloped ones. The principle of Panchsheel is a fine example of a synthesis between the nationalism and internationalism, but for this peaceful co-existence itself is not enough. Active cooperation is more important.

## MEANS OF INTERNATIONAL EDUCATION

In order to encourage the growth of internationalism, it is necessary to make suitable amendments and modifications in the objectives of education, in the syllabus, and the methods of teaching. The following suggestions have been put forward :

### (a) Aims of education

With the intention of spreading international feeling, the following aims of education should be paid special attention :

1. *Development of independent thinking* : Education must help every student to think for himself so that he should not blindly accept every statement favourable to his own country, and blindly reject everything in favour of another. He must be able to arrive at an independent judgement of the worth of some fact relating to his own country or another.

2. *Developing a feeling of world citizenship* : Education must also seek to teach children that they are citizens of a world state. When this feeling is developed in them, they will have no difficulty in rising above national interests and understanding international interests, which they will try to achieve.

3. *Creating faith in humanity* : Rabindra Nath Tagore, the strongest supporter of internationalism among the contemporary Indian educational philosophers, based his concept of internationalism upon the philosophical background of humanitarianism. Humanity is the true religion of human beings, while all the great religions are only different forms of it. All great religions have placed great stress upon the equality of human beings. Human perfection has been accepted as the goal of human life. Once this concept is understood, it becomes easy to have faith in humanity and to love all human beings irrespective of their country.

**(b) Syllabi**

The following changes in syllabi are suggested, if an international feeling is to be created :

1. All syllabi should include paintings, literature, music, etc., which are typical of different countries.

2. The children should be acquainted with all attempts at humanitarian work carried out in every part of the world.

3. Efforts should be made to overcome narrow-mindedness and blind faith in children through a scientific education.

4. The teaching of geography should be supplemented with knowledge of the singleness of the world.

5. The teaching of history should concentrate primarily on the efforts of great figures who have contributed to the history of the world.

6. In teaching civics, the educator should explain to the students not only the rights of a citizen but also the rights and duties of a person to the international community as a whole.

7. Teaching should not be restricted to bookish teaching alone, but must also extend to visits to different parts of the country and also to other countries.

8. Pen-friendship should also be encouraged.

**(c) Methods of Teaching**

Certain suggestions about the changes and improvements in syllabi also imply some changes in teaching methods, if education is to have an international impact. The points to be noted in this connection are :

1. *Stress on World Citizenship* : During the process of teaching, it is desirable to stress points which may help in evolving an all encompassing love and world citizenship.

2. *Stress on Similarities* : The teaching of history, geography and civics should concentrate not upon the differences between and tensions among nations but on

the similarities so that sympathy for other nations and nationals is created in the mind of the educand.

3. *International Viewpoint of Education* : But an international viewpoint cannot he generated in the educand if the educator himself lacks it. When the educator is possessed of it, he will inspire the educand through his conversations, his ideas, training and by setting an example. Hence, the first step in the process is to educate the educator.

4. *International Contact*: The various committees for the various sciences and arts that are constituted at the university level should be encouraged to develop contact with national and international institutions of the same kind. What is really required is international contact at all levels of life and among people of every walk of life, scientists, scholars, literary figures, teachers, doctors, in fact every profession. Such contacts can be evolved by international meetings of local committees concerned with different professions and also through mutual exchange of scholars and learned people.

Finally, it has also been suggested that every national plan of education, in every country, must make a specific provision for developing international feeling through education. Educators and educational institutions should be given specific instructions concerning this. Only this will awaken sufficient enthusiasm in local institutions, and only thus can the aim of international education be fulfilled.

## MEANS OF SPREADING INTERNATIONAL EDUCATION

Apart from the formal education of colleges and schools, certain other media can also be useful in spreading international feeling, the major ones being :

1. **Pen-friendship** : Quite a few of the contemporary magazines, in all parts of the world, more particularly, the magazines meant for children and adolescents carry this kind of information. Such magazines publish the reader's interests, age, hobbies, other relevant information and sometimes even a photograph of the person interested in pen-friendship. Thus many children and adolescents form pen-friends in all parts of the world, and later on exchange pictures, postal stamps, books and other things. Pen-friendship is thus the most important means of increasing feeling for people of different parts of the world.

2. **Exchange of gifts** : Another modern practice is the sending of gifts by the children of one country to the children of other countries. India for example, has gifted elephants to the children of other nations. Such actions strengthen international feeling by attracting children of one country to another. Sometimes, some gift packets are also distributed in schools. These packets contain things that the children can use. It is only natural that when the children get these gift packets, they harbour kind and friendly feelings for the donor. The American Redcross distributes such gift parcels among Indian children from time to time.

3. **International competitions** : Now-a-days cultural competitions over the display of dance, drama, art, music, etc., take on an international colour because people from many countries participate in them. This brings people into contact

with the result that the world seems like a vast home.

4. **International exhibitions** : Such exhibitions also play an important part in promoting international understanding, because they help to acquaint people with the art and culture of different countries.

5. **Cine films** : People derive a lot of information by seeing foreign films, because they see their mode of living. Besides, it also encourages the feeling that human beings are the same everywhere, in their happiness, pain, pleasure, problems, joys and sorrows. This helps international understanding.

6. **Radio and television** : Radio and television play practically the same role as films because foreign programmes help the audience to understand life in other parts of the world.

7. **Literature** : Now-a-days, the literature of almost every country is available in every other country of the world. This can help in increasing acquaintance with life as it is lived in different countries. In addition to such literature certain books specialize in compiling the stories of lives, characters, interesting incidents and surprising objects in various parts of the world. This is a kind of international literature.

8. **Contribution of universities** : Finally, it can be said that universities are the most important medium of propagating international education because they provide opportunities for the meeting of artists, scientists, literary figures and scholars. This creates international understanding at a very high level.

9. **Various institutions of U.N.O.** : Many institutions of U. N. O. more particularly, UNESCO, are engaged in directly and consciously promoting international understanding and the growth of international feeling. It is desirable that their sphere should be further expanded, and that more nations should participate in their programmes so that their objectives can be achieved more easily.

**Multi-Culture Society in India**

India is a big country in which one finds groups distinguished from each other on the basis of language, religion, race, mode of dress, etc. There are numerous racial groups living in different parts of the country who not only possess different cultures, but possess cultures which do not resemble civilized groups. One finds differences of living standards, languages, style of dress, etc. among the people living in different parts of the country, but even more remarkable is the difference in values of life and ideas. In fact, that which is called Indian culture is not a single culture, but a composite culture made up of the synthesis of numerous cultures. This was born even before Aryan civilization, and other cultures have added to it from time to time. In view of the numerous instances of conflict which have been seen recently due to linguism, regionalism, communalism, casteism, etc., it can be said that schools have failed to create unity and mutual sympathy among the different groups. These influences are also seen constantly working in the country in the garb of partiality for a person of one's own region. This had led many educationists to reflect upon this issue and to give valuable suggestions.

## SUGGESTIONS FOR INTER-CULTURAL UNDERSTANDING

Inter-cultural understanding implies particular attitude, the attitude of understanding members of another culture, of recognising their merits, of sympathising and being liberal towards them. And since India contains many different cultures, inter-cultural understanding is essential, for in its absence, conflict can never be curtailed. This inter-cultural understanding can be created through education. An emotional unity is the first essential thing for this. Besides, in the absence of inter-cultural understanding, it is impossible to generate a genuine internationalism which is necessary in view of the substantial differences between the numerous cultures found in different parts of the world. And, as long as human beings do not rise above their petty differences and understand all human beings to be members of the same group, and learn to appreciate other cultures, international understanding cannot be created. The following suggestions are put forward for creating inter-cultural understanding:

1. **Study of Cultural anthropology** : Cultural anthropology, one branch of anthropology, provides knowledge of the origin of various cultures, their development and their inner content. By studying the fundamental elements of this discipline, educands can comprehend the different cultural patterns and characteristics which are found. By studying the origins of various cultures, they will be able to understand that differences in culture arise out of the different circumstances in which the cultures are born. This will lead to a more charitable and liberal attitude to cultural differences.

2. **Encouragement to tourism** : Travelling to different parts of the country is a valuable experience in that it helps one to realise that despite the obvious differences in various groups, all of them are Indians. This promotes inter-cultural understanding.

3. **Encouraging mutual meetings** : Indian universities regularly organise cultural programmes in which students from different universities present cultural shows. Such meetings give the young people to meet young people of other cultural groups, with the result that they get a chance to understand the other culture. This helps to free their minds of narrow thinking.

4. **Propagating the theory of unity in diversity** ; People who believe either in the destruction of diversity in order to create uniformity or in the destruction of unity to maintain diversity forget that unity in diversity is a natural characteristic of human society as well as of the entire creation. Happiness lies in following this principle. If this principle is accepted, internationalism will be encouraged, but not at the cost of nationalism. Today, all the different cultures that are growing in the country must be allowed to flourish. None of them should be destroyed, because each represents a specific pattern of adjustment with the environment existing at a particular place, and hence it has its own value. Each culture is the product of the local conditions, climate and natural environment, and represents an adjustment to that environment. Therefore, each culture must be given the opportunity to grow in future. But this does not necessarily imply that the country will inevitably be

divided into numerous different cultural groups or that this should be allowed to happen. Cultural unity can be promoted even after maintaining cultural variety and identity. This cultural unity can be created by using education to promote inter-cultural understanding. If people can be made to realise that both unity or conformity and diversity or individuality are part of the theory of unity in diversity, it will be possible to take care of and eradicate much of the prejudices, partiality, differences, etc., that arise out of cultural differences.

In addition to the above measures, it is possible to utilize many other things for the purpose of creating inter-cultural understanding. Young men and women can, for example, be encouraged to establish contact with members of other cultures through the medium of pen-friendship. Even inter-cultural marriages can be of immense value in this respect. It is possible to create situations in which members of different cultures come into contact with each other. Tourism, in particular, should be encouraged. Young students can tour the country in groups and thus acquaint themselves with the different cultures existing in remote parts of the country. It is possible to generate a liberal, sympathetic and kind-hearted attitude towards other cultures among the younger generations through the medium of magazines, literary publications intended for the young, and other similar channels. Exhibitions of literature and art can achieve the same thing. Films can also make valuable contributions in this respect. Besides, once the teachers themselves have understood the importance of this aim of education, they will provide many illustrations to their students to create inter-cultural understanding.

## QUESTIONS FOR EXERCISE

1. Explain fully the meaning of "education for international understanding." Describe a few activities which can be undertaken in your school for its development.
2. "Internationalism is a synonym for humanism, with the emphasis on what is universal in man — his striving for self-expression within the large community and for its ultimate benefit. National contributions must not be glossed over by internationalism in education. On the contrary, they will be stressed, just as individual contributions are stressed in democratic society. But those contributions will be stressed as part of man's larger heritage and not as a nation's jealously guarded monopoly." Formulate and comment on, some of the issues relating to nationalism and internationalism in education which the author has raised.
3. Suggest some measures for developing inter-cultural understanding through education among various groups in India.

# 37

# EDUCATION FOR DEMOCRACY

Aldous Huxley has remarked,'' If your aim is liberty and democracy, then you must teach people the arts of being free and of governing themselves.'' Democracy can never be successful, in the event of lack of education. In a democracy the government is composed of the elected representatives of the people and if the people are uneducated they can never elect the right leaders and consequently can never create the right kind of government. In fact, it is impossible even to hope for democracy in the absence of education. It is difficult to expect a citizen to behave responsibly if he is not even aware of his rights and duties. Bertrand Russell has commented, ''Democracy in its modern form would be quite impossible in a nation where many men cannot read.'' The truth of the matter is that education is a prerequisite of democracy. Only after proper education should the citizen be invested with his democratic rights. As Fichte, the German philosopher has commented, ''Only the nation which has first solved in actual practice the problem of educating perfect men will then solve the problem of the perfect state.'' Although Fichte made this comment in the context of autocratic states, it cannot be doubted that the perfection of even a democratic state can be judged only by the extent to which it contains educated people. As Hetherington puts it, ''Democratic government, at least, demands an educated people.'' Throwing light on the objectives of education in the 1949 meeting of the Universities Commission, Dr. Radhakrishnan stressed the fact that the democratic state recognises the importance of the individual, and it is the process of development of this individual which is called education. Hence, education is absolutely necessary for establishing a democratic society. Dewey has pointed out that democracy is inconceivable without education, because education can generate and instil the qualities which democracy demands as a prerequisite. Philosophers of the ancient Greek city state were aware of the significance of education. Both Plato and Aristotle laid stress on the importance of education for the success of democracy. Ernest Barker comments, ''To Plato education was the most important function of the state and they particularly advocated for producing the philosopher kings to improve the men's minds for becoming virtuous beings.'' Plato, in his famous text, *The Republic*, stressed not only the importance of education for democracy but even formulated a plan for the education of men and women which made all kinds of development physical, mental, moral and aesthetic — possible. Aristotle was of the opinion that the aim of the state is to make possible the achievement of the highest moral level and this can be reached through education alone. Thus, education is the most important function of the state. From one point of view, the state itself is a school in which the individual learns citizenship. These truths were known not only to the Ancient Greeks but also to Indian thinkers of ancient times. Hermitages and places of worship were used as schools in which the sages tried to produce ideal citizens who could become useful members of society. But the modern age needs democratic education far more than was needed in ancient Greece or ancient India because modern democracies are so vast and their problems so complex that the education of citizens is even more imperative today.

## IMPORTANCE OF EDUCATION IN DEMOCRACY

The importance of education for a democratic state is fairly evident from the foregoing account. The following points can be stressed in this connection :

1. **Knowledge of rights and duties** : If democracy is to be a success, it is essential that every citizen should be aware of his rights and duties because only then can he take active productive part in the affairs of the state. This knowledge of rights and duties can be obtained only through education. Education socializes the individual so that then he develops consciousness of duty.

2. **Development of humane qualities** : If the ideal of brotherhood is to be achieved by a democratic state, it is necessary for it to develop humane qualities in its members. Kant's moral concepts, quoted earlier, throw important light on this. Only through education such qualities as a high moral character, sociability, benevolence, patience, pity, sympathy and brotherhood, etc., can be developed in the individual.

3. **Faith in democratic ideals** : In order to make democracy a success, it is essential that its citizens must have faith in the democratic ideals. And this can be brought about only when they are adequately educated because it is only the educated person who realizes that the sole purpose of life is not the satisfaction of gross physical desires. The ideals of freedom, liberty, brotherhood, are more valuable and necessary. No one but the educated individual can understand the circumstances and needs of another person before passing judgement on him. Only such a person can accept the ideal of equality after recognizing human values as being the end to be achieved.

4. **Fulfilment of political duties** : In a democracy the government is elected by the people, and hence the responsibility for electing a good government devolves upon them. And, if the people are unable to understand their political rights or to fulfil their political responsibilities, it is foolish to hope for a democratic government. This ability to recognise where one's duty lies can come only through education. Educated people can properly assess the qualities and shortcomings of the various individuals who are fighting the elections, and of the various political parties and their plans and polices which they profess. In India, in the absence of education the ignorant people are persuaded to vote for the wrong person, with the result that the government of the country has failed time and again. Corruption is rampant.

The Mudaliar Report points out that if democracy is anything more than voting blindly, then every individual must accept the task of independently thinking about all social, political and economic problems before deciding upon the party he wishes to support. But this is possible only when the entire electorate is educated to think independently.

5. **Protection and transmission of culture** : In any state, ideals can be achieved only when change is accompanied by a parallel continuity, and this continuity with the past is maintained only through culture, the social heritage, which is passed on to the new generation through the medium of education. Hence, education is also required for transmitting culture to future generations and for protecting it.

6. **Preventing exploitation** : The ideals of democracy are opposed to exploitation of every kind, but if political, social and economic exploitation is to be eliminated from society, it is essential to have universal and compulsory education. In its absence, the rich and powerful people will never give up their advantage and habit, while the poor will never become sufficiently conscious of their rights or their ability to organize together and counter this exploitation. Educated people in a country are aware of their rights and they have the intelligence and training to fight exploitation or violation of their rights. Hence, education is the only real foundation on which democracy can be based.

## EDUCATION FOR DEMOCRACY IN INDIA

### Democracy in India

India is not merely a modern democratic state but a country which is traditionally inclined towards democracy. A democratic constitution was adopted after independence. In 1938 Jawahar Lal Nehru had said, "The Indian Constitution seeks to establish a popular government in the country on the basis of democratic principles outlined earlier. For this every citizen must participate in the administration, through his right to vote and to be elected. Every individual is guaranteed and given equal status and opportunity, because no one is discriminated against on the basis of religion, race, caste, community, sex, or on any other grounds. The government is responsible to the people and its elected representatives."

### Provisions in Indian Constitution

In order to achieve this objective of democracy, education is as necessary in India as anywhere, else, a truth which the Indian people have been quick to realise. In the words of F. W. Thames, "Education is no exotic in India. There has been no country where the love of learning had so early an origin or has exercised. so lasting and powerful an influence. From the simple poet of the Vedic age to the Bengali philosopher of the present day there has been an uninterrupted succession of teachers and scholars." Not only did the Indian Constitution accept the ideals of democracy, it considered education the prime responsibility of the state. In Article 45 of the Constitution it has been stated that every state must arrange for the provision of free and compulsory education to all children upto the age of 14, within ten years of the date of inception of the Constitution. After the achievement of independence, a new phase began in the history of education. Articles 29 and 30 of the Constitution give fundamental rights 'to' every individual in connection with education and cultural development. According to article 20, every Indian national living in any part of India will have the right to maintain his own specific language, script and his culture. No person can be refused right of admission to any educational institution, established by the state, by reason of religion, race, caste, language or any other similar consideration. According to article 30, every minority community will have the right to establish and maintain educational institutions of its own choice, irrespective of whether the minority is a linguistic or religious one. The state will also not refuse aid to any such institution created by a religious or linguistic minority. Articles 45 and 46 determine the policy for education as part and parcel of the directive principles. According to article 45, the state will make every effort to provide free and compulsory education, within ten years, to every child below the age of 14. According to article 46, the state will pay special attention to the educational and economic interests of all backward classes, especially the scheduled castes and scheduled tribes. It also entrusts the State with the duty of protecting such tribes from social injustice and exploitation of every kind. The Indian Constitution laid the foundation for a federal government in which the functions of the State Government have some duties with respect to education. It has been realised that there must be coordination between the central and state authority on education for a balanced development of the country. The modern Indian state is a welfare state whose objective is the complete development of its people. This welfare can be achieved only through education. Little surprise therefore if all the leaders of the nation stress the importance of education as first step to improving the future of the nation.

## VIEWS OF SECONDARY EDUCATION COMMISSION

The democratic ideals which the existing educational policy is trying to achieve have been outlined most precisely in the Secondary Education Commission's explanation of the objectives of education:

1. **Development of democratic citizenship** : The success of democracy depends largely upon the people's awareness of their rights and duties and the extent to which people fulfil their responsibilities. Education aims at developing this ability between right and wrong. He can understand social, economic and political issues, and reflect on the possibility of solving such problems. He can decide upon the political party of the leadership which should be entrusted with the task of forming a government and undertaking administration. He does this after thinking on the problems facing the country and considering the ability of each group or leader to face such problems. He can express his ideas and suggestions through lectures, essays, articles, etc. He can organize new movements or constitute various kinds of committees to solve the problems facing the country. It is the duty of the state to insist upon a syllabus which can be expected to generate such democratic awareness among the children being educated.

2. **Training in skilful living** : Democracy can be said to have succeeded only

if it can translate the democratic ideals to its essential. It is desirable to develop such social qualities as collective feeling, cooperation, discipline, tolerance, sympathy, brotherhood, etc. in the individual. Education must also aim to create faith in social justice and the willingness to rebel against injustice. Education helps people in adjusting to each other, and the educated individual is generally tolerant and liberal. Although he may differ from other people in their opinions, he has the ability. Hence, education is the only means of removing the obstacles in the path of democracy, and also for achieving some adjustment between people who differ from each other in respect of language, race, caste, religion, sex, etc.

3. **Development of personality** : The success of a democratic society also depends upon whether mature men and women form the majority or minority in its population. Democracy can succeed only if most of its members have developed mature personalities, because a mature person has gone through physical, mental, social, ethical and spiritual development. Hence, education should aim at the development of all aspects of the educands' personality through various kinds of training. Keeping this in view, most schools and colleges now provide many kinds of extra-curricular training, which supplements all that is taught as part of curriculum.

4. **Developing vocational skill** : The Secondary Education Commission has pointed out that another aim of education is to develop some vocational skill in the educand. No nation can progress in the absence of economic progress. The first duty of the state is to provide a system and means of education which imparts some vocational and professional skills to the educands so that they can earn their livelihood at the same time as they contribute to the nation's economic growth. The country urgently needs skilled craftsmen, engineers, doctors, teachers and administrators. For this, specialized colleges are required. Every child should be given the right to choose a profession of his own liking, and he should be given the opportunity to acquire the highest training and education in this profession.

5. **Developing leadership** : The success of a democracy depends upon the capabilities of the leadership. The democratic government is a decentralized government, and for that reason it requires skilled leadership at many different levels of administration. The democratic government is run by the elected representatives of the people, who should be possessed of special qualities. Expert leadership is required for development and progress in every sphere — political, social, economic, artistic, scientific and cultural. Education should aim at evolving such leadership, because without doing this education cannot make any real contribution to democracy, for, then it is leaving unfulfilled one of its important responsibilities. The element of leadership can be encouraged through many kinds of curricular and extra-curricular activities in schools and colleges.

## QUESTIONS FOR EXERCISE

1. "Democracy without education is blind." Explain and discuss the need and importance of education in democracy.
2. How can education be used to establish democracy in India? Discuss the views of Secondary Education Commission and Indian Universities Commission in this connection.

# 38

# EDUCATION FOR MODERNIZATION

### Modernization function of education

S. N. Eisenstadt has rightly pointed out, "Perhaps the best starting point for the analysis of the characteristics in the educational institutions in modern societies is the pattern of demands for and the supply of educational services that tended to develop with modernization." In the words of Yogendra Singh, "...education has been one of the most influential instruments of modernization in India. It has led to the mobilization of people's responsible for the growth of an enlightened intelligentsia which carried forward not only a movement for independence but also a relentless struggle for social and cultural reforms."

### Meaning of Modernization

The most important function of education is modernization. Modernization is a comprehensive concept aimed at capturing and describing the transition of a society from medieval to modern culture. It stands for progress beyond tradition. Modernization, according to some sociologists, is based upon European and American models. As compared to Urbanization, Industrialization, Westernization and Europeanization, modernization presents a more complex process and a more complex result. In the intellectual sphere it is an awareness that it is possible to see a rational explanation of pysical and social phenomena. Thus, it is represented by positivism and empiricism and rationalism. In the field of religion it is expressed in secularism. Its approach is multiple. In philosophy it is expressed in humanist thought. It includes social mobilization and differentiation and specialization in individual and institutional activities. In political field it stands for democratization. In ecology it is characterized by advancing degree of urbanization.

### Symptoms of Modernization

But the most important feature of modernization as related to education is cultural. In cultural sphere its symptoms have been pointed out by A.R. Desai as follows:

1. Growing differentiation of the major secular or cultural system, "The spread of literacy and secular education: a more complex intellectual and institutional system for the cultivation and advancement of specialized roles based on intellectual disciplines."

2. Emergence of a new cultural outlook, characterized by emphasis on progress and improvement, on happiness and spontaneous abilities and, feelings, on the development of individuality as a value, and efficiency.

3. Emergence of a new personality orientation, traits and characteristics revealed in greater ability to adjust to the broadening societal horizons: some ego-flexibility; widening spheres of interests; growing potential empathy with other people and situations; a growing evaluation of self-advancement and mobility; a growing emphasis on the present as the meaningful temporal dimension of human existence; a growing awareness of dignity of others and an increased disposition to respect them; a growing awareness in the individual that 'his world is calculable, that people and institutions around him can be relied on to fulfil their delegation and responsibilities,' 'growing faith to fulfil their delegation and responsibilities,' 'growing faith in sciences and technology and growing awareness' that, 'rewards should be according to contribution and not according to either whim or special properties of person not relating to his contribution'.

4. Finally, modernization implies, 'the ability of society to develop an institutional structure capable of adjusting to continually changing problems and demands.' The emergence of such a challenge is the result of modernization.

**Modernization through Education**

Education is the most important instrument of modernization since modernization includes the following :

1. Directed change in the system of attitudes, beliefs and values and also in the institutional complex to enhance the acceptability of modern technology and its organizational and operational framework.

2 Growth of the infrastructure essential to the adaptation to technology of foreign origin to specific national needs.

3. Laying the foundations of institutions and organizations which could, in time, assume responsibility for independent innovation and technological growth to the country's needs and problems.

**Functions of Education**

In view of the above mentioned changes required by modernization the functions of education in this direction may be achieved by the following :

1. *Alternatives to tradition* : By enlarging the cognitive map of those exposed to it, education suggests alternatives to attraction, bringing into focus the rewards implicit in them, and indicates roughly at least the paths through which the new goals with their attendant regards can be achieved. It broadens mental horizons, raises expectations and predisposes people to make experiments.

2. *Socialization* : As an instrument of socialization it can project new images and values.. Purposively used, it can be a help in obliterating attitudes and behaviour patterns that are dysfunctional programmes of modernization.

3. *National Consciousness* : By providing ideological articulation it can

promote the development of national consciousness and can help people see their needs and their problems in a national perspective. This can stimulate the creation of a national consensus at least on major issues.

4. *Educated Elite* : Education provides a highway to elite status on the educated. The educated provide a reference model to the masses, who, in imitation of the former, take the first steps away from tradition. Modernizing elites are almost always the products of modern or semi-modern school/university systems.

5. *Problem-solving leadership* : Scientists and technicians, management experts and administrators with the requisite knowledge and skill, can only be expected to emerge out of the educational system. Large-scale programmes of modernization demand specialists of several types at different levels, and look to the education system for a steady flow of technocrats, planners and managers to operate them.

6. *Mobility multiplier* : Although its impact is on the immobility of thought-ways in the long run it does alter rigid forms of social stratification. Modernization requires both types of mobility.

In sum, with proper planning and under efficient direction, education can make meaningful contribution of the attainment of modernization. It can be harnessed to diffuse attitudes and ideologies required for the adoption of modern technology and its associated values and organizational premises, to provide personnel to operate and sustain the programmes of modernization, and to create capabilities for adaptation and origination of new technology.

## MODERNIZATION OF INSTITUTIONAL EDUCATION

### Review of Studies

Researches have been conducted in West and India about the role of educational institutions in bringing about modernization. Most of them have shown a positive correlation between the two. However, Saunders in his study *Education and Modernization in Brazil* has found that it undermines modernity. He remarks: 'Brazilian schools, especially at the primary level where their impact on personality development is greatest, tend to stifle rather than develop the personality traits on which modernization depends, and from which the society must draw its innovators.' Learner in his research work *The Passsing of Traditional Society : Modernising the Middle East (1963)*, on the basis of his study with adult samples of six developing countries, asserted that literacy is the basic personal skill underlying the modernization process. Joseph A. Kahl in his research, *The Measurement of Modernism: A study of Values in Brazil and Mexico* (University of Texas Press 1968), pointed out significant correlation between education and modernization. Reporting results of the Harward's project on the social and cultural aspects of economic development, covering Argentina, Chili, India, Pakistan, Israel and Nigeria, Inkeles concluded that, 'Education is the most powerful factor in making men modern'. In their study based on 5 national probability samples of adult age, 20 and older, drawn from the U.S.A., Finland, Japan, Mexico and Costa Rica, Waisanen and Kumata, concluded positive relationship between education and various indicators of modernity.

## School and Modernity

Examining the immediate effects of schooling on people's modernity Armer and Youtz conclude, "Western education leads to the modernization of perspective in traditional, non-industrial societies." After a study of 591 seventeen years old males in Kano City in Nigeria they maintain, "Western education does, indeed, have a definite effect on value orientations of youth that is largely independent of test factor." This has been collaborated by S. L. Sharma in his work *Modernizing Effects of University Education* published by Indian Council of Social Science Research in 1979. This conclusion has been again supported by articles in a special number of International *Journal of Comparative Sociology* (1974, XIV, 3-4). In this special number, researches conducted independently in various parts of the world, showed remarkable uniformity in concluding that schooling promotes attitudinal modernity in developing societies.

## Higher Education and Modernization

Besides the relation of schooling and modernization researches have been conducted about the effect of higher education on modernity. Williamson studying university students in United States, Germany, Japan and Columbia concluded that while Americans and Columbians are at the conservative the Japanese are on the other end of the scale of rationalism — traditionalism developed by Kahl. Similar researches were conducted by some other notable sociologists in the West including Silberman (1970), Greer (1972), Smith and Inkeles (1966), Sack (1973), etc. In India studies concerning schooling and social change were conducted by A.R. Desai (1952), G.S. Bhatnagar (1972), and Margaret L. Cormack (1961). Cormack made a full length study of Indian students concerning social change. She concluded, "They are not considering values, attitudes and attitudinal change. They are concerned with certificates, degrees and employment." Thus, Cormack maintained negative correlation between higher education and social change in India. She found little evidence of change orientation among her respondents. Similar conclusion was reached by B.V. Shah (1964), in his study *Social Change among College Students of Gujarat* (Baroda : Maharaja Sayaji Rao University). Y.B. Damely found correlation between higher education and individuation, a trait of modernization. But he himself admits, "It is not a study of the nature of the student's behaviour or thinking." M. S. Gore, I.P. Desai and Suma Chitnis found encouraging evidence of the relation between education and modernization. According to them, "The state, sex, and educational level of the respondents were all important variables in determining the modernity of student sample." Similar conclusion was reached by Malik and Marquitte in their study *Changing Social Values of College Students in the Punjab*. They concluded that, "...an overwhelming majority of Punjab youth favours the abolition of such traditional institutions as caste and untouchability and strongly approves of a general social revolution in India." In his book *Education in Social Change* Sullivan found that, "Factors other than experience at a particular training college appear to be operative in changing that students' outlook towards traditional social practices."

**Modernizing Effects of University Education**

The latest study in this connection was however made by Dr. S.L. Sharma published by ICSSR (1979) under the title *Modernizing Effects of University Education*.. On the basis of a study of 3437 students in the 34 teaching departments of Punjab University during the academic year 1973-74 Dr. Sharma reached the following important conclusions concerning the relationship of modernization and education:

1. The level of higher education is of consequence as an explanatory variable of student modernity.
2. There is the lowest percentage of moderns in the humanities, followed by social sciences and professionals with the highest percentage in the science faculty.
3. Males are more modern than females.
4. High status students are more modern than low status students.
5. There is a significant and positive correspondence between level of student modernity and that of 'their reference teacher, provided the latter preferred character-building role, over other roles, favoured no social distance in their relations, with students and reported greater interpersonal interaction with students.
6. There is a weak though positive relationship between years of hostel exposure and modernity's course.
7. Age is found to be inversely related to student modernity. Boys outscored girls in modernity.
8. Caste has no bearing on modernity.
9. A significantly larger percentage of high modernity cases hails from medium size families with 4 to 6 numbers.
10. Family type has no association with modernity.
11. Socio-economic status of the family has a significant though weak positive relationship with modernity.
12. Father's education and occupation are only weakly related to student modernity.
13. Father's income has a moderately strong positive association with modernity.
14. Students with early urban background are not more modern than those with rural background.
15. Those who have lived longer in urban setting are more modern than those with fewer years of urban dwelling.
16. The initial exposure to cosmopolitan city like Chandigarh makes not much difference in modernity.
17. Duration of urban exposure positively associated with modernity.

18. Early residential background and modernism of the city have no influence on student modernity.
19. There is a significant and positive relationship between media exposure and modernity.
20. There is a strong positive relationship between extent of exposure to other cultures and level of modernity.
21. Constant exposure to other culture significantly increases the negative effect of education on modernity.
22. The convent and or public school education students are more modern than the government and/or aided school educated.
23. The type of schooling is the best predictor of modernity with the convent or public school educated being most modern.
24. Early socialization variables' account for greater in student modernity than the later socialization variables.
25. Development variables are more powerful than structural variables in explaining students modernity.

On the basis of the above conclusion Dr. S.L. Sharma points out inverse relationship between the level of higher education and the student modernity. He gives the following reasons for this surprising fact:

1. The present higher education leads to mere transmission of information to the neglect of inculcating ability to think of oneself. It stresses mere skill acquisition to the neglect of generating this position, for skill formation. It neglects character trainings and stresses mere certification for white-collar Jobs.
2. The system of higher education in India lacks an articulate social ideal.
3. The present educational system has not changed the light of goals set by the Constitution of free India.
4. The present system of education is not a source of characterological transformation.
5. The course content of the present higher education does not lead to modernization.
6. The cognitive and value content in conjuction with the social context of the present higher education is not relevant to the cultivation of modernity.
7. Our teachers are not so modern as to influence the student. They are not interested in character-building and social training. They are unsure of what the community expects from them. The persistent authoritarian orientation limits the power of teachers to act as agents of student modernity.
8. The objective conditions in our educational institutions such' as over-crowded classes, low teacher-pupil ratio, impersonal character of teacher-

taught relationship, render the task of change of orientation on the part of the teacher the more difficult. Small classes are better for such influence than large and unwieldy classes.

9. The lack of freedom for the teacher to design his own courses restrict considerably his potential for induction for social change. In the words of Dr. S.L. Sharma, "Our teachers thus presented a case of double failure as socializers of student modernity; first, they lacked strong modernity orientation and second, they failed to modify their role orientation so as to bring in line with modern norms."
10. The extra academic component of campus climate restricts its relevance to modernity.
11. Routinization of educational experience is a possible reason for the failure of higher education as a modernizer.
12. The overgrown structural format of higher education is a significant reason for its failure to modernize.
13. The built-in traits of present higher education such as underemphasis on the value element in its course content are responsible for its poor performance.

Dr. Sharma suggests the following three objectives as the aims of higher education to make it a better instrument of modernization :

1. To prepare skilled manpower for a developing economy;
2. To re-socialize people in the values conducive to socio-economic development.
3. To inculcate in man a creative self-awareness, and ability to think for himself and a sense of critical judgement.

He suggested that three areas should be particularly modernized : the re-orientation of the content, the recasting of teaching-learning nexus, and improving the quality of education. The quality of early education should be improved. Group extra-curricular activities should be encouraged; A secular rational and egalitarian man should be created. To conclude, "Besides providing the highly skilled manpower to a technico-industrial economy, higher education in our view can lay down the foundation of socio-economic development in the following ways : by imparting to the younger genration the requisite psychological dispositions which are regarded as helpful for development; (2) by instilling in students a reflective ability and a capacity to make rational decision."

## TWO PATTERNS OF MODERNIZATION

In his paper *Social Change and Educational Policy* published in *The Sociology of Education In India (NCERT 1967),* Professor A. R. Desai accepts two patterns of modernization of a traditional society pointed out by Don Martindale — exogenous and endogenous. He defines these two patterns by pointing out, that, "An exogenous factor is one arising outside the social system." Both these factors initiate and shape social change. They determine the nature of leadership and its basic aim. These in their turn determine the objectives of education, the structure of the machinery of education, technical and other means of spread, the allocation of finances of education and nature of personnel executing it. Historically, the modernization process worked differently in the capitalist and the non-capitalist countries. In U. S. A., it grew in three phases — merchantilist, *laissez faire* and monopoly. It developed a massive formal education system. This system, though basically the same, changed according to changing circumstances in each country. Not only in Europe but also in Africa, Asia and Latin America the modernization process transformed the politico-economic and socio-cultural structures. However, the colonial hold on these nations was maintained. Thus, modernization in colonial countries was brought about by the foreign rulers, an exogenous factor. In communist countries, on the other hand, modernization developed on non-capitalist lines aiming the establishment of a social structure based upon collective ownership and meeting the assessed needs of the citizen. After the Second World War these countries developed a modern educational system different from that envolved in capitalist countries. The countries liberated from colonial subjugation engaged in modernization according to their specific conditions aiming at overcoming backwardness by rapid industrialization and social institutional reconstruction. According to Professor A.R. Desai, "The two patterns of modernization, *viz*., modernization on the capitalist and the non-capitalist basis have the following implications for their educational system:

(a) They provide different aims and approaches to the content of education and to the communication process.

(b) They result in different attitudes towards education.

(c) They determine different methods of providing finances for education.

(d) They also generate different patterns of organization of education.

In capitalist countries education was considered commodity purchased by the consumer at different prices in the market. Thus, it depends on the purchasing capacity of the family and group that the individual gets a particular type of education. In non-capitalist countries, however, eduction was considered a vital need and a fundamental right and therefore provided as free communal service by the society. Besides the aims and approaches and attitudes, the methods of providing finance for education also differed in capitalist and non-capitalist countries. In capitalist countries finances for education were provided by individual, private societies, endowments and the government. Thus, the government is one of the competing financiers though being the supreme it frames laws to regulate education market. It reserves certain aspects of education which are essential for the community. It also takes such measures as are required to safeguard the educational interests of the handicapped and backward groups.. In non-capitalist countries, however, the entire responsibility for educational finance is the burden of the state. Finally, there are two partners of organization of education in capitalist and non-capitalist societies. In the former it is made of an amalgam of the heterogeneous bodies and groups providing finances. In non-capitalist countries there are no diversities and conflicts in several agencies controlling education as the total control is in the hands of the state in the name of the society.

## QUESTIONS FOR EXERCISE

1. Write short note on Education and Modernization.
2. Show the relationship of modernization and education in the context of Institutional education.
3. Discuss the educational implication of the two patterns of modernization.

# 39

# EDUCATION IN INDIA TODAY

**Resume**

The structure of educational services in India was somewhat loose and undefined in the early British period. With the issue of Woods Despatch in 1854, about 20 years after Macaulay's minute advocating the use of English language and Western literature as the main form of education in India, Departments of Education were set up in the various provinces. They undertook the supervision of schools established by the government or private agencies as also the gradual conversion and absorption of indigenous primary institutions in the system of education. The training of teachers, often drawn from the indigenous schools themselves, and the preparation of a few basic texts to be used in these schools were undertaken in this connection. In 1857, three universities were established at Calcutta, Bombay and Madras in order to undertake the work of examining the teaching done in government as well as private, mostly missionary, institutions, at the high school, F.A. and B.A. levels. This set the essentially examination-dominated tone of Indian education for the succeeding century. The affiliating character of the universities enabled private enterprise, primarily missionary, in the first instance, but local Indian managements from about 1880 onwards, to organise a large number of institutions. While adhering to the formal syllabus for purpose of instruction examination, it had thus become possible for different institutions to have their own specific religious or cultural climate. After the Indian Education Commission, 1882 (Hunter Commission), had recommended withdrawal of active government leadership in opening schools and encouragement of private enterprise, this trend became even more predominant. However, poor state support in terms of finance did very often lead to poor quality in instruction.

One consequence of the emergence of private managements and simultaneous grants to graduates of franchise in university elections towards the end of nineteenth century, was an increasingly Indian composition of university bodies and strong reflection of nationalist sentiments in the fields of education and culture.

Early in the 20th century, the Swadeshi Movement in Bengal, as also the reformist as well as the radical trend of the nationalist movement in Maharashtra, represented by Ranade-Gokhale and Tilak, respectively had their reflection on education. A little later, Arya Samaj in Punjab also called for the development of a national system of education under which the gurukuls were formed and Vedic learning was emphasised. The Bengal movement for national education led to the establishment of technical institutions, the strongest of which today constitutes the Jadavpur University at Calcutta. Muslim and Hindu sentiments led to the establishment of the Muslim University (growing out of the earlier Muslim Anglo-Oriental College at Aligarh) and the Banaras Hindu University founded by the late Pt. Malaviya.

The next big wave of nationalist activity in education came after Gandhiji's call for a boycott of British educational system in 1920. The rebel Jamia Millia Islamia at Aligarh, which was later transferred to Delhi, the Gujarat Vidyapeeth, Kashi Vidyapeeth, Tilak Vidyapeeth and an earlier National University sponsored by Mrs. Annie Besant and some liberal educationists, along with a large number of national schools, were efforts to liberate education from official control and to change its content.

Emphasis on practical activity related to national reconstruction and on study of the indigenous and national problems and culture were the two key points in the programmes of the various national movements in education. However, the great bulk of educational activity continued along the broad lines of the officially sponsored university and school education even as they influenced the content of education in a somewhat nationalist direction.

Police-making and Legislation in Education

Education being a State subject in the Constitution, annual meetings of the Central Advisory Board of Education and the Conference of State Ministers of Education, supported by Conference of State Secretaries of Education, have been important media for formulation of educational policy. As is understandable, these policies are framed within the broad limits laid down in the Five-Year Plan where not only the rough magnitude of resources available for education, but also the general direction of growth is set out. Plan proposals for educational development are formulated by a working group set up jointly by the Planning Commission and the Ministry of Education and discussed with State governments. On the other hand, the Central government has a number of advisory boards in the field of women's education, secondary education, education of the handicapped and the blind, etc.

The government of India have set up the National Council of Educational Research and Training to develop improvement activities in the whole range of school education such as production of new model text-books for adoption by States, devising of improved techniques of examinations for adoption by the State Boards of Secondary Education and by schools, research in appropriate areas, e.g., testing, guidance, school organisation, supervision and inspection of schools, etc., which may lay the basis for better practices in education. The Central Ministry of Education also supports the creation of State Institutes of Education and other agencies like Bureau of Educational and Vocational Guidance, Institutes of Science

Education, Institutes of English, and Examination Reform Bureau to bring about improvement in their respective fields.

The most important pieces of legislation in the field of education have been the Primary Education Acts passed about 1961 in various States where such Acts were not already enforced. This enables States to employ compulsion. The approach, however, has been not punitive, but one of providing schools to all children and persuading parents. The regulation of secondary education and of private education in most States is through States Acts, setting up Boards of Secondary Education which lay down examination curricula, conditions of recognitions of institutions, etc. In many cases, States have undertaken supervisory functions vis-a-vis private managing bodies of institutions largely in order to protect the interest of teachers in respect of security of service and conditions of management.

Universities are set up by Acts and receive grants from the State governments though there has recently been some felling that they (the governments) might, on the one hand, be encroaching too much on the autonomy and privileges of academic institutions and, on the other, setting up universities without due consideration of the resources a available and educational needs. It has, therefore, been felt that the State governments should consult the University Grants Commission which provides grants for developmental purposes and which has itself been set up by an Act of Parliament to exercise the Union government's responsibility for maintenance of standards in higher education. Education is not yet a justiciable right, that is, no citizen can claim education from the State in a court of law. The provision of education upto the age of 14 has been mentioned in the Directive Principles chapter of the Indian Constitution.

Some legislation has impinged on the private bodies, particularly, religious and the denominational groups. The Constitution permits the minorities to set up institutions of their own choice and the State's right to legislate is limit to that extent.

**International Contacts**

International organisations involved in education in India have been mainly the United nations Educational, Scientific and Cultural Organisation (U.N.E.S.C.O.) and the United Nations Children's Emergency Fund (U.N.I.C.E.F.). The International Labour Organisation (I.L.O.) pay attention to technical and vocational training and the Food and Agricultural Organisation (F.A.O.) have recently paid attention to agricultural education and some farm-oriented literacy programmes in connection with increases in agricultural productivity. U.N.E.S.C.O. stated as the continuation of an earlier International League of Intellectual Co-operation which mainly stressed extension among the intellectual contacts of the world. However, during the past 6 years, with the growth in the numbers of new under-developed nations, which have become independent, and with increasing attention to the growth gap between the rich and the poor nations of the world, the activities of U.N.E.S.C.O. have been taken a developmental character. Thus, technical support in educational planning, improvement of methods and curricula, teaching-training, equalisation of access to education and women's education have figured in its programme.

The main point to note about the activities of most of the U.N. Organisations is that a great part of their assistance is available in the form of services of experts, equipment and training fellowships. Substantive support for the programme in the country has still to be found necessarily from national finances, except in cases like U.N.I.C.E.F. mid-day meals programme. This is also a characteristic of all the activities of the United nations Special Fund, now United Nations Development Programme, whose activities may be treated as pre-investment programmes preparing the ground for fruitful investment of capital in economic development programmes of under-developed countries. The support of Special Fund has mainly been available to programmes of technical training on the job training, etc. The activities of U.N.I.C.E.F. have covered a wider ground besides supporting U.N.E.S.C.O. work in the fields already mentioned. It has been willing to sponsor assistance programmes for school-meals, school medical services and recently, studies in problems of wastage, and greater co-ordination of school programmes with the community's life and needs, etc.

There is also a certain amount of bilateral assistance mainly from the United States through its Agency for International Development and the U.S. Educational Foundation in India, and also through Colombo Plan and other agreements with other countries. The Colombo Plan, in particular, is a programme of mutual assistance among nations so that India not only receives but also gives help of a technical nature to countries which need it. The Soviet Union has co-operated mainly in technical and higher scientific education by providing staff and consultants in this area and joint publication of text-books for schools as well as higher technical institutions.

### Control Over Education

In India today, while the various States of the country are made responsible for progress of education in their respective areas, the Centre also shares some responsibility in some fields of education. According to 1976 Constitution amendment some of the subjects of education have been placed under joint responsibility of the States and the Centre. The Centre is responsible for determining the standard of higher research, science education, technical education and higher education. Aligarh Muslim University, Banaras Hindu University, Hyderabad University, Jawaharlal Nehru University, Delhi, Visva Bharati University, Shantiniketan and North Eastern Hill University, Shillong and some other centres of higher learning come under the direct control of the Central government. All educational institutes, scientific and technological institutes of national importance are run on the finances obtained from the Centre. Hence these are under the control of the Central Ministry of Education. Educational planning and education of the backward classes are also the responsibility of the Centre.

### Central Bodies of Education

In order to carry out its responsibilities in the area of education the Central government has established the University Grants Commission, I.T.T.'s (Indian Technological Institutes), N.C.E.R.T. (National of Educational Research and Training), etc. For education and research in engineering the Central government has established five national technological institutes. Besides, there are 15 regional engineering colleges, four management institutes, four technological teachers training institutes and about 350 Central schools run by the Central government.

## THE NATIONAL EDUCATION POLICY

In July 1978 a conference of State education ministers was held at Delhi. The conference unanimously decided that the following fields of education should be developed:

1. To make primary education universal.
2. Structure of education.
3. Adult education.
4. Arts and culture.
5. Physical education and Sports.

The Central education ministry appointed ad-hoc committees for each of these fields of education. The work is being done on the recommendation of these committees.

## EDUCATIONAL STRUCTURE

The Education Commission of 1964-66 recommended the implementation of the 10+2+3 system of education i.e., ten years of high school, two years of higher secondary and three years of undergraduate education. In 1968 this pattern has been recognised as the national pattern. Andhra Pradesh, Assam, Bihar, Gujarat, Karnatak, Kerala, Maharashtra, Tamilnadu, Orissa, Nagaland, Sikkim, Manipur, Meghalaya, Tripura, Andaman Nicobar Islands, Chandigarh, Dadra, Nagar Haveli, Delhi, Goa, Daman, Diu, Lacca Islands and Mizoram have accepted this pattern. Himachal Pradesh, Rajasthan, Uttar Pradesh, Punjab, Haryana and Madhya Pradesh, too, have accepted this pattern in principle and they need some more time to implement it.

### Primary Education

In all the States of the country primary education has been made free and compulsory. Primary education is taken care of both by the government and the local institutions run by private organisations and local bodies. Except in U.P., Orissa and West Bengal education up to the VIII class, too, is free. In these three States education up to the VIII class is free for girls only. In Bihar, Manipur, Meghalaya, Nagaland, Tripura and Sikkim the free education law has not yet been passed. In all the centrally governed areas this law has been passed and implemented also.

**Middle School**

In the beginning of the sixth five year Plan, i.e. by 1978-79 especial efforts were made for making primary education for the children between 6 and 11 years of age compulsory, instead of trying for making the junior high or middle class education (i.e. from classes 5 or 6 to 7 to 8) compulsory. It was decided that during the sixth five year Plan, i.e. from 1978-83, primary education and middle school education would be made universal within ten years. Informal and part-time education was considered necessary for those children who have not taken admission in schools for some reasons. So it was planned that the Centre would give financial assistance to those States in which there were about four crores and 18 lakhs unregistered children.

**Secondary Education**

In Tamilnadu, Kerala, Gujarat, Andhra Pradesh, Arunachal Pradesh, Andaman and Nicobar Islands and Lacca Islands, secondary education has been declared free. In Nagaland, Jammu and Kashmir, Dadar and Nagar Haveli and Pondicherry no fees are charged in government secondary schools. In Madhya Pradesh, Manipur, Orissa, Rajasthan, Tripura and Uttar Pradesh secondary education for girls has been made free. For the children of scheduled castes and tribal classes secondary education is free in all the States of the country. Their children are given stipends also for their education.

**Higher Education**

All education including higher education has, in response to a recognisable tendency in the Indian national movement for over half a century, been considered to be the constitutional prerogative of the State. Universities are set up by law, by State legislatures with formal as well as much practical authonomy. However, in the special powers of the State Governor as Chancellor, in the State's control of government grants to universities and, recently, in certain States through reconstitution of university bodies as well as on account of the private as well as government management of colleges affiliated to them, their autonomy suffers some limitations. The essential feeling of national unity is, in this matter, properly expressed in the provision of our Constitution that the maintenance and improvement of standards of higher education will be the responsibility of the government of India. For discharging this responsibility, the government has neither resorted to straight control by itself as, for instance, is the case in U.S.S.R., Germany and even France, nor gone to the American extreme of leaving it to voluntary accreditation associations of higher institutions. Somewhat on the British model, it has set up a University Grants Commission (U.G.C.) to disburse central finances to universities and to discharge the responsibility regarding maintenance of standards. Unlike the British Committee, however, the commission in India has a somewhat greater affinity to government styles and methods, presumably on account of general predominance of such styles and methods in our society. Similarly, the Indian U.G.C. had, among its members, heads of universities, i.e. Vice Chancellors, in contrast to university professors who sit on the British University Grants Committee

Research grants from bodies like the Indian Council of Medical Research, the Council of Scientific and Industrial Research, the Research Programmes Committee of the Planning Commission, the National Council of Educational Research and Training, etc., also affect the control and the morale of higher institutions. Disbursement of funds and formulation of policy also come, in their respective fields, from the All-India Council for Technical Education, the Indian Council of Agricultural Research, etc. The Indian Medical Council inspects medical institutions but does not disburse grants for which the State governments make appropriate arrangements.

## EXPANSION OF EDUCATION

### Primary and Secondary

Phenomenal expansion has taken place in the field of education since Independence. The number of schools increased from 5,30,000 in 1950-51 to 8,21,988 in 1992-93. The enrolment in schools increased from about 2.4 crore in 1950-51 to about 16.07 crore in 1992-93. Since Independence the gross enrolment ratios have gone up many times and have reached 105.5 per cent in classes I-V and 67.5 per cent in classes VI-VIII. the number of universities (including deemed universities) has increased from 25 at the time of Independence to 207 and the number of colleges from about 700 to 8545 by 1992-93. In addition there are 1040 polytechnics. The student enrolment in universities and colleges increased from about two lakhs at the time of Independence to 44.18 lakhs in 1991-92. The literacy rate as per the 1991 census is 52.11 per cent compared to 20 per cent in 1947.

With quantitative expansion of educational facilities, there is now a greater emphasis on qualitative improvement. Before 1976, education was largely the responsibility of States, the Central government being only concerned with certain areas like coordination and determination of standards in technical and higher education, etc. In 1976, through a Constitutional Amendment education became the joint responsibility of the Centre and the States.

Universalisation of elementary education, eradication of illiteracy in the age group of 15 to 35 and strengthening of vocational education (VE) so as to relate it to the emerging needs in the urban and rural settings are the major thrust areas of the Eighth Plan in the education sector. Utilisation of formal, non-formal and open channels of learning would be the strategy for this purpose. The changed approach, improved methodology of teaching, increased participation of NGOs and student volunteers have infused a new vitality into the literacy programme and have given it a fresh momentum. The aim would be to impart a similar vitality and momentum to the universal elementary education programme with a definite edge in its favour. The Eight Five Year Plan strategy for universalisation of elementary education envisages adoption of disaggregated target setting and decentralised planning. District specific plans for universalisation of elementary education are proposed to be drawn within the strategy frame of microplanning through people's participation and introduction of minimum levels of learning.

**Higher Education**

At present higher education is imparted through 137 universities of which 12 are under Central and the rest under State administration. The total number of colleges in the country is 8210. Besides, there are 34 institutions deemed as universities. The number of students is 50.07 lakhs and the number of teachers is 2.86 lakhs.

## VOCATIONAL AND TECHNICAL EDUCATION

The government has established the following four institutes for meeting the requirements of specialised workers:

1. Higher Training Institute, Madras.
2. Foreman Training Institute, Bangalore.
3. Central Employees Training and Research Institute, Calcutta.
4. Institute of Higher Training in Electronics, Hyderabad.

The progress of primary and secondary education in India may be assessed from the following table.

### INCREASE IN ADMISSIONS

In lakhs

| | Primary | Secondary |
|---|---|---|
| 1960-61 | 350 | 07 |
| 1968-69 | 544 | 125 |
| 1970-80 | 716 | 193 |
| 1982-83 | 795 | 236 |
| 1984-85 | 856 | 262 |
| 1986-87 | 900 | 288 |
| 1987-88 | 929 | 300 |
| 1988-89 | 957 | 309 |
| 1989-90 | 973 | 322 |
| 1991-92 | 1016 | 345 |
| 1992-93 | 1054 | 387 |

Seven Central training institutes have been opened for preparing teachers under the Directorate of Employment and Training. In 750 polytechnics 90,000 trainees are admitted every year for acquiring practical experience regarding production, construction, experimentation and development. The successful trainees are awarded diplomas in engineering, technology and some non-technical areas. These institutes give three years' training. For the part-time trainees the period of training is four years.

Up to 1983-84 about 30 polytechnics have opened for giving training in engineering and technology to those women who are leading poor life due to unfavourable social and economic conditions.

Engineering colleges teaching courses leading to degrees in engineering to those persons who want to serve as engineers in engineering and technological vocations. Today there are 300 such engineering colleges in which about 65,000 students are receiving education in various branches of engineering. For postgraduate education in engineering there are 76 institutes in which about 11,000 students are admitted every year. For part-time students these institutes offer four year course. In the engineering colleges affiliated to some universities graduate and post-graduate degree courses in management and vocational administration are taught. The State Technical Education Board evaluates the working of the various industrial training institutes and polytechnics spread in the respective States.

There are six national institutes known as I.I.Ts (Indian Institute of Technology) established at six places, viz., Bombay, Bangalore, Kanpur, Khadakpur, Madras and Delhi. In the Bangalore I.I.T.2,000 post-graduate students and 1.500 research scholars are admitted every year. In the remaining five institutes about 7,200 students are admitted every year. In addition to these five institutes there are 70 other engineering colleges and engineering faculties of universities admitting 3,500 students every year for education in engineering. For giving training in various branches of engineering and technology there are 15 regional colleges, technical institutes and polytechnics. There are various centres giving training in the various branches of mining and metalurgy. Some institutes give training also along with work. These institutes offer 5½ years degree course and 3½ years diploma course. Four training centres have been opened for training of teachers of engineering.

## TEACHING IN EDUCATION

### Four Years Degree Course in Education

A new direction has been given to teachers' training by introducing a four years degree course in Education on the pattern followed in U.S.A. There are four regional colleges of education in the country situated at Mysore, Bhubaneswar, Bhopal and Ajmer, besides the Kurukshetra University in Haryana (which has been discontinued now) where too this degree course has been introduced with the object of turning out efficient teachers. This move has been started on the plea that nine months' teachers' training imparted to graduates and post-graduates is not adequate to make the trainee an efficient teacher. Consequently, a four years degree course after High School has been introduced in education with the hope that the future teachers will be fully trained to become efficient teachers. This degree course is divided into three main parts which are as follows:

1. General and Liberal Education.
2. Specialised Education and

3. Professional Education.

**1. General and Liberal Education**

The object of this part of education is to develop in the future teacher such qualities as may help him to develop the personality and character of his students in a manner which may enrich their country and the humanity at large To achieve this proficiency he will have to study the following subjects:

1. Languages — regional and the English language
2. Social Sciences
3. Mathematic
4. Natural Sciences
5. Arts and Crafts
6. Health and Physical Education.

**2. Specialised Education**

The future teacher must acquire a thorough knowledge of the subject which he intends to teach his students. The teachers of High School standard have to teach more than one subject. So any teacher of this standard must possess a knowledge of a number of subjects. They are, therefore, given specialised education in some subjects.

**3. Professional Education**

Under this part the future teacher is taught subjects of educational psychology, educational philosophy, social science, history of education, problems of education and principles of guidance and evaluation.

## 2. CORRESPONDENCE SCHOOL AND COURSE

There are many persons in India who had to give up education due to certain circumstances beyond their control, although they possessed a strong desire to pursue their studies further. Correspondence schools are meant for persons of this category. In Delhi a Directorate of Correspondence Course was opened in 1962 for the first time in the country and in this way a way was opened to make higher education available to any citizen who desired to be educated. Such schools exist in countries like Japan, U.S.A., Russia, England and some other countries. They have proved a success there. In these schools lessons are prepared by very able teachers. The answers to these questions are carefully examined and improved and then returned to the students along with the next lesson. The Directorate has declared that the curriculum, examination and degree awarded will be the same as is given to the students of Delhi University. We need such correspondence schools in large number in the country. Himachal Pradesh University, Simla, too, has started correspondence courses for B. Ed., M. Ed. and other subjects. Many other universities in the country are now planning to start correspondence courses for degree classes.

## 3. REGIONAL COLLEGE OF EDUCATION

For regional colleges of education have been set up at Ajmer, Mysore,

Bhuvneshwar and Bhopal in order to prepare teachers for multi-purpose schools. These colleges have been opened on the recommendation of Secondary Education Commission of 1953. The colleges started functioning in July 1963.

**Aims of Regional Colleges**

1. To prepare teachers for multi-purpose schools.
2. To train teachers for science, agriculture, commerce, home-science, sculpture, arts and crafts.
3. To provide in service training to teachers and supervisors engaged in teaching profession in multi-purpose schools.
4. To run a Model Demonstration Multi-purpose schools.
5. To function as regional centre for extension services.
6. To conduct research for improving teaching methods.
7. To conduct research in teachers education and implement new methods of teaching evolved as the result of research.

**Expansion of Regional Colleges**

The regions covered by different regional colleges are given as below:

| | | |
|---|---|---|
| Mysore | — | Southern regions — Karnatk, Kerala, Tamilnadu and Andhra Pradesh. |
| Bhopal | — | Western regions — Madhya Pradesh, Gujrat and Maharashtra. |
| Ajmer | — | Northern regions — Rajasthan, Delhi, Himachal Pradesh, Uttar Pradesh, Punjab, Haryana, Jammu and Kashmir. |
| Bhubaneswar | — | Eastern region — Orissa, Bihar, Assam, West Bengal, Manipur, Tripura, Nefa and connected regions. |

**Programme of Regional Colleges**

1. Four years course for training science and technology teachers.
2. One year course for training teachers in commerce, art and crafts, (in colleges in Bhopal and Bhubaneswar), agriculture, science, home science (for colleges in Mysore and Ajmer) and technology.
3. In service training programme.
4. One to two years diploma course and two years degree course for the teachers of sculpture.

## CENTRAL SCHOOLS

These schools have been opened for the children of those Union government employees whose jobs are transferable (who are transferred from one place to other). These schools have been opened on the recommendations of Second Pay Commission. These schools prepare students for the higher secondary education curriculum and examinations, as prescribed by the Central Board of Secondary Education, Delhi. In these schools the children of the following categories of people are admitted:

1. Those employees of the Union government who are often transferred from one place to another.
2. Defence personnel.
3. Employees of the All India Services.
4. Employees of the autonomous bodies aided by the Union government.
5. Floating and local population.

**Finances at Central Schools**

The Union Ministry of Education is responsible to bear the expenditure incurred over these schools. Education is free up to eighth class. The fee for classes IX, X and XI is Rs. 6, Rs. 7 and Rs. 8 respectively. No fee is charged from the boys of scheduled castes. The medium of instruction is both English and Hindi in these schools. These schools exist in all the States in the country.

At present there are 796 central schools with seven lakh students and 41712 employees. During 1993-94 additional 25 schools were sanctioned.

## N.C.E.R.T.

The National Council of Educational Research and Training (N.C.E.R.T.) was established in September 1961 in New Delhi as an autonomous body. Qualitative improvement and excellence in school education and teacher education are some of its major objectives. To achieve them, the N.C.E.R.T. undertakes programmes related to research, development, training, extension and dissemination of educational information through its constituent departments — the C.I.E.T., the Regional Colleges of Education at Ajmer, Bhopal, Bhubaneswar and Mysore and 17 field offices located all over the country.

The N.C.E.R.T. continued to coordinate and monitor activities related to the U.N.I.C.E.F.-assisted projects in elementary and non-formal education and U.N.F.P.A.- assisted National Population Education Project (school and non-formal education). The N.C.E.R.T. maintains effective liaison with State education authorities and State level institutions for providing academic inputs to school education system.

During 1992-93, major achievements of N.C.E.R.T. were directed towards Early Childhood Care and Education (E.C.C.E.), Universalisation of Elementary Education (U.E.E.), Minimum Levels of Learning (M.L.L.), orientation of content and process of education at the school stage, improvement of science education in school, computer literacy, vocationalisation of education, teacher education, education of SCs/STs and minorities, education for women's equality, education of the disabled children, utilisation of educational technology, educational survey and data processing, National Talent Search Scholarship, promotion of educational research and publication of textbooks for C.B.S.E. affiliated schools in the country.

N.C.E.R.T. develops curricula, syllabi and prepare textbooks for classes I-XII. The syllabi prepared by the N.C.E.R.T. from the basis for prescription of scheme of studies by Central Board of Secondary Education (C.B.S.E.) for the students of schools affiliated to the board. The syllabi and textbooks so prepared by N.C.E.R.T. are given to State/UT agencies for use in their schools after adoption/adaptation. It also develops instructional material for childhood education and training packages for teacher educators and supervisory personnel. N.C.E.R.T. orgtanises Jawaharlal Nehru National Science Exhibition every year in which a large number of school students from all over the country participate. The council produces science kits for the use of schools students. It prepares comprehensive guidelines for curriculum evaluation and school-industry linkages as well as for pre-service and in service education of teacher on vocationalisation of education. Training courses for the officials involved in the Integrated Education Programme for Disabled Children are also conducted by the N.C.E.R.T.

## SPECIAL RESEARCH ORGANISATIONS

Indian Council of Historical Research, New Delhi, set up in 1972, enunciates and implements a national policy on historical research and encourages scientific writing of history. It operates research projects, provides financial support of research projects by individual scholars, awards fellowship and undertakes publication and translation work.

Indian Council of Philosophical Research which started functioning from 1981 with offices in New Delhi and Lucknow, reviews the progress of research in philosophy from time to time, sponsors or assists projects of programmes of research in philosophy, gives financial assistance to institutions and individuals to conduct research in philosophy and allied disciplines.

Indian Institute of Advanced Study, Shimla, set up in 1965, is a residential centre for advanced research in humanities, social sciences and natural sciences. It is a community of scholars engaged in exploring new frontiers of knowledge aimed at making major conceptual development and offering interdisciplinary perspectives on questions of contemporary relevance.

Indian Council of Social Science Research, New Delhi, is an autonomous body for promoting and coordinating social science research. Its main functions are to review the progress of social science research, give advice on research activities in government or outside, sponsor research programmes and give grants to institutions and individuals for research in social sciences.

## THE U.G.C.

Coordination and determination of standards in higher education is a subject in the Union List and, hence, a special responsibility of the Central government. This responsibility is discharged mainly through University Grants Commission

(U.G.C.), which was established in 1956 under an Act of Parliament to take measures for promotion and coordination of university education and determination and maintenance of standards in teaching, examination and research in universities. To fulfil its objectives, the commission can enquire, among other things, into financial needs of universities, allocate and disburse grants to them; establish and maintain common services and facilities, recommend measures for improvement of university education and give advice on allocation of grants and establishment of new universities. U.G.C. has approved 111 colleges for autonomous status—23 in Andhra Pradesh, 44 in Tamilnadu, 30 in Madhya Pradesh, five each in Rajasthan and Orissa, two each in Gujarat and Uttar Pradesh.

## LITERACY

According to 1991 census the literacy rate in India increased to 52.2 per cent in 1991 from 43.56 per cent in 1981, an increase of 8.65 per cent. Where the literacy among males increased 13 per cent literacy among women increased by 6.45 per cent. The number of literates (aged seven and above in 1991 at 3,593 lakhs compares very well with the number of literates at 2,357 lakhs in 1981. The number of illiterates in 1991 was 3,289 lakhs which is a marginal increase from 3,289 lakhs which is a marginal increase from 3,053 lakhs in 1981. The increase in the number of literates in 1991 over 1981 was 1,236 lakhs whereas the corresponding increase in the number of illiterates was 236 lakhs only. Kerala (82.8 per cent) tops the literacy rate followed by Mizoram (82.27 per cent), Lakshdweep (81.78 per cent) and Chandigarh (77.81 per cent). At the end of the ladder are Bihar (38.48 per cent) and Dadra and Nagar Haveli (40.71 per cent). The increase in female literacy rate has been very significant in the States/Union Territory of Sikkim (19.29 per cent), Lakshadweep (17.59), Nagaland (14.45 per cent), Daman and Diu (12.90 per cent), Haryana (13.57 per cent), Manipur (13 per cent), Andaman and Nicobar Islands (12.26 per cent), Pondicherry (12.63 per cent), Tripura (11.65 per cent), and Kerala (10.47 per cent). The literacy rate is above the all India level of 52.21 per cent in case of 22 States/UTs but eight States viz. Bihar, Rajasthan, Arunachal Pradesh, Madhya Pradesh, Uttar Pradesh, Andhra Pradesh, Meghalaya, Orissa and Union Territory of Dadra and Nagar Haveli are still below the threshold level of literacy i.e. 50 per cent. All these States/UTs except Meghalaya are also below the all India level in case of female literacy.

## ADULT EDUCATION

The National Literacy Mission (NLM) was launched in 1988 with the objective of imparting functional literacy to 800 lakh adult illiterates in the age-group 15-35 by 1995. The implementation of programmes under the NLM has showed that eradication of illiteracy is not a utopian idea but possible, feasible and achievable. The most important development that has taken place under the NLM is the near ascendancy of the campaign mode in the adult education programmes in the country. After experimenting with successive number of alternative models of adult education programmes we have finally settled down to one which has given us hope and faith that literacy can be overcome in a time bound manner with planned and coordinated efforts and with mobilisation of people belonging to all sections of the society.

Campaigns for total literacy constitute the major thrust and initiative in the mission, they also constitute the principle strategy. In the heels of success of Ernakulam and Kerala experiments for achieving full literacy, these campaigns for total literacy have generated certain characteristic features which make them unique and distinguish them from other programmes. They are area specific, time-bound, voluntary-based, cost-effective and outcome-oriented. Total literacy campaigns have been launched in 258 districts of the country covering over 520 lakh illiterate persons. Eighty districts have commenced post literacy campaigns.

The thrust in all programmes of adult education is now on adoption of area approach, continuous environment building for literacy through Jathas, street plays, nukkad nataks, T.V., radio, newspapers, folk art forms, etc. and use of motivation oriented teaching/learning materials produced under the new technique of Improved Pace and Content of Learning (I.P.C.L.).

## NATIONAL POPULATION EDUCATION PROJECT

The objective of inculcating the message of small family norms and other population related issues in the minds of school and college students and the clientele of adult and non-formal education is being achieved through National Population Education Project. The National Population Education Programme is now being implemented through three projects of School and Non-Formal Education, Higher Education and Adult Education.

Since its inception in 1980, National Population Education Project (N.P.E.P.) has covered much ground towards achieving its main objective of institutionalising population education in the school education system. During the second cycle (1986-90), the main focus has been on consolidation of project's multidimensional activities and further expansion of its network. The project is currently running in 29 States/UTs. During the Seventh Plan, it is proposed to direct substantially and systematically the N.P.E.P. activities towards the non-formal sector.

## SCHOLARSHIPS

The Department of Education funds several scholarship/fellowship programmes for Indian students for higher education including some offered by other governments. These include the national Scholarship Scheme, a special coaching scheme for scheduled castes and scheduled tribes students, a scheme of scholarships to help students of non-Hindi speaking States studying Hindi, research scholarships for Indian classical languages and scholarships to enable talented rural children to continue secondary education. These programmes are administered through the State governments. A new programme of prestigious fellowships for Postgraduate studies in India and abroad named Jawaharlal Nehru Fellowships have recently been introduced.

Scholarships for advanced or specialised studies are offered under the provisions of cultural exchange programmes, bilateral agreements. Commonwealth scholarships/fellowships plan and ad hoc scholarship offers received from different countries. These scholarships are mostly for Ph. D (Doctoral) and Post-doctoral specialisation for which the minimum eligibility requirement is a Masters degree.

## BOOKS

### National Book Trust

The National Book Trust (N.B.T.), India, an autonomous organisation under the Department of Education, Ministry of Human Resource Development, plays an important role in book promotion programmes. The National Book Trust publishes low priced books on a variety of subjects including physical environment and culture of India, folklore, popular science, biographies and books for children, adults and neo-literates. Publishing translations of significant creative writings in various Indian languages is a major activity. The trust has published over 6,000 titles in 13 languages. During 1993-94 the trust published more than 500 titles.

The N.B.T. subsidises publication of economically priced books for higher education. Besides subsidy to the publisher, the trust pays an attractive royalty directly to the author. Under this scheme, the N.B.T. has subsidised about 800 titles. The trust also provides financial assistance to private publishers and voluntary agencies for producing quality low-priced books for children, neo-literates and school drop-outs.

N.B.T. organises book fairs, festivals and exhibitions, seminars, symposia and workshops to promote interaction amongst readers, writers, intellectuals, publishers, booksellers, etc. During the year 1993-94 the trust has organised children's book fairs at Guwahati (October 10-18, 1992) and New Delhi (January 2-10, 1993); book festivals at Bhubaneswar (October 31 - November 8, 1992) and Visakhapatnam (November 28 - December 6, 1992); and the National Book Fair at Bangalore (January 30 - February 7, 1993).

Since 1989, the trust has been promoting the celebration of national Book Week on all-India scale. The trust has taken up pilot projects for establishing Readers' Clubs in schools of Bangalore, Guwahati and Bhubaneswar. On behalf of the Ministry of Human Resource Development, the National Book Trust participates in various international book fairs and exhibitions and puts up exhibits of contemporary Indian books.

### Import Policy for Books

Under the new policy announced by the Ministry of Commerce with effect from April 1, 1992, any person/organisation is free to import books on educational, scientific and technical subjects without any restrictions.

### Copyright

Copyright protection is governed by the Indian Copyright Act, 1957. The Copyright Act has been amended thrice in 1983, 1984 and lastly in 1992 to extend the term of Copyright from 50-60 years. A comprehensive review of the Act has been made and two Bills—the Copyright (Second Amendment) Bill, 1992 and the Copyright Cess Bill, 1992 were introduced in the Lok Sabha in July 1992 to amend the Act further.

**Raja Rammohan Roy National Agency for I.S.B.N.**

The International Standard Book Numbering System (I.S.B.N.) is an international system by which a distinct identifying number is assigned to each book. The I.S.B.N. system introduced in 1985 is still in its infancy in India but is already proving useful to the book trade, libraries, information systems and research scholars. Since 1985 up to March 31, 1994 more than 2367 publishers have been registered under the system. The National Agency also brings out National Catalogue of I.S.B.N. titles annually.

## PROMOTION OF LANGUAGES

The government encourages development of all Indian languages including classical, modern and tribal. Its policy lays emphasis on training of teachers in relation to adoption of the three-language formula and production of university-level textbooks with a view to facilitating media switch over from English to regional languages. In order to assist non-Hindi speaking States/Union territories to effectively implement the three-language formula, support for provision on facilities for teaching of Hindi in these States/UTs is provided by sanctioning financial assistance for appointment of Hindi teachers in schools and for establishment of Hindi teachers training colleges in these States/UTs, under a Centrally sponsored scheme. The grant-in-aid is provided mainly to assist the consolidation and further development of Hindi teacher training colleges in non-Hindi speaking States/Union territories and to a limited extent, to assist the setting up of a new institution in such areas which are in need of such assistance. Assistance is also given to voluntary organisations for enabling them to hold Hindi teaching classes, conducting research on methodology of its teaching and providing Hindi books to various organisations. Various schemes are in operation to promote and develop tribal, classical, modern Indian languages and prepare and publish books, dictionaries, research and instructional material besides training of teachers in Hindi. Through the Kendriya Hindi Sansthan, Agra, the government of India promotes development of improved methodology for teaching Hindi to the non-Hindi speaking students. Central Hindi Directorate runs programmes relating to purchase and publication of books and their free distribution to non-Hindi speaking States and to the Indian missions.

The Commission for Scientific and Technical Terminology, New Delhi, prepares and publishes definitional dictionaries and terminology in various disciplines and Pan-Indian terminology. Hindi-English glossaries in basic sciences, humanities, social sciences and applied sciences, university level textbooks in agriculture and engineering and other subjects are also published. Fifty scholarships are awarded every year to foreign students for studying Hindi in Kendriya Hindi Sansthan, Agra.

**Modern Indian Languages**

Financial assistance is given to voluntary organisations and individuals to bring out publications like encyclopaedias, dictionaries, books of knowledge, original writing on linguistic, literary, indological, social anthropological and cultural themes, critical editions of old manuscripts, etc., for the development of modern Indian languages. Grants are also given for holding literary conferences, seminars and exhibitions besides, purchasing copies of printed publications. States are given special help for the production of university level books in the regional languages. The Bureau for Promotion of Urdu was set up in 1969. Apart from working as a secretariat to the Taraqqi-e-Urdu Board which advises the government on development of Urdu, it also develops educational literature in Urdu. It has established 39 calligraphy centres where training is given to students in Kitabat.

Government also provides facilities for study of languages other than mother tongue. For this, the Central Institute of Indian Languages (C.I.I.L.), Mysore, conducts research in the areas of language analysis, language pedagogy, language technology and language use. Study of tribal languages is one of its important functions. It runs six regional language centres at Bhubaneswar, Mysore, Patiala, Pune, Solan and Lucknow to help meet the demand for trained teachers to implement the three-language formula and one extension centre at Guwahati to do research for development of tribal languages of north-eastern region.

**English and Foreign Languages**

The Central Institute of English and Foreign Languages (C.I.E.F.L.), Hyderabad, set up as an autonomous body in 1958 is engaged in bringing out qualitative improvement in teaching of English. Subsequently, teaching of major foreign languages, viz. Russian, German, French and Arabic and their literatures was also included in its activities. In 1973 it was declared to be an institution of higher learning deemed-to-be a university. It has two regional centres at Shillong and Lucknow.

Financial assistance is also provided to States for setting up C.I.E.F.L.'s district centres for English with a view to improving the standard of English language, teaching and learning. These centres aim at imparting training to teachers of English in their areas through orientation courses. Under another scheme, financial assistance is given to regional and State institutes of English for strengthening their programmes of training with respect to improving standard of English language teaching.

**Sanskrit and Other Classical Languages**

There are many schemes for propagation, popularisation and development of Sanskrit and other classical languages like Arabic and Persian. These include schemes for financial assistance to State governments and voluntary Sanskrit organisations, development of Sanskrit institutions run by voluntary organisations into Adarsh Sanskrit Pathshalas, for incentives to retired scholars as Shastra Chudamani pandits for publication of original writings of contemporary authors, editing and publication of rare manuscripts and catalogues of manuscripts, reprinting of important out-of-print Sanskrit texts, promotion of oral Vedic tradition, vocational training to products of Sanskrit Pathshalas, national awards to eminent Sanskrit, Arabic and Persian scholars and preparation/publication of Sanskrit dictionaries.

Registered organisations engaged in the development and propagation of Sanskrit are given recurring and non-recurring grants for salary of teachers, scholarships to students, construction and repair of buildings, library books, research projects, etc., up to 75 per cent of the approved expenditure. About 700 voluntary institutions conducting courses on traditional Sanskrit education and about 200 institutions working in the field of propagation and promotion of Arabic/Persian are benefited under this scheme every year. Institutions having potential for greater development are identified and brought under the scheme of Adarsh Sanskrit Mahavidyalayas and Shodh Sansthans. At present, such Mahavidyalayas and Shodh Sansthans are being assisted. Under the scheme of Certificate of Honour to Sanskrit, Arabic and Persian scholars, 15 eminent Sanskrit scholars and three each in Arabic and Persian are honoured by the President every year. They are also given a grant of Rs 10,000 per year for life.

Department of Education also conducts an all-India Vedic convention (through R.V.V.P.) and an all-India Sanskrit elocution contest every year where scholars in different Shastras and a team of eight contestants from all States are invited with a view to identifying the rare Veda Shakhas and their repositories, devising ways and means for preserving the oral traditions and encouraging extempore speech on classical subjects. As a special measure to preserve oral tradition of Vedic studies, a scheme was introduced in 1978 under which each Swadhyayin is expected to train two students each below 12 years, one of them being his own son or near relative in a particular Veda Shakha. The scholar gets an honorarium of Rs 1,250 and the student Rs 175 per month. In all, 21 such units are receiving assistance. Seven of them were set up after the Vedic convention held in Indore in November 1987. Rashtriya Veda Vidya Pratishthan has been set up with the objective of preserving and developing all aspects of Vedic studies. For this, the Pratishthan undertakes various activities such as supporting traditional Vedic institutions and scholars by providing fellowships, scholarships, etc. Similarly, there are 26 institutions which are given 95 per cent grant for popularising Vedic education. Government is also providing financial assistance to eight Veda units which are engaged in the preservation of oral tradition of Vedic recitation.

Under Shastra Chudamani scheme, young scholars are given in-depth coaching in Kendriya Vidyapeethas/Adarsh Sanskrit Mahavidyalayas, etc. in various disciplines by utilising services of eminent services of eminent elderly scholars. These scholars are appointed on a monthly honorarium of Rs 1,000.

Rashtriya Sanskrit Sansthan an autonomous organisation under the Ministry with its headquarters at Delhi, exercises academic and administrative control over seven Kendriya Sanskrit Vidyapeethas at Jammu, Allahabad, Guruvayoor. Puri, Jaipur, Lucknow and Sringeri where Sanskrit education in traditional Shastras and research in various fields is conducted. Vidyapeethas of Delhi and Tirupati, were declared deemed-to-be universities in 1987. The Sansthan also conducts examination from Prathma to Vidyayaridhi (Ph.D) and Vachaspati (D.Litt.) and in addition to its own institutions over 50 other institutions all over the country are affiliated to it.

Under the Centrally sponsored scheme of Development of Sanskrit 100 per cent grant is given to the State governments/UTs for (a) financial assistance up to Rs. 4,000 per annum to eminent Sanskrit scholars in indigent circumstances; (b) for appointment of teachers for teaching selected modern subjects in the traditional Sanskrit Pathshalas; (c) for providing facilities for teaching Sanskrit in high and higher secondary schools; (d) for scholarships to students studying Sanskrit in order to attract good students in IX to XII classes; and (e) for their own schemes for promotion of Sanskrit.

**Resources for Education**

Promotion of quality and equity are no less resource initiative than quantitative expansion of institutions. The budgetary outlays on education, of the Centre and States, had steadily increased from 1.2 per cent of GNP in 1950-51 to 3.5 per cent in 1990-91.

## MAHILA SAMAKHYA

A Central scheme 'Mahila Samakhya' was launched in April 1989. This programme seeks to mobilise rural women for education through Mahila Sanghas in each of the village concerned. This is a Central scheme where full financial assistance is provided to Mahila Samakhya societies in Karnataka, Uttar Pradesh, Gujarat and Andhra Pradesh set up under the chairmanship of the concerned State Education Secretary. The Minister of Education in the state is the president of the society. As an Indo-Dutch programme, it receives cent per cent assistance from the government of Netherlands. Essentially, the programme revolves around Mahila Sanghas where women are mobilised around issues like access to health, education, water, information about development programmes, general information about their immediate environment, and above all, issues related to their personality and self-image in society. The programme tries to facilitate critical reflection and analysis which would encourage women to take active interest in issues that affect their daily life. The focus of the programme is on generating demand for education and introducing innovative educational inputs for pre-school, non-formal, adult and continuing education.

## BIHAR EDUCATION PROJECT

The Bihar Education Project (B.E.P.) is a programme of educational reconstruction for bringing about fundamental change in the education system in Bihar. As a comprehensive basic education project, it covers the elementary school system; the non-formal education system; early childhood care and education; women's education and development; and post literacy, continuing education and inculcation of basic skills for survival and general well being. It is a joint project of Central and State government which U.N.I.C.E.F. is also assisting. The project is implemented through an autonomous state level society with the partnership of State government, the Centre, U.N.I.C.E.F., teachers representatives and N.G.Os active in the field. The Chief Minister is Chairman of the society. The executive responsibility vests with the State Project Director. The project is currently under implementation in Ranchi, Rohtas, Chatra, Sitamarhi, Muzaffarpur, West Champaran and Singhboom district.

## LOK JUMBISH : PEOPLE'S MOVEMENT FOR EDUCATION FOR ALL

An innovative educational project called 'Lok Jumbish: People's Movement for Education for All, Rajasthan with assistance from Swedish International Development Authority (S.I.D.A.) has been taken up in Rajasthan. The basic objective of the project is to achieve education for all by the year 2000 through people's mobilisation and their participation. The project presupposes that creation of a people's movement would generate a stimulus for human development which, in turn, would lead to a basic socio-economic change. Lok Jumbish concentrates on primary education.

## SHIKSHA KARMI PROJECT

The Shiksha Karmi Project is being implemented since 1987 in Rajasthan with the assistance from the Swedish International Development Authority (S.I.D.A.). Its aim is universalisation of primary education in selected remote and socio-economically backward villages of the State.

The project identifies teacher absenteeism as a major obstacle in achieving the objective of universalisation. It accordingly, envisages substitution of the primary school teacher in single teacher schools by a team of two locally resident educational workers called 'Shiksha Karmi'.

## U.N.E.S.C.O. AND INTERNATIONAL COOPERATION

Since the inception of the United nations Educational Scientific and Cultural Organisation (U.N.E.S.C.O.), India has been in the forefront in promoting the ideals and objectives of the organisation. The Indian National Commission for Cooperation with U.N.E.S.C.O. set up in 1949 in compliance with Article 7 of the Constitution of U.N.E.S.C.O., is the apex advisory, executive, liaison, information and coordinating body at the national level. It has been playing an active role in U.N.E.S.C.O.'s work particularly in the formulation and execution of its programme in collaborating with national commissions of Asia and the Pacific region.

During 1991-92, India extended its cooperation of U.N.E.S.C.O. and its regional offices through participation in numerous workshops, symposia and conferences, organising national, regional and inter-regional activities in the country in area of competence of U.N.E.S.C.O., arranging placement of U.N.E.S.C.O. fellows in Indian institutions, implementing projects under the participation programme of U.N.E.S.C.O. and administration of U.N.E.S.C.O. Coupons scheme.

### External Academic Relations

External academic relations both bilateral and multilateral perform a significant role in international deplomacy. With a view to deepen India's academic interaction with important countries, the educational component of the cultural exchange programmes and other bilateral arrangements is being explored to encourage studies regarding India and Indology in foreign universities. A dialogue has been established to concretise new ideas in this area with our missions in China, Pakistan, Japan, U.S.A., Germany, Bhutan, France, etc.

### U.N.E.S.C.O. Clubs and Associated Schools

The U.N.E.S.C.O. clubs, constituted mainly in educational institutions, are voluntary bodies engaged in the promotion of aims and objectives of the organisation. The associated schools are educational institutions which are directly linked with U.N.E.S.C.O. Secretariat for participation in the Associated School Project for undertaking activities relating to education for international understanding, cooperation and peace. Thirtyseven scholls and teacher training institutions from India are enlisted with U.N.E.S.C.O. under the project.

## BORDER AREA DEVELOPMENT PROGRAMME (B.A.D.P.)

Border Area Development Programme (B.A.D.P.) is implemented in the border States of Gujarat, Jammu and Kashmir, Punjab and Rajasthan covering 18 border districts and 79 border blocks. Financial assistance was rendered to the States under this programme in all priority areas of education such as universalisation of elementary education, improvement of secondary education, vocational education, culture and sports besides establishment of ITIs and polytechnics.

## EDUCATION OF WOMEN

Enrolment of girls as a ratio of total enrolment during 1991-92 is only 39 per cent at primary stage, 33 per cent at middle stage and 28 per cent at higher education stage. All out efforts were made during the period for improving girls/women's participation in education. Under the Scheme of Operation Blackboard, government has provided assistance since 1987-88 for creation of 1,22,890 posts of primary school teachers mainly to be filled by women. According to the latest reports, 1,02,587 posts of teachers have been filled up of which 48.52 per cent are women teachers. Ninety per cent assistance was given for N.F.E. centres meant for girls. The cumulative number of N.F.E. centres for girls is 82,000. The 'Mahila Samakhya' (Education for Women's Equality) Project has been under implementation. By conscious action, admission of girls to the extent of 28.44 per cent in Navodaya Vidyalayas has been ensured. Special attention was given to enrolment of women in adult education centres. In the Total Literacy Campaigns (T.L.Cs), the theme of empowerment of women is receiving special focus. The women learners under T.L.Cs out number male learners.

## EDUCATION OF SCHEDULED CASTES AND SCHEDULED TRIBES

The year 1990-91 was the centenary year of Dr. B.R. Ambedkar. The National Committee which was set up under the chairmanship of the then Prime Minister, decided that the programmes for the development of SCs and STs would continue up to the year 1993-94. Department of Education has issued instructions to organisations under its control to take up programmes and activities for celebrating the birth centenary in a befitting manner and extend these activities to the current year also. The programme includes panel discussion, seminars, essay competitions, publications of Dr. Ambedkar's biography and anthology of his works, creation of chairs of Baba Saheb Dr. B.R. Ambedkar, philosophy and thoughts in universities, inclusion of Baba Saheb's thoughts in the textbooks, etc.

The thrust on removal of disparities and equalisation of educational opportunities by catering to specific needs of SCs and STs continued. Under the schemes of 'Operation Blackboard', non-formal education adult education, etc., States were advised to give high priority to selection of blocks which have large concentration of SCs and STs.

The revised Programme of Action (P.O.A.) 1992 prepared in pursuance of the modified National Policy on Education (N.P.E.), 1986 provides for continuance of the existing education programmes for SCs and STs with stress on improving literacy increasing enrolment and reducing drop-out rates among SCs/STs. The scheme of upgradation of merit of SC/ST students started in 1987-88 continued to be implemented through States/UTs. Under this scheme, remedial coaching is given to SCs and STs in classes IX-X and special coaching in classes XI and XII for preparing them for competitive examinations.

Other facilities like reservation of seats in educational institutions (15 per cent of SCs and 7.5 per cent for STs), relaxation in qualifying marks in entrance examinations, reservation in pre-matric scholarships, freeships in Kendriya Vidyalayas, reservation in university level research fellowships, research associationships, teacher fellowships, etc. were continued.

The Indian Institutes of Technology operate a scheme under which candidates belonging to SCs and STs, who fail in the Joint Entrance Examination by very slender margin of marks are given further training and admitted to relevant courses.

## EDUCATION OF MINORITIES

Under 15-Point Programme, University Grants Commission continued to implement the scheme of providing assistance to universities and colleges for coaching students from educationally backward minorities. The scheme is being revamped. It will be expanded to cover minority concentration areas as well as non-minority concentration areas for remedial and enrichment coaching. One of the proposals under consideration is to get the minority students coached for the higher studies through reputed private coaching institutions as is being done in the case of SC/ST students. The programme of review of textbooks from the point of view of communal harmony, secularism and national integration is being implemented by the National Council of Educational Research and Training (N.C.E.R.T.) and State governments. All the 41 minority concentration districts identified by the Programme of Action, (1986) have been covered by community polytechnics and their extension centres under 15-Point programme.

The revised Programme of Action 1992 envisages several short, medium, and long term measures for the improvement of minorities' education. In pursuance of these programmes, a scheme of financial assistance to voluntary organisations for modernisation of Madrasa education has been prepared to encourage traditional institutions like Madrasas and Maktabs by giving financial assistance to introduce science, mathematics, social studies and modern Indian languages like Hindi and English.

Another new scheme of Area Intensive Programme for educationally backward minorities has also been prepared to provide assistance to State governments and voluntary organisations for taking up programmes for educationally backward minorities, not covered by the on-going programmes. The Eighth Five Year Plan provision for the scheme is Rs. 16.27 crore.

Up to March 1993 the facility of coaching was availed by 41002 candidates under the coaching scheme for competitive examinations started in 1984 and at present being carried on in 21 universities and 32 colleges. During 1992-93 the number of successful candidates was 2650. The scheme was modified in March 1993. In the programme of teachers' training for minorities, so far 450 principals and 950 teachers have been trained.

## STIPENDS FOR FOREIGN STUDENTS

The Central government grants various stipends to foreign students for education and training in India. Under the general cultural scholarship programme every year about 200 stipends are given to foreign students of Asia and Africa. Scholarships to foreign students are generally given in the areas of engineering, agriculture, medicine, technology and humanities. According to the 1972-73 plan it has been decided to award stipends to about 100 students of Bangladesh every year. During 1983-84 about 300 students of Bangladesh have been studying in India. There is a provision for granting stipends for studies to foreign students of those countries which maintain friendly relationship with us. Under this provision the following are the plans worth mentioning:

1. The plan of exchange of stipendship.
2. The plan of Common Wealth fellowship or stipendship.
3. Technological co-operation and stipendship under the Colombo plan.

## YOUTH SERVICES IN INDIA

In India there are many Youth Services which work towards promoting physical, mental, social and cultural development of our youths. Below we are hinting at some of these services:

*Nehru Youth Centre*. There are about 255 Nehru Youth Centres in the various

States and Union territories which engage student and non-student youths in activities leading to national reconstruction. Constructive work for youths between 15 and 35 years of age, informal education, competitive sports and games, physical training, spreading literacy, health education and cleanliness, community service work and land improvement work are the main activities of these centres.

*National Service Scheme*. This scheme was enforced in 1969 for undergraduate boys and girls. Their chief activities are co-operation in spreading literacy, constructive work through free labour (Shramadan), planting trees, cleaning dirty colonies, first-aid and organising hospitals.

*All India Board of Sports and Games*. This board has been established for promoting physical, mental, moral and social developments of the youths. This board has appointed a committee of sports and games which sends suggestions to universities, schools of various States, State boards of sports and games and federations of sports and games. It is on the advice of this national board that players are sent to foreign countries to participate in international games and sports. The board also advises to invite foreign teams to play in our country. Competitions and training camps for national championship are organised by this board. The State boards of sports and games are given grant on the advice of this board. Physical training facilities and centres for games and sports in rural areas are organised by the board. This board determines the national policy regarding sports and games. According to the Parliament directive of 1968 sports and games programmes are organised occasionally throughout the whole country.

Besides the above board at the centre, there is another National Organisation of Sports which gives training in sports and games to the selected youths of universities and colleges in the country. This organisation holds camps also. The University Grants Commission and Indian University Organisation exercises some control over the National Organisation of Sports and Games. The following two institutions are playing leading roles in the field of physical development of youths of the country:

(1) The Netaji Subhash National Institute of Sports Patiala.

(2) Lakshmibai National College of Physical Education, Gwalior.

The Netaji Subhash National Institute of Sports at Patiala runs two years postgraduate diploma in sports and games in addition to a graduate course in the same. Foreigners also obtain training in sports and games at this institute. The Nehru Youth Centre and the National Board of Sports and Games co-operate with this institute in running national training plans at various regional centres of sports and games.

The College at Gwalior offers three years graduate course in physical education, sports and games. For employees a three years summer course is also run by this college.

In 1959 a National Physical Efficiency programme was instituted. Afterwards this programme was called the national capacity programme. Those participating in this programme are grouped into four classes — sub-junior, junior, senior and adult. The Gwalior College runs this programme through various training institutions.

## QUESTIONS FOR EXERCISE

1. Write an essay on Education in Modern India.
2. Write short note on (i) N.C.E.R.T., (ii) Central Schools, (iii) Education of Women, and (iv) The U.G.C.

# QUESTION BANK

## (A) ESSAY TYPE QUESTIONS

1. What are the difficulties in implementing the constitutional provision for universal compulsory education?
2. Discuss as to how far the constitutional provisions for universal compulsory education have been implemented in our country.
3. What are the difficulties faced by the Governments (Centre and the States) in the matter of universal provision of school facilities?
4. What measures may be taken for improving the quality of primary education?
5. Examine the problems involved in improving the quality of primary education by the State.
6. Explain how the Home, the Community and the State can contribute to the quality of primary education.
7. Suggest the various measures that can be taken to overcome Wastage and Stagnation in education.
8. What are the causes for Wastage and Stagnation in primary education ?
9. Describe the measures taken by the State to curtail Wastage and Stagnation in primary education.
10. Suggest how the quality of secondary education can be improved to meet more effectively the needs of present day society.
11. It is said widely nowadays that the upgrading of the syllabus of secondary education has added to the burdens of the average and below average children. Comment on this view giving pedagogic reasoning.
12. In the new pattern of 10+2+3 education what are the purposes and objectives of Higher Secondary schools?
13. Describe how Secondary Education can lead to the total development of the personality of the pupils.
14. Describe the problems involved in maintaining standards in higher education.
15. Examine the importance of higher education in our effort towards national development.
16. What measures will lead to the qualitative development of higher education?

17. It is said, in a democratic country, admission to higher education should not be selective. Comment on this view giving your reasoned arguments.
18. What are the defects of the various selection procedures used in higher education in your State? Suggest suitable remedies.
19. What should be the criteria for selecting candidates for training as teachers at the primary and secondary levels?
20. What are the major weaknesses noted in the existing system of teachers at various levels?
21. Discuss the suggestions of the Kothari Commission Report for improving the quality of teacher education at the secondary level.
22. Discuss the importance of increasing the professional efficiency of teachers with regard to qualitative improvement of education.
23. Explain the role of teachers, parents and the community with regard to maintenance of professional code of ethics for teacher.
24. Discuss the importance of in-service education of teachers for maintaining quality in education and indicate the role played by SCERT and NCERT in this matter.
25. Outline the 'Work-Experience' programme of the ten year school curriculum as formulated by the NCERT.
26. What are the essential qualities and features of a good text-book at the secondary level?
27. Discuss the various recommendations of the Kothari Education Commission on improving the lot of text-books.
28. Describe briefly the problems involved in the expansion of education of girls at all levels.
29. Suggest definite measures for overcoming the problems faced in co-educational institutions.
30. Describe the different categories of handicapped children and point out what are the special facilities required for their education.
31. Describe the facilities available for the education of handicapped children through the services of many agencies.
32. Examine the value of diversified courses at the +2 stage of education in the context of the country's development.
33. Describe the state of vocational education in our country, highlighting the problems faced therein.
34. Discuss the need, value and problems associated with the issue of channelising students to different streams based on their aptitudes.
35. What are the practical difficulties in implementing the examination reform proposals submitted by different commission reports?

36. Describe the pattern and organisation of Secondary Education which was examined by the Secondary Education Commission (1952-54).
37. Review any three aims of education as formulated by the Secondary Education Commission.
38. How did the members of the Secondary Education Commission (1952-54) justify the need for the diversification of courses of the secondary level?
39. Spell out the causes for the slow progress of Technical Education in the first half of the twentieth century.
40. What are the four distinct types of students to whom Technical Education has to cater?
41. Summarize briefly any two main recommendations of the Secondary Education Commission towards improving quality of text-books.
42. Comment on the national objectives of education enumerated by the Kothari Commission.
43. Enumerate the various steps recommended by the Kothari Commission to strengthen social and national integration.
44. Evaluate the language policy recommended by the Kothari Commission to promote national and emotional integration
45. Comment on the recommendations of Kothari Commission to develop social, moral and spiritual values in school and colleges.
46. Describe briefly the recommendations of the Kothari Commission on the structure of the educational system.
47. The Kothari Commission has laid great emphasis on teacher's status. What are the steps recommended by Kothari Commission to improve the condition of work and service of teachers?
48. "Most teachers in secondary schools in India have neither the proper background nor basic qualification in the subject they teach." What are the measures suggested by the Kothari Commission to change this deplorable state of affairs?
49. Outline the suggestions given by the Kothari Commission to improve professional education.
50. Discuss any two of the recommendations of the Kothari Commission to solve the problem of unemployment.
51. Describe the measures outlined by the Kothari Commission to facilitate Equalization of Educational Opportunities with reference to:

    (a) Handicapped Children.

    (b) Women.

    (c) Backward classes and tribes.
52. Summarize the guiding principles, as enunciated by the Education Commission in evolving a workable three language formula in the schools.

53. Formulate in broad terms the functions of Universities in the modern world.
54. Specify the broad objectives of Higher Education as stated by Education Commission (1966).
55. Critically examine the recommendations of Kothari Education Commission regarding —
    (a) Teaching methods in Higher Education.
    (b) Medium of instruction in Higher Education.
56. Evaluate the Education Commission's suggestions regarding,
    (a) need for quick action to liquidate illiteracy,
    (b) the programmes for literary education.
57. What should in your opinion be the objective of education at the secondary level?
58. Draw up a list of objectives of education at the University level.
59. What measures have been undertaken by the Centre as well as the State Government in the matter of provision of equal opportunities to all in education?
60. Categorically state recommendations offered by the Kothari Education Commission towards equalisation of educational opportunities at the school level.
61. Trace the important contours of our language policy from 1952 to 1976.
62. Quote reasons for the non-acceptance of Hindi as the "lingua franca" of India by a certain section of the Indian people.

## (B) SHORT ANSWER QUESTIONS

1. Describe the constitutional provision for universal compulsory primary education.
2. Mention any three difficulties in the implementation of the constitutional provision for universal compulsory education.
3. Mention any five difficulties in the matter of universal retention of pupils.
4. Show how the school improvement schemes benefit the primary pupils.
5. What constitutes wastage in primary education?
6. What are the causes for Stagnation in primary education?
7. Account for the need for upgrading the Secondary School syllabus.
8. Show how the Secondary syllabus can be upgraded in any one of your elective subjects with reference to any one unit.
9. Examine the place of Work-Experience in Secondary Schools.
10. Show how the teacher can contribute to the total development of personality of the secondary pupils.

11. Identify the problems faced in the maintenance of standards in higher education.
12. What should be the criteria for selecting candidates for training as teachers at the primary level?
13. What should be the criteria for selecting candidates for training as teachers at the secondary level?
14. What are the suggestions of the Kothari Commission with regard to removing the isolation of teacher education from Universities.
15. What are the functions of the State Boards of Teacher Education, as suggested by the Kothari Commission?
16. Comment on the statement of Kothari Commission Report, "the destiny of India is shaped in the classrooms."
17. What is the significance of the celebration of Teachers' Day?
18. Discuss the need and importance of a professional code of ethics for teachers.
19. Explain the need and value of in-service education of teachers.
20. Mention the various agencies responsible for in-service education of teachers.
21. Discuss the role of NCERT in the in-service education of teachers.
22. Explain the value of Summer Institutes for teachers.
23. Name the professional organisation of teachers in your State.
24. Discuss the role of professional organisations with regard to in-service education of teachers.
25. Name three programmes meant for arresting the growth of illiteracy in your country.
26. Describe the role of the Universities in adult education programmes.
27. Give an account of functional literacy programme.
28. What are the features of Social Education?
29. Discuss the value of Correspondence Courses and Continuing Education.
30. State the values of Continuing Education.
31. Mention the contribution of All India Radio in the promotion of adult education in your State.
32. Mention the contribution of the Television Programmes in the promotion of adult education in your State.
33. Assess the value of daily newspapers in the regional languages for promoting adult education.
34. Describe any five important conditions necessary for the success of literacy programmes.
35. Discuss the special features of the literature for 'neo-literates'.

36. Describe the difficulties experienced in the implementation of the three-language formula.
37. Describe the working and implications of the modified three-language formula.
38. Discuss the place of English in the 10-year school curriculum.
39. Discuss the place of regional language in the 10-year school curriculum.
40. Discuss the place of Hindi in the 10-year school curriculum.
41. Discuss the relative importance of Hindi and English in the 10-year school curriculum.
42. Establish the need for including 'work-experience' in any scheme of education.
43. Point out the merits and demerits of nationalisation of text-books.
44. What is the role of NCERT in text-book preparation?
45. Discuss the value of staff-student relationship from the point of view of the character development of school children.
46. What are the problems faced in the matter of enrolment and retention of girls in schools?
47. Weigh the merits and demerits of co-education.
48. Name the agencies that are involved in the education of the handicapped children.
49. Explain the need for diversification at the + 2 stage of education.
50. Specify ten areas for diversified studies at + 2 stage.
51. Explain the concept of vocational education with special reference to the needs for growing economy of our country.
52. Explain the basic principles of vocational guidance.
53. What are the functions of the State Evaluation Unit according to the Kothari Commission?
54. What are the problems of internal assessment?
55. Enumerate any three significant achievements of the U.G.C. within the first years of its inception.
56. State any three terms of reference regarding the appointment of the Secondary Education Commission.
57. What was the view held by the Secondary Education Commission with reference to the development of personality of pupil in Secondary schools?
58. What is the future of intermediate colleges as envisaged by the Secondary Education Commission?
59. Enumerate any three basic principles of curriculum construction recommended by the Secondary Education Commission (1952).
60. Spell out any three objectives to be achieved through the introduction of work-experience.

61. Bearing in mind the suggestions of the Kothari Commission draw up a programme to relate education to productivity.
62. In what ways can social and national service be made effective making it obligatory for all students at all levels?
63. Make three practical suggestions to promote moral and spiritual values among the secondary school pupils.
64. Detail any two recommendations of the Education Commission (1966) to improve conditions of work and service teachers.
65. Give any four points recommended by the Education Commission (1966) to remove the existing isolation of Teacher Education from schools. Point out what the training colleges have done in the past ten years to remove this isolation.
66. State categorically the measure our teacher associations have chalked out to improve professional efficiency as suggested by the Kothari Commission.
67. Enumerate the steps as suggested by the Education Commission (1966) to be taken at the national level to improve the standards of Teacher Education.
68. List two steps recommended by the Kothari Commission for the expansion of training facilities in teacher training institutes.
69. Give any three enrolment policies in Secondary and Higher Education recommended by the Kothari Commission.
70. Specify three main recommendations of the Kothari Commission to provide for equalisation of educational opportunities.
71. List any two types of inequalities found in the field of education as mentioned by the Kothari Commission.
72. Enumerate three interesting points that emerge from a scrutiny of enrolments in Higher Education.
73. Distinguish part-time education from own-time education.
74. Mention three advantages of Correspondence Courses for home study.
75. Indicate the role of universities in promoting adult education.
76. Mention the role played by the NCERT in the qualitative improvement of teachers.
77. What provision has been made for continuing education for the propagation of Adult Education.?
78. Comment on the extent to which co-education can help to solve the problem of illiteracy among women.
79. List the qualities of a good text-book.
80. Enumerate the distinct advantage of production of books by the State.
81. Bring out the limitations of text-books.

82. What are the recommendations of the Kothari Commission with reference to education and modernisation.
83. List the national objectives of education spelt out by the Kothari Commission.
84. Enumerate the first three major objectives of education of the Kothari Commission.

# BIBLIOGRAPHY


Altekar, A.S., 1957, Varanasi, *Education in India,* Nawal Kishore and Bros.

Agaham, Wiliard, *A Time for Teaching,* New York : Harper and Row,1964.

Aiyar, S.P., "Education and the Traditional Society in India", *General Eduation Quarterly* (Vol. III, No. 1) October, 1965.

Anderson, C. Arnold. *The Social Context of Educational Planning,* Paris, International Institute of Educational Planning, UNESCO, 1968 (Fundamentals of Educational Planning No. 5).

"The Modernization of Education", in *Modernization, The Dynamics of Growth,* Myron Weiner (ed.), Madras, Higginbothams, 1967.

Appadorai, A., "Integration Council and Its Task", *The Hindustasn Times,* June 20, 1968.

Archer, R.L., *Rousseau on Education,* New York, Longmans, Green and Co., 1912.

Arnstine, Donald, *Philosophy of Education : Learning and Schooling,* New York. Harper and Row, 1967.

Bardis, Panos D., "Education and Sociology in the United States of America", *Sociological Bulletin* (Vol. XIV, No. 2), September 1965.

Barnett, George and Jack Otis, *Corporate Society and Education : The Philosophy of Elijah Jordan,* Ann Arbor, Michigan : University of Michigan : Press, 1962, 1961.

Battle, Jean Allen, *Culture and Education for the Contemporary World,* Columbus, Ohio : C.E. Merrill Publishing Co., 1969.

Biddle, Brue J., et. al. *Essays on the Social System of Education,* Columbia, Missouri : University of Missouri, 1966.

Brookover, W.B., *A Sociology of Education,* New York, American Book Co., 1955.

Burnett John, *Aristotle on Education,* 5th ed. Cambridge, Massachusetts : Harvard University Press, 1928.

Burns, H.W. (Ed.), *Education and the Development of Nation,* Syracuse, Syracuse University Press, 1963.

Butts, Robert F., *A Cultural History of Education : Reassessing Our Educational Traditions*, 1st ed., New York and London : McGraw Hill Book Co., Inc., 1947.

Cale, Luella, *A History of Education* : *Socrates on Montessori*, New York : Holt, Rinehart & Winston, Inc. 1950.

Coleman, J.S., (Ed.) *Education and Political Development,* Princeton, Princeton University Press, 1965.

Damle, Y.B., "Socialisation for an Unknown Future" — paper presented to the *Seminar on "Higher Education, Technology and Social Change"* (December 1-3, 1966). New Delhi Indian Institute of Technology, Department of Humanities and Social Sciences, 1966.

——, "Education and Social Values" — paper presented to the *'Conference of Indian Sociologists'* (October 14-16, 1967) Bombay, Indian Sociological Society, 1967.

Deva Indra, "Contemporary Technology and the Image of Man"— paper presented to the seminar on *"Higher Education, Technology and Social Change"* (December 1-3, 1966). New Delhi, Indian Institute of Technology, Department of Humanities and Social Sciences, 1966.

Deutsch, Martin., "Early Social Environment: Its Influence on School Adaptation," in *The Social Dropout,* Washington, National Education Association, 1964.

Dewey, John, *Democracy and Education : An Introduction to Philosophy of Education,* New York, G.P. Putnam's Sons, 1939.

"Educational and Traditional Values — A Symposium," *Education Quarterly* (Vol., 15, No. 58), June 1963, pp. 64-105 (See especially the contributions of Zakir Hussain, Mulk Raj Anand, Kamla Devi Chattopadhyaya and A.R. Wadia).

Eisenstadt, S.N., *From Generation to Generation,* Chicago, Free Press, 1956.

Elkin, Frederick, *The Child and Society,* New York, Random House, 1960.

Erickson, Erick H., (Ed.) *Youth : Change and Challenge,* New York, Basic Books, 1963.

Eron, Leonard D., et. al. "Social Class : Parental Punishment for Aggression and Child Aggression" *Child Development* (Vol. XXXIV, No. 4), December 1963.

Fletcher, S.S. and J. Welton., *Froebel's Chief Writings on Education,* New York : Longmans, Green & Co., 1912.

Forbes, Clarence A., *Greek Physical Education*. New York : Century Co., 1929.

Garforth, E.W., *Education and Social Purpose*. London, Oldburire, 1962.

Gittler, Joseph B., *Review of Sociology : Analysis of a Decade,* New York, John Wiley & Sons, 1957.

Goel, B.S., "Caste and Class Tensions in Indian Education", *Conspectus* (New Delhi, Indian International Centre, Vol., No. 4), 1966.

Goodman, Paul, "The Universal Trap", in *Social Foundation of Education : Current Issues and Research in Education*. Dorothy Westby-Gibson (Ed.), New York, Free Press, 1967.

Gore, M.S., Desai, I.P. and Chitnis, Suma, *Papers in Sociology of Education in India,* New Delhi, National Council of Educational Research and Training, 1967.

Gottlleb, David, "Social Class, Achievement, and College-going Experience", *The School Review* (Vol. LXXX, No. 3), Autumn 1962.

Government of India, *Emotional Integration Committee : Preliminary Report,* New Delhi, Ministry of Education, 1962.

Hansen, Donald A., "The Responsibility of the Sociologist of Education", *Harvard Educational Review* (33), Summer 1963, p. 313.

——, "The Uncomfortable Relation of Sociology and Education" in *On Education: Sociological Perspectives,* Donald A. Hansen and Joel E. Gerstl (eds.), New York, John Wiley and Sons, 1967, p. 22.

Harley, Ruth, E., "Sex-Role Pressures and the Socialisation of the Male Child", *Psychological Reports* (Vol. V), 1959.

Herriott, Robert E., "Some Social Determinants of Educational Aspirations", *Harvard Educational Review* (Vol. XXXIII, No. 2). Spring 1963.

Husen, Trosten, "Home Background and Behaviour in the Classroom Situation", *Research Bulletin,* No. 5, Stockholm Institute of Education, University of Stockholm, January 1956.

India, *Education and National Development : Report of the Commission* (1964-66), New Delhi, Ministry of Education, Government of India, 1966.

India, Ministry of Education, *Education in India* (Successive Years).

India, Ministry of Education, 1958, *Indian University Administration : Report of a Conference of Vice-Chancellors* (Delhi).

India, Ministry of Education, 1954, *Report of the International Team on Secondary Education* (Delhi).

India, National Council of Educational Research and Training 1963-64, Physics, *The Physical Sciences Study Committee Text on High School Physics* (Delhi).

India, *Report of the National Committee on Women's Education,* Ministry of Education, Government of India, 1959.

India, *Post-War Education Development in India,* Report by the Central Advisory Board of Education, New Delhi, January 1944.

India, *Report of the University Education Commission : 1948-49,* Vol. I, Government of India Press, Simla, 1949.

India, National Council of Educational Research and Training, *Review of Education in India : 1947-61,* Ministry of Education, New Delhi, 1961.

Inkeles, Alex and David H. Smith, 1974, *Becoming Modern,* Cambridge : Harvard University Press.

Inkeles, Alex, 1973. "*The School as a Context for Modernization.*"

International Journal of Comparative Sociology XIV (3-4) : 163-179.

Jindal, B.L., 1979. *School Type and Student Modernity*, Field-work Monograph (Mimeographed). Chandigarh : Punjab University.

John, V.V., "The Freedom to Teachers", *The Hindustan Times,* November 10, December 1966.

Jesselyn, Irene M., *The Happy Child,* New York, Random House, 1965.

Kabir, Humayun, *The Indian Heritage,* London, Asia Publishing House, 1962.

Kahl, Joseph, A., "Educational and Occupational Aspiration of Common Man Boys", *Harvard Educational Review* (Vol. XXIII, No. 3), Summer 1963.

Kerber, August and Smith, Wilfred (Eds.), *Educational Issue in Changing Society,* Detroit, Wayne State University Press.

Kimball, Solon T., "An Anthropological View ofLearning", *In Social Foundations of Education : Current Readings from the Behaviour Sciences* (ed.), New York, Macmillan 1966, Vol. 266-271.

Kirk, Robert N., "Educating Slum Children in London," *School and Society* (Vol. 93, No. 2250), March 20, 1965.

Kohn, Melvin L., "Social Class and Parental Values", *American Journal of Sociology* (Vol. LXIV), 1959.

Kenyon, Frederic G., *Books and Readers in Ancient Greece and Rome*, New York, Oxford University Press, 1932.

Lawrence, Evelyn, ed. *Friedrich Froebel and English Education,* New York, Philosophical Library, 1953.

Marrou, Henri I., *A History of Education in Antiquity,* Translated by George Lamb, New York, Sheed and Ward, 1956.

Mallery, David., *High School Students Speak Out,* New York, Harper and Brother, 1902.

McClelland, David C., et. al., *Talent and Society : New Perspectives in the Identification of Talent,* Princeton, N.J., D. Van Nostrand Co., 1958.

Mannheim, Karl and Stewart, W.A.C., *An Introduction to the Sociology of Education,* London, Routledge and Kegan, 1962.

McClelland, David C., *The Achieving Society,* Princetion, D. Van Nostrand Co., 1961.

Mead, Margaret and Wolfenstein, Martha (Eds.), *Childhood in Contemporary Cultures,* Chicago, University of Chicago Press, 1955.

Mehta, Prayag, *Achievement Motivation in High School Students,* New Delhi, N.C.E.R.T. 1969.

Mekeel, Scudder, "Education, Child-Training and Culture," in *Education and the Social Order,* Blaine E. Marcer and Edvin V. Carr (eds.), New York, Rinehart and Co. 1968.

Mukerji, Shridhar N., *Higher Education and Rural India*, Baroda, India : Acharya Book Depot, 1956.

Mukherjee, Kartick C., *Underdevelopment, Educational Policy and Planning,* Bombay and New York, Asia Publishing House, 1967.

Mukherjee, D.P., *Problems of Indian Youth : A Collection of Papers,* Lucknow, 1945.

Munshi, K.B., *Foundations of Indian Culture,* Bombay, Bhartiya Vidya Bhawan, 1962.

Phillips, H.W., *Sociology and the Planning of Education in Relation to Development,* Paris, U.N.E.S.C.O., 1964.

Poignant, R., *The Relations of Educational Plans to Economic and Social Planning,* Paris, International Institute of Educational Planning, 1967.

——, *Social Change in Modern India,* Bombay, Allied Publishers, 1966.

Radha Kumud Mukherji, 1951. Delhi, *Ancient Indian Education* (Motilal Banarsidas).

Radhakrishnan, S., *An Idealist View of Life,* London, George Allen and Unwin, 1951.

——, *Freedom and Culture,* Madras, G.A. Natesan and Co., 1952.

Rai, Lala Lajpat, *The Problems of National Education in India,* Delhi, Publications Division, 1968.

Raj, Krishna, "Thought on Tradition and Modernity", *Quest* (41), April-June, 1964.

Ramanathan, G., *Education Planning and National Integration,* Bombay, Asia Publishing House, 1965.

Rawat P.L., *History of Indian Education* (3rd Ed.), Ram Prasad and Sons, 1963.

Rodehover, Myles W., Axtell, William B., and Gross, Richard E., *The Sociology of the School,* New York, Thomas Y. Crowell Co., 1957.

Ruhela, S.P., *Sociology of Education : A Review of Researches and Priorities,* New Delhi, National Institute of Education, Department of Foundations of Education, 1967 (Mimeographed).

——, *A Pre-view of the Seminar on Sociology of the Teaching Profession in India* — A Paper presented to the Seminar held at the Tata Institute of Social Sciences, Bombay, February 5-10, 1968 (Mimeographed).

——, *A Note on the Researchable Topics in Sociology of Education in India* — A Paper presented to the Jamia Millia Teachers' College Seminar on 'Educational Sociology,' December 24-26, 1968 (Mimeographed).

——, *Field Studies in Sociology of Education,* New Delhi, National Council of Educational Research and Training.

Ruhela, S.P. (Ed.), *Sociology of the Teaching Profession in India,* New Delhi, National Council of Educational Research and Training, 1970.

"Research Needs in the Sociology of Education" in *Research Needs in the Study of Education,* U. Shanker and S.P. Ahluwalia (Eds.), Kurukshetra, Kurukshetra University, 1968, pp. 17-25.

Rugg, Harold O., *Culture and Education in America,* New York, Harcourt, Brace and Co., 1931.

Ryan, Patric J., *Historical Foundations of Public,* Education Dubuque, Iowa, W.C. Brown and Co., 1968.

Samuel, R.H. and R. Hinton Thomas, *Education and Society in Modern Germany,* London, Routledge and Kegan Paul Ltd., 1949.

Saiyidain, K.G., *The Humanist Tradition in Indian Educational Thought,* Bombay, Asia Publishing House, 1960.

Sexton, Patricia, *The American School : Its Social Context.* Englewood Cliffs, New Jersey, Prentice-Hall, 1967.

Shah, A.B. and Rao, C.R.M. (eds.), *Tradition and Modernity in India,* Bombay, Manaktalas, 1965.

Shah, A.B., *Planning for Democracy and other Essays.* Bombay, Manaktalas 1967.

Shah, B.V., "Sociology of Education — An Attempt at Definition and Scope," *Sociological Bulletin* (Vol. XIV, No. 2), September 1965, p. 65.

Sharma, R.N., *Philosophy of Education,* Atlantic, Delhi, 1996.

Sharma, S.L., *Modernizing Effects of University Education.* ICSSR. New Delhi, 1979.

Silber, Kate., *Pestalozzi, the Man and His Work, London,* Routledge and Kegan Paul, 1965.

Sinha, M.R. (ed.), *The Struggles of Modern India,* Bombay, Asian Studies Press, 1967.

Stanley, William O., *Education and Social Integration,* New York, Columbia University, Teacher's College, 1953.

Vadekar, D.D., "The Indian Traditional Values and their Indications for Education in India in the Age of Modern Science and Technology", *The Journal of the University of Poona, Humanities Section* (23), 1965.

Vakil, C.N., "National Integration : The Common Language" (Part I), *Times of India,* July 13, 1961.

Waller, Willard., *The Sociology of Teaching,* New York : Wiley and Sons, 1932.

Ward, Herbert, *The Educational System of England and Wales and its Recent History,* Cambridge University Press, 1935.

Westby-Gibson D. (Ed.), *Social Foundations of Education : Current Issues and Research,* New York, Free Press, 1967.